D0949423

POPS:

*Paul Whiteman,
King of Jazz*

POPS:

Paul Whiteman, King of Jazz

by

THOMAS A. DeLONG

New Century Publishers, Inc.

Printing Code
11   12   13   14   15   16

Library of Congress Cataloging in Publication Data

DeLong, Thomas A.
  Pops: Paul Whiteman, king of jazz.

  Bibliography: p.
  1. Whiteman, Paul, 1890–1967. 2. Conductors (Music)—
United States—Biography. I. Title.
ML422.W4D4   1983   785.42′092′4 [B]   83-19291
ISBN 0-8329-0264-0

To Katharine
and our parents
S. & H.A.D.
L. & F.D.C.

Contents

Preface

Strike Up The Band—those words might have been coined with Paul Whiteman in mind. He took the center of the stage to give the downbeat inaugurating a new era in popular music. The bandstand took on new luster and glamor, along with a new sound and a novel tempo, when Whiteman stepped on the podium at the very beginning of the 1920's. First he augmented a dance band with more and better-trained musicians. Then he supplied them with special arrangements. And before long he expanded the repertoire by introducing greater musical variety. His polished ensemble may be called the first of the big bands as we know them today. Certainly by 1924 Whiteman's group was listened to and sought after more than any other musical organization in the United States.

Whiteman stood out as a music maker of gigantic proportions. He built an incredibly large and successful aggregation, which shaped the Jazz Age. He embraced virtually every facet of show business. A pioneer and an innovator, Paul Whiteman moved in the right direction at crucial moments in the rise and development of this century's forms of mass entertainment. His influence was felt in recording studios, over radio, in theaters and concert halls, on movie sound stages, and on television screens.

Furthermore, he never ceased spotting talent in its formative stages. Hiring these musicians at top dollar, he showcased an array of instrumentalists and singers who made their mark in a highly competitive profession. He also sought innovative material for his troupe to perform. Composers, arrangers, and writers with backgrounds in both popular music and classical music—or somewhere in between—were warmly welcomed and encouraged to contribute to Whiteman's programs.

Paul Whiteman's commitment to music and musicians was total. His life was lived in the spotlight of theaters and night clubs, the microphones of radio stations and recording studios, in rehearsals, auditions, and backstage meetings, and on the road by train or bus.

Week after week, month after month, Whiteman was "public

property.'' His whole life, particularly during the 1920's and 1930's, was spent on a podium. The elements of the private man paled by comparison with the big, boisterous, and bountiful Pops who was rarely out of the public eye.

This, then, is the story of Paul Whiteman, his musicians and his music—all of which came together to shape an unparalleled epoch in American entertainment.

Acknowledgments

During a long career Paul Whiteman avoided writing letters whenever possible. His fast-paced life—characterized by frequent road trips, late-night engagements, and almost daily rehearsals—necessitated quick communication. Whiteman reached for a telephone, jotted down brief notes for telegrams, chatted backstage or across a restaurant table. Written material in his own hand is therefore scarce. He was, however, pursued by newspaper reporters and magazine writers. He made good copy and never missed an opportunity to toss out a zesty phrase or anecdote.

Much of Whiteman's business files have long since disappeared. Luckily he gave most of his scores, recordings, radio transcriptions, films, press books, programs, television tapes, and other memorabilia to Williams College to form the Whiteman Collection. Its associate curator, Carl Johnson, gave generous and enthusiastic help in making available this extensive array of Whiteman material and provided invaluable insights and manifold suggestions on the life and times of Pops. Both Professor Irwin Shainman, of the Williams Department of History and curator of the Whiteman Collection, and his predecessor, Dr. Roy Lamson, were generous with their recollections of the establishment and growth of this center for the study of American popular music.

By the 1980's only a handful of musicians from the Whiteman orchestra of the Jazz Age survive. Kurt Dieterle, the long-time concertmaster, and Bill Challis, chief arranger, made immeasurable contributions to the manuscript. I am also grateful to Ken Darby both for sharing his vivid recollections and for making available his own extensive and unique archives of the Whiteman years. Ira Gershwin also allowed me to examine his large treasure trove of material concerning the musical theater and concert hall.

Whiteman's last manager, Peter Dean, was of enormous help in depicting Whiteman's later years. To Ward Byron, Whiteman's longtime friend and associate goes the greatest measure of appreciation. Without his steadfast encouragement and energetic support, this biography of his beloved and colorful companion would not have come about.

Many of Whiteman's family, associates, friends, and fans provided a wealth of dates, facts, stories, and memories. They are Durelle Alexander, Alan Andrews, Kay Armen, Eugenie Baird, Jeanne Bargy, Virginia MacLean Bargy, Helen M. Black, Vet Boswell, George Burns, Thurlow O. Cannon, Carroll Carroll, Alda Whiteman Chalenor, Rocky Clark, Phil Cohan, Jack Cordaro, Ivy Livingston Crawford, Dr. William Crawford, Emery Davis, Clark Dennis, David Diamond, Carol Ellis Digges, Morton Downey, Al Duffy, George Eells, Philip R. Evans, Michael Feinstein, Joe Franklin, Stan Freeman, Jack Fulton, Leonore Gershwin, Kitty Lang Good, John Green, Nat Greenburg, Anna Lempton Grofé, Cindy Haas, Thomas Haas, Thornton Hagert, Wilbur Hall, George Hart, John Hauser, Howard W. Hays, Justin Herman, Ken Hopkins, Elizabeth Lennox Hughes, Paul Hutcoe, Ed Jablonski, Helen Jepson, Brooke Johns, Dorothy Kemble, Andy Kirk, Roy Lamson, Paul Lavalle, Mort Lewis, Les Lieber, Ron Livingston, Stephen Longstreet, William Losch, John W. Mackay, Russell Markert, Deena Meiner, Paul Mertz, Brenda Miller, Peter Mintun, George Morrison, Jr., Ken Murray, Lyn Murray, Abe Olman, Richard Osk, Glenn Osser, Cay Bowes Paisley, Nino Pantano, William Payne, Leonard Pennario, Gerald H. Phipps, Carl Pingitore, Rosa Rio, Buddy and Marshall Robbins, John Roberts, Lanny Ross, Vincent Rowe, Brian Rust, Phil Schapiro, Irwin Shainman, Joe Showler, Harry Sosnik, John P. Stevens, Richard M. Sudhalter, Dana Suesse, Kay Swift, Glenhall Taylor, Charlie Teagarden, Mrs. Frankie L. Thomas, Jane Vance, Larry Wagner, Fred Waring, Buddy Weed, Alvy West, Margo Whiteman, Earl Wild, Howard Wiley, Mark Woods. Many others fielded questions and led me to important sources of information.

Dozens of institutions and organizations supplied material essential to the Whiteman story and to describe the tempo of the times. They include Colorado Historical Society; Denver Symphony Orchestra and A. P. Cady; Division of Education of Denver Public Schools; San Francisco Public Library; California Historical Society and Jocelyn A. Moss; West Alexander (Ohio) Archive and Mrs. Joe Gilbert; New York Public Library; Fort Worth Museum of Science & History; Chicago Public Library; Chicago Historical Society, Forbes Library; Northampton, Mass.; Fairfield (Conn.) Public Library; Elmer Ellis Library of University of Missouri at Columbia; The Museum of Broadcasting, New York; Lincoln Center for the Performing Arts, New York; Broadcast Pioneers and Catharine Heinz, Washington, D.C.; Pequot Library and Stanley Crane, Southport, Conn.; Pacific Pioneer Broadcasters, Hollywood; ASCAP; Utah State Historical Society and Steven R. Wood; The Songwriters Hall of Fame and Frankie MacCormack, New York; American Federation of Musicians, Local 802 and 47; KRMA-TV, Denver; Monmouth-Evergreen Records; Bucks County Historical Society, Doylestown, Pa.; Walt Disney Studios and Bill Latham, Burbank, Calif.; Bridgeport (Conn.) Public Library; Special thanks go to the University of Wyoming at Laramie and Dr. Gene M. Gressley and Emmett D. Chisum for providing access to the papers of the late Charles Strickfaden.

A number of publications offered additional help from their reference libraries: *Variety;* the Los Angeles *Times*; *Better Homes and Gardens; The Rotarian; US Magazine* and Lynn Dorsey; the Detroit *Free Press;* the Daytona Beach *News-Journal;* the Chicago *Sun-Times* and Larry Bartkus; the Miami *Herald;* the Boston *Globe; Rocky Mountain News;* the New York *Daily News;* and Associated Newspapers Group Limited, London.

I am also indebted to Bobbe Siegel, Ruth Hein, and Robin Little for their skillful professional know-how. To my wife Katharine go high accolades for her inestimable time and talents in preparing a finished manuscript.

POPS:

*Paul Whiteman,
King of Jazz*

1

Fear and Jubilation

As the three men walked slowly up Forty-Second Street through the swirling snow, they were startled to see the crowds milling around the main entrance to Aeolian Hall, the venerable auditorium for classical concerts. They had expected a fair-sized audience, of course. Some would attend out of curiosity, and the novelty seekers would come, and there were bound to be some jazz fans. More than likely, there also would be a few people of the kind who yearn to see a celebrity fail—make a total fool of himself. But no one had expected crowds like this. Were all these people actually coming to hear the innovative concert that had been slapped together at such short notice? The three musicians did not know whether to be relieved or more worried than ever.

The tall, portly man, who had appeared calmest until now, came to a dead stop. Paul Whiteman stared at his two companions, George Gershwin and Zez Confrey. He looked bewildered. He was on the verge of turning and walking away from his own brash experiment in modern music. It was all Gershwin and Confrey could do to steer him to the stage entrance. At the door he stopped again, shook himself free, and walked in alone.

Whiteman had made an impressive name for himself. Now, in 1924, he was New York's most popular bandleader, the head of the Palais Royal musicians. But at this moment he was as fearful as if the impending performance were his first. Once again he was gripped by the doubts that had nearly paralyzed his will on more than one previous occasion. Why had he made the insane decision to stage this concert? Almost on a whim he had chosen to stake his reputation in this town of sophisticated theater patrons and concertgoers. He had plunged ahead and rented Aeolian Hall, he had commissioned George Gershwin and Victor Herbert to provide new compositions, he had reorganized his band into a symphonic dance orchestra, he had rehearsed feverishly. Would anyone approve? Would anyone care?

Why was he gambling his career on this crazy, quixotic undertaking? God knows it wasn't for the money. He was making over $3,000 a week, a very real fortune for 1924.

Out there the current Broadway season offered frightening competition—too much, far too much, competition. Theatergoers had the choice of such plays as *Abie's Irish Rose* and *Wildflower. St. Joan*—George Bernard Shaw's latest work—and Kaufman and Connelly's *Beggar on Horseback* were scheduled to open later in the week. The mecca of vaudeville, the Palace, headlined musical-comedy stars Julia Sanderson and Frank Crumit. A new edition of the *Ziegfeld Follies* starred comedian Fanny Brice and dancer Ann Pennington. The Hippodrome offered its usual potpourri, which currently included the Albertina Rasch Ballet, singers Nellie and Sara Kouns, the Vincent Lopez Orchestra, trained seals, champion ropers, clowns, and equestrians.

Cecil B. DeMille's *The Ten Commandments* was shown twice a day. John Barrymore's latest movie, *Beau Brummel,* was about to open. The Rivoli was featuring Dr. Lee De Forest's new Phonofilm synchronized-sound movies with such "talking" segments as the Gettysburg Address recited by actor Frank McGlynn. Siegfried Wagner was appearing as guest conductor at the Metropolitan Opera House. In Aeolian Hall, Whiteman's concert was to be followed later in the week by Bruno Walter and the New York Symphony, performing works by Handel, Haydn, and Beethoven.

Inside the hall Whiteman greeted the house manager and walked slowly to his dressing room. How could he have been so brash as to expect to please both jazz lovers and the devotees of the classics? True, he had been talking for years about a concert of symphonic jazz; but it was only when he heard that Vincent Lopez, a rival bandleader, was planning a concert of American music at the Metropolitan Opera House that he sprang into action. He was determined he would not be bested by his rival in the headline-grabbing dance-band razzle-dazzle. Immediately he had started looking for a hall to hold his jazz concert. He had to move fast if he was going to beat out Lopez. Finally Aeolian Hall agreed to rent to him. The only available date was Lincoln's Birthday, 1924. Whiteman quickly began planning what turned out to be one of the most momentous events in the history of twentieth-century American music.

He was almost in a state of nervous collapse by the time he finished dressing. He mumbled that he was sick, that he needed his doctor. Twenty minutes before the concert was to begin, he grabbed his overcoat and went out to see what was happening on the street. What he found nearly scared him to death. Years later he described the scene.

> There I gazed upon a picture that should have imparted new vigor to my wilting confidence. It was snowing, but men and women were fighting to get into the door, pulling and mauling each other as they do sometimes at a baseball game, or a prize fight, or in the subway . . . I wondered if I had come to the right entrance . . . I went backstage again, more scared than ever. Black fear possessed me. Now that the audience had come, did I really have something to offer them?

His terror grew when he spotted a number of world-renowned musicians making their way through the crowded lobby—Igor Stravinsky, John McCormack, Victor Herbert, Mary Garden, Leopold Stokowski, Sergei Rachmaninoff, Walter Damrosch, Jascha Heifetz, Fritz Kreisler, Amelita Galli-Curci, Alma Gluck. He was well aware that most of them had received complimentary tickets as part of his promotional campaign. So had the score of music critics milling about outside. What Whiteman couldn't understand was why all of them had come to hear this invasion of syncopated jazz into the hallowed halls of Heifetz and Paderewski.

Gershwin, who was featured as soloist in the premiere of his new composition for piano and orchestra, remained backstage, calm and composed as the house filled to capacity. Gershwin, successful as a composer of popular tunes, and Paul had occasionally talked about bringing concertized jazz into Carnegie or Aeolian Hall. Just five weeks earlier, Whiteman had reminded Gershwin of a longstanding promise that he would write a piece for Paul's group. Gershwin felt he would need six months to develop a major concert work, but Paul insisted that he honor his word. "You better stop talking like one of those symphony types," he said. "Hot or cold, the body goes out on Lincoln's Birthday."

Trained in the methods of Tin Pan Alley, Gershwin worked swiftly. He chose the rhapsody form, with its elastic and free-flowing structure, to meet the impossible deadline. He began to set down notes during a rail trip to Boston. The rattling, steely rhythm of the train so stimulated him that much of it worked its way into the rhapsody. His brother Ira Gershwin suggested he include an andante piece composed two years earlier. The work for solo piano was completed in about three weeks. Whiteman's arranger, Ferde Grofé, virtually looked over Gershwin's shoulder as he wrote. When Gershwin finished a page of music, Grofé took it away to orchestrate it. He also suggested instrumentation, jotting down the names of Whiteman's key players to remind Gershwin of their individual styles. At one point Gershwin wanted to take out the broad melodic section, but Grofé persuaded him to keep it.

As Whiteman's talented arranger worked feverishly to complete each page and deliver it to the conductor, the orchestra rehearsed the composition piecemeal.

"When Gershwin dotted the last note, we were only one dot behind him," Whiteman later recalled.

Gershwin had wanted to call his work "American Rhapsody." It was Ira who named the composition. Inspired by Whistler's paintings "Harmony in Gray and Green" and "Nocturne in Blue and Green" at the Metropolitan Museum of Art, Ira suggested *Rhapsody in Blue*.

Grofé's rough score left his hands one week before the concert. Because the composition called for more strings and brass than the Whiteman band contained, Paul hired eight violinists, two French horn players, and a performer on the double bass. Some of Whiteman's musicians, more at ease with the tempo of the foxtrot, teased the classically trained newcomers. After a few sessions with the Gershwin score, the symphonic players had the last laugh as the Palais Royal contingent stumbled through several key passages. Whiteman's fears increased with each rehearsal.

In the last weeks before the concert, he met with his manager, Hugh C. Ernst, and with Gilbert Seldes to prepare notes for a twelve-page printed program. Whiteman wanted to emphasize the experimental and educational nature of the event. "Mr. Whiteman,'' the program noted, "intends to point out the tremendous strides which have been made in popular music from the day of discordant popular music which sprang into existence about ten years ago, to the really melodious music of today, which—for no good reason—is still called Jazz.''

Whiteman was cautious. The program's introductory notes ended with the statement, "If after the concert you decide that the music of today is worthless and harmful, it is your duty to stamp it down. If it is not, then we welcome anyone eager to assist in its development.''

Backstage, Paul thumbed through the program as the time for the opening number approached. He paced the floor as he anxiously contemplated the ordeal to come. Except for the opening number, he would be conducting an unusually long and varied concert. To establish the theme—the evolution of jazz music—he had decided to open with a version of the 1917 "Livery Stable Blues,'' played by five musicians, without conductor, in a raw, raucous arrangement.

Still in his dressing room, he heard the sudden hush and then the strains of the first number. He wanted a drink. God, how he wanted a drink. Listening to the wailing of the blues, he tried to concentrate on the symphony he was about to conduct. Instead, he found himself brooding over all the past battles with his father, the incessant disapproval, the old, bitter realization that even fame and money and critical success would never vindicate him, never erase the verdict of failure in his father's mind. What kind of musician abandons the classics to play cheap popular tunes? Wilberforce Whiteman could tell you what kind. Wilberforce Whiteman— teacher of music, teacher of real music, not modern trash—he could tell you what kind. A failure. A wastrel. A lazy, drinking, womanizing ingrate.

And now here was the son of Wilberforce Whiteman, preparing to stride on stage and conduct the music that symbolized everything his family hated. Here was Paul Whiteman—balding, overweight as always, sweating nervously, afraid of heights, afraid of closed spaces, afraid of disapproval, afraid even to prove his father wrong.

The music ended and the sound of applause rose. Paul Whiteman stood up and left his dressing room, mumbling. What he said is unknown. In all probability, it was a nervously defiant answer to the old, angry family rhetoric: "A goddamn original musician, that's what kind. A goddamn good musician. I'll show you what kind of musician . . ."

As the applause died, a numb Paul Whiteman arrived on stage with the rest of his Palais Royal orchestra to demonstrate up-to-date syncopated scoring of jazz through a rendition of "Mama Loves Papa."

During the playing of the first few pieces, Whiteman's anxiety abated somewhat. He found himself conducting almost automatically, thinking ahead to the more ambitious selections that were to come.

After "Mama Loves Papa," the orchestra presented a comic interpretation to show that the origin of "Yes, We Have No Bananas" could be found in parts of a half-dozen well-known songs and classical themes. The first four notes, for example, were so akin to the Hallelujah Chorus in Handel's *Messiah* that in 1923 its publishers had won a plagiarism suit against the composers of the popular number. Whiteman's next item on the program demonstrated another facet of the close relationships between one kind of music and another. Called "So This Is Venice," it was Whiteman's adaptation of the familiar "Carnival of Venice," with reed virtuoso Ross Gorman as soloist on several instruments.

A change of pace, which affirmed Whiteman's showmanship, was the rendition of the first number he had ever recorded, "Whispering," in its pure form and properly scored, in comparison to the delectable "hot" or jazzed-up version of the recording.

Composer Zez Confrey took the center of the stage as solo pianist in a medley of popular airs, followed by his innovative and comic "Kitten on the Keys." The next selection, a foxtrot adaptation of "The Volga Boat Song" called "Russian Rose," displayed Ferde Grofé's singular contributions to the group. Three Irving Berlin tunes, including "Alexander's Ragtime Band," closed the first half of the concert. It was going well enough, Whiteman thought, yet the anxiety was returning. He began to realize that his concert-hall debut was too ambitious for one program. He could feel the audience becoming restless.

During intermission he retreated to his dressing room. The concert was running too long. Four selections remained, including Victor Herbert's suite and Gershwin's rhapsody. Well, there was no turning back now. Might as well plunge ahead, and the critics be damned. If only the hall weren't so overheated. How could it be so cold outside and so hot in here? He wondered if people would begin to leave.

The second half opened with Whiteman leading Herbert's first work for jazz orchestra—a novel adventure into unfamiliar territory for the composer of *Naughty Marietta* and *Babes in Toyland.* As the conductor concentrated on the music, his anxiety now began turning to exhilaration. Waving his long baton, he felt a tinge of pride at last. Now he *could* tell his father back in Denver that a cabaret bandleader could dream of a symphony-hall debut, that a jazz artist *was* an artist, that a pop musician could mount a concert podium before one of the most prestigious and discriminating audiences in the world. Wilberforce Whiteman, director of music in Denver's public schools, had been wrong after all to throw up his hands over his son's determination to play ragtime and jazz rather than remain with the San Francisco Symphony. The old man had, of course, reluctantly acknowledged that there might be money in jazz, but how could a son of his associate with "those jazz people"?

Well now, Paul thought, he had "made a lady of jazz."

Fear had turned to exhilaration. Very soon now, the exhilaration would fade, replaced by numb defiance—or numb retreat, perhaps. Out of the corner of his eye, Whiteman could see several people leaving the overheated hall, just as he had feared. He caught a glimpse of the upper balcony, where clusters of standees were fanning themselves with programs. The crowded auditorium was a sweat box. Whiteman and his musicians felt trickles of perspiration underneath their layers of winter clothing. Later they learned that the ventilating system had broken down. Heat and fatigue permeated the hall. How much longer would the audience stay?

When it was Gershwin's turn, he stepped to the piano, eagerly sat down at the keyboard, and nodded to Whiteman. An opening cadenza by Ross Gorman on the clarinet grabbed the attention of the audience at once, and they never lost interest throughout the crisp, exciting, and moving piano passages and orchestral interludes.

Full of emotion and relief, Whiteman found himself crying. When he regained his composure, he was eleven pages along. For the rest of his life he could not tell how he had conducted that far in a semiconscious state.

The listeners remained on the edge of their seats until the rhapsody's explosive coda. Gershwin bowed to thunderous applause, reverberating from the upper reaches of the second balcony down to the first row of the orchestra. Fear was forgotten. He was jubilant. He came back for three curtain calls before the program could continue.

With this concert Gershwin and Whiteman added a new chapter to America's musical history. "There was realization of the irresistible vitality and genuineness of much of the music heard," wrote the *New York Times* critic Olin Downes the following morning. Gershwin's *Rhapsody in Blue,* he noted, was no mere dance tune. "It is an idea, or several ideas correlated and combined in varying and well contrasted rhythms that immediately intrigue the hearer. This, in essence, is fresh and new, and full of future promise."

Variety called the concert "brilliant." Whiteman, the trade journal pointed out, had started something he should not be permitted to abandon. "The maestro proves conclusively that the dance orchestra or the band or the jazz craze, or any of other names it has been identified with, will never die. It is part of modern American culture and an absolute necessity."

Overnight, Paul Whiteman was crowned King of Syncopation, King of Jazz Rhythm, King of Jazz. Before long he brought his concertized arrangements of both the classics and current tunes to tens of millions, first by personal appearances and recordings, then over radio and in films, and finally by way of television and high-fidelity discs.

Whiteman continued to seek new Gershwins by commissioning an unusual array of composers, ranging from Igor Stravinsky and Aaron Copland to Duke Ellington and Richard Rodgers. His experimental concerts attracted music fans for the next twenty years. His quest for talented young musicians and entertainers lasted for the rest of his life and brought into his fold such performers as Bing Crosby, Mildred Bailey, Johnny Mercer, Helen Jepson, Jack Teagarden, Bix Beiderbecke, Buddy Weed, Joan Edwards, and the Dorseys.

Through the 1920s, the Great Depression, the Second World War, and the 1950s, Whiteman stood at the forefront of American music, setting the tempo of the times. Away from the limelight, he suffered personal disappointments and family tragedies. Chronic overweight and a drinking problem plagued him much of his life; but these battles—some won, some lost—never stifled his drive to enlarge the frontiers of modern music.

Whiteman remained a master showman of the twentieth century, dean of popular music, the admired Pops to friends and fans, until his death at the age of seventy-seven in December 1967. For nearly forty years he was the unparalleled catalyst for music makers, an unsurpassed impresario of mass entertainment, a Pied Piper larger than life. Paul Whiteman embodied an exuberance and urgency that reflected America's frontier spirit—a zest as natural and solid as the Rocky Mountains that had shadowed his birth.

2

Frontier Stock

By 1890, the year Paul Whiteman was born, Colorado had been in the Union for fourteen years. Some thirty years earlier the discovery of gold near Pike's Peak had drawn a wave of prospectors, speculators, con men, and camp followers, accelerating the taming of the wilderness. These Rocky Mountain gold seekers soon found silver and lead deposits, but only a handful would fulfill their dreams of ending up with a king's ransom. However, both millionaire and disappointed adventurer chose to settle in the small but growing territorial capital called Denver City.

Denver might have remained a city of modest size. Instead, it hurried to equal, rival, and surpass the cities of the West and many in the East. Soon Denver would rank as the richest, fastest-growing metropolis between St. Louis and San Francisco. Once its citizens had built railroads, banks, and mills, they turned to opulent homes, grandiose theaters, and excellent schools.

Just as the frontier days ended, the young city's educational system acquired what would prove to be a dynamic power in the city. In 1888 Wilberforce J. Whiteman accepted a position teaching music in the Denver public schools. The wiry, ascetic-looking teacher had already spent two years on the faculty of a school in Greeley, Colorado, before his new assignment took him some 50 miles south to the state capital. With him were his twenty-two-year-old wife, Elfrida, and their two-year-old daughter, Ferne.

Wilberforce came from a prosperous family of farmers that had arrived in the Colonies with a land grant in western Virginia from

12

King George. Each generation moved slowly westward with the frontier. By the 1840s Wilberforce's parents had settled in Preble County, Ohio, some 35 miles west of Dayton. The sixth of seven children, Wilberforce was born on the Whiteman farm near Fairhaven in 1857. Sons and daughters were educated, and special attention was paid to the art of music and the playing of the piano and violin. When Wilberforce exhibited unusual talent, they encouraged him to pursue a career in music. He saved several hundred dollars to study at the College of Organists in London for a year. Wilberforce returned home with outstanding credits—very few midwestern teachers of music in the 1880s had studied abroad.

His first job was in Iowa where he taught in the adjacent towns of Bedford and College Springs. There he met sixteen-year-old Elfrida Dallison, a statuesque, auburn-haired girl who was one of his first pupils. They were married a year later, on December 4, 1883.

His older brother John Whiteman had just settled in the new state of Colorado as music teacher in the Normal School at Greeley. Wilberforce visited him and soon was hired to teach in a local school. After a year or so, thirty-year-old Wilberforce began looking for even greener musical fields and applied for a teaching job in Denver.

In Denver, the Whiteman family prospered. Both Wilberforce and Elfrida, an accomplished singer, gave private music lessons in their home on South First Street. Along with his work in the schools, Wilberforce also was musical director at Trinity Methodist Church. In 1894 he became superintendent of music education for the entire Denver school system, a post he held for thirty years. In that capacity he talked the city's taxpayers into financing more music courses in the schools and persuaded a local philanthropist to donate instruments for students who could not afford to buy their own. In the community he organized amateur orchestras and planned oratorio concerts at which these orchestras played.

As a teacher and educator, he was well-liked throughout the schools. It is an interesting sidelight that among his pupils he numbered Jimmie Lunceford and Andy Kirk, both of whom eventually became well-known leaders of swing bands.

But most of this activity was still in the future when a second child was born to Wilberforce and Elfrida Whiteman on March 28, 1890. The baby, a boy they named Paul Samuel, delighted his parents; they took special pride in his solid chubbiness.

According to family chroniclers, Paul's fascination with music began very early. He would stop crying whenever music was played, he wiggled his toes in time to the piano, and when he was a toddler, he could imitate all manner of musical instruments with eerie precision.

When the baby was less than a year old, his parents wheeled him to a picnic in a carriage that also held Wilberforce's violin and a large watermelon. At some point during the outing, the family parked it on an incline; unattended, the carriage rolled down a hill. Little Paul and the unusually heavy cargo came to an abrupt stop at the bottom of the slope. There are two versions of what his parents saw when they rushed to the carriage. According to one, Paul prophetically grabbed his father's violin. Others claim he clutched the watermelon. Either account was a sign of the future. It was not the last violin or the last melon that Paul would hold in his hands.

Paul was given a miniature fiddle when he was three. Under his father's tutelage he was soon sawing away at several tunes. When he was six, he received a Christmas present that would shape his future—a quarter-size violin. Paul never forgot that Christmas. Many years later, in 1946, he told an interviewer from *Parents' Magazine*, "My eyes almost popped as I saw the shape of the gift which I knew was a violin, and naturally I could hardly interest myself in the other gifts . . . I suppose right then and there that must have been the very beginning of my interest in a musical career."

Getting Paul to practice was another matter, however. When the hated hour approached, he was always somewhere else, gone to play ball or swim. He also loved guns and practiced his markmanship with real dedication—something that could hardly be said of his daily bout with the violin. By the time he was ten, Paul could shoot the head off a garter snake at long range with a .22.

When Wilberforce finally understood the situation, he moved swiftly. Paul and his violin were locked into his mother's sewing room. He threatened to run away; nobody paid attention except to make certain that he was promptly and securely locked in. After several weeks of spending an hour a day with his mother's sewing machine as his sole companion, the eleven-year-old boy lifted up his violin and smashed it over the offending machine. He sat down and awaited his fate.

When Wilberforce saw the ruined $60 fiddle that evening, Paul was ordered to the woodshed for disciplining. For the next two years he mowed lawns to pay his father back. To the end of his days the smell of newly-cut grass made Paul remember that confining sewing room and the rage he felt at having been imprisoned there. Meanwhile, the determined professor provided another violin, so that Paul would not miss even an hour of practice. Viola lessons were added to violin lessons, and as Paul's skills on both instruments grew, he became determined to be a first-rate string player.

Mowing lawns and practicing were suspended the summer Paul was twelve. The healthy, active boy was stricken with typhoid fever. The disease took its toll: much of Paul's hair fell out and never grew back. While he was recovering, he developed a ravenous appetite. The craving for food did not disappear once he was pronounced well. Paul soon weighed far more than the normal twelve-year-old, and he did not lose the pounds as he shot up. By the time Paul was fifteen, he was over six feet tall and weighed 180 pounds. The illness left Paul an unhappy legacy—chronic weight problems as well as baldness for the rest of his life.

When he returned to school, Paul was more restless than ever. A below-average student, he had given up plans to become a mechanical engineer, a career chosen by his father. As Paul ignored homework and played hooky with his cronies, he became involved in real mischief, which eventually got him into trouble with the law.

One night Paul and a buddy were caught greasing the city's trolley tracks with butter and were brought before Judge Ben Lindsey, then presiding over Denver's juvenile court. (Lindsey gained national notoriety in the 1930s with his book, *Companionate Marriage,* in which he advocated that couples contemplating marriage live together first.) Also waiting to come before the judge was another juvenile prankster—Gene Fowler, the later journalist and biographer. Paul advised the other boy to tell the truth as the best policy with this particular judge. In fact, Lindsey's only sentence for both offenders was to ask them to report to him every Friday for two months. Fowler and Whiteman often joined forces in mischief-making.

Surprisingly, Wilberforce Whiteman—now known as "the Professor" throughout the city—took a much more lenient view of his son's hijinks than he did of skipped violin or viola practice. He did, however, set up a routine of daily lessons and chores designed to leave Paul with little free time. Boxing lessons were only one of the numerous activities. As it happened, the Professor was an expert pugilist and put on the gloves with young Paul every day. "It'll take some of that fat off," he'd chant as he danced around, jabbing at Paul, getting ready to move in with his memorable one-two punch that consistently floored his son.

Paul became more and more alienated. He began to rebel against the household restrictions. At school his attitude was reflected in failing grades. His rebellious streak led to confrontations with teachers and administrators; he shifted from school to school, usually at the request of authorities. He later admitted having gone to nearly every school in town, including three different high schools between 1903 and 1907. Through all his scholastic floundering, Paul kept playing the viola. It was going to be the solution to all his problems. At sixteen he was skilled enough to be accepted as a member of the local musicians' union.

Paul frequently found paying jobs with Denver's professional musicians. The young man joined Raffaelo Cavallo's orchestra, playing evening concerts on the mezzanine of Denver's famed Brown Palace Hotel. Often Paul changed his clothes, walked across the street, and played in the pit for musical revues at the Broadway Theater. Occasionally he also played with the Stewart Opera Company, and the Professor called on him for the special orchestras and choruses he so liked to organize and direct.

In 1908, Wilberforce Whiteman was asked to prepare a musical program for an appearance by William Howard Taft, then a presidential candidate, at the new City Auditorium. A platform standing about 17 feet above the audience, the chorus, and the orchestra was erected at the center of the hall. The musicians, including Paul, were seated at floor level and to one side of the flag-draped rostrum. The Professor stood on the platform high above his performers to direct "The Star-Spangled Banner."

Taft, who weighed some 300 pounds, worked his way onto the high rostrum to address the crowd. Following his forceful plea for tariff revision and greater conservation measures, the portly candidate maneuvered his way down from the lofty platform to floor level. Professor Whiteman rose to direct his musicians and the audience in a patriotic tune. As he lifted his baton, the platform gave way.

At the same moment Paul looked up to catch the beat, but could not see his father anywhere. He gasped, but before he had time to jump from his chair, Wilberforce popped out from beneath the platform, colorful bunting draped over his head and shoulders. His only concern was that his players should not miss a beat.

Paul's jobs finally put money in his pocket. He spent it on hearty meals downtown and dates with local young women. His work also financed the purchase of a motorcycle. Now he could begin the serious pursuit of some of the girls who attended the dances he played at. His campaign began on an alarming note. He talked one young lady into letting him take her home on his new motorcycle. They settled comfortably on the porch swing, and Paul was about to place his arm about the girl. At that very moment a signal bell went off inside the house and lights flashed. Paul heard the sound of heavy boots clattering down the stairs. Thinking that he had set off some kind of alarm to warn against suitors, Paul raced off just as a huge man came running through the front door.

Afterward Paul learned that the commotion had had nothing to do with his amorous designs. The father of his would-be sweetheart, a fire-department captain, had a signal connection in his bedroom tied into the alarm system at the fire house. The experience dampened Paul's spirits only for a short while. Some forty years later Gene Fowler recalled Whiteman's discovery of the opposite sex with some amusement. "Paul was never able to concentrate on any one girl. Each of his romances, however, was violent while it lasted and kept him in a condition of worried excitement."

In 1907 Paul landed his first steady job as a violist. He was hired by the Denver Symphony Orchestra and its conductor Raffaelo Cavallo. Whiteman had just finished East Denver High School and was enrolled at the University of Denver for several courses. "But I only took physics, football, and my lunch," Paul said years later to a Denver reporter, speaking of his short tenure on campus.

In spite of a modest but steady income, the future King of Jazz was usually in debt. This situation bothered his father, who finally insisted that Paul go into business. A symphony musician would never make enough money to live the way Paul wanted, the Professor argued.

Paul obediently looked for a job and found one with a real estate firm. One of his first clients was an elderly lady whom he drove in a horse and buggy to look at several houses that were up for sale. Two hours later he was back at the real estate office.

"You will have to get someone else to do it," he told his boss. "The cheapest house cost $2,500, and that would take her last cent. I won't do it."

Young Paul then tried his hand at driving a taxicab. Auto taxis, newly introduced in Denver, quickly replaced the horse and carriage. Most of his calls took him to Market Street, the city's red-light district—an area he knew well. Taxi driving did not last long, either. "The engine valves were too musical; the sound led me back to the viola." Paul returned to music.

3

Symphonic Chords

In 1908 America was in the middle of "the good years," that period of peace and prosperity that lasted from 1900 to the outbreak of the First World War. At the turn of the century the country had fought briefly with Spain over its island possessions. When the war ended, the United States was recognized to be a major world force. In Washington a young, dynamic president, Theodore Roosevelt, held the reins of government. St. Louis had heralded the centennial of the Louisiana Purchase with a memorable fair. San Francisco had survived a devastating earthquake and fire. The Wright brothers had proved that man could fly. Admiral Peary and Dr. Frederick Cook were racing each other to the North Pole. A very real exuberance brightened the early 1900s. And popular music and entertainment played no small part in creating this spirit of optimism.

On Broadway, *The Ziegfeld Follies of 1908,* which opened in June, starred Nora Bayes and Jack Norworth singing their own composition, "Shine On, Harvest Moon." For an encore they belted out another of their songs, "Take Me Out to the Ball Game." Gus Edwards's nostalgic *School Days* and Oscar Straus's captivating *A Waltz Dream* drew large audiences to the Great White Way.

The musical *Three Twins* opened for a spectacular run of 288 performances, made possible in part by its show-stopping melody, "Cuddle Up a Little Closer." George M. Cohan wrote the music for three shows that season and starred in one of them, *The Yankee*

19

Prince. Fritzi Scheff, Bert Williams, Anna Held, Trixie Friganza, and Joe Howard all saw their names in lights.

From Broadway to the Golden Gate, people were humming and singing "Sunbonnet Sue," "Pony Boy," "Sweetest Maid of All," "Yama-Yama Man," "Rose of the World," "In the Garden of My Heart," "Up in a Balloon," "Down in Jungle Town," and "To the End of the World with You."

Touring companies brought many of Broadway's biggest hit musicals to Denver, and Paul frequently managed to get free tickets or passes from other musicians or press agents. Most of the new popular tunes—especially those with a ragtime beat—never made it past the front steps to the Whiteman home; Wilberforce disliked ragtime and jazz. Still, when his son became a household name, the old Professor remarked, "I still don't like jazz, but I must admit my boy Paul plays it better than the others."

Paul's mother, more than her husband, understood Paul's growing interest in the Broadway show tunes and Tin Pan Alley melodies. To Elfrida and Paul, music was fun, not merely business or a serious profession. They made room in their lives for spontaneous and carefree interludes of singing "By the Light of the Silvery Moon," "Meet Me Tonight in Dreamland," and "Down by the Old Mill Stream," accompanied on the piano in the front parlor—but only when the Professor left the house.

Elfrida Whiteman continued to sing in community concerts and oratorios, with occasional engagements as far away as Philadelphia and Boston. She was asked to be a regular soloist with the Trinity Church Choir, which Wilberforce directed. Trinity's special annual program—often augmented by more than 250 singers—became a major event on the city's musical calendar.

The Professor took great pride in planning bigger and more elaborate musical affairs. It became the talk of Denver when Wilberforce Whiteman gathered some 750 school orchestra players and more than 2,000 singers for a performance of a Gilbert and Sullivan operetta to raise money to buy additional musical instruments and keep them in repair.

The ordeal of organizing this mammoth concert led him to the brink of a nervous collapse. Wilberforce gathered up his family and herded them to their nearby mountain lodge. He was certain that a respite from the constant demands of teaching, coaching, and performing would restore his health. But a week passed without improvement.

Then at breakfast one morning the Professor leaned across and spoke to Paul in a choked voice. "I don't like the way you are holding your mouth."

Paul made no reply. He and his sister had been warned repeatedly not to excite their overwrought father.

Wilberforce repeated in a high voice, "I said I don't like the way you are holding your mouth. Put it back the way it ought to be."

Paul stood up and left the table.

The Professor jumped to his feet, grabbed a chair, and broke it across his son's broad shoulders. As Paul walked quickly toward the door, his father shouted after him, "And don't think you'll ever be old enough or big enough to lick me!"

Oddly enough, this open show of violence and hostility seemed to mark the beginning of Wilberforce's recovery. In a little over a month he was able to return to the city and resume work. Paul had certainly been made aware that his devil-may-care attitude and late-night carousing had contributed to the Professor's breakdown.

It became more and more evident that Paul could not conform to his father's strict Victorian morals. After most performances at the Manhattan Beach Theatre, Paul went out on the town, usually accompanied by a chorus girl. There was a never-ending supply of companions, furnished by the touring companies. The inevitable happened. One singer caught Paul's eye and he asked her out. They met every night after the show, and by the end of the one-week run they had made up their minds to marry.

The young woman, Nellie Stack, had joined the road show in New York, where she lived with her mother. Six or seven years older than Paul, who was just eighteen, she easily persuaded Paul to elope. Years later, when he was asked why they had married, he shrugged his shoulders. "Maybe she thought my father would give us money. I don't know. But it seemed like a good idea at the time." Their honeymoon was brief. Two days later Nellie was off on the road again with her show. Paul made plans to join her in New York. They agreed to keep the marriage a secret.

Toward the end of the year Paul persuaded his father to let him go to New York to investigate the possibilities of studying music there. Wilberforce gave him train fare and money for a hotel room.

Two weeks later Paul returned to Denver. He seemed unusually quiet and crestfallen and said that he had no further plans to leave town.

About a year later, in January 1910, the postman delivered a letter postmarked Brooklyn, New York, which cleared up the mystery of Paul's New York visit. Wilberforce opened the envelope to find a one-page letter written by a John O'Hanlon.

> Dear Sir,
> Miss Nellie Stack . . . has given me instructions to write to you, asking to have her marriage to your son Paul Whiteman annulled.

Wilberforce's jaw dropped in amazement. He read on:

> As you are doubtlessly aware, he was a minor when the ceremony was performed and it would be no great trouble to you to have the annulment procured. This will save a great deal of trouble to you and Miss Stack. She has asked me to do this before she takes proceedings, and she will have to take proceedings against you as your son is a minor.

When nineteen-year-old Paul returned home that evening, he had a lot of explaining to do. He told his father about meeting Nellie Stack, their brief courtship, and the impulsive decision to elope. "We planned to start our married life in New York where Nellie's mother runs a theatrical boarding house. That's the real reason why I went to New York. Well, when I got there, Nellie said she didn't want to be married and didn't want to see me any more. She told me that I'd better get the marriage annulled real fast. But I didn't have the nerve to tell you and Mom. I was hoping Nellie would forget."

Wilberforce realized that an annulment was indeed the only answer. Paul was under age. Miss Stack would only make trouble if Wilberforce did not agree. It was obvious that the alluring Nellie had no intention of settling down as Mrs. Paul Whiteman.

So Nellie passed out of Paul's life. But sixteen years later, in the wake of Paul's international fame and mounting fortune, Nellie and her mother Celia reappeared. His former mother-in-law sued Paul for $10,000 in damages, claiming that he had deserted her daughter six months after their marriage in 1908. Shortly thereafter Nellie had allegedly borne a child, who lived for only six months. Mrs. Stack stated that she paid the infant's hospital and doctor bills and funeral expenses at Paul's request and that he had agreed to repay her.

The case was heard in March 1926. The judge denied an application by Paul's lawyer to examine Mrs. Stack before the trial. Whiteman contended that the suit was outlawed by the statute of limitations, and he denied any past promise to Nellie's mother to send her money. Just as the case was about to go to trial (and Paul to sail for Europe), Paul's lawyer advised him to settle out of court and end the gossip and speculation. Paul paid Mrs. Stack $7,750. The settlement ended the public airing of a sorry episode from his past—one that all the Whitemans had tried to forget.

By the time Paul's marriage was annulled, he was no longer a teenager. But Wilberforce complained that he still acted like one and that he was headed for more trouble. The Professor felt it was time for his son to pull himself together and do something with his life. Paul could play well enough to hold down the first violist's chair with the Denver Symphony, Wilberforce pointed out, but he should devote more time to his music and perhaps give private violin and viola lessons to help make ends meet.

Matters came to a head one morning when twenty-four-year-old Paul overheard his father talking to his mother. "I've had just about enough of that son of ours. He's become a lazy, good-for-nothing parasite. We've given him a good home for over twenty years, a fine education, the best musical training. But he just can't seem to get started or stick with anything very long. All he thinks about are girls, vaudeville shows, and drinking with his pals between rehearsals. It seems our son is set upon not amounting to anything."

His mother said sadly, "He's only floundering until he can find his proper place in the world."

"We've done all we could to help him find his proper place," the Professor replied. "The truth is, I don't want him around any longer."

Paul fled to his room. His father was right—it was time he made his own way. A few years earlier, he had briefly left Denver to play in a resort hotel orchestra at Hot Springs, Arkansas, but had returned home. Paul packed, gathered up his viola and violin, and went downstairs, headed for the front door. He stopped in his tracks; his mother was in the entrance hall.

"I heard what Pop said about me, and he's right. It *is* time I make something of myself. I'm leaving Denver. I'll write you when I settle down. Don't worry . . . good-bye, Mom." Paul paused. "And say good-bye to Dad for me."

Paul's mother kissed him and reached into her pocket. He'd need money, she said, and she happened to have taken some out of the bank only yesterday. Elfrida handed Paul several hundred dollars and watched as he closed the door behind him.

Paul was to learn later that the professor had staged the conversation with his wife in the hope that they could force their drifting, aimless son to take some action.

For some months in 1914 Paul had been reading about musical activities on the West Coast in *The Etude* and other music journals. San Francisco's symphony orchestra, the magazines noted, had attracted larger and more enthusiastic audiences every year since its first performance in 1911, when Henry Hadley, its conductor, had scored a triumph with works by Tchaikovsky, Liszt, and Haydn. The growing orchestra was adding full-time musicians and increasing its subscriptions. There were good prospects for other jobs, too; the city was looking for musicians for the Panama–Pacific Exposition, scheduled to open in San Francisco in early 1915.

Paul talked with his friend Fred Baker, a violinist, about working in San Francisco. They agreed that the exposition to celebrate the opening of the Panama Canal would increase their chances of getting work. Besides, the big fair sounded like fun for footloose bachelors.

Fred and Paul boarded a train for California. Paul carried both his violin and his viola. He immediately went to the symphony office hoping for an audition. Though he was told that there were no openings, Paul was determined. His viola at his side, he sat in the lobby of the hotel where the orchestra manager was staying. When he saw the manager he picked up the viola and began to play, ignoring the astonished other guests. Impressed by Paul's playing, the manager found a place for him (and Fred Baker, too) in another orchestra, which was performing at the Union Pacific Railroad exhibit on the fairgrounds.

During the run of the exposition, the eighty-piece orchestra was led by a number of guest conductors, including Frederick Stock, Carl Busch, Walter Damrosch, and Victor Herbert. Herbert enjoyed the company of fellow musicians and often gathered a group of players for support at a local restaurant. Paul usually joined them. The renowned composer was struck by the young violist's capacity for beer and steak—Paul was one of the few musicians who could match Herbert's own capacity for food and drink.

Before the end of the festival summer Paul had performed works by a remarkably broad range of composers, from Bach through Brahms to Richard Strauss and Camille Saint-Saëns. He also participated in a Beethoven Festival of Music, which brought together a hundred musicians and the soloists Ernestine Schumann-Heink and Paul Althouse in a program at the Civic Auditorium to celebrate the unveiling of a monument to Beethoven.

Before the close of the 1915 Exposition, Paul again tried to get a job with the symphony. This time he succeeded. He signed a contract that guaranteed sixteen weeks of employment during the 1915–1916 season at a salary of $25 per week. The new conductor, Alfred Hertz, began rehearsing the orchestra in the fall for its opening concert at San Francisco's Cort Theatre on December 17.

One of ten viola players, Whiteman worked hard under the dynamic maestro. His association with the symphony led to engagements with the San Francisco People's Orchestra, a smaller group of symphony musicians. Giulio Minetti directed this orchestra in frequent concerts for school children throughout the city. He also asked Whiteman to join his highly acclaimed Minetti String Quartet.

With Paul in the ranks, mischief and pranks broke up many serious and sedate occasions. Chester Hazlett, a talented clarinetist and saxophonist, was a willing accomplice.

Just before one performance of *The Sorcerer's Apprentice*, it was Hazlett who asked Paul to hold out his hands, palms up, then placed an egg in each. As the bassoonist prepared to play the beginning notes of the introductory theme, Hazlett ordered his friend to break the eggs in the bell of the large, convoluted instrument, which jutted past Paul's shoulder. Paul hesitated and then dropped the two eggs down the bassoon bell.

Maestro Hertz nodded at the bassoonist, giving him his cue. A barely audible gurgle was heard. The bassoonist blew harder. His eyes nearly popped behind his glasses. Hertz scowled as he beat the silent air in a vain effort to raise notes from the instrument. The gurgling caused an outbreak of stifled guffaws and chuckles on stage. Only the timely entrance of other sections of the orchestra silenced the spreading laughter and prevented the entire performance from collapsing.

Paul signed a contract for another season with the symphony.

At the same time, he organized a small seven-piece orchestra to play for ice skaters at a rink near Post and Sutter Streets. Outfitted in band uniforms, the musicians were stationed on a balcony overlooking the skating arena. The entertainment featured professional skaters, who performed everything from ballet to barrel jumps. Patrons were encouraged to try their skills between shows. Whiteman and his men played the usual waltzes associated with ice palaces, including "Over the Waves" and "The Beautiful Blue Danube." From time to time, however, he departed from the usual repertoire. Paul kept the skaters on their toes by trying ragtime novelties. The audience welcomed the change of tempo, and Paul's first attempt at conducting succeeded admirably. Paul and his six musicians, whose identities are now lost, were forced to disband within a year only because there were not enough jobs to keep them busy and in the money.

Paul turned to playing with hotel orchestras and salon ensembles to add to his modest salary from the symphony. Conductor Rudy Sieger engaged him for the fashionable Fairmont Hotel, noted for its outstanding menu and fine dinner music. The men performed on a gold-draped balcony in the high-ceilinged dining salon. Dressed in dinner jackets and starched shirtfronts, they could be seen only from the waist up. History does not record what Paul and his friends did or did not wear below the waist.

The Fairmont was the setting for the yearly Greenway Ball, hosted by the colorful and free-spending Ned Greenway, who had made a fortune selling champagne. To entertain his many friends, he hired the entire San Francisco Symphony to play for dancing. Franz Meyer, a German-born violinist and cellist, conducted with his bow.

Toward the end of the ball, a dowager waltzed by the bandstand. She paused to remark, "Oh, Mr. Meyer, we are having a wonderful evening. Your music is marvelous. I knew you played the cello; I have heard you many times with the symphony. But I had no idea you played the violin."

Meyer replied in broken English, "Oh, sure. Mit my concerts I play der cello. Mit my balls der violin." Paul heard the maestro's reply and exploded with laughter.

Paul also worked at the St. Francis Hotel where many musicians stayed during concert engagements. Paul met Eugene Ysaye during one of the great violinist's visits to the city. Ysaye and Paul, together with a few other symphony members, played Viennese waltzes until the early hours of the morning. Paul later claimed that he based his first arrangements on the general pattern of the Viennese waltz— that is, a striking introduction, a series of sparkling modulations throughout, and another striking effect in the coda. Speaking of his very early orchestrations, he commented, "I developed the theme and variations type of arrangement, based partly on the classic form and partly on the plain common sense belief that you must play the song through at least once, to have the audience know what you are doing."

During Paul's third season with the San Francisco Symphony he began to think of the viola as a poor relation to the violin and of questionable importance to the orchestra. Pitched a fifth below the violin, the viola would have to be 50 percent larger than the violin to maintain its tonal brilliance. Unfortunately a viola that size could not be played unless it was handled like a cello. Essentially the instrument yielded few advantages to its player. The violin outshone its slightly bigger sister, gaining all the best solo parts.

During a performance of Sibelius's *Valse Triste* Paul's viola had only two notes to the bar to play. "After about ten years of having different conductors try to get something different into those two notes," he complained, "I knew the viola could not stack up against the violin. In 'Valse' there was a boop-boop and peep-peep. I was the peep-peep guy. I needed to go into a freer form of music."

He decided to resign from the symphony orchestra at the end of the season in early 1918. Paul had heard a lot of jazz in San Francisco, where it was the latest rage. Jazz promised nothing worse in the way of dollars earned and perhaps the chance of something better. Being a classical musician in San Francisco did not provide a living. Two jobs were necessary to make ends meet.

"Jazz was beginning to be popular," Paul recounted to musicologists years later, "and I made the surprising discovery that, while I was able to earn only $40 a week in the symphony, I could get $90 playing what was then called 'jazz' fiddle. The music was often sketchy, the arrangements inexpert, and a great deal was left for the player to improvise."

Whiteman joined the orchestra at Tait's Café, one of the city's most popular gathering places for jazz enthusiasts. He played only two evenings. The next night John Tait fired him because he could not play jazz the way the rest of the musicians did. "You can't jazz, that's all," he said; Paul just wasn't good enough. The string

musician, who had played the classic symphony and opera repertoire, failed to measure up to the popular beat.

"This made me mad, and I was determined to find out why."

Paul spent more and more of this free time—and by now he had
plenty of it—in the jazz cafés and dance dives on San Francisco's
Barbary Coast. This notorious waterfront district had become the
jazz center of the West Coast during the years before the First
World War. Jazz screeched and bellowed from smoke-filled, beer-
fumed cabarets and saloons. Here, Paul thought, he could learn
what jazz was about, could discover the hang of it. He would keep
at it even if it took a year.

Night after night he visited the restaurants and backrooms where
jazz was being played. He had no money for food and drink—only
a very presentable dress suit, left over from his symphony days.
Wearing this, he cut a highly prosperous-looking figure, and there
was no way that a head waiter could tell that he had not a dime in
his broadcloth pocket. Paul would appear when the music was at
its height. He would hang around near the entrance as though waiting for someone, but actually he was studying jazz and jazz players.
If necessary, he would make up a name and say that he was joining
that person's table when his friends arrived. The drawback was
that this ruse could be used only once in each restaurant or café.

These lean days brought encouragement from his mother and his
sister, who had married before his abrupt departure from Denver.
Like Elfrida, Ferne possessed an excellent contralto voice. She
had studied extensively and was a respected and well-paid teacher;
Ferne's husband was the St. Louis representative of the Seaboard
Railroad. When her letters to San Francisco contained money to
tide Paul over, therefore, he knew that he could wait to pay her
back.

In his furnished room on Jones Street, Paul worked on experimental orchestrations. With violin, paper, and pencil, he struggled
through his rudimentary jazz studies. After many attempts Paul
finally worked out an orchestration. He soon discovered that "faking" or improvising was what jazz outfits relied upon. That is, they
had no scores; each player worked out his part for himself, "faking"
as he went along. Essentially there were no jazz orchestrations.
That was the classically trained Paul's first discovery. He would
try to change the situation.

As 1918 presaged a new era, Paul continued to prowl San Francisco's many music meccas from the Barbary Coast to Nob Hill. On a visit to the Fairmont Hotel he took particular note of an innovative young bandleader, Art Hickman. Deemphasizing the prevailing brassy texture, Hickman had added more saxophones to his group, giving a lush but jazzy sound to his music. The dominant tonal effect of the additional two or three saxophones pleased Paul.

Paul was now convinced that, without losing spontaneity, lighter popular music could be played from prepared sheets by expert players, with the same accuracy and precision demanded in the symphony orchestra. At the same time he did not want to lose whatever flavor came from the jazz improvisations that were derived from free-flowing sessions, where the players extemporized on their parts. Paul believed that many players in those "jam" sessions "invented" particularly clever variations, which had to be carefully noted and preserved so that they could be integrated into an orchestration.

"Up to that time, there had never been a jazz orchestration," Paul wrote some years later in his book *Jazz*. "I made the first, and started into the jazz orchestra business. That sounds simple, but it wasn't. The first hundred days of any business have their discouragements and there was nobody hankering for the opportunity to finance my jazz band—not after I got myself fired because I couldn't jazz."

Gradually Paul collected a handful of musicians. He wanted to be sure that the people he brought into his jazz group knew what he was trying to do. He recognized that neither the general run of jazz players nor the more traditional symphony musicians were suited to his purpose. He needed musically trained young people who were, in his words, "ambitious, slightly discontented, and willing to adventure a little."

Paul also managed to borrow a few hundred dollars from his sister and his friends to guarantee his employees, salaries. At last he had both the money and the men. He marshalled his resources, started rehearsals, and began looking for auditions and bookings. But he did not reckon on the prolonged war in Europe.

4

On the March

Whiteman tried to enlist in 1917 during the first year of America's involvement in the war. But recruiters took one look and turned him down. By now he weighed almost 300 pounds; by the rules he was unfit for "combatant purposes."

Paul plodded in and out of recruiting stations in San Francisco until the Navy finally agreed to put him in uniform if he would enlist as a bandmaster. Born and raised far distant from any ocean, he grew up with a landlubber's contempt for the sea. Nevertheless, in the spring of 1918 he was sworn into limited service compatible with his civilian experience. His first order: find a tailor to fit his large frame into a seaman's uniform. The new sailor hired a suitmaker who managed to accommodate his large size with a fairly acceptable outfit while still adhering to regulations. But the standard measurements of the traditional square collar were inadequate to cover his broad back; instead, the collar hung straight down between his shoulder blades. On seeing the odd collar, his commanding officer ordered it rescaled in proportion to the rest of his uniform.

Whiteman was assigned to Mare Island Naval Station in San Francisco Bay with orders to organize and train an orchestra of sailors. Called the Naval Training Camp Symphony, it included a number of musicians who had played in San Francisco cafés and hotels, such as Tait's and Victoria's. Among the recruits were two sidemen who would be heard from in a big way as civilians—saxophonist Rudy Wiedoeft and pianist–conductor Paul Ash.

An undated note to his mother reveals Paul's initial experiences in uniform. It is one of his few surviving letters.

My Dearest Mother,
   You ask what my duties are. Well at the present nothing. I have charge of the upper barracks and just boss the other fellows. The meals are fine by the way. The Sailors call it chow. But when I get out of here I am to lead the vaudeville show and play viola in a string quartette. I don't have to play in the band so it is very soft unless I get shipped on a boat. Then I shall have to take up a brass instrument but it isn't likely. I shall have to leave for a while. I get out of Detention a week from Monday. The Bandmaster is very nice to me. He's come to see me a couple of times and is going to give me leave for 5 days. . . .
   Give me Ferne's and Paul's address as I want to write them and you write me often. Love to both you and Father.
                                                                    Paul

Paul's morale-boosting outfit played practically every Red Cross event and Liberty Loan drive in and near Mare Island. It also performed regularly at Sunday services and motion-picture shows. A special assignment, accompaniment for an original all-Navy show called *The Rose of Queretaro*, raised money for the Naval Auxiliary Relief during a two-week run in downtown San Francisco.
   By the end of four months Whiteman and his men had played for every conceivable wartime event or program. In spite of his dislike for the high seas, Paul, envious of the war's heroes and restless with morale-building chores while many contemporaries were risking their lives, applied for an overseas assignment. The commanding officer at Mare Island turned him down because he lacked combat training and fitness. Instead, Paul was assigned to a submarine chaser off the coast. Paul welcomed the change; he was assigned regular seaman duties aboard the vessel.
   His assignment came to an unexpected and tragic end. An explosion ripped apart the ship's boiler room, killing ten men. Paul counted the days until his return to shore, his fear of boats now firmly entrenched.
   A week or so after Paul had rejoined his musicians, the Mare Island bugle sounded "cease firing," signaling the end of the war

on November 11. Paul's time in uniform had provided him with valuable experience as a bandleader. It had also given him ample opportunity to try out his ideas for orchestrations. "Best of all," Paul later admitted, "we had discipline, so that the trombonist couldn't get off practice whenever he had been out late the night before and the French horn player never dared pipe a word about headaches. And I learned something about being disciplined as well as disciplining. I was paid $42 a month and got it a good deal more regularly than later when I was paying other men forty times that."

At the close of the war Paul moved back to San Francisco, into a rooming house at 17 Powell Street. He had made something of a mark as a naval conductor, and he quickly put his contacts to use. The owner of Neptune's Palace, a cabaret on the Barbary Coast, suggested that he gather a handful of former Navy musicians to form a dance band. Paul put together a sextet—violin, saxophone, banjo, accordion, drums, and piano. Neptune's Palace attracted a rowdy, free-spending crowd made up largely of returning service-men and waterfront seamen. The availability of several dozen unescorted women to drink and dance with added to the allure. In a short time they all knew Whiteman—whom they called "Tiny"—and were eager to dance to his jazzy, fast-tempo tunes.

Paul, too, learned a few things about the restaurant business from watching the waiters. They carried out a quick maneuver to oust a belligerent customer. Two waiters would usher him to the back of the dance hall and shove him through a camouflaged section of the wall. Behind the panel was a laundry chute, which sent the surprised patron sliding down to the street below. The waiters also had orders to remove all glasses, full or empty, whenever imbibers got up from a table. Regular customers knew the ropes; they grabbed their drinks and finished the contents before trotting off to the dance floor.

Early in 1919 Paul's old friend Rudy Sieger called him from the Fairmont Hotel. "I'd like you to take charge of the dance orchestra. The hotel is planning to open a new room called Rainbow Lane. You can pick eight or nine men, including four sax players. My only suggestion is to include a great trumpet player I heard in Los Angeles. He'd be tops on the fast ragtime stuff you like."

"What's his name?" asked Paul.

"Henry Busse."

Paul had already met Busse. His musical ability was well known in San Francisco.

Paul Whiteman and his orchestra opened at the Fairmont a month later. They were well received by what was then the fashionable crowd. Paul later described this opportunity as a stopgap in his career. Readjustment to civilian life hadn't been easy. He actually missed the discipline of the military; it had relieved him from facing many decisions.

Now he was breaking in new musicians and new arrangements, and the effort was taking its toll in ways he could not fathom. As the orchestra's manager, arranger, and leader, he felt that he lacked the skill necessary to juggle the three jobs. At the Rainbow Lane he would leave his post at the end of a set and when he was out of sight, he would, for no apparent reason, cry for ten minutes or so. He would pull himself together, return to the bandstand, and curse himself for his lack of control. Was it fear of failure?

As the situation continued, he gave up drinking, hoping for improvement in his condition. He also suffered from frequent back pain. The several doctors he consulted could only suggest a long rest. Paul found it impossible to quit worrying. He began to spend all his free time in bed. He even lost considerable weight—some hundred pounds in three months. His nerve, ambition, and health all seemed in jeopardy. Finally, he quit the Fairmont. After a bright beginning, Paul's orchestra broke up almost before it had begun.

Removed from the pressures of backstage planning, auditions, negotiations, and the ordeal of public appearances, Paul came to grips with himself. He admitted that his profession entailed long, fatiguing hours and daily work in crowded, noisy rooms. There was no way to avoid these strains. He also realized that living this life in a pressurized goldfish bowl, he had developed certain phobias. He now feared close quarters and heights, so that tall buildings and elevators were torture to him. In later years airplanes would affect him the same way. Given his profession, there was no way he could avoid travel or skyscrapers, and facing the inevitable triggered bouts of heavy drinking. Whenever his schedule allowed sufficient time off, Paul escaped to the unfettered outdoors and the open countryside.

Once again Rudy Sieger came to his aid. His boss, the owner of the Fairmont, had also acquired the Belvedere, a hotel in fashionable Santa Barbara. Rudy recommended Whiteman for the job of music director. Paul now felt able to resume work on a bandstand, and he was eager to start the job. The only drawback he faced was recruiting a new group of musicians outside of San Francisco. Fortunately several of his friends agreed to join him; they were pianist C. Welborn Jackson, trumpeter Frank Siegrist, and cellist Ralph Eliaser.

The music program at the Belvedere stressed dinner dances, society hops, and almost daily tea dances. Every Sunday evening Paul's Belvedere Quartette gave well-attended concerts of light classical numbers, such as excerpts from *Aida* and *Lucia di Lammermoor* or Edward Grieg's *Solveig's Lament*. At the end Paul always included one or two of the latest Tin Pan Alley hits from New York.

Time nearly stood still amid the verandas, gardens, and public rooms of the handsome resort hotel. Even the visit of a European monarch was taken in stride. When Albert, King of the Belgians, appeared, the nonplussed hotel manager escorted him to various Belvedere attractions, including the dining room, where the Whiteman ensemble was playing. Paul and his musicians made a vivid impression on the king. Later in the season, during Albert's visit to Pasadena, Paul's group was ordered to play for the king there at the Maryland Hotel. Paul had won over the first of his many royal and loyal fans.

While he was playing at the Maryland, Paul also made an impression on at least one critic. In the first review ever devoted to Whiteman's music, *California Life* magazine wrote, "He surely is a jazz artist extraordinary, for he is overflowing with rhythm, and his dance music is the most intoxicating, rhythmic, and effervescing product I have ever heard."

Regal disciples and ecstatic critics notwithstanding, Paul needed money to keep his men together, especially for the hours of rehearsal he considered important. In order to pay his men for these sessions, Paul was forced to play in a dance hall on the beach. His pay consisted of silver dollars dropped into a can attached to a railing in front of the band.

Help was on the way, however, in the form of John Hernan, who had been impressed by Paul's conducting in Santa Barbara and Pasadena. He guaranteed the musicians' first month's salaries if Paul got an orchestra together for the Alexandria Hotel in Los Angeles. Paul jumped at the offer, assuring Hernan that his outfit was working hard to perfect a new and distinctive sound.

In late 1919, just a year after his discharge from the Navy, Paul and his orchestra opened in Los Angeles. This group was the beginning of what would one day be called the "original" Whiteman band.

On the advice of Hernan, the owner's right-hand man, the 700-room Alexandria signed Whiteman for twelve weeks, starting at $650 a week. The contract called for nine men, contained an option for work at other hotels under the same ownership, and provided for an increase in pay for any employment in the East.

Paul used his advance wisely. He hired his eight musicians on a cooperative basis. The band members participated in all proceeds, with one share for each of the players and two for Paul as conductor, violinist, business manager, and organizer. The plan got results. Paul's musicians eagerly worked at giving the best possible performances—which, in turn, meant steady income for one and all.

This "original" group consisted of pianist Charles Caldwell, drummer Harold McDonald, trombonist Buster Johnson, bass player J. K. Wallace, trumpeter Henry Busse, saxophonists Leslie Canfield and Charles Dornberger, and banjoist Mike Pingitore.

Mike often claimed that he had been with the Whiteman band longer than its leader. He reported for the first rehearsal before anyone else, including Paul, who was a half-hour late. A short, hunchbacked man with a perpetual smile, Mike had been crippled since birth. His left leg, five inches shorter than his right, required special shoes. Paul called Mike his good luck charm and kept him in the band for thirty years as banjoist, part-time librarian, and general assistant. Pingitore's artistry on the banjo—especially his fast and dextrous figure-eight and circle strokes—became familiar to anyone who heard the Whiteman orchestra.

As a professional musician, Mike often spelled his last name "Pingatore" because he thought that this form was easier to pronounce. Just before linking up with Whiteman, Mike had led an all-girl band at the Venice Pier near Santa Monica. In the early 1920s he made the tenor banjo an important and versatile part of a dance orchestra. He also revamped the instrument by extending the neck and repositioning the pegs. He went into partnership with a major banjo manufacturer and earned sizable royalties for a number of years.

Henry Busse rejoined Whiteman in Los Angeles. The Dutch-born trumpet player had led his own five-piece band a few years earlier in Buffalo, then had worked in composor Vincent Rose's band in California, where Busse met Whiteman. The star brass player stayed for nearly ten years, until a battle with Paul sent him off to organize his own orchestra. Busse helped to compose two early Whiteman hits, "Wang Wang Blues" and "Hot Lips," which became Busse's theme. He succeeded on his own in hotels and theaters for over twenty years with a good commercial band that featured his "shuffle rhythm."

When pianist Charles Caldwell left the original nine shortly after the opening at the Alexandria, Paul's friend Ferde Grofé took his place. Although born in New York, Ferde had left the city as a youngster to live in Germany with his widowed mother but returned to the United States to attend high school and college. Ferde had studied the piano, viola, and composition and had played with the Los Angeles Symphony. He drifted into popular music for probably the same reasons as Paul. Their paths crossed in 1915 when Ferde was playing piano at the Portola Louvre in San Francisco. Paul dropped by to hear Grofé's jazz improvisations and orchestrations. Whiteman liked Grofé's arrangements, particularly his reworking of symphonic themes into dance tunes. That Ferde could more fully utilize this talent and at the same time beef up the instrumental outpourings of Paul's relatively inexperienced orchestra struck Whiteman as the best of two worlds. He convinced Grofé to cast his lot with the Alexandria Hotel outfit.

On opening night Whiteman and his men took their place on the bandstand. As he nervously looked out at the clusters of neatly set tables, Paul spied a number of people he had played for in Santa Barbara and Pasadena. During the first set, the room began to fill up, and he was stunned to see Mabel Normand, Harold Lloyd, Charlie Chaplin, Fatty Arbuckle, Blanche Sweet, Wallace Reid, and Gloria Swanson. Every star in Hollywood seemed to have come. The entire movie colony was eager to pass judgment on the orchestra and its conductor. Paul's music instantly captivated the Hollywood crowd. Before the evening ended, comedian Fatty Arbuckle grabbed a set of drumsticks and sat in for drummer Harold McDonald. Matinee idol Wally Reid borrowed Leslie Canfield's sax to blow some notes. The irrepressible Chaplin jumped onto the bandstand and, grabbing a violin bow, mimicked Paul's style of conducting.

By all standards the debut was an unqualified success. Paul's brisk, energetic arrangements and his flamboyant podium personality caught the attention of the first-nighters. Jazz had been a blatant and raucous upstart; according to one writer, Whiteman's well-honed ensemble "whispered its heresies." The Whiteman sound had a certain lilt that captured and held the attention of people who were occupied with eating, drinking, talking, and dancing. His fans came back again and again, and spread the news of the mesmerizing Whiteman music.

Soon the movie colony invited Paul and his musicians to its lavish parties—not just to play but often as guests. Marshal Neilan, a film director, helped the group to earn extra money by playing mood music on the silent-movie sets. Neilan also urged Paul to think about opening in New York as part of a Ziegfeld show. He offered to deposit $10,000 in Paul's bank account to take the band East for a tryout with the great Flo Ziegfeld. But Paul decided to stay in Los Angeles; his contract at the Alexandria had been sweetened and extended as the hotel saw the cover charge receipts rise from $300 to $1,200 a day.

Paul reveled in the Hollywood hijinks and enjoyed hobnobbing with the free-spending celebrities. With extra money in his pockets, he amused himself in childlike ways. His neighbor in the Hollywood Hills, Tom Mix, regularly invited him to markmanship contests inside his house and Whiteman reciprocated. Fortified by a magnum of champagne, the pair shot .45-caliber pistols at knicknacks in one or the other living room and den. A day or so later, after the broken bric-a-brac had been replaced, they would start shooting all over again. Paul joked that the walls of their two houses came to contain enough lead to keep them anchored to the ground even in the path of a Kansas tornado.

With all the success and publicity, Paul was barely scraping by from week to week on his two shares from the cooperative plan and after repaying his loans. One of the reasons was that whenever a musician threatened to accept a better offer, Paul took something off his own proceeds to give the disgruntled player a bit more to keep him satisfied and on the "team." In 1920, when Whiteman began to make records regularly, the men began to resent the cooperative plan. A musician who played two notes in an entire number was given the same money as the man who played five or six instruments and worked throughout the session. The arrangement was abandoned immediately, and after that time Paul paid each musician a commensurate straight salary. From then on Paul began to make money for himself.

The popularity of Whiteman's music, which kept him in the same location for such a long time, led to a need for a steady flow of new arrangements. But as conductor, violinist, organizer, and business manager of the unit, he had less and less time to devote to orchestration. At times he used the publishers' stock arrangements with only minor changes; on other occasions Ferde Grofé contributed his considerable talents. Paul and Ferde often worked on ideas together, discussing a song's possibilities, deciding on variations in tonal textures, and talking over thematic embellishments. Whenever any of the sidemen were present at such discussions, they were free to toss in their suggestions, and some of their ideas were incorporated in Ferde's drafts. At the next rehearsal the arrangement was given a thorough reading, and final additions and improvements were made. Ferde wrote down every change to arrive at the fixed and final version. From then on the number was played exactly the same way, and audiences enjoyed the same tonal texture and rhythmic effects, whether at the first or the 500th performance.

Ferde Grofé wasted little time in turning out new arrangements. Among them was "Johnny's Tune," composed by John Schonberger. Later this melody acquired lyrics, and as "Whispering," it became one of the biggest hits of 1920. That same year a young real estate dealer in Beverly Hills had his first song published and asked Paul to introduce it at the Alexandria. Paul liked the melody and soon had couples dancing to "Coral Sea" night after night. The composer, Nacio Herb Brown, later quit his job and began writing songs for early talking pictures. His later resounding successes included "Broadway Melody," "Pagan Love Song," and "You Were Meant for Me."

Hit songs with outstanding arrangements made Whiteman a bigger attraction and built for him an ever larger following. One of his admirers was Herbert K. Somborn, a minor motion-picture distributor who had just married Gloria Swanson. They had spent their honeymoon at the Alexandria and danced to Paul's music. Somborn—who eventually left the movie business to open the Brown Derby restaurant—felt that Paul only needed a push in the right direction and a bit more confidence. Somborn's uncle, S. W. Straus, owner of the Alexandria, was about to open the Ambassador in Atlantic City. Somborn persuaded Straus to bring Whiteman East for the new hotel.

When Straus offered Whiteman's nine men $1,200 a week, he

had no intention of paying the band's train fares and other traveling expenses. Whiteman explained that he had not been able to save any money. If Straus wanted him and his orchestra, the only way they could open at the Ambassador was for the hotel to lend him at least $2,500. Straus ultimately advanced the group $2,600 but ruled out any pay raises until the loan had been repaid.

Over 3,000 miles separated Hollywood from Atlantic City. No eager fans awaited Whiteman's arrival. In the East no one seemed to care that night after night he had played to a room full of enthusiastic movie stars.

5

Dance Craze

In the 1920s conventioneers and honeymooners flocked to Atlantic City. No other resort in the East—with the exception of Niagara Falls—attracted so many newlyweds and salesmen. They added to the daily crowd of tourists strolling along the four-mile Boardwalk and the oceanfront piers, where sea breezes mixed with the aroma of popcorn, saltwater taffy, and tap beer, and the sound of the surf blended into the music provided by carrousel calliopes, player pianos, and hotel orchestras. There was no lack of diversion or entertainment. Midway games, vaudeville shows, industrial exhibits, band concerts, motion pictures, and rolling chairs enticed vacationers and businessmen. From morning swimming and sun bathing to midnight dining and dancing, the seemingly endless variety often overwhelmed new arrivals, whether they had come to play or to work.

Paul's band reached Atlantic City after four days on a New York-bound cross-country express and a day on a local New Jersey train. Paul's orchestra now included two new sax players—Hale "Pee Wee" Byers and Gus Mueller—and a new string bassist, Sam Heiss. They replaced Leslie Canfield, Charles Dornberger, and Spike Wallace, respectively, all of whom had chosen to stay in Los Angeles.

Most of the musicians had never crossed the Mississippi before; it was Paul's second trip East. They found the Ambassador far up the Boardwalk, off the beaten track. The hotel manager welcomed them, although he worried about offering the Whiteman band as

40

his opening musical attraction; better-known orchestras were playing at more conveniently located and more established hotels. To reassure him, Whiteman began rehearsals immediately, hoping to make a favorable impression at least on the hotel staff. Almost at once his gang became homesick for California. The musicians missed the wholehearted camaraderie of the West. Several decided to return to Los Angeles, but Paul persuaded them to stick with the group.

Whiteman opened at the Ambassador in the late spring of 1920. His debut in the resort city featured the carefully worked-out Grofé arrangements of well-known classical and semi-classical numbers, popular Tin-Pan Alley tunes, and several new songs. The music barely caused a ripple along the oceanfront. Few of the diners stayed past dessert and even fewer gravitated to the dance floor.

The first week or two at the Ambassador were heartbreaking to Paul. Customers stayed away and business was virtually nonexistent. After his huge success in Los Angeles, he felt totally let down.

Then, one gloomy afternoon, an attractive couple came into the almost empty dining room. When the music started, they danced. They stayed for an hour or more, not missing a single opportunity to enjoy Paul's music. The following day the couple returned bringing several friends. Again the group stayed and stayed, obviously entranced with "Avalon," "Japanese Sandman," and other lilting foxtrots. The following evening the couple brought still more guests. Soon the tables began to fill up and business started to grow.

"We never spoke to the girl nor she to us, but we knew she was press-agenting us all over town," Paul later wrote in *Jazz*, "All we have ever known about her is that she had yellow hair and brown eyes and danced like a wood nymph."

The growing crowds and receipts at the hotel lifted the musicians out of their doldrums. On Saturday nights they now played for over 1,000 guests. Paul did well enough at the Ambassador to begin to repay Straus for the travel advance.

As summer approached and the oceanfront hotels and rooming houses filled to capacity, another stroke of luck came Paul's way. The annual convention of the Victor Phonograph Company met in Atlantic City. A number of salesmen breezed into the Ambassador for lunch and heard Whiteman play. They were impressed with the group's unusual rhythmic and tonal treatment of such favorites as

"My Heart at Thy Sweet Voice" from *Samson and Delilah*, the Meditation from *Thais*, and "Dance of the Hours" from *La Gioconda*. As a result, they urged their bosses at Victor to listen to this new group from California.

Paul's story, from his chapter "Growing Pains" in *Jazz*, has Victor executive Calvin Childs listening to the orchestra at the Ambassador and a few days later offering a two-year recording contract. Other sources claim that Paul was signed by a company underling without any official okay and that Childs reluctantly agreed to record the group. Whatever the preliminary details, the recording was, as Paul said, "The beginning of so many unbelievable cyclonic happenings that we began to get used to miracles."

In 1920 the phonograph-record business was inching up to $100 million for the year. Victor stood out as the leader, with annual sales of $50 million. It was in 1920 that Caruso made his last record for Victor and Toscanini his first. The company could easily afford to take a chance on Paul Whiteman and his orchestra.

Paul's contract specified a fixed payment of $50 to him for each side recorded. The musicians got $25 apiece. No royalties would be paid. In fact, very few artists, outside of Victor Red Seal's classical repertoire, were given more than a flat recording fee.

No sooner was the ink dry on his Victor contract than Paul started to worry about everything that could go wrong during the recording session. Victor scheduled a trial waxing session at its Camden, New Jersey, plant for early July. Paul postponed the date. A second session was planned; again, Paul canceled. A third date was set. Totally inexperienced in the ways of recording, Paul had become so scared of facing the unfamiliar acoustical recording horn that he was almost hoping Victor would cancel the deal. There was no one to turn to for advice. None of his musicians had ever faced a recording machine. Finally, on August 9, Whiteman and the band entered the large Camden complex and located the small recording room. Paul had worried so much that he had made his musicians memorize every note. Whiteman made four records in two hours without using a sheet of printed music.

Of the four selections cut that day only "Wang Wang Blues" was acceptable. The others—"Japanese Sandman," "Avalon," and "Whispering"—were spoiled by the audible curses of the musicians whenever they made a mistake. The engineers also had problems with Hale Byers's shrill and overpowering soprano sax. Whiteman was asked to return in ten days for a second attempt. At that session on August 19, studio engineers approved "Japanese Sandman" on its fourth run and "Dance of the Hours" on its third. "Avalon" was not attempted. "Whispering," with an added slide-whistle chorus by an outside musician named Warren Luce, again failed to measure up after six tries. "Come back in four days and we'll work on it some more," the Victor technicians told Paul.

On August 23, the band regrouped in Camden for the third time in two weeks. Both "Avalon" and a new tune, "Anytime, Anyday, Anywhere," were waxed without mishap. "Whispering," which Paul had played hundreds of times over the past eight months, evaded capture on takes one and two. The third run-through—actually the ninth matrix since the first session—made the grade. During his entire first year of recording, Paul was faced with an unusually high number of rejected takes.

Pressings of "Whispering," with its flip side of "Japanese Sandman," began to leave Victor's shipping department in September. Victor mounted a full-scale promotional and sales campaign to get a hearing for the disc, which the executives believed would be a big seller. They did not wait for the publication of the regular monthly catalog to announce the newest release. Dealers received special notice of Paul Whiteman and his Ambassador Orchestra, and this new type of modern dance music. By early October the Whiteman record was in dealer bins throughout the country and was attracting a steady stream of record buyers.

In its November catalog, Victor officially introduced Whiteman as a Victor artist. It ran a full-page description of the orchestra, its brisk and beautiful arrangements, and its unusual instrumental effects, along with a portrait of Paul by the famous photographer, Bachrach. The publication also introduced Whiteman's second record—a twelve-inch disc of "Avalon," backed by "Dance of the Hours" (now retitled "Best Ever Medley"). Victor had already realized the tremendous popularity of Whiteman; it issued the record with a list price of $1.35—fifty cents more than the ten-inch "Whispering." In December 1920 the company brought out Paul's very first pressing, "Wang Wang Blues," along with "Anytime, Anyday, Anywhere," recorded on August 23. Starting in early 1921, Victor released one or two Whiteman discs a month. Within four months the phonograph maker had sold tens of thousands of Paul's records—and the demand grew.

As the summer drew to a close in Atlantic City, Whiteman continued to fill the Ambassador with a growing number of fans. Straus, who had become one of them, wanted Whiteman orchestras installed in his cross-country chain. He suggested that Paul's arrangements be copied for similar groups at each of his big hotels. Wherever his customers traveled, he said, he wanted them to know that they could always hear the Whiteman sound. Though it was a novel idea, it struck Straus as a simple task to hire, rehearse, and manage a string of Whiteman offshoots. But to Paul, who had worked several years to find the ideal players and to develop the right instrumentation and arrangements, the proposal had limited merit. Though such an undertaking might make big money for both Whiteman and Straus, Paul took a dim view of diluting his budding, and still regional, success by branching out in assembly-line style. He promised to think the proposal over while Straus took a short trip to Europe.

When Straus returned, he had more ideas for Paul's men. They should all be dressed in Hungarian peasant outfits, with Paul wearing the brightest, most elaborate gypsy costume ever designed. Or, thought Straus, perhaps they should create a Bavarian-looking dance band, in red jackets, lederhosen, and long woolen socks. Many of Paul's men could be replaced with German or Hungarian players to make the group more authentic.

Paul didn't speak for a long moment. "You've been good to me, S. W., but I've got the band I've always wanted now. My records are starting to sell well, and everyone thinks we should go to New York in the fall. I gave up concert work because there were a lot of players better than me. I wanted to do more than play viola or second fiddle stuck away in the back row of an orchestra. Besides, who would want to look up at a bandstand and see a fat fiddler in leather britches?"

As the season at the Ambassador neared the end, Paul received a flurry of offers from owners of cafés and restaurants. Dining-and-dancing spots in New York were eager to book him, enticed by his enormous success in Atlantic City. Theatrical producers Lee and Jake Shubert also wanted Paul as an attraction on the Century Roof in New York. He had an opportunity to stick with Straus and work his hotel chain, but New York beckoned with its offer of more money and a chance to tackle Broadway.

Paul and Straus parted friends. Straus, with his $2,600 loan repaid and mounting ballroom receipts, had seen his newest hotel successfully launched.

Prohibition, which went into effect in January 1920, hardly inaugurated an era of clear thinking and clean living, as the Anti-Saloon League of New York had prophesied it would. Violation of the law began immediately and continued unabated for the next fourteen years. Rum-running boats and speakeasies sprang up overnight. Drinking increased in spite of the ban on manufacture, sale, and consumption of liquor.

This period was the heyday of the carbaret and the nightclub. Ben Selvin was leading an orchestra at the Moulin Rouge; Sam Lanin, at Roseland; Arnold Johnson, at Reisenweber's; Bill Munro, at the Café de Paris. Farther uptown, at Fifty-Ninth Street and Fifth Avenue, Joseph C. Smith conducted the Hotel Plaza orchestra; he also was virtually the only contributor of dance records to Victor, having just cut "Left All Alone Again Blues" and a medley from the Ziegfeld Follies for that label.

The bidding from New York cafés and hotels for the Whiteman band was overwhelming. But the Palais Royal restaurant won Paul's services at a weekly salary of $1,600 for a three-month run beginning in mid-September 1920. Paul's first preparation for his opening was to move the existing bandstand from a palm-sheltered balcony above the floor to the dance floor itself. "We've got to be close to the people, the dancers," he said. "Up in that jungle perch, they'll think we're a bunch of monkeys."

The club's owners objected, insisting that New York's social set did not mingle with musicians.

"We're pretty social ourselves," Paul replied. "Most of my boys are college guys. We dress well and know our p's and q's. We met a lot of New Yorkers in Atlantic City, and they'll probably be your customers. They're used to talking with us. Besides Al Jolson is gonna be here opening night, and he promised to sing. But he won't do it if the band's out in left field hanging from the roof."

The owners relented. Paul even persuaded the manager that there was no need to add big-name acts in a floor show. "We don't want that window dressing. If we stick to business and play the best we know how, New York will take to us without a lot of fanfare."

On opening night, head waiter Louis Cantoni—who had a reputation for knowing the Social Register, Dun and Bradstreet ratings, and the show business Who's Who—welcomed a capacity crowd of New Yorkers. Paul and his men were an immediate hit; the first set lasted over two hours because the dancers refused to leave the floor.

Night after night Whiteman and his orchestra dispensed the newest and most danceable music in town. As Hollywood had adopted him, so did New York. Paul's salary soon jumped to $2,500 a week, and his original twelve-week engagement grew into a four-year stint at a steadily mounting fee.

On October 25 over a hundred Victor record dealers came to the Palais Royal to thank the band for the tremendous public acceptance of the Whiteman records. A few days earlier Paul had recorded two more songs—"Honolulu Eyes" and "Darling"—and Victor was scheduling more sessions in New York during November. As 1920 ended, it was clear that Paul and his men had risen in less than a year from an obscure regional outfit with few prospects to a nationally acclaimed band with unlimited horizons.

Hardly a week passed without Paul's picture in the papers. His round face with its pencil-thin moustache, double chin, and deep widow's peak became well known. Soon these features were captured in a distinctive pencil sketch—a copyrighted illustration that would identify Paul for the rest of his life.

Vaudeville scouts pursued him with contracts. Broadway booking agents offered him lucrative deals. Victor rushed him into its recording studios month after month. Party givers offered enormous sums for his services. Song pluggers, press agents, reporters, tour managers, composers—all became a part of his days and nights.

As Whiteman's popularity and earnings soared, he acquired an enterprising agent named Harry Fitzgerald. Along with Hugh Ernst, Paul's manager, Fitzgerald urged Whiteman to consider satellite bands under the Whiteman banner. Paul changed his mind about spinning off orchestras and he began to organize bands of nine or ten instruments at other cabarets and clubs and aboard luxury liners. By October 1922 he had nineteen orchestras working out of his office at 158 West Forty-Fifth Street. As their popularity waned, the number of these units gradually decreased. By the end of the 1920s none was left bearing the Whiteman name.

That year Paul decided to collaborate with Ferde Grofé on writing the music to a number which the band could introduce and popularize. It evolved into "Wonderful One," with lyrics by Dorothy Terriss (who also wrote the words to another big seller, "Three

O'Clock in the Morning"). An instant hit and perennial favorite, "Wonderful One" was Whiteman's only major effort at songwriting, and a highly successful one. Paul's name did appear as a collaborator on at least five less successful tunes of the 1920s: "I Never Knew," "Madeline Be Mine," "When the One You Love Loves You," "Charlestonette," and "Flamin' Mamie." But in all probability he was cut in for royalties in return for building interest for the songs from his bandstand—a common practice of the day.

Not long after the Palais Royal opening, sax player Gus Mueller came to Paul. Distressed at his inability to read music scores, the New Orleans musician told Paul that he simply could not stand all the work the band put in over a sheet of music. Gus was not lazy or stubborn; he worried about losing his special knack of playing Dixieland and jazz. If he learned to read music well, he explained, he might forget how to improvise.

Paul replaced Gus with Ross Gorman, then thirty years old. A sax and clarinet player, he had started in vaudeville as a youngster at the turn of century. By 1915 he led his own Novelty Syncopaters and began mastering as many instruments as he could. He joined Harry Yerkes's well-known orchestra in 1919 and stayed two years. He recorded extensively with the Virginians, a band recruited from Whiteman musicians and other popular dance groups of the 1920s. With the hiring of Gorman, Paul added a unique talent. Ross played virtually every reed instrument ever devised and a half-dozen others. As a result, Ross and Paul regularly featured what was known as "doubling"—that is, one man playing various instruments during one set. This practice spread from Whiteman's band to almost every major outfit in the music business.

No one equaled Gorman in the incredible number of instruments he could play and play well. But the addition of Don Clark to the Palais Royal group meant that Paul gained a sax man who also played the cello for luncheon concerts. Urbane and well-educated, Clark was heir to an insurance fortune in California. When he joined he brought his gold-plated saxophone and a valet who polished and laid it out nightly with his dress clothes.

Other personnel changes soon left only Paul, Mike Pingitore, Henry Busse, and Harold McDonald of the original Los Angeles nine. By 1922 Tom Gott was added on second trumpet; Sam Lewis took over trombonist Buster Johnson's chair; Jack Barsby filled Sam Heiss's shoes as tuba; and string bass player Henry "Jack"

Lange joined as second pianist. Ferde Grofé, who just missed being among the original nine players, now was busier than ever with orchestral arrangements, and he required an assistant at the piano. When Lange left in 1922, pianist Phil Ohman came in and, in turn, was succeeded by Phil Boutelje. A violinist—initially Fred Cook, then George Tjorde, and Mario Perry—was signed up, as Paul gradually put aside his violin to concentrate on conducting.

A young Irish tenor named Morton Downey joined Whiteman's musicians in 1921. He had been performing in New York neighborhood theaters and speakeasies, where he was heard by Hugh Ernst, who urged Paul to audition the nineteen-year-old singer. Paul reluctantly agreed, then signed Downey for $75 a week as a band vocalist. Audiences were still hesitant to accept a singer with an orchestra. Vocalists were considered semi-musicians sitting on a bandstand without much to do. Downey and Whiteman gradually changed this attitude. But at the outset Downey did not perform with the Palais Royal group. Young Downey served a sea-going apprenticeship with the newly-formed Whiteman Orchestra on the *S.S. Leviathan.* Eventually he made over twenty trips to Europe and achieved his first measure of fame as "The Tenor of the High C's."

Downey first began making regular appearances with the main Whiteman group in 1923, during its first concert tour in England. During the *Leviathan*'s layover at Southampton, Downey joined the band in London for a week of engagements. Soon Whiteman took him off the ship to do featured numbers with the orchestra in New York. By 1924 Downey was consistently on stage although he rarely performed. During the Aeolian Hall concert that February he sat with the orchestra though he did not sing.

Paul still felt that it was necessary for Downey to hold a musical instrument between vocal selections. He put a reedless saxophone in the singer's hand, then moved him to a French horn. But when a composition called for a French horn, Morton had to pantomime alongside the real player. No one could tell whether Morton or the real French horn soloist was actually playing. To keep Downey from an occasional toot on the horn, Whiteman had him stuff towels or toilet paper into the bell.

Audiences gradually accepted the presence on the bandstand of someone who only sang. Downey's rendition of "Emeralda," by

Phil Boutelje, and of "Macushla" brought him increasing recognition. His singing of "Wonderful One" did much to popularize the tune Grofé and Whiteman had collaborated on.

Morton's weekly take doubled to $150 by 1925. So convinced was Paul that Downey was scheming with every theater manager and producer to leave Whiteman for bigger money that he fired the singer. Downey quickly joined a Ziegfeld show in Florida before going into vaudeville with a single act. Network radio contracts followed, and Morton Downey became one of the biggest and most successful popular singers on the air. He remembered his years with Whiteman kindly as "invaluable training with the very best in the band business."

In September 1921, the first anniversary of Paul's debut in New York, Harry Fitzgerald persuaded E. F. Albee, the vaudeville magnate, to spend $900 a week to feature the band at the Palace Theatre. Show-business professionals believed that a dance band would make an absurd and noncommercial vaudeville act. Ticket buyers, they thought, wanted performers—singers, dancers, jugglers, comedians, acrobats—but not mere music makers, playing for twenty minutes to an audience that didn't even have a place to dance.

Albee gambled on a week's run, adding to the bill hoofers Louis and Charlie Mosconi, toe dancer Bessie Clayton, and the Avon Comedy Four. When Paul opened at a Monday matinee, he was visibly ill at ease. Just before the curtain went up, he was close to a nervous collapse. The thought of facing a demanding Palace audience rekindled all his old feelings of insecurity, leaving him overly sensitive to what he saw as his shortcomings as a bandleader and musician. He had never before played in a theater, and without any previous experience of vaudeville, he was now expected to play in the ultimate variety house, the Palace on Broadway. But at the very last minute he managed to pull himself together and face the audience—without makeup and in need of a shave.

Reviewers criticized the act's lack of showmanship, but they noted the repeated call for encores. The band was a smash, and the engagement was extended to five weeks. When the theater wanted the group back for another run, after a short break, Paul raised his fee to $2,750 a week. He played the Palace another month before deciding to end the engagement. Though Albee was insistent that he stay, Paul and his men, who had taken New York by storm, feared that they would wear out their welcome among the bigtime vaudeville fans. Albee, angered and annoyed, signed up Vincent Lopez instead.

Dozens of theaters in the city wanted Whiteman on their bill. Paul was reluctant, however, to commit the band to engagements that interfered with his nightly Palais Royal schedule or his frequent recording sessions. But by the summer of 1922 he succumbed to a really tempting offer to appear in a Broadway show.

George White had produced his first revue, which he called *Scandals,* in 1919, after dancing in several Ziegfeld shows. The first edition of the *Scandals* ran four months. But the 1920 production caught on and ran for nearly a year, chiefly because a new composer wrote the music for the show. The 1921 *Scandals* brought more of George Gershwin's music, including "Drifting Along with the Tide."

George White planned the 1922 edition for a late-August opening. The Ziegfeld Follies of that year had bowed in June with a cast headed by Will Rogers, Gilda Gray, Gallagher and Shean, and Mary Eaton. Irving Berlin's *Music Box Revue* had signed William Gaxton, Charlotte Greenwood, and Clark and McCullough for a fall run. Also in rehearsal was *The Passing Show of 1922,* with Willie and Eugene Howard and Fred Allen.

White was facing stiff competition. His newest revue had to be outstanding. He had lined up comedian W. C. Fields as his star, and Gershwin had agreed to write the music once again. But White still needed a special attraction. He approached Whiteman with the idea of making Paul and his orchestra part of the production. The Globe Theatre was only a few blocks from the Palais Royal, so that the numbers could be integrated into the show in a way that would not cut into Whiteman's regular appearances at the popular night spot.

Gershwin, one of New York's popular and indefatigable men-about-town, frequented the Palais Royal to enjoy Paul's orchestra. Whiteman played George's music, and the two soon met one evening between dance sets. Both welcomed a chance to work together in the *Scandals of 1922.* Gershwin's jazzy "I'll Build a Stairway to Paradise," sung by Winnie Lightner and conducted by Whiteman from the pit, stopped the show. "He made my song live with a vigor that almost floored me," Gershwin is quoted as saying in *The Gershwins* by Robert Kimball and Alfred Simon. "There was no stopping Stairway to Paradise once Whiteman got his brasses into it.'' Paul also played a vividly orchestrated medley of the Gershwin score—"I Found a Four Leaf Clover" was one of its hits—during the intermission.

George White's *Scandals of 1922* also introduced the first of George Gershwin's more serious works written in a jazz idiom. *Blue Monday Blues,* a one-act opera, told the story of two black lovers, the man's infidelity, and the woman's murder of him. Gershwin wrote the music to a *Frankie and Johnny* plot, and Buddy DeSylva added lyrics to what became the arias "Blue Monday Blues," "I'm Going to See My Mother," and "Has Anyone Seen My Joe?" George White himself danced in the production. Whiteman conducted from the pit.

The audience was taken aback when the capsule opera—which ran for twenty-five minutes—was presented right after the first intermission. The melancholy, moody work was nothing like what they expected in a musical revue; Charles Darnton, the music critic for the *New York World*, described it the next day as "the most dismal, stupid, and incredible black sketch that has probably ever been perpetuated."

White immediately cut the number from the show. But three years later it resurfaced at Carnegie Hall in a concert version under the new title *135th Street*. Benny Fields and Blossom Seeley sang the leading roles, and once again Whiteman conducted the work, which Grofé had reorchestrated. In 1925 the critics paid more attention to the performance because Gershwin had already written *Rhapsody in Blue* for Whiteman; they thought no better of it. "My association with Whiteman in this show I am sure had something to do with Paul's asking me to write a composition for his first jazz concert," George wrote years later. "There is no doubt that this was my start in the field of more serious music."

The *Scandals* brought together these two fast-rising innovators of music in the 1920s. Gershwin and Whiteman became good friends though hardly intimates; Paul never moved in Gershwin's close circle. He did attend George's large parties, and when Gershwin moved to his new Riverside Drive penthouse in 1928, Whiteman could certainly be found there, along with Ferde Grofé, Fred and Adele Astaire, Walter Damrosch, music publisher Max Dreyfus, and Ira and Leonore Gershwin.

New York's "Four Hundred" had discovered Whiteman and his

orchestra at the Palais Royal. They now had to have him and his music for their parties, and he soon vied with conductor Meyer Davis for any season's top-flight social gatherings. Evalyn Walsh McLean, the owner of the Hope diamond, and her husband threw a New Year's ball in Washington for which she hired the orchestras of both Whiteman and Davis, each alternating sets from opposite sides of the room.

Whiteman, however, preferred conducting for an audience not made up of private partygoers, and in later years he committed himself to fewer and fewer such dates. Even when, as a new arrival on the New York party scene in the early 1920s, Whiteman took his orchestra to private engagements for princely fees, he considered his men more than mere hired hands, on a par with waiters and busboys. He refused to let them be hidden behind potted palms, thick hedges, or large screens. When he played at the home of John T. Dorrance, heir to the Campbell Soup fortune, Paul insisted that he and his musicians eat with the guests, not with the servants in the pantry, as was the custom. In fact, Paul did more to gain social acceptance for dance-band musicians than any other conductor of his day.

Society hostesses considered Paul a "catch"; so did Broadway chorus girls. He was always pursued by a bevy of chorines, who sought to share the spotlight with him and thus to advance their careers. They also enjoyed his conviviality and largesse. Paul was one of the town's big spenders in a madcap era.

In 1921 Paul was so smitten by a mesmerizing showgirl that he could not take his eyes off her. It seems that he told none of his friends about her. One day he simply brought her to a rehearsal and introduced Alfrica Smith as his wife. Nicknamed Jimmie, she had no more theater credentials than had Paul's first wife. This second marriage to yet another comely chorus beauty lasted a month or so. Years later Paul referred to it as one of his "mini-marriages." By 1922 Paul was again a bachelor, no better and no worse for the brief encounter.

Before long a young dancer he had first met in San Francisco reentered his social life. Paul had been introduced to Mildred Vanderhoff while he was conducting his band at the Fairmont Hotel, though they may already have met during Paul's stint with the San Francisco Symphony, where her father, Herbert Vanderhoff, also played. Mildred was an interpretive dancer, using the stage name

Vanda Hoff. During the First World War she came to New York to appear in Ziegfeld's *Midnight Frolics* at the New Amsterdam Roof, and in 1920 she was featured dancer in *Carnival,* starring Ed Wynn. The lithe, graceful Vanda also appeared in the popular Vincent Youmans and Ira Gershwin musical, *Two Little Girls in Blue*.

Paul and Vanda became reacquainted in New York, when he was at the height of his popularity. In spite of two failed marriages, Paul could not wait to tie the knot with still another showgirl. He proposed, twenty-four-year-old Vanda accepted, and they were married at City Hall on November 4, 1922. Witnesses to the ceremony included members of Paul's orchestra. The bride put aside her career and took up housekeeping at Paul's apartment on West Seventy-Fifth Street.

6

Music Exporter

After two and a half years in New York Paul felt that now was the time to get away from Broadway for a while. Jazz was not taken seriously in America. But, he knew, anything coming from Europe was put on a high pedestal. There were singers and instrumentalists who were unable to get a hearing in the United States until they had studied or performed in France, Germany, or Italy, where they had gained what the public seemed to want them to have—foreign approval.

Paul's plans had been given a boost the previous summer, when the honeymooning Lord and Lady Mountbatten had spent many of their hours in New York dancing at the Palais Royal. Mountbatten had been especially enthusiastic about Paul's brand of music and had insisted that London—and most especially the dashing Prince of Wales—must be given a chance to hear the band. Paul reflected that his orchestra would be given more serious consideration if it, too, had a European stamp of approval. He decided to risk leaving New York's limelight for four or five months and using his own money to pay traveling expenses for his band. He contracted to appear in a revue, *Brighter London,* beginning in March 1923, at a fee of $7,500 a week. Though this was three times his fee at the Palais Royal, he had no assurance that the engagement would last more than a week. His advisers in the William Morris talent agency urged him to take the risk and go. They pointed to the growing sales of phonograph records throughout Britain and the prestige in the wake of probable acclaim in London.

Not long after passage was booked, Mike Pingitore fell ill. Paul cast about for a substitute banjo player. Harry Reser, a recent arrival from Ohio, agreed to fill in. Paul was impressed by Reser's ability to sightread as well as his skills as a soloist. As it turned out, the British audiences delighted in his exuberance and technical ability. He returned home with the signature on his banjo head of no less than the king, George V.

There was a "terrified lump" in Paul's throat as the *S.S. President Harding* passed the Statue of Liberty. Paul and the gang were a strictly American bunch; most of them had never been abroad. Paul immediately grew seasick, adding to his doubts about whether the trip would be worth the time and expense. He could hardly wait for the ship to reach England.

The moment the *President Harding* docked in Liverpool, Paul was the center of attention. His coming had been widely discussed in the British press and debated in government. A representative of the British Ministry of Labour met the ship to suggest that Paul and the band turn right around. It was pointed out that they did not have working papers. Paul cabled to the United States Secretary of Labor for help.

There was real fear on the part of British officials that increasing popularity of American jazz would flood the country with American bands and players. British musicians were not well trained in banjos and saxophones, key instruments of the "new" music. Paul realized that the entire controversy was based on the belief that the appearance of this band would be very successful. Though he found such faith flattering, he pointed out to Grofé that it was cold comfort if they were not allowed to play.

The imbroglio was eventually resolved, Whiteman and his band being given permission to perform in *Brighter London* but forbidden to accept any other engagements. But after the revue, which opened in tryouts in Liverpool on March 19 and moved to London on March 28, received good reviews, other managers sought Paul's services. Eventually the Ministry of Labour allowed the Grafton Galleries, a popular London nightclub, to hire the Whiteman band if it also paid the wages of an equal number of British musicians. Paul employed only a few of them.

"Our recruits never seemed to get the hang of jazz," Paul observed. "There was something about it that was absolutely foreign to them. Perhaps they took it too seriously." One day at rehearsal he asked one of the British musicians, "Can you ad lib?"

"Certainly," answered the man, rather annoyed. "I can ad lib anything you write."

These newly acquired musicians read and played music very well, according to Paul. But they seemed to lack the spontaneity, the exuberance, the courage for jazz.

Brighter London played to a full house week after week. "I do not think it is too much to say that what Johann Strauss was in the playing of waltzes, Paul Whiteman is in the playing of modern dance music," wrote Francis Toye, music editor of *The Sphere,* sister magazine of *The London Illustrated News.* "They do some odious things, and at times they make some unpleasant noises, but even then their performance is clever and amazing. And when they play softly, as, for instance, in a foxtrot based on Korsakoff's *Sadko,* they are absolutely delightful. Never in my life have I witnessed such a display of rhythmical virtuosity."

With Paul's success in *Brighter London* and his nightly engagement at the Grafton Galleries following the stage appearance, his visit to England began to stretch from weeks to months. Even Vanda had time to prepare a dancing routine, which she performed at the Grafton Galleries.

True to his word, Lord Mountbatten welcomed Paul to London with a party to introduce Paul's music to the Prince of Wales. The Mountbattens invited only thirty guests, all members of the royal family. Paul had another of his attacks of stage fright; he was so nervous that he couldn't tell the prince from his brothers—the Dukes of Kent, York, and Gloucester. "Be natural," advised Mountbatten. "Just be yourself."

The prince instantly took to Paul, the musicians, and their danceable rhythm. He complimented drummer Harold McDonald on his technique and picked up a few pointers. The prince confessed his fondness for bagpipes, ukulele, and drums. But dancing was his first love; he was extraordinarily good at it.

After the Mountbattens' gala, the prince came to the Grafton Galleries many times to hear Paul play. On a number of occasions Paul also entertained at the prince's private parties.

"We all addressed his Highness quite informally as Prince," Paul recalled in *Jazz*. "He once remarked upon this habit of Americans who, he says, Prince him until he feels like barking. He never reminded you that he was a prince, but you never forgot it. The quality I liked most in young Edward Albert was his consideration for others. I saw a hundred instances of it with his personal attendants and others who served him. He noticed a saxophonist was absent one night and asked solicitously if he were ill. When next he saw the man, he remembered to inquire about his grippe."

Though the Prince of Wales often insisted that he wanted to pay for Paul's appearances, Whiteman reminded him that he had come to London initially to play for him and considered it honor enough to have that privilege. He did not mention that the terms of his work permit would not allow a fee in any case. Paul's compensation from the Grafton Galleries alone was filling the Whiteman coffers handsomely. Paul shared in the club receipts, and as a result, this cavalier from America could afford to act—and dress and eat—in a royal manner.

Paul's musicians, too, were living like princelings. They bought striped trousers and cutaways, plus-fours, Argyle socks, and sweaters. They attended sporting events from cricket matches to steeplechase races. They borrowed colorful runabouts for jaunts in the English countryside. They explored the city's pubs and music halls. Paul was especially fond of London's large bathtubs. Years later, the memory inspired him to install king-size fixtures, including an extra-large "throne," at his New Jersey country home.

Paul also spent hours exploring London's great restaurants, where roast beef and steak were daily fare. Cocktails, beer, and wine came with every meal. Paul had almost forgotten the joy of ordering drinks in a land that knew no Prohibition. His waistline soon expanded; by the time he left England, he had gained some 40 pounds, pushing his weight well over 300.

The orchestra played at a number of benefit shows and regimental balls. All its appearances captivated audiences and critics—except a performance at Albert Hall to aid a military hospital. The group followed a seventy-piece orchestra in the enormous auditorium not known for its acoustics. The audience greeted the Whiteman selections, played by sixteen men, with cold silence. There was no applause. At the London Hippodrome the band had been given ovations, but the vast Albert Hall was just too big for the group; and it did sound awful by comparison. The hardest blow of all was delivered by the man who had requested Paul's services for the benefit. The sponsor told Whiteman that his orchestra was without doubt the worst he had ever heard. Paul could only think that people seldom appreciate what they get for nothing.

When the London season reached its peak in early summer, Paul remained the popular ambassador of American jazzdom. He decided that before returning to New York, he would host a large party for all his new British friends as well as for the cast of *Brighter London.* The guest list grew to include the show's backstage crew, the staff at the Grafton Galleries, and the press, as well as other acquaintances. Of course Lord and Lady Mountbatten were sent an invitation, although cynics cautioned Paul that the British upper crust would not appear at a backstage bash. Paul took over the basement of the Hippodrome and brought in hundreds of pounds of American-style hot dogs and spareribs, plus barrels of German beer. The farewell celebration which, indeed, included the Mountbattens (but not the Prince of Wales), started on a Saturday after the last show. Twenty-four hours later many of the guests were still toasting Paul and his musicians, whose thoughts were on home and the bright lights of Broadway.

At midsummer, after five months in England, Paul and Vanda and the band joined 1,550 passengers of the *S.S. Leviathan* bound for New York. On August 13, as the ocean liner sailed into the harbor and passed the Statue of Liberty, every musician in the city seemed to be waiting to greet Whiteman with a syncopated welcome. Paul looked up from the deck to see a small band playing in an airplane above the ship. From another plane a skywriter had spelled out "Hello Paul" against the blue sky. Steaming toward the *Leviathan,* the *S.S. Tourist* held hundreds of fans, clustered around six orchestras joined to serenade the returning jazz king. In the water a half-dozen musicians wearing life savers added additional notes to the cacophony.

Mayor John Hylan sent an aide to meet Paul and his men, as did the police commissioner. On Pier 86, at the foot of West Forty-Sixth Street, the reception continued with more bands and more fans. Representatives from the Victor company and from the American Federation of Musicians joined theater owners and performers to crown Whiteman King of Syncopation. The celebration continued that evening at the Waldorf-Astoria Hotel, where 400 people toasted Paul. On the dais at the dinner were George M.

Cohan, New Jersey Senator Edward Edwards, publisher Frank Crowninshield, Irving Berlin, John Philip Sousa, and Victor Herbert. When Paul rose to respond to the many welcoming remarks, tears were rolling down his cheeks. "For a moment," Paul wrote in *Jazz*, "I forgot any cynicism I had felt about the false value of the European label in America. Cynicism doesn't take deep root in an American, anyway. I only felt happy, touched, almost overcome by the warm-hearted generosity of our welcome home. It seemed to me then that everybody understood me, that my orchestra was a real success, that there was nothing in the future but sunshine and roses."

Two nights later *Little Jessie James* opened on Broadway, with "a genuine Paul Whiteman orchestra led by Ernest Cutting: in the pit." Other Whiteman units had sprung up at New York's Club Royal and the Café de Paris. Barney Rapp was leading a Whiteman's Romance of Rhythm Orchestra on tour, and in vaudeville Coletta Ryan held a baton over Whiteman's Saxophone Sextette. Paul himself—"The Maestro Who Symphonized Syncopation"—reopened at the Palais Royal to a following that was larger and more enthusiastic than ever.

Flo Ziegfeld courted Whiteman for his upcoming extravaganza, starring one of the biggest of his many headliners, Fanny Brice. All of Ziegfeld's *Follies* since 1914 had opened in June, but the 1923 edition was scheduled to bow at the New Amsterdam in October. Along with the beloved Fanny, he had lined up Ann Pennington and Bert and Betty Wheeler. Victor Herbert and Rudolf Friml were working on the music; Joseph Urban was designing the elaborate sets. Ziegfeld wanted to perk up the show with the biggest name in dance music. Although the production ran 333 performances, it was a hackneyed edition. There was little doubt that Whiteman's orchestra contributed the best musical number when it teamed with dancer Ann Pennington and banjo-playing Brooke Johns on "Take, Oh Take Those Lips Away," which Harry Tierney and Joseph McCarthy contributed.

The demand for Whiteman recordings showed no signs of slackening. "Whispering" had already sold well over a million copies (its sales eventually reached two and a half million), and "Three O'Clock in the Morning"—a waltz recorded in August 1922—was approaching the million mark. By the fall of 1923 Paul and the band had gone to the Victor studios more than seventy times in three years, often three or four times a month. In England they had two sessions at Victor's studio in Middlesex to wax "Chassonette," "Tell Me with a Melody," "The Merry Widow Waltz," and "Just One More Chance" for His Master's Voice label.

Paul's orchestra became one of the earliest to add a vocal chorus to dance records. Before 1922, discs of popular bands featured only the melody; no lyrics were sung during the two-to-three-minute arrangement. Ted Lewis and Vincent Lopez were among the very first to record vocal segments. In January 1923, Billy Murray vocalized on Whiteman's recording of the comedy song, "Mr. Gallagher and Mr. Shean." Later that year the American Quartet, featuring Murray and Frank Croxton, sang the chorus on "Last Night on the Back Porch." Gradually more and more of Paul's records featured such vocalists as Ed Smalle, Franklyn Baur, Lewis James, and Billy Murray, all of whom were on call as part of Victor's stable of singers. But the bulk of Whiteman hits—"Chicago," "Carolina in the Morning," "Say It with Music," "By the Shalimar"—came out as pure orchestral numbers. Not many record buyers were ready to accept dance music with an integrated vocal break.

Whiteman's sprightly foxtrots seemed to be in a class by themselves. Most of them had a rollicking manner, with calm interludes. The arrangements sparkled with excellent sax, brass, and banjo highlights. Ferde Grofé contrived outstanding themes, at the same time that he incorporated unexpected rhythmic effects and skillful modulations. He and Whiteman were continually experimenting. A solo sax would carry a melody as brass chords played softly in the background. Then the trumpet entered, supported by saxophones. A softly strummed banjo and deftly fingered piano, underscored by a light brush on a snare drum, would all mark the beat.

Members of the orchestra—especially the brass and reeds—were also increasing their own virtuosity, reaching for higher top notes, experimenting with various types of mutes, practicing more agile fingering techniques, executing more precise slap-tongue or flutter-tongue effects.

In the percussion section, Paul took on a skilled new player. George Marsh replaced his original drummer, Hal McDonald, in the fall of 1923. McDonald, however, would reappear on Paul's bandstand before the decade ended.

A number of classical artists were taking a close look at popular music, especially jazz. Fritz Kreisler added a jazz tune to his concert tours. Jascha Heifetz and Efrem Zimbalist played "Kitten on the Keys" on their violins. Tenor Charles Hubbard had sung a jazz tune at the Fourth of July concert in Paris in 1923. John Alden Carpenter had given a jazz beat to his music for the ballet "Krazy Kat." However, it was soprano Eva Gautier who included jazz in the dignity of a song recital. In November 1923 she added a segment of so-called jazz songs to a program otherwise made up of works by Bartok, Bellini, Purcell, and Hindemith. Thus Gautier became the first important artist to include American popular songs in a formal concert program, set in respectable Aeolian Hall.

Whiteman was in the audience and took special notice. George Gershwin accompanied Eva's serious and skillful renditions of "Alexander's Ragtime Band," "Swanee," "I'll Build a Stairway to Paradise," "Carolina in the Morning," and "Innocent Ingenue Baby." A performer of modern songs, Gautier "respectabilized" current Tin Pan Alley tunes. Her widely acclaimed excursion into what the critic and composer Deems Taylor called "our own folk music" sparked Paul's interest in a similar undertaking. He moved quickly.

When Paul told his men about his plans for a concert of modern American music—stressing their contributions to its development—they were eager to hone their talents for the challenging program. Paul outlined the purpose of the forthcoming concert. He believed that tremendous strides had been made in popular music since the early days of jazz around the turn of the century, which his predilection for smooth orchestration made him hear as discordant. Nevertheless, he recognized jazz as true American folk music and a product of black musicians. While he appreciated Negro syncopation, he realized that his musical arena lay near the middle of the road. It was his intention to show, with the assistance of his orchestra, what he saw as the rapid progress of a primitive form (the first piece on his program had not been composed until 1917) toward the melodious artfulness of the early 1920s, which was still called jazz although it had become a somewhat different kind of music in the process of being tamed on its way to the ballroom and the concert hall.

By late 1923 Paul had little time for second thoughts about his foray into a concert hall. Vincent Lopez had announced his own plans for a jazz concert, and now there was no turning back for

Paul. Lopez should not be the first to give a full-fledged concert of popular music.

Paul rehearsed his Palais Royal orchestra whenever he could, usually in the early hours of the morning after the club closed. He knew that the outfit had to be near-perfect to play on a concert stage. Every moment available for rehearsal was crucial; the challenging program would include major new works by George Gershwin and Victor Herbert. As the year came to a close, Paul invited many of the city's leading newspaper critics and musicologists— including Leonard Liebling, John Tasker Howard, Deems Taylor, and Pitts Sanborn—to a series of luncheons at the Palais Royal, where he proceeded to explain what the concert hoped to achieve. To his immense satisfaction, he found them interested in his undertaking and understanding of his goal. Some offered helpful suggestions; all wished him well, and almost to a man, they promised to be at Aeolian Hall on February 12.

For the concert Paul had to add nine instrumentalists to his orchestra. Seven violinists—including Alex Drasein, Bert Hirsch, and Kurt Dieterle—and two French horn players were recruited. Paul now had twenty-three musicians on his payroll and prepared to take the music world by storm.

As the year ended, the editors of *Vanity Fair* magazine nominated Paul for inclusion in the publication's prestigious annual Hall of Fame. Paul joined three writers—Ring Lardner, Marcel Proust, and the Comtesse De Noailles—and actress-philanthropist Eleanor Robson Belmont in the group of notable achievers. Paul's nomination read, "Because he began his musical career, at the age of nineteen, as a violin player in the Denver Symphony Orchestra; because, when thirty, he created the first dance orchestra with symphonic effects; because he first used the saxophone and banjo to maintain tempo and rhythm; and because he makes the most infectious phonograph records."

Soon 1924 added new words and accolades to future nominations.

7

Jazz Treatment

At the end of the unusual concert, on February 12, 1924, well-wishers streamed toward Paul's dressing room in Aeolian Hall. Victor Herbert, Otto Kahn, Fritz Kreisler, and others were eager to congratulate Whiteman on his professional triumph. Many youthful music enthusiasts—such as John Green, Sam Marks, and Teddy Thomas—tried to congratulate both Paul and Gershwin on the electrifying performance of *Rhapsody in Blue*. Others sought out soloists Zez Confrey and Ross Gorman to compliment them on their part in the program of contemporary American music.

After nearly four hours on the podium, Paul was exhausted. He would read the official word on the concert in the morning. The reviews in the New York papers were enthusiastic and encouraging, although not uniformly complimentary. The *Sun* called the program a "long, strong, musical cocktail" and noted that Whiteman "has some amazing musicians under him and he shines out as an extraordinarily well-rounded musician." Lawrence Gilman of the *Tribune* described Paul's experiment as an "uproarious success." He went on to say that the music "conspicuously possesses superb vitality and ingenuity of rhythm, mastery of level and beautiful effects of timbre. For jazz," he continued, "is basically a kind of rhythm plus a kind of instrumentation." The melody, however, failed to impress him. "It seems to me that this music is only half alive. Its gorgeous vitality of rhythm and instrumental color is impaired by melodic and harmonic anemia of the most pernicious kind." Gilman approved of the arrangements and the sounds of the

63

orchestra, but the choice of selections, including *Rhapsody,* left him less than enthusiastic.

Writing in the *World* a week after the concert, Deems Taylor analyzed the *Rhapsody* as "possessing at least two themes of genuine musical worth and displaying a latent ability on the part of this young composer to say something in his chosen idiom." Gershwin's work, he added, projected an "occasional sacrifice of appropriate scoring to momentary effect and a lack of continuity in the musical structure."

W. J. Henderson of the *Herald* described Whiteman "as a born conductor and a musical personality of force and courage who is to be congratulated on his adventure and the admirable result he obtained in proving the euphony of the jazz orchestra." The *Times's* Olin Downes painted a vivid picture of Paul's conducting. "He trembles, wobbles, quivers—a piece of jazz jelly, conducting the orchestra with the back of the trouser of the right leg, and the face of a mandarin the while."

There was little doubt that Paul Whiteman had brought new meaning and perspective to the realm of American popular music. Moreover, the Aeolian Hall concert changed his life and the direction of his orchestra virtually overnight.

Within days Paul's office telephone rang incessantly with offers of concert tours, promotional schemes, private party bids, and proposals for personal appearances. The size of his orchestra and the number of people on his staff started to grow. *Rhapsody in Blue* became his signature tune and his theme song. Victor planned recordings of the *Rhapsody* and other concert selections, to be released with Whiteman's dance music. Paul's nights at the Palais Royal were numbered as cities throughout the country demanded his music in person. It was not too long before his personal income quadrupled to over $400,000 a year.

Undoubtedly Paul's determination to bring his dance music into a concert hall stemmed in part from his father's condescending view of his son's work. "He can't conduct," the Professor had exclaimed time after time. "Besides, it's not real music, just some honkytonk outpourings that don't mean a thing in the long run." When Paul mounted the podium of Aeolian Hall on February 12, 1924, Wilberforce could no longer deny that his son was conducting an orchestra in surroundings that echoed the great masters of the classical repertoire. It was a far cry from Tait's Café and the Ambassador Lounge—even from the highbrow Palais Royal.

Whiteman had taken a giant step, one that thrust him onto a lofty platform and permanently placed him on a level that was stimulating and challenging at times and at others unnerving and enervating. There was no turning back. "I was forced into a situation and couldn't back out," he admitted forty years later to a reporter with the *Miami Herald*.

In the spreading wake of acclaim Whiteman assumed the mantle of spokesman for popular music, the foremost authority on jazz. He, more than any other individual, had successfully traveled the road from smoke-filled backrooms to gilt-draped concert halls, bringing a new sound to a vast range of listeners.

There was no disputing the fact that modern dance music owed much of its sophistication to Whiteman. He was directly responsible for the artistic recognition now given to jazz and for many of its instrumental methods. His influence was obvious in numerous orchestras. Whiteman was, however, the agent rather than the initiator of the force that raised him. "Somebody had to do it," he often said.

Paul always stated that there was no secret about his "method" of bringing jazz into the sphere of dance orchestration. "It's not patented," he pointed out. Nor did he claim to be a composer; he frankly told other dance orchestra leaders, "You can do it, too, provided you are a trained musician instead of a trickster."

Nor was this something good musicians should scorn to be concerned with, he often explained. "All classical music consists, in the final analysis, of the folk themes of peasants which have been built into sophisticated art. Our dance music, with a few possible exceptions, had thus far been America's one original contribution to the music of the world."

Dance music, buoyed by the spread of phonograph records and the new, persistent sounds of radio, had entered on a heyday. The roots of southern jazz arrived in the cities of the North in such groups as the Original Dixieland Jazz Band and King Oliver's Dixie Syncopators—featuring Louis Armstrong's trumpet. Ted Lewis, who became popularly recognized by the sound of his raucous clarinet and his cry to the audience, "Is everybody happy?" had never lacked for bookings since starting his band in New York in 1917.

In and around Philadelphia, Paul Specht, Fred Waring, and Art and Ted Weems developed distinctive styles. Working in Chicago before and immediately after the First World War, Isham Jones and Edgar Benson gained renown for the bands they led. Carleton Coon's and Joe Sanders's Night Hawks played to capacity audiences in the Muehlebach Hotel in Kansas City. Ted Fio Rito and Jean Goldkette led bands in the Midwest. And George Olsen played the new music on the West Coast.

Vincent Lopez, however, came closest to Whiteman in achieving popularity as leader of a dance band. Born in Brooklyn in 1894, Lopez abandoned his studies for the priesthood after three years and took a job as a saloon pianist. He got his start as a bandleader at a Broadway restaurant. In 1920 he cut his first record, "Bluin' the Blues," for Edison. Whiteman's closest rival, Lopez built his initial popularity through a long engagement at Manhattan's Pennsylvania Hotel and by late-night radio remotes directly from his bandstand. In 1924 he followed Whiteman's Aeolian Hall "experiment" with a jazz concert of his own. On November 23, at the Metropolitan Opera House, Lopez made his move to challenge the King of Jazz.

To match Paul's commissioning of Gershwin, Lopez brought in an original jazz composition by W. C. Handy, whose "St. Louis Blues" Vincent had introduced. Called "The Evolution of the Blues," the work suffered from a lack of focus, since it consisted largely of a number of well-known blues themes strung along one after the other, with no attempt at variation or development. Lopez played a potpourri of orchestral pieces—"Russian Fantasy," "By the Waters of Minnetonka," "Indian Love Song," "Cielito Lindo," and "Scheherezade." He added songs by Irving Berlin and Vincent Youmans, jazz numbers by Fletcher Henderson and Henry Souvaine, and a fantasy of themes by Sir Arthur Sullivan. "Pell Street," from a suite by Emerson Whithorne, attracted the most attention as a distinctly original attempt at concertized jazz. As a featured soloist, Lopez hired a harmonica player he had discovered demonstrating the instrument at Wurlitzer's—Borrah Minevitch, who played an operatic aria and a jazz number to prove that the mouth harmonica should be taken seriously.

Lopez increased his band to symphonic size and spent over $2,500 merely to have music arranged and copied. But all the trouble and expense to top Whiteman did little for Lopez, and he had no *Rhapsody in Blue* to show for his efforts.

"Whiteman! Whiteman!" Lopez exclaimed to his manager as the concert bills piled up. "Why am I always chasing after him, anyway? From now on, I don't care what Whiteman does. I'm going to be concerned with what only one orchestra leader does—and his name is Vincent Lopez."

But other bandleaders did keep a sharp eye on Whiteman. Harry Yerkes and his Syncopating Symphonists attempted to claim Paul's title with their jazz concert at Aeolian Hall in 1925. Eric Delamarter, assistant conductor of the Chicago Symphony Orchestra, conducted a jazz concert at the Wanamaker Store in Philadelphia on a sweltering evening in June of that same year. Other popular leaders copied Whiteman by heading for Europe to keep club and concert dates. Abe Lyman, Hal Kemp, Ted Lewis, Noble Sissle, Eubie Blake, Isham Jones, and Vincent Lopez made successful forays abroad in the mid-1920s. To a man, every conductor took advantage of any opportunity to record and bring wider exposure to his orchestra.

But it was the big man with the big band—Paul Whiteman—who was recognized by the public as the one who had "married" jazz to classical music. Crowned the arbiter between jazz and symphonic music, he responded to the times. In the 1940s Paul said that the universal popularity of jazz could never have happened except for "an era of wonderful nonsense" following the First World War. "I was a product of those times." So Whiteman became the public symbol of jazz in a period when every political or cultural event had to have its hero or heroine. Baseball fielded its Sultan of Swat, Babe Ruth. Movies made Clara Bow the ultimate It Girl. Lindbergh flew the Atlantic to become aviation's Lone Eagle. Valentino emerged on the silent screen as the Great Lover. Politics proclaimed Al Smith the Happy Warrior. And Whiteman was crowned the King of Jazz.

This epithet stuck throughout the Roaring Twenties, and it continued to follow his name for the rest of his long career. Paul claimed not to have personally capitalized on his title or its appeal and drawing power. Yet he could not deny that it sold tickets. He never dissociated himself from such billing, and when he bowed in motion pictures in 1930, it was in *The King of Jazz,* a revue containing biographical elements of how he came to "discover" jazz and to take it from the "melting pot" of many nationalities and folk tunes.

Nevertheless Paul was the first to acknowledge the enormous gap between the genuine world of jazz and the public adoption of the term. His was a "respectable" quasi jazz or soft jazz orchestra; though it included a number of jazz musicians, they were generally subordinated to the band's special symphonic jazz arrangements. Paul once remarked to a would-be biographer, "I know as much about real jazz as F. Scott Fitzgerald did about the Jazz Age."

What he did know about jazz worked for him, and worked very well indeed. Paul called jazz a method of rhythm and counterpoint, of using tones and of using the color of sound. "Almost anything can be played by a jazz group on jazz instruments in the jazz manner," he frequently remarked to musicologists. "Anything can be jazzed—that is, subjected to jazz treatment. With a very few but important exceptions, jazz is not what is said; it is the manner of saying it . . . with a twist, with a bang, with a rhythm."

Paul also referred to jazz as the spirit of a new country, an expression of the soul of America. Jazz, he noted, stirred the whole body, increasing the heartbeat, raising the temperature, quickening respiration, and making all the senses more acute. Jazz had the power to take people out of a dull world, to shake them up, to give them an intoxication of rhythm and movement that makes them happy, makes them better, makes them live more intensely. It did no harm to anyone.

New worlds awaited Whiteman in 1924. A vast throng had been turned away at the Aeolian box office on February 12. Now these disappointed listeners had to be pacified. Paul arranged a second concert to take place three weeks later. Entrepreneurs who had scoffed at the idea of a jazz concert read the reports of the second sell-out performance and bid even higher for Whiteman's services. On April 13 the program was presented at Philadelphia's Academy of Music.

F. C. Coppicus of the Metropolitan Musical Bureau convinced Paul that the country was eager to see him in action. Whiteman signed for a concert tour that spring. The contract called for $10,000 a week; Paul personally got $2,000 outright and the first $1,000 or any part of it over a weekly box office of $10,000. Coppicus received the second $1,000. Any receipts beyond $12,000 were split 70/30, with Whiteman on the long end.

Before the tour began, Whiteman and Gershwin gave New Yorkers another opportunity to share in the experiment of modern music. Ticket buyers jammed Carnegie Hall on April 21 for a concert to benefit the musical scholarship fund of the American Academy in Rome. Again enthusiastic audiences cheered, particularly roaring their approval of the humor and inventiveness of Zez Confrey at the keyboard and the originality and imagination of Gershwin in performing his *Rhapsody*. There were many and prolonged encores for the soloists. Meanwhile Coppicus moved ahead with his plans for a short, intensive tour.

At the same time Paul ordered the design and construction of a special set with a glittering metallic backdrop and with white bentwood chairs for the players. Joseph Urban, Ziegfeld's production genius, worked out a spectacular three-tier platform of dove gray with a curved shell, which enclosed the regal maestro from the waist down in what was described as resembling an ocean liner's smokestack. Perhaps, struck by Olin Downes's comment on his conducting with the back of the right trouser leg, Paul realized that his habit of fidgeting might distract from a serious performance. He therefore blocked the view—at an overall cost of some $6,000.

Paul also started to work on perpetuating and improving on his unmistakable sound—a distinctive trademark regardless of the inevitable personnel changes. He first dropped two violins, leaving the section with six instead of eight. He replaced them with a saxophone—bringing a fourth to the orchestra—and a cymbalom, a Hungarian invention whose tones are produced by drumming upon its strings with felt-tipped sticks. This percussion instrument was dropped later in the year, but the four-sax section remained and became a key component of many big bands, especially with the emergence of swing in the 1930s.

Gershwin agreed to join the orchestra on the spring tour for as many engagements as possible. The Aeolian Hall program (minus Edward Elgar's "Pomp and Circumstance" which had actually closed the concert) was recreated beginning at Rochester's Convention Hall on May 15. From upstate New York, Gershwin traveled to Pittsburgh, Cleveland, Indianapolis, and St. Louis. Between May 15 and June 1 the troupe played thirteen cities in the United States and Toronto, Ottawa, and Montreal.

On the morning of the May 30 performance in Toronto, Paul received a telephone call from New York informing him that, after eighteen months of marriage, he had become a father. Vanda had given birth to a son, a solidly plump offspring his parents named Paul Samuel Whiteman, Jr. The musicians began their celebration of the heir's arrival before the evening concert and continued it through the night at bars and bordellos, courtesy of the jubilant Paul, Sr.

Gershwin had left the troupe before the Canadian leg of the tour to work on the score for George White's *Scandals*. Milton Rettenberg, a recent Columbia Law School graduate, filled in. Reputedly the second person to play *Rhapsody in Blue,* he had borrowed the original manuscript from its composer and copied it. Actually, Gershwin did not get around to copyrighting the Grofé arrangement until June 12, 1924. Copyrighted as an "unpublished" composition, the actual deposit at the Library of Congress in Washington was merely a few pages of manuscript excerpts.

Gershwin believed that the *Rhapsody* would enjoy only brief popularity, especially because it was not a dance tune. He was surprised when his music publisher Max Dreyfus decided to publish it in the wake of the incredible excitement the piece aroused in New York. Both George and his brother Ira wondered who would want to play the difficult piece or, more to the point, want to buy the music.

The sheet music of *Rhapsody in Blue: For Jazz Band and Piano* carried a publication date of December 31, 1924. The front cover depicted a modernistic design utilizing the colors red, purple, and blue. The piece was dedicated to Whiteman. In 1927 Harms published an arrangement for solo piano. The earliest known copyright of an instrumental arrangement, a score for symphonic band, is dated May 27, 1938.

Gershwin rejoined Whiteman's orchestra on June 10 to record *Rhapsody in Blue* at Victor's New York studios. The selection was released on two twelve-inch discs. That same month Paul added eight numbers to the Victor catalog, including "Suite of Serenades," "Song of Songs," "By the Waters of Minnetonka," and "San."

Whiteman's agenda grew a little lighter by late June. The band spent the summer rehearsing five different programs for another concert tour scheduled for the fall and winter. Paul and Vanda rented a summer place at Hewlett, Long Island, twenty miles from Manhattan and close to the Atlantic shore. They converted a barn on the property into a rehearsal hall with workable lighting effects and scenery grids. Now Paul could spend more time with his family.

The orchestra completed its existing agreement with the Palais Royal before settling down in the country. Within weeks after Paul's departure the club was sold to new owners. It failed immediately, and creditors padlocked the once flourishing café. The closing eliminated the need for Paul to interrupt his 1924–1925 tour for a midwinter engagement in New York.

That same summer Whiteman hired Jimmy Gillespie away from Vincent Lopez. Gillespie had been Lopez's manager and in that capacity had been sent to shepherd a junior orchestra of boys under eighteen on a cross-country tour. Whiteman recalled Gillespie to New York as a publicity representative who would hold down the fort in the city while Whiteman took his band on the extensive tour of one-night stands.

But soon after Gillespie joined Whiteman, Paul had other ideas of how Gillespie could be useful. Whiteman was haunted by the fact that, no matter how much money his band earned and how high his personal income was, he was always short. He suspected that he was being cheated. Would Gillespie straighten out his finances and handle his money? For the next seven years Gillespie traveled with Whiteman and held the purse strings for the million-dollar operation.

By August, Whiteman and his musicians were ready to try out their tour program at Atlantic City. The concert at the Garden Pier drew an enormous crowd, including the arrangers of every dance orchestra playing on the Boardwalk. Ross Gorman on "So This Is Venice," Mike Pingitore on "Linger Awhile," Morton Downey on "Emeralda," and Milton Rettenberg on *Rhapsody,* all stopped the show. The applause at the end was so insistent that Paul was forced to respond not only with a short speech, but also with his old standard, "Song of India."

In the midst of confirming the itinerary for the fall tour, packing stage equipment, ordering custom-made suits, and waxing a handful of new records, Paul and the orchestra were delighted to receive a request to play at the year's biggest social event—undoubtedly one of the grandest parties of the 1920s.

On August 29, the thirty-year-old Prince of Wales arrived in Manhattan for a two-month visit to the United States and Canada.

His New York host, James A. Burden, turned over his home on Long Island to the prince, and an endless round of sports and entertainment began for the world's most eligible bachelor. "My American hosts spared no expense in demonstrating the splendor of a modern industrial republic," he later wrote in his autobiography, *A King's Story*. The most elaborate of these all-night parties took place on September 6 at the 600-acre Long Island estate of postal-telegraph magnate Clarence H. Mackay. The prince spent the day of the dinner dance at Mackay's vast country place. In the afternoon he played several games of squash and then strolled through the formal gardens and viewed the large collection of armor and tapestries. As darkness fell, dozens of maids and footmen prepared for the guests. Paul and his musicians arrived during a last-minute check of the blue electric lights positioned in the maple trees lining the mile-long winding road leading to the French chateau.

"Guards were everywhere," Paul wrote in *Jazz,* "and the invitation cards were watched as if they had been jewels, for it was a safe bet that a lot of the city's 'celebrity hunters' would try to force their way in. The prince, on the occasion of this, his second visit, had become more popular and more interesting than ever, so that he was not allowed even breathing time away from watching eyes. But Mr. Mackay was determined he should have at least one partly undisturbed evening."

Nearly a thousand guests attended the ball. While *The New York Times* suggested that there were roughly a hundred gate crashers, Mackay's teenage son, John, who observed the party, doubted that anyone managed to get past the front gates without proper identification and a bona fide invitation. The prince was cordial to everyone and bowed frequently as he made his first tour of the dancing rooms. Every time he came on the dance floor, every woman there watched him with wistful eyes.

Because Mackay wanted the music to go on without interruptions, Paul divided his orchestra into two groups that played alternately. The prince rarely left the dance floor, spending as much as twenty minutes with each of his numerous partners. At one point Paul led his musicians in a march around the hall, weaving in and out of the collection of shadowy figures in medieval armor.

Edward greeted Paul warmly and throughout the night asked for favorite selections. Among them was "Leave Me Alone," a tune he had come to like during his American visit. He also asked Paul if he would send him the recently released record of *Rhapsody in Blue*.

The prince left the party at two-thirty in the morning, but the music continued on to nearly dawn. The choice of Whiteman, a favorite of the future king since *Brighter London* days, added immeasurably to the success of the gala ball. Paul left the baronial hilltop with a hefty check for $6,000 and an unsurpassed reputation for music making among the country's fabled rich.

8

Book 'Em and Hook 'Em

Traveling with the Whiteman band combined the more colorful aspects of touring with a ball club, a minstrel troupe, and a three-ring circus. Paul took to the road in two special Pullman cars plus a baggage car laden with over eighty trunks, two white-veneer concert grand pianos, some $10,000 worth of Buescher Company instruments, and drayloads of scenic and electrical effects.

The departure from Pennsylvania Station was always a gala event, which the public clamored to see. Photographers posed Paul and the band with showgirls in furs or chaps and cowboy hats or bathing suits. Paul was often snapped wearing the uniforms and hats of the engineer, the fireman, the conductor, and the switchman (complete with lantern). As always, he was cooperative. "Publicity never hurt anybody who didn't hurt it first," was his motto.

Every long journey was interrupted by station stops in small towns, where welcoming committees waited. A goodly segment of a town's people jammed around the train, peering into windows, seeking autographs, taking pictures, and shooting questions. Paul was obliging, and the public reacted in kind. He maintained one rule: he accepted no compositions or manuscripts. And he made one promise: he would come back someday.

The troupe moved from city to city like a huge sideshow. When the group arrived at a town where a concert was to be held, a parade would begin, a brass band accompanying Whiteman and his men as they rode in open touring cars with a police escort. They were hailed and feted with all the ballyhoo the Jazz Age could muster.

The best was none too good for such a rich and famous gang. It was well known that Whiteman paid his men no less than $150 a week, or nearly $8,000 a year. Many received over $300 a week, and a few as much as $400. Whiteman gave wages that were double what any other band in the entire country paid and at least ten times the average American worker's salary. With solid 1920s dollars filling their pockets, these men lived high, wide, and handsome on the road. A free-spending gang, they were a railroad porter's dream, a restaurant waiter's prayer.

Until the spring tour of 1924 Whiteman had rarely left New York for any extended time. Two years earlier, when the Palais Royal closed for renovations, Paul had taken his band to Chicago's Trianon Ballroom. Six nights' work netted $25,000, a record high in the band business. There had also been the trip to England. But on the whole his New York commitment kept Paul close to Times Square. All that changed quickly; for the rest of the decade the Whiteman troupe lived out of a trunk.

Paul traveled in a Pullman drawing room that also served as a meeting area. He only shared the room for one night, when he asked Jimmy Gillespie to stay with him so that they could talk business and budgets into the small hours. Paul's claustrophobia made it impossible for him to sleep with the window closed; he felt smothered. That wintery night he opened the window as wide as possible, asked the porter for extra blankets, and encased his feet in woolen socks. As the night grew colder after the two had retired, Paul spread his large raccoon coat over the blankets and quickly went back to sleep. Snow, cinders, and dirt blew in. Gillespie shivered and coughed until dawn. One day was enough; he moved into another compartment. The word was out, and no one stayed in the drawing-room car after the last drink.

Playing in a traveling band was not easy for Whiteman and his men. The work was not only hard; it also took them away from their families and put strain on many marriages. "You must be ready to go anywhere the orchestra goes," Paul would advise job seekers. "You must be ready to toil in the recording room of a phonograph company up to show time, then rehearse between shows, and practice by yourself the rest of the night."

It was in 1924 that Paul struck on the idea of special tours, with themes that would truly "book 'em and hook 'em." In September of that year Whiteman and the orchestra left on a fifty-five-day junket with a program that featured only American numbers—"especially arranged and scored with as much thought and ingenuity and feeling for orchestral effect as has even been given to the great symphonies." The Whiteman repertory included three new pieces by Eastwood Lane, a largely self-taught musician. They were "Persimmon Pucker," "A Minuet for Betty Schuyler," and "Sea Burial." Ferde Grofé also contributed a new work, called "Flavoring a Selection with Borrowed Themes."

All Paul's printed programs that fall issued a general invitation to musicians to compose special works for his orchestra. Whiteman was going to make every effort to create an American tradition of music, not influenced by any foreign school. But it became increasingly evident that the task would fall chiefly on Ferde Grofé's shoulders.

The tour ended on November 13, when the Whiteman train pulled into Grand Central Station at eight-twenty-six in the morning. The men had the rest of the day off—their first in nearly two months. But the following afternoon they were back on the bandstand, rehearsing for a concert at Carnegie Hall that same evening.

The program featured Gershwin and his *Rhapsody;* a new Grofé composition "Broadway Night"; and two pieces for piano written and played by Mana-Zucca, "The Zouave's Drill" and "Valse Brilliante." The program described Mme. Mana-Zucca—whose real name was Augusta Zuckermann—as an American composer of over 400 published compositions.

New York audiences not only packed Carnegie Hall, but also trooped to hear Whiteman at Aeolian Hall, the Brooklyn Academy of Music, and the Metropolitan Opera House. Boston concertgoers also had an opportunity to judge the phenomenon and Paul's orchestra when they came with Gershwin to Symphony Hall on December 4. One Boston paper described the sold-out concert as a "sensational jazz carnival."

Then, on January 1, the orchestra regrouped for a winter and spring tour as far afield as Los Angeles. Vanda joined Paul on this trip, but during an incredibly fast-moving sixteen weeks they were lucky to have one free day together.

Paul's old friends from the West Coast warmly welcomed him back after five years. In Los Angeles dozens of people from the movie colony greeted the band on its first visit since the days of the Alexandria Hotel. Paul gave a concert at the La Monica Ballroom on the Santa Monica Pier, partied a little, and then boarded a train north.

Whiteman's arrival in San Francisco took on the trappings of a city holiday. The San Francisco Municipal Band gave Paul a loud and brassy hello in Oakland, to the tune of "California, Here I Come." The band, newspapermen, and hundreds of fans trailed Paul as though he were the original Pied Piper. He and a bunch of local musicians boarded the ferry across the bay for a round of concerts. At the Ferry Building the mayor, the police chief, and the city's well-known orchestra leaders rolled out the red carpet for its adopted son. At the Fairmont Hotel, the "birthplace" of Paul's band, Local #6 of the American Federation of Musicians joined the city fathers in honoring the Whiteman orchestra at a gala banquet.

The band turned in the direction of home on March 2, with concert dates en route. At midmonth Paul reached Denver and had a happy reunion with his mother and father and sister. They had not been together in over five years. Paul introduced Vanda to the family and proudly produced pictures of Paul, Jr.

His father had never heard the band on stage, although he had most of Paul's recordings. His engagements at Denver's American Theater and Hiawatha Gardens, and a concert at Colorado Springs' Broadmoor Hotel gave the entire Whiteman family an opportunity to share in Paul's success on the podium. The Professor was forced to acknowledge that Paul had done well with his "jazzed up" music.

Paul and Vanda stayed with the elder Whitemans at their new ranch outside of the city. When the Professor had retired the previous year, Paul had built Elfrida and Wilberforce a house on 320 acres near a small village fifteen miles from Denver. The Whitemans were anxious to show Paul and his men the new place—"the house that jazz built."

The second half of the tour led through Kansas, Missouri, Nebraska, Iowa, South Dakota, Minnesota, and Wisconsin to Illinois. The band arrived back in New York on Sunday, May 3—four months after leaving on the coast-to-coast tour. On Tuesday, Wednesday, and Thursday of that week Paul returned to Victor's recording studios to cut a batch of new releases for dance fans.

While the Whiteman troupe had been on the road, Columbia and Victor had begun recording by a recently developed electrical process. Both companies decided to keep the revolutionary method secret for a while. They were afraid that publicizing it would make their earlier records out of date and unsaleable. The public was unaware of the transition for many months.

Inside the recording companies, however, the change was rapid and startling. The electrical microphone could capture the full range of musical instruments, from the softest pianissimo to a loud forte. Gone were the recording horns that looked like megaphones. Unnecessary was the maneuvering a musician had to go through for a solo passage, getting him close to the horn to play directly into it.

Paul and the band journeyed to Camden, where the research-and-development department had converted the old cramped acoustical quarters into a spacious, well-designed studio. Paul and his men made a half-dozen trips to Camden that summer to put the new Orthophonic process to use in recording such tunes of 1925 as "Let Me Linger Longer in Your Arms," "Footloose," "You Forgot to Remember," and "Ukulele Lady." In September they cut Willard Robison's "Peaceful Valley," a melody that became closely identified with Paul. With the new process the Whiteman band sounded fuller and more natural, and Victor made plans to increase the number of discs, using Paul's talented sidemen on solos. The musicians relished the long hours in the studios; recordings added $5,000 or more a year to each man's income.

The original band had grown from nine to twelve, then fifteen, and since the first experimental concert, to at least twenty-five men. The expansion brought personnel changes that reflected the group's thrust into concert halls and theaters.

Violinist Kurt Dieterle had left a trio playing theater music to join the orchestra for *Rhapsody in Blue*. Kurt recalled that he heard the Whiteman sound for the first time during a summer in Cooperstown, New York, where he listened to "Whispering" in a local record store. The distinctive sound and innovative arrangement caught his attention. When Paul approached him, Kurt readily agreed to join the new string section. By the mid-1920s, he was concertmaster. Reed player Charles Strickfaden brought unusual musical talent and dedication to the band. Both joined the orchestra in 1924 and remained until the mid-1930s—the glory years of the Whiteman organization.

Paul called Strickfaden his quadruple threat because he was master of clarinet, saxophone, oboe, and English horn. But music was not his sole occupation; in later years he built a fortune through real estate investments, a restaurant business, and airline operations. He was also an accomplished writer, skilled photographer, and all-around sportsman.

When West Coast scouts told Paul about trombonist Wilbur Hall and his unusual comedy routine, Whiteman wired Hall to come East. Willie doubled on the violin and the trombone, and Paul quickly built him into the novelty act for his theater bookings. He would play "The Farmer Took Another Load Away" on the trombone, go on to "Pop, Goes the Weasel" or "Turkey in the Straw" on the fiddle, and end with "The Stars and Stripes Forever" on a bicycle pump. Occasionally Hall used a lamp shade as a substitute mute, holding it against the bell of his instrument by thrusting his thumb through the hole left for the lamp socket. Musicologist Henry O. Osgood marveled at his agility in playing such tunes as "Nola" at an astonishing pace, employing double tonguing, triple tonguing, and false positioning and manipulating the slide with a speed defying normal physical dexterity. The extraordinary routine never failed to bring down the house. Paul upped Willie's weekly salary to $350—the second highest in the band. Only Ferde Grofé topped him at $375.

All-around reedman Ross Gorman had recently left Whiteman to lead his own orchestra in the newest of Earl Carroll *Vanities*. In need of a top-flight replacement, Paul approached his old friend from the San Francisco Symphony, Chester Hazlett, whose classical training and experience qualified him for the Whiteman sound. Because Hazlett felt that, as a serious musician, he was unlikely to pass muster in a jazz group, he turned down Paul's offer. He reconsidered, however, in view of a weekly draw of $250 and a chance to work with his old buddy. Chet Hazlett became a star soloist with Whiteman in the 1920s and remained with him for eight years.

As Grofé turned more and more to arranging, his regular piano-playing chores were turned over to a new musician, Harry Perrella. He was a concert-trained pianist of unusual ability, who performed the *Rhapsody* on the third tour—better than Gershwin himself, according to many who heard him.

Another keyboard artist was discovered right after a concert in

St. Joseph, Missouri, in 1925. At the conclusion of the program a woman barged into Paul's dressing room as he was changing into street clothes.

"I want you to hear a local young man play the piano. He's outstanding."

"Look," answered Paul, "I'm tired after a performance. I don't really think I can."

"I won't let you go unless you listen," she insisted, grabbing away his clean shirt. "You don't get your shirt unless you agree to hear this boy play."

"Come on, Kurt," Paul said to his concertmaster who was watching the scene with some alarm. "We'll go and hear this guy."

Paul and Kurt sauntered over to a backstage piano as the woman beckoned a tall young man to the piano bench. "Hello, Mr. Whiteman, I'm Raymond Turner." He sat down and started to play.

Whiteman was immediately impressed and asked for more. "But I can't run these stagehands into overtime. Let's find another place with a good piano."

They arranged to go to a nearby home which boasted of a fine concert grand. Ray Turner played for an hour. During the session Paul would ask, "Play something classical for me," or "Do you know the latest popular jazz?"

Both Kurt and Jimmy Gillespie, who had come along, asked what he thought he could do with Turner.

"I am thinking about adding a second piano. If I do, he'll soon hear from me."

The next day the St. Joseph newspapers ran a headline, "Ray Turner to Join Paul Whiteman." The headline became a reality some months later, when Paul hired Turner.

By mid-1925, Whiteman's orchestra had expanded to twenty-eight men and included a greatly enlarged string section. The musicians were:

VIOLIN: Kurt Dieterle, Mario Perry, James McKillop, Paul Daven, Charles Gaylord, Irving Achtel.
VIOLA: John Bowman, Julius Mindel.
CELLO: Frank Leoncavallo, William Schuman.
STRING BASS: Walter Bell (who had played with Whiteman in the San Francisco Symphony).
TROMBONE: Wilbur Hall, Roy Maxon, Boyce Cullen.

Victor advertised the February 12, 1924, concert in Aeolian Hall along with the Whiteman recording orchestra. *(Whiteman Collection, Williams College)*

(Below, left) Wilberforce and Elfrida Whiteman with daughter, Ferne, shortly after moving to Denver in 1888. *(Courtesy of Margaret L. Whiteman)*

(Below, right) Paul Whiteman faces a camera for the first time, in 1890. *(Courtesy of Margaret L. Whiteman)*

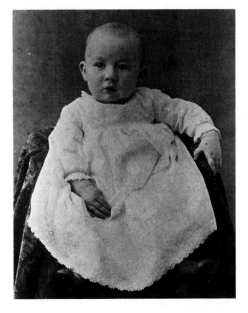

The young string player held a chair in the Denver Symphony Orchestra. *(Courtesy of Margaret L. Whiteman)*

In the years before the First World War, Paul (left front) earned extra money playing for orchestras in theaters and ballrooms, including the Arlington Hotel in Hot Springs, Arkansas. *(Courtesy of Margaret L. Whiteman)*

Classical music pushed aside, Paul, as a Navy bandmaster, organized a ragtime combo among his military musicians. *(Courtesy of Jack Fulton)*

Paul's first postwar orchestra, with Henry Busse and Mike Pingitore, successfully opened at the Alexandria Hotel in Los Angeles in December 1919. *(Courtesy of Margaret L. Whiteman)*

In August 1920 Paul traveled from Atlantic City to Camden, N.J., to record the first of hundreds of tunes for Victor. *(Courtesy of Margaret L. Whiteman)*

By 1922—the midpoint of the four-year engagement at the Palais Royal—the Whiteman orchestra had grown to twelve players. (*Courtesy of Margaret L. Whiteman*)

Paul and Vanda sail for England in 1923 for the first concert tour abroad. *(Courtesy of Margaret L. Whiteman)*

Floating musicians in New York harbor welcome their hero back from his 1923 European tour. The combo nearly drowned in a sudden swell near the arriving S. S. *Leviathan*. *(Courtesy of Margaret L. Whiteman)*

Vincent Lopez sparked Paul's interest in planning the 1924 concert at Aeolian Hall. Lopez later mounted a similar program. His popular orchestra included B. A. Rolfe on trumpet (third from right), who organized the rival Lucky Strike Dance Orchestra shortly afterward. *(Author's Collection)*

The augmented concert orchestra rehearses for the Aeolian Hall program. Whiteman added eight violinists—including Alex Drasein, Kurt Dieterle, and Bert Hirsch—and two French horn players to the Palais Royal regulars. *(Courtesy of Margaret L. Whiteman)*

In a publicity stunt Paul spars with Babe Ruth as the athletic-club trainer and John Philip Sousa look on. *(Courtesy of Margaret L. Whiteman)*

With the success of the Aeolian Hall concert, Paul's orchestra expanded to twenty-five musicians and played from this three-tier set with a curved, shell-like podium. *(Courtesy of Margaret L. Whiteman)*

The Whiteman orchestra arrives in St. Louis for a concert on May 21, 1924. Paul stands between his mother and the star tour attraction, George Gershwin. *(Courtesy of Margaret L. Whiteman)*

The House That Jazz Built: The Colorado farm Paul gave his parents in 1924. *(Courtesy of Jeann Bargy)*

The King of Jazz acquires a princeling when Paul, Jr., is born in 1924. Violin lessons follow shortly. *(Courtesy of Margaret L. Whiteman)*

Paul moves ahead with plans for a second experimental concert in December 1925. George Gershwin (right) with Deems Taylor (left), Ferde Grofé, and Blossom Seeley study the reorchestration of *Blue Monday*, retitled *135th Street* for the Carnegie Hall program. *(Courtesy of Ira Gershwin)*

TRUMPET: Henry Busse, Frank Siegrest, Teddy Bartell.
SAXOPHONE: Chester Hazlett, Hal McLean, Charles
Strickfaden, E. Lyle Sharpe.
BANJO: Mike Pingitore.
GUITAR: Austin Young.
BASS: John Sperzel.
DRUMS: George Marsh.
PIANO: Harry Perrella, Ray Turner. (Ferde Grofé was now
a full-time arranger, filling in as pianist only when
necessary.)

New York audiences awaited the return of the nationally acclaimed conductor–showman and his large group of talented musicians. Only the city's largest entertainment arena could do justice
to the Whiteman concert orchestra. Paul moved the band into the
Hippodrome at Forty-Third Street and Sixth Avenue on May 11,
1925. He received $7,000, a record weekly figure only matched once
before by Sarah Bernhardt. This vaudeville engagement represented
a challenge to the outfit: could these musicians come before the $1
public and click with Paul's advanced ideas of syncopation as they
had with the top-hat, $3 concert crowd? It became apparent that
Paul could bridge both audiences when he scored at the Hippodrome
with a program of popular numbers stamped with a trademark dis-
tinctively his own. Abel Green explained it in *Variety*.

It is syncopation scored to a symphonic degree approaching
a rhapsody in color and yet replete with all the nerve-tingly,
feet-tickling barbaric rhythm in existence. And then to show
it's not all four-four stuff, Whiteman takes Isham Jones'
"Spain," a tango, and dresses it up like a symphony and
changes pace with a familiar waltz which is scored into an
offering of rare charm.

Whiteman packed the Hippodrome for three weeks. There was
no question that his foray into concert halls had not diminished his
basic mass appeal. "There are too many American families with
standing orders at their Victor shops for all new Whiteman recordings to necessitate any doubt about that," Abel Green noted.
"Whiteman can keep the Hip open well into the summer with his
aptness for shifting programs." An added attraction during the run

gave Paul's men a chance to ham it up in a skit called "Pre-Historic Jazz." Wearing caveman costumes, they spoofed "jazz" in a Stone Age cabaret (cover charge: fifty rocks) with Henry Busse as "a big butter-and-egg man from the Ark." Paul's resounding drawing power brought him back to the Hippodrome on Labor Day for a seven-day run. He again opened to one of the biggest daily grosses in the history of vaudeville, and when the week ended, the house had taken in $45,000.

Paul varied his program with a cleverly mounted closing number, "Meet the Boys." Highlighting the individual specialties of his soloists, this number proved to be a show stopper. It started Paul thinking about more specialty acts from within his band. In its review *Variety* concluded that "one just watches the Whiteman band, listens to it and ponders, then realizes why Paul Whiteman is the highest paid performer in the history of vaudeville."

In the time between the two Hippodrome runs, Paul kept busy in recording studios and on the road. His band packed many auditoriums, armories, and community halls in New England, New Jersey, and Pennsylvania as jazz-bent youth danced its way through the Roaring Twenties. That summer Paul's fans foxtrotted to the tune of $60,000—practically a drop in the Whiteman bucket in those halcyon days.

As the fall of 1925 approached, Paul told his managers, "You book 'em, we'll hook 'em." And so they did with well over eighty dates in twelve weeks. The now familiar railroad lines were again used: the Missouri Pacific, Santa Fe, Union Pacific, Rock Island, B & O, New York Central, Boston & Maine, Delaware & Lackawanna.

Whiteman was enthusiastically received everywhere, but no greater acclaim awaited him than in Chicago. On October 11 he opened at the Auditorium Theater with several new works by American composers, including Grofé and two Chicagoans, Leo Sowerby and John Alden Carpenter. Sowerby contributed a symphony for orchestra and metronome; Carpenter, a jazz piece.

Sowerby's *Monotony* made a visual impression, but as a composition it left listeners utterly confused. For its premiere Whiteman, ever the showman, installed an enormous time-beating metronome in front of the band. The musicians were dressed in blue smocks and helmets of papier-mâché decorated with cogwheels. To add to the bizarre appearance, he had them paint their faces blue. Sowerby ignored all conventional time signatures, devising the impossible one of five third-notes to the bar. The morass of sound seemed increased by the scarcity of character. "The resulting performance," Charlie Strickfaden recalled, "was a tug of war between conductor and orchestra." A distinguished organist and composer of religious music, Sowerby had turned out a pseudo-modern work of little merit—a piece of *Monotony* and despair.

John Alden Carpenter offered *A Little Piece of Jazz* to his hometown audience. But nothing lifted this composition above the jazz works heard daily and little was recognizable as coming from the composer of *The Birthday of the Infanta* or his very clever *Perambulator* suite, first performed by the Chicago Symphony in 1915.

The new American selection that was most favorably received was Grofé's *Mississippi Suite*. This novel tone poem, or journey in sound, had many moments of musical and imaginative inspiration. Some descriptive setting was indicated by the titles of the four selections: "Father of the Waters," "Huckleberry Finn," "Old Creole Days," and "Mardi Gras." Grofé's first major success in serious music, the suite became a perennial favorite with light concert orchestras. This work was Grofé's first step in an independent career as composer and conductor. He continued to work for Whiteman as an arranger and orchestrator, but he rarely went on the road after this time.

During 1925 Paul was continually urging Gershwin to write another important piece for a full-scale Whiteman concert, but George seemed uninterested. The fact was that he had set out to complete a work commissioned by Walter Damrosch and the New York Symphony Orchestra. His *Concerto in F*, the eagerly anticipated follow-up to *Rhapsody in Blue*, premiered at Carnegie Hall in early December, with Gershwin at the piano. His contemporaries thought it less exciting than the *Rhapsody*, but it added a serious new work to the repertoire of contemporary American music, liberating it from its ties to rigid formula.

George suggested that Paul reintroduce *Blue Monday* if he wanted to include something of his in a second experimental concert. Paul agreed that rudimentary Gershwin was better than no Gershwin at all. He moved ahead with plans for a Carnegie Hall program on December 29, 1925. The rejected jazz opera from the *Scandals* was reorchestrated by Grofé and renamed *135th Street* for its concert premiere. The vocal parts were recast to put two vaudevillians—Blossom Seeley and Benny Fields—and musical comedy star Charles Hart in the leads.

Paul added Grofé's own *Mississippi Suite* to the program. The principal new selection came from one of Paul's most enthusiastic admirers, the highly regarded music critic Deems Taylor, whose career had taken a new direction. *Circus Days* was an early attempt at symphonic composition, and Paul made the most of this premiere. He instructed Grofé to give it the Whiteman touch. "Make the lions and all those circus animals pop out of the score," he insisted. "Make it witty, and use all the men and their instruments. It's a good composition, but without our players it probably doesn't stand much of a chance."

Excited by Taylor's work, the Carnegie Hall audience "roared" its approval. When it came time for a curtain call, Taylor was nowhere to be found. Paul made an appearance: "I've no doubt he was just as scared as I was," he told the crowd.

Gershwin's revamped opera also pleased the listeners. They clapped to the music, and many left the performance humming. While the music was interesting and dramatic, with snatches of genuine blues, Carnegie Hall was far from an ideal setting for it. To see the wicked heroine wailing over the body of her dead lover on the stage apron, just behind the figure of Paul as he wiggled his ample backside and waved his arms, was an unfortunate sight, especially to the press. Disappointing though it was in many ways, the work demonstrated Gershwin's potential as an imaginative creator of operatic material. In the eyes of the public that night, Whiteman and Gershwin were an unbeatable team in the concert hall.

Both ended the year with flying colors. George made his debut with the New York Symphony, playing his *Concerto in F*. He composed the music for several shows, made a handful of recordings and piano rolls, and had plans for an extensive visit to Europe the following year.

Paul, too, could point to a banner year, with appearances in nearly 300 cities and towns, more than twenty-five new records, a half-dozen new works commissioned and played, and a major vaudeville act. And even after he had paid his musicians and all expenses for seven or eight months on the road, Paul's income was still at a staggering $800,000. Although the big money poured in for many more years, Paul never topped 1925 in dollars earned or miles traveled.

9

Flabby and Coarse, Quick and Shrewd

In 1926 a profile in *The New Yorker* described Paul Whiteman at the age of thirty-six as "a man flabby, virile, quick, coarse, untidy, and sleek, with a hard core of shrewdness in an envelope of sentimentalism, striped ties, perspiration, and fine musical instincts."

But one thing was clear. Whiteman had made himself the foremost exponent of an immensely important development in music. The public looked to this mountain of a man as the King of Jazz. His kingdom had spread from back-alley honkytonks to Boardwalk bistros, from Broadway cafés to Main Street parlors. Jazz was leaving its stamp on a decade that would, in turn, call itself the Jazz Age.

As the Pied Piper of syncopation, Paul held sway over legions of loyal subjects. As the purveyor of savage sounds to many others, he faced brickbats from near and afar. Scores of educators, ministers, editors, and legislators and countless parents flared up at his music and what it was doing to America's youth. By the mid-1920s criticism came from many quarters.

"The jazz band view of life is wrecking the American home," remarked a well-known professor. "The jazz spirit of the times is causing many suicides," declared a leading doctor. "Jazz music causes drunkenness," noted a metropolitan preacher. "Jazz is cheating the home, since folks are spending on dances and cafés the money they might otherwise spend on home appliances and improvements," remarked a famous economist. "Jazz has doubled insanity in the United States," stated a learned physician.

In one small Nebraska town jazz was classed a public nuisance. A Harvard football coach told the Boston Chamber of Commerce that jazz parties were sapping the strength of American youth. In Kansas a historian even found in jazz a new cause for the fall of the Roman Empire.

Possibly the most stinging attack on jazz—at least among musicians—came from an English music critic, Ernest Newman of *The London Sunday Times*.

> Your typical jazz composer or jazz enthusiast is merely a musical illiterate who is absurdly pleased with little things because he does not know how little they are. Jazz has no composers in the full sense of the term. The brains of the whole lot of them put together would not fill the lining of Johann Strauss's hat. At present jazz is not an art, but an industry: the whirring of a standardized machine endlessly turning out a standardized article. The thing is dead from the neck up.

By 1926 Paul was accustomed to unfavorable remarks, but hardly to a stinging invective of such intensity aimed, to all intents and purposes, directly at him as the King of Jazz. "I would sooner fill the lining of Johann Strauss's high hat than wear one," he replied to a *Variety* reporter. "Let supposedly astute critics take off their high hats long enough to recognize the possibilities of a brown derby."

Paul was not so far removed from the days of his own youthful escapades, and the charges of desecrating music, wrecking home life, menacing young people, and throwing an entire nation into criminal ways hurt. It led to Paul's writing a book, partially intended as self-justification. *Jazz,* published in early 1926, was to answer the questions people asked about its beginnings, growth, and future and Paul's connection with it. He shared his position in the opening chapter.

> I certainly haven't tried to be literary for I am no writer, but only the conductor of a jazz orchestra. I sincerely believe in jazz. I think it expresses the spirit of America and I feel sure that it has a future—more of future than of past or present. I want to help that future pan out. Other Americans ought to be willing to give jazz a respectful hearing. If this effort of mine helps toward that end, I shall be satisfied.

Paul's decision to write on jazz was encouraged by his press agent, Estella Karn. She shared an apartment with a young writer from Missouri who desperately needed a job. Estella, a former newspaperwoman and circus promoter, persuaded Paul to use her struggling protege as coauthor. Mary Margaret McBride, welcomed the assignment, and in spite of Paul's incredibly full schedule, she mined sufficient material from him to produce a 300-page account of the Whiteman saga and jazz up to the mid-1920s. She often trailed Paul on his travels, notebook and pencil in hand. At the end of a long day and night she would sit at his bedside and ask him questions.

Published by the Curtis Company, *Jazz* also ran in the *Saturday Evening Post* as a three-part series in 1926. A few years later, Mary Margaret turned to radio as a homey talk-show commentator. By 1936 she and Estella Karn were highly successful business partners in radio. Once again the astute Paul had played an important part in launching the careers of talented individuals—though in this case it happened away from the bandstand.

The Whiteman–McBride book arrived at book stores within weeks of a volume by Henry G. Osgood, *So This Is Jazz*. That book was the first significant attempt to set down an account of the origin, history, and development of jazz music: "a story," noted Osgood, "for the reader who would like to know a little something more about what he has been enjoying—or detesting—for the last decade."

In his foreword the New York critic admitted the difficulty of obtaining accurate and authenticated information about the origins of jazz, recent as these beginnings were. "It is only since H.R.H. [the Prince of Wales] struck up a speaking acquaintance with Paul Whiteman and George Gershwin was invited to dinner at Mrs. Astor's that jazz has become an Art. In the early days an occasional young reporter would drag a story about jazz out of one of its exponents, serving it up with a sauce of his own imagination that might heighten its picturesqueness, though sure to lessen its accuracy." At heart Osgood's book was a eulogy of Whiteman and Gershwin.

Supporters of Whiteman and his orchestra gave many and varied signs of approval. Leopold Stokowski occupied a box at a Whiteman concert in Philadelphia. After the program he assigned to the controversial jazz music a definite and unquestioned place among the legacies that would be handed down by the first generation of the twentieth century. "Jazz has come to stay," stated the conductor of the Philadelphia Orchestra. "It is an expression of the times, the breathless, energetic, superactive times in which we are living."

It was known that composer Arnold Schönberg had a complete collection of Whiteman records in the early 1920s. He frequently played a new record fifteen times or more in succession in an effort to analyze the use of the various instruments.

Sergei Rachmaninoff, the Russian composer and pianist, heard Whiteman in Providence. "He has the finest orchestra of its size I have ever heard. I have long been an admirer of his work, and each month I send to my daughter in Europe the Victor records made by his remarkable organization. This may certainly be called authentic American music, for it can be heard nowhere else that I know of."

In a 1924 interview for a feature in *Etude* magazine called "Where Is Jazz Leading America?" humorist George Ade said, "It can be a dreadful disturbance to the atmosphere when perpetrated by a cluster of small-town blacksmiths and sheet-metal workers, but it becomes inspiring and almost uplifting under the magical treatment of Paul Whiteman and some of his confreres. If the Paul Whiteman boys play 'jazz,' then I am in favor of that particular variety of 'jazz.' "

From Wall Street, financier Otto Kahn paid tribute to jazz in a speech to the Brooklyn Chamber of Commerce.

> It is easy enough to deride or disparage that thing, but any movement which, in its rhythm and in other respects, bears so obviously the American imprint, which has divulged new instrumental colors and values, has taken so firm a footing in our country, and is an object of such great interest to foreign musicians visiting here—any such movement has a just claim to be taken seriously. There is a vast amount of talent among players and composers of jazz.

Soon Kahn, chairman of the Metropolitan Opera Company, announced that he would be glad to consider a jazz opera at the venerable house. Irving Berlin and Kahn met in Florida and talked on the subject. Berlin said that he would "give his right arm" to compose a syncopated opera suitable to the repertory of the Met, but he did not feel that he was technically equipped for such a work.

Jerome Kern, with a half-dozen Broadway hits to his credit, claimed that he had declined a similar attempt when Kahn wrote to him. Otto looked to Gershwin as the third most promising composer of a jazz opera on a grand scale. He fulfilled that promise in the 1930s with *Porgy and Bess*.

Paul's defense of jazz filled trade journals and general-interest magazines week after week. *The New York Times Magazine* even ran Paul's byline feature on what he called "the folk music of the machine age." No scholar or academician or writer, however, he was happy to return to the road as the country's leading exponent of the "new art." In January 1926 the band left New York for a ten-week tour to forty-four cities, again leading to California. The band played many one-nighters. After a concert at the Houston City Auditorium, the men packed up their instruments, hailed cabs, and set up at the Hotel Rice for a dance beginning just before midnight. By the time of their arrival at San Francisco's Automobile Show, they were relieved to stay in one place for eight consecutive days. The 1926 show was the West Coast's biggest exhibition of cars, and Whiteman and his orchestra were given an enormous amount of publicity. Whiteman played every afternoon and evening. The job called for five and a half hours of music each day, for which Whiteman was paid $550 an hour, or more than $3,000 a day. Many visitors to the show gave the latest automobile models short shrift and simply stood watching and listening to Whiteman.

Paul rarely passed up an opportunity to be near an automobile, especially the newest, fastest, and sportiest Stutz, Paige, or Duesenberg. One year, when the Pontiac Division of General Motors asked him to open its new all-glass showroom in Detroit, he made very sure that Jimmy Gillespie fitted the date into his schedule. The entire band was hired for a week, to play and to mingle with prospective car buyers as subtle salesmen. At the close of the engagement, Kurt Dieterle was surprised to receive a new Pontiac for having helped to sell the most cars. One of the more famous visitors to the showroom was Eddie Rickenbacker, the flyer. A great fan of Whiteman, he mentioned to the Fisher brothers and their associates at General Motors that it was his ambition to sit at a table with a glass of champagne and listen to Paul's band. The following day Rickenbacker was ushered into the empty ballroom of Detroit's Book-Cadillac Hotel. There, on the bandstand, stood Paul with his orchestra. He gave the downbeat to "Moonlight and

Roses'' as a waiter popped the cork on a bottle of champagne for the flying ace. Toast followed toast, music filled the air, and the best of times was had by all.

While in San Francisco, Whiteman also acquired a new musician for the band—Jack Fulton. Two years earlier the Victor Company had signed up George Olsen and his lively dance orchestra. Among its earliest recordings was the hit from Jerome Kern's 1925 smash musical, *Sunny*. The tune "Who" captured the spirit of the rollicking good times; Olsen's version was impressive, largely because of vocalists Fran Frey, Bob Rice, and Jack Fulton.

Fulton, who had caught Paul's ear, was also a good trombonist. Paul made an offer at once, but Fulton liked the Olsen group and decided to stick with it. Paul always left the door open when he was turned down by a musician. He would try again, and usually he succeeded. Fulton's clear, high-range tenor voice was worth waiting for.

When Roy Maxon left the band while Paul was in San Francisco, he lost a veteran trombonist, who had replaced Sam Lewis in 1923. Paul approached Fulton with another solid proposal. This time Fulton came aboard just as the band left California for dates in the Midwest and a tail-end gig in Florida.

Paul's path also crossed with a former student of his father. Violinist Matty Malneck had left Colorado to work in Los Angeles with Glenn Miller. He wound up with Glen Oswald's Serenaders, then jumped into Gene James's band at San Francisco's Palace Hotel. Paul dined there during a break from the auto exhibit and heard a sample of Matty's soloing on his hot fiddle. Paul invited him to his ringside table. The outcome was that Malneck accepted Paul's offer of $150 a week—a boost from the $95 James was paying him at the Palace. Matty gave notice and two weeks later came East to catch up with Whiteman.

If Paul could move cars, why not real estate? Florida land speculators knew that wherever Whiteman's music went, dollar bills were sure to follow. Paul's music makers in that southern playground would attract the kind of people who had money to spend.

The Florida land boom had already brought nearly two million people to the state's Gold Coast. Its pristine beaches with their lush tropical backdrop suggested a life of luxury and grandeur. Developers seized upon the theme of good times and quick money as they prepared to divide tracts of land into lots for sale. Tales of riches spread north and west and even overseas, where, it was reported, the French Riviera was nearly deserted as affluent Europeans booked passage for the United States and a stake in Miami Beach or Palm Beach. An ocean-front lot that had sold at $800 before the boom now fetched $65,000.

Paul and the band arrived in Miami during the peak of the land frenzy. On their first night beneath the sheltering palms, they helped open the new and luxurious Biltmore Hotel. The following day real estate developers at nearby Coral Gables welcomed the musicians to their "romance land where sunshine smiles, where snow and ice are but memories." The band was employed in every possible way to stimulate land sales that promised "dividends in health and cash." They played for dancers at Tahiti Beach, for sportsmen at the Biscayne Kennel Club, for golfers at the Coral Gables Country Club, and for students and faculty at the University of Miami. Day after day for five weeks the band gave out with the latest tunes and wove in many choruses of "Moon Over Miami," "When the Moon Shines Over Coral Gables," and "Tamiami Trail." Promotional photographers made the most of the daily serenades. The band posed for countless pictures, including a memorable shot of all the men playing their instruments while bathing in the resort's famous Venetian pool. Even the tuba player was up to his valves in water.

The Florida land bubble burst later that same year. Nearly every speculator and investor lost his shirt. Several decades passed before Florida recovered and began attracting outsiders to its sandy shores again. How many parcels of land Paul and his men actually matched up with buyers is long forgotten. Paul often commented, "You know, I bet I'm the only guy who *didn't* buy land in Coral Gables in 1926."

It was spring when the Whiteman band returned to New York, but there was little time to enjoy the city. For a solid week, except for one day off, the band was confined to the Victor studios. The company had brought in vocalists Franklyn Baur, Lewis James, Elliott Shaw, and Gladys Rice to participate in the Grofé arrangements. The dozen sides recorded included the first waxing of Grofé's *Mississippi Suite.*

Between sessions the men and their families busily packed for yet another long journey. On March 31 the Whiteman troupe boarded the *S.S. Berengaria.* A second European trip was in the making, and once again Paul had misgivings about leaving the

country, especially so soon after an extended absence from Manhattan. And he certainly did not like leaving Paul, Jr., behind.

The Whiteman party consisted of nearly fifty travelers—Paul
himself, Vanda, twenty-eight musicians (including three or four
hired for only this trip), a dozen wives, a handful of children, and
Jimmy Gillespie. At the first roll of the large ship, when New York
was barely out of sight, Paul retreated to his stateroom with a magnum of champagne. Stewards delivered bottle after bottle as the
vessel steamed eastward. Paul spent most of his waking hours
drinking to deaden his very real fear of ships. He solemnly announced that alcohol stopped him from being seasick. One midnight
while in his cups, he was found perched on a deck rail and reeling
from side to side. He was coaxed off the precarious outpost. "Why
did you have to go and get me down?" he asked as he was pulled
safely to the deck. "I can swim."

As the ship neared England, Paul rounded up a half-dozen musicians to play selections at the traditional Seamen's Fund benefit.
The entertainment proved a highlight of the voyage, and passengers
were generous with applause and donations. Paul wondered if the
audiences he was about to face in Great Britain—the first leg of
the tour—would be as warm and receptive.

Three years had passed since his last visit to England, and at
least a half-dozen American dance bands had toured Europe in the
interim. Had the British shifted their loyalty to some of his rivals
from the United States? Would the Prince of Wales and Mountbattens still be as hospitable? What effect would the serious labor
disturbances have on the box office?

An irritable and worrisome Paul walked down the gangplank in
Southamptom carrying his usual baggage of qualms and quirks. He
had some real cause for concern. A work permit had been issued
only on Paul's assurance to the Ministry of Labour that no British
musicians would lose work. While the band was on the high seas,
the British musicians' union learned that the Kit Kat Club in London
had engaged Paul—for a reported $10,000 a week—and planned
also to use the band at the Tivoli Theatre. Thus, the regular theater
orchestra would be furloughed without pay. The union protested.
The Tivoli manager and the Minister of Labour conferred. Just before Paul disembarked, all parties were reassured once again that
no regular musicians would be out of work. "We are to play on
the Tivoli stage an extra turn. The regular orchestra will still ac-

company the films, so they will not be affected by us," Whiteman declared. He also eased the minds of the British by promising that he would not jazz up the immortal melodies of classical composers. "Every musician must realize it is impossible to change the tune of classical music without robbing it of its beauty and grandeur." His protestation made no mention of his habit of syncopating the classics.

Paul's British fans were impatient to hear the *Rhapsody in Blue*. The Gershwin composition was featured on nearly every program of the tour. Indeed, Whiteman's conducting of the piece had been a major factor in bringing the band back to Europe. *Rhapsody* was almost as familiar on that side of the Atlantic as an artistic evocation of American jazz as it was in the States.

Paul's worries proved unfounded by the conclusion of his opening concert in the Royal Albert Hall on April 11. A capacity audience of 10,000, packing the auditorium from pit to dome, exploded in a deafening roar. Clapping, shouting, and whistling filled the air, and hats were tossed high above the clamoring throng. Paul beamed. He seemed ten feet tall and the master of all he surveyed. Once again Paul had taken London by storm. Now he could relax between performances, have some fun, and enjoy spending the money that filled his pockets day after day.

Sell-out engagements in London sparked standing-room-only crowds in Liverpool, Birmingham, Manchester, Glasgow, Edinburgh, Newcastle, and Brighton. The flush of success led the men to rent apartments complete with housemen and butlers in London's fashionable sections. Local tailors rubbed their hands in anticipation of their visits. To complete their debonair outfits, several of the group bought walking sticks with gold and silver heads. Paul and Vanda took to the roads in their Marmon touring car, which they had brought over on the *Berengaria*. Maneuvering the luxurious seven-passenger auto on English roadways required nerve and concentration. Paul often turned the task over to Kurt Dieterle. The car also came in handy when the general strike was called in early May. Transport and railway workers joined striking coal miners, as did employees in heavy industry and utilities. When millions of workers walked off their jobs, volunteers were recruited to drive trains and trucks. Amid the national crisis, Paul's musicians frequently borrowed bicycles and pedaled to work along the streets and byways.

Playing at the popular Kit Kat Club from nine-thirty to twelve-thirty every night reacquainted Paul with Britain's social leaders. The Prince of Wales once more became a regular patron of the cabaret, often sitting in on the drums and staying until closing time. Paul accepted invitations from the landed gentry for shooting parties at their manor houses. These affairs usually began and ended in a hearty round of drinks. For one of his concerts in Scotland, Paul arrived backstage inebriated. He all but lurched on stage, and during many numbers he carried on a conversation with members of the audience seated in the front rows. It was one of the few blemishes on a highly acclaimed tour.

In London the orchestra may have scored a first when British Victor decided to record the Albert Hall concert live before an audience. Engineers installed microphones in the auditorium, and the sound was transmitted to studios in a London suburb. Among the recorded selections were "Valencia," "St. Louis Blues," "You Forgot to Remember," *Rhapsody in Blue,* and "Lady Be Good." It was a pioneer attempt to record the Whiteman outfit in action in its usual setting, but the sides failed to measure up to studio quality and were never released.

In June, Whiteman crossed the Channel to the Continent. The general strike had caused the cancellation of several concerts, giving the orchestra a week or two of leisure. Paul wanted to see Vienna, the home of sparkling music. Franz Lehar welcomed him to the Austrian capital with a luncheon in Whiteman's honor. Paul made headlines by remarking to his host and his guests that jazz "is a handsome child trying to make its way in the world. Everybody is interested in him wherever he goes."

A number of composers who heard of Paul's presence in Vienna brought him material to audition. Among the compositions he heard was a piece by a German dentist, Robert Katscher. A successful writer for the musical stage, with *Wunderbar* to his credit, Katscher had composed a hauntingly beautiful tune called "Madonna du bist schöner als der Sonnenschein." Paul liked the song immediately, realizing its tremendous appeal as a concert selection as well as a dance number. A young reporter in Vienna by the name of Billy Wilder had been instrumental in bringing "Madonna" to Whiteman. He wrote a series of articles on Whiteman, and with his impressive knowledge of jazz, he seems to have charmed Whiteman in spite of a language barrier. Wilder and Paul made a tour of the Vienna night spots, and he traveled with Paul to Berlin to serve as a German-speaking guide during the concerts there.

Paul first played "Madonna" in Berlin at a concert in the Schauspielhaus. Katscher had already planned to attend, without any notion that his piece would be on the program. In fact, Paul did not decide to include it until the last minute. There was no printed arrangement; a sheet with the melody line was handed out, the rest worked out in an ad-lib arrangement on stage. Paul asked Harry Perrella to devise some sort of introduction on the piano. The first chorus went to the violins; the second, to trumpeter Henry Busse, who improvised and added a mute. The hastily worked-out parts came together in a short and lively reprise by the entire orchestra. The audience went wild, and the surprised dentist-composer found himself an instant celebrity. After Whiteman returned to the United States, Buddy DeSylva added English lyrics to "Madonna" to make it "When Day Is Done"—today a classic.

Paul would always remember his stay in Berlin. Fritz Kreisler attended several rehearsals of the orchestra. (He also showed Paul the sights of the German capital; one night, in a traditional drinking ceremony, students, holding tankards of beer, formed two rows outside the stage door and made Paul drink right and left as he passed between them.) Composer Otto Lindemann submitted his new foxtrot, "I Could Fall in Love with You," to Paul. German music publishers printed special editions of the compositions featured by the orchestra with Paul's face on the sheet-music covers. The German press took a fancy to Whiteman; the *Berliner Zeitung* hired a plane to show the band the German capital from the air.

In spite of the enthusiasm, the Whiteman orchestra met its first noticeable resistance in Berlin. Though audiences were enthusiastic, Paul fretted over their lack of warmth and spirit. He was accustomed to a greater outpouring of affection. German critics found the Whiteman instrumentation and virtuosity of the players worthy of high praise; but they felt that in most instances the instrumentation was more important than the music itself. The *Boersen Zeitung* commented, "We Germans heard jazz yesterday for the first time. It will not become popular in Germany, for it does not suit the folk character, but it is a magic note from another world and cannot be dismissed contemptuously as 'negro music.'"

Academically Whiteman impressed the German establishment, but overall his music was put down as coarse, unpleasant, and

empty. Postwar neo-nationalists looked askance on any foreign influence, even in music. Soon the ruling factions would discourage
any such inroads from abroad.

The Dutch found it otherwise; they were thrilled by the Whiteman
sound. Paul was the great American jazz hero and, for the moment,
the most popular man in Holland. Audiences packed the concert
hall in Amsterdam while Whiteman played "Tiger Rag" and "Valencia."

During the long European tour Paul gave the band several weeks
of vacation. When it regrouped with restored vitality, Paul noticed
the improvement—the music seemed fresher. After the first concert
he remarked, "You boys play better in Europe; we should come
here more often."

From the back row of the bandstand a voice was heard. "We
should vacation more often. It would make us all into virtuosos!"

At the height of the tourist influx the Whiteman musicians joined
thousands of their countrymen in Paris. The orchestra opened at
the Champs Élysées theater in mid-July and concurrently played
at night at the Café des Ambassadeurs. Paul appeared there with
Florence Mills, the overnight singing sensation of the Eubie Blake–
Noble Sissle musical, *Shuffle Along.* Producer Lew Lesile had taken
her to Europe and staged her vehicle, *Dixie to Broadway,* as a co-
attraction with Whiteman. The supper and dance club, which seated
a thousand, never grossed less than $35,000 a week that summer.
Such opening night luminaries as the Dolly Sisters, Nita Naldi,
Constance Talmadge, and Grace Moore glided about the dance floor
in the latest Parisian fashions.

French audiences raved about Paul's show. His music familiar-
ized the country with the latest popular style from abroad. Parisian
avant-garde composers, including Arthur Honegger and Darius
Milhaud, made note of the Whiteman repertoire as serious musicians argued its pros and cons at many sidewalk cafés. Only a year
or two earlier the French government had expelled American jazz
players in response to protests by French musicians, who feared
that the foreigners were taking jobs from them. Now they seemed
even hospitable to Yankee artists in their midst.

Paul gave Europeans his music. In exchange he tested every native dish and brew, from Yorkshire pudding and paté de fois gras
to Scotch whisky and Rhine wine. A news photographer snapped
the multichinned balloon-shaped Paul in Berlin as he held up a

foamy stein of German beer. The picture, evocative of freely flowing spirits and heaped platters of rich dishes, caused readers of roto-gravure sections of New York papers to wonder if the King of Jazz were eating, rather than playing, his way through Europe. Even his men noticed that stage floors creaked a bit more when Paul walked to the podium.

From every hotel Paul sent a postcard or wire to his parents, who were taking care of two-year-old Paul, Jr. Paul's usual method of communicating—a quick telephone call—was impossible. He bought toys for Paul, Jr., and remembered Elfrida and the Professor by sending things for the ranch. From Berlin he shipped iris; from Amsterdam, tulips; from London, English ivy. Over the next ten years he shipped plants and bushes and trees to the ranch from nurseries all over the world. At the same time Paul and the Professor stocked the place with black and white animals, reflecting the keys of a piano. They included white chickens, holstein cows, a dal-matian, and a pair of parakeets with black spots.

On July 24 the band boarded the boat train to Le Havre, where the troupe boarded the *S.S. Rotterdam*. They had been away from New York for nearly four months. Family, friends, mistresses, bill collectors, and especially the Victor executives were waiting for them. At the pier in Hoboken 300 admirers and a band welcomed Whiteman.

"How well you look," said Vanda, who had returned to the States a month earlier, to be with the baby. "You've put on weight, have-n't you?"

"And how!" replied Paul. "Can you imagine being able to get the finest Pilsener at four cents a stein and *not* getting fat?"

After clearing customs, the Whiteman party entered six auto-mobiles bearing large posters proclaiming, "Welcome home, Paul Whiteman." The cars, covered with multicolored streamers, crossed on the Lackawanna ferry to Twenty-Third Street and were met by two motorcycle policemen, who escorted them to City Hall.

As Paul and his party left their cars to walk towards Mayor Jimmy Walker's office, Paul spotted a bunch of small boys wading in the pool at the base of the statue of Civic Virtue. He turned to Vanda. "That pool reminds me of the old swimming hole. Gee, I'd sure like to join those kids."

"You'd certainly create a sensation."

"Go on, I dare you," said a bystander.

Without another word, Paul began to climb over the spiked iron fence surrounding the pool and the statue. But he had not allowed for his added weight. It took the help of two policemen to negotiate the fence. Some of the boys offered to dive for coins.

"You mean pennies?" asked Paul.

"Naw, quarters," came an indignant chorus.

So quarters they got.

Inside City Hall, Mayor Walker greeted his friend. Paul told him about the tour of Europe and the good times on his travels.

"It's no use offering you the freedom of the city," the Mayor remarked. "It's already yours."

Paul responded by assuring His Honor that the orchestra was always at the city's disposal; to prove it he would give a concert the following Sunday in Central Park for as many as would come. More than 15,000 people crowded the Mall to welcome back their genial jazz potentate.

10

Magnet For Talent

The days and nights of wonderful nonsense of the late 1920s captivated the American public. Everyone was eager to hear of the latest pastime, fad, gimmick, stunt, or invention that appeared in the daily headlines. Good times were everywhere. Growing prosperity beckoned everybody. Every day was more and more taken up with leisure activity. Speed, too, was essential in travel, sports, movies, music, drinking, and living.

Paul kept up with the spirited, fun-seeking pace. He was more than part of a crazy, madcap era; he added to it with all his weight and wherewithal.

Walking along Fifty-Seventh Street in New York, Paul noticed a Duesenberg in a showroom window. He was told that it cost $14,500 and could be ready in a couple of hours. He said, "I'll take it."

Forgetting his new Duesenberg, Paul decided to take a group of friends from New York to Alaska by train. The party got only as far as San Francisco. There the booze ran out, and Paul began to sober up.

Jimmy Walker and Whiteman engaged in a spur-of-the-moment boxing bout when their scheduled game of handball was called because it was too cold to play outdoors. The mayor weighed in at 150, Paul at more than 250 pounds. Paul went down for the count in the second round. He explained that the bout was part of his weight-reducing program, because he was afraid that the excess baggage would make his next trip to Europe unprofitable.

Looking like an admiral, Paul led a thousand-piece band from the back seat of a car in a Knights Templar parade along Broadway.

Paul and his trumpeter, Henry Busse, drank a case of champagne every night for nineteen nights. Alone, Paul set a record of a hundred pint bottles of beer at one sitting.

Paul could do just about anything and get away with it. The press and police usually looked the other way when he departed from his kingly bearing or broke the law. He was rarely given a speeding ticket although he drove like a demon. Nearly every traffic cop on his commuting route recognized his big, sporty car and waved him by, ignoring his violations.

The accent was on dash and action as the last quarter of the 1920s unraveled. Just a year or two earlier, in 1924 and 1925, the pace had been less frenzied when Paul had given concerts in auditoriums and civic halls, but by 1925 most ticket buyers were heading to theaters booking film and stage presentations. Paul knew that his concert programs had reached most of the major cities in the country at least once. To maintain his preeminence and popularity, he had to revamp his itinerary and his band.

It was time to be more theatrical, more showy, more jazzy. By mid-1926 Paul knew that, without losing the solid commercial basis he had developed in little more than six years, he needed more than his characteristic "touch of jazz." He would build a small jazz contingent into the orchestra. Violinist Matty Malneck and Teddy Bartell constituted an established nucleus. Paul was determined to expand it carefully with new men and new arrangements.

He looked to black musicians, recognizing their contributions to the evolution of jazz. Since they were masters at improvised jazz, they had written down little of it. Most black musicians were denied entry into the commercial mainstream. Though jazz was black people's music, they had to delegate its widespread performance to less proficient commercial groups who, for the most part, made the big money and best-selling records. Black music, as well as the men who played it, had already influenced what was taking place in the dominant sector of popular music, as Irving Berlin had proved with "Alexander's Ragtime Band" early in the century.

The true jazz center was not Times Square but Harlem, the black area of New York. During the boom years the best jazz bands played there and received plenty of attention from white visitors and sightseers who sought out hot jazz. This audience spent money freely in the black clubs, usually owned by whites. Paul was hardly alone in visiting Harlem and stopping by Connie's Inn and the Cotton Club. Both places catered to white customers; usually blacks were admitted only as entertainers or waiters.

Paul, however, had his eye on two black bands that spent a good deal of time downtown. Fletcher Henderson led one of the best of them at Roseland, a popular dance hall off Broadway. He appeared off and on for over twenty years, starting in 1919, a year before Paul first came to the Palais Royal. Henderson's renditions of "Down Hearted Blues" and "Sugar Foot Stomp" helped to popularize jazz to white audiences. In 1924 he had contributed a jazz number to Lopez's concert at the Metropolitan Opera House.

During these years Duke Ellington began a long engagement at the old Hollywood Café at Forty-Ninth Street and Broadway. Renamed the Kentucky Club and wired for late-night remotes by radio station WHN, it became an "in" place to go, especially after the other clubs around town had closed for the night.

Paul and his musicians were regular listeners to Ellington's five-piece band. Paul and Ferde Grofé spent many hours studying the Duke and his "East St. Louis Toodle-oo," "Black and Tan Fantasy," and "Creole Love Call." Paul urged Ferde to make notes of what Ellington's outfit was playing, but Grofé had little or no success at capturing its distinctive sound and syncopation. When Ellington left the Kentucky Club for the uptown Cotton Club in 1927, Paul and Ferde were seen there frequently. Again they admitted that they couldn't steal even two bars of the Duke's amazing music.

Paul and Ferde saw in Ellington the first American composer-musician to catch the true jazz spirit. Duke, in turn, respected Whiteman for breaking down barriers with his soft jazz approach. He praised Paul for leading a comparatively lighthearted revolt on behalf of syncopation by young people of the 1920s amid the surviving restraints of the pre-First World War social order. "They embraced music which Paul Whiteman had made whiter," Duke later wrote of jazz's migration from black band to acceptable mainstream aggregations. "I used to hear Whiteman records taking the snobbishness out of the music and opening the doors for musicians."

Paul also had his eye on Eubie Blake as a special bandstand attraction. Good friends, Whiteman and Blake admired each other's talents. Paul had high regard for Blake, Ellington, and Henderson and thought seriously of bringing them and some of their musicians into his orchestra. He pointed out to his managers and advisers that the technical know-how and spirit of these performers could bring some real verve into the Whiteman band.

But his idea met with resistance based on the customs of the day. A racially mixed band would not be accepted in the South and not even in other parts of the country, including New England. Bookings would be withdrawn and lost. Traveling arrangements would become impossibly complicated as well—few hotels would allow blacks through the front door. Adding black musicians might spice up the Whiteman sound; but it wasn't good box office.

Paul bowed to this logic, but he found a way out. He would bring that special rhythm and syncopation to his followers by hiring black composers and arrangers. Don Redman, an alto sax player who had transformed Fletcher Henderson's band into one of the most expressive jazz groups in the country, began to prepare arrangements for Paul. Redman's orchestration of "Whiteman Stomp," written by Fats Waller as a bright, fast-tempo tune and "Sensation Stomp," had sparked Paul's interest in Don. Whiteman hired him to submit twenty similar arrangements at $100 each, an amount double the going fee.

A more prolific orchestrator for Whiteman was William Grant Still. Paul met him through Jack Robbins, a music publisher, who gave Whiteman one of Still's arrangements without identifying the musician. Paul liked the piece immediately. Still did not immediately join Whiteman as a staff arranger. In a year or so, he was chosen to orchestrate popular ballads for Paul's radio broadcasts which had become frequent by then. Still, who had studied at Oberlin College and the New England Conservatory of Music, made over a hundred arrangements for Paul. The pioneering black composer called his association with Whiteman his "school of experience" because it offered him a chance to experiment with different orchestral colors and tones and to hear the results of his experimentation quickly. He left Whiteman with a backlog of practical information not found in any textbook. His 1931 *Afro-American Symphony* is regarded as the first work of its kind by a black composer. He was also the first black musician to conduct a major American orchestra, the Los Angeles Philharmonic, in the Hollywood Bowl in 1936.

William Grant Still admired Paul as a musician and liked him as a person. Still also considered Whiteman a good and responsible businessman, who paid his associates well and promptly, something that was not always true in the music business.

Dozens of musicians applied for jobs every day at Paul's New York office during the 1920s. At the same time his managers, musicians, and friends scouted around for him. They made mental note of any players who would be assets to the organization. When he had an opening, Paul would reach for the person who seemed likely to fill the slot best. By mid-1926 he was reaching for star jazz material more intensely than at any time and the word was out.

After Labor Day, Whiteman arranged another tour. Instead of undertaking the grueling one-night stands of previous seasons, he signed a contract with the Paramount-Publix Theatre chain for bookings lasting a week or two in movie theaters in most cities, and longer in Los Angeles, San Francisco, and Chicago. The agreement called for three shows a day between film presentations. For his services for eighteen months the chain paid him $9,500 a week, with a guarantee of forty weeks of work a year. The contract allowed the band to play at one dance in each city; Paul received 50 percent of the profits from these extra dates.

Work in motion-picture theaters necessitated a revamping of the band into a small-scale variety-show unit. Fred Waring, Irving Aaronson, and Horace Heidt had had great success on the movie-chain circuit by designing their material to appeal to a cross section of the country's mass audiences, rather than a narrower, more discriminating segment of music enthusiasts. Paul placed his new emphasis on popular vocal numbers and novelty jazz acts.

The orchestra was also regrouped to eliminate violas, cellos, and bassoons (the French horns had long since been dropped). Instrumentalists who could also sing were increasingly featured on vocals. Violinist Charles Gaylord and guitarist Austin "Skin" Young frequently joined trombonist Jack Fulton to form a singing trio. Wilbur Hall and his slide trombone plus bicycle pump held the spotlight as a comic act. Bartell and Malneck contributed instrumental jazz solos.

In September, after the customary rush to record enough selections for release during the band's absence from New York, the men boarded their two special railroad cars. The train also hooked on a seventy-foot baggage car to carry musical instruments, scenery, electrical equipment, and a wardrobe consisting of four changes. A stage crew and a piano tuner joined the troupe. Before leaving, Paul turned over last-minute details to Gillespie and his staff so that he himself could travel ahead for a short visit with his parents. Busse and Malneck went along on the brief family reunion at the ranch outside Denver. They rejoined the band in Los Angeles, where it opened on September 18 at the palatial Million Dollar Theatre. The audience response was overwhelming. The men enjoyed accolades as crowds filled the house for weeks.

During the Los Angeles run Whiteman picked up a singer who stayed with him the better part of four years and turned out to be Whiteman's greatest discovery. Jimmy Gillespie actually found the young baritone at the nearby Metropolitan Theatre. He was part of a two-man singing and dancing act of Crosby and Rinker. Jimmy described the duo to Paul. "One of them plays a piano and the other bangs on a cymbal."

"Oh boy, I need them like I need another chin," replied Paul.

"But they're different. You've got to hear these two guys."

"If you think they're the bees' knees, bring 'em to me."

Bing Crosby and Al Rinker had left their homes in Spokane in a beat-up Ford bound for Los Angeles. Al's sister, Mildred Bailey, who was working as a singer in a nightclub, had written an enthusiastic letter about the chances for young performers in and around the film capital. She thought that Al and Bing might land a job in a neighborhood theater or club. Mildred arranged an audition for them and they got a booking with a musical revue touring the outskirts of Los Angeles. Though it folded in Santa Barbara, Bing and Al were lucky; they got another booking in Paramount-Publix's downtown Metropolitan Theatre, where some of the Whiteman band saw their act.

A week or so earlier, Bing and Al had gone to Union Station to watch the band's arrival and then caught Whiteman's show at the Million Dollar Theatre. They were mesmerized. Bing was particularly impressed with Skin Young's full-range singing style and fast rhythms.

Crosby and Rinker went backstage to Paul's dressing room. Paul was sitting on an ottoman, wearing a silk dressing gown, eating caviar from a large bowl, and drinking champagne. As Crosby later noted in *Call Me Lucky,* Paul had all the trappings of success. "When you can eat a pound of caviar and drink champagne in your dressing room in the middle of the day, you've reached the pinnacle." This is the place for me, Bing knew at once. Al, too, was on cloud nine. But he recalled Paul as having an ordinary lunch with beer, not champagne.

According to Bing's autobiography, they sang several numbers. On the other hand, Al claimed that Paul came right to the point without an audition.

Paul offered the two $300 a week for the pair, with additional pay for recordings. The agreement gave Whiteman the option to book the team independently from the band. Crosby and Rinker finished their local stint, headed north for a break in Spokane to rest up, and then joined Whiteman in Chicago in mid-December. The Chicago *Daily News* erroneously called the two California "finds" Bing Rinker and Bill Crosby.

Paul had given Bing and Al a pep talk before they bowed with the band. "Music's the same all over. They liked you in Los Angeles, and they'll like you in Chicago. Just do your stuff the way you've always done it."

He introduced the pair by casually telling the audience, "I want to introduce two young fellas who are joining my band. I picked them up in an ice cream parlor in Walla Walla, Washington." He struck exactly the right note. Rinker and Crosby went out, did their stuff, and went over very big. Their act added even more zing to the band. But audiences in the East would soon have a different reaction.

Before leaving Chicago, Paul made a half-dozen recordings. They included Bing's and Al's first disc for Whiteman, "Wistful and Blue," an arrangement by Matty Malneck. In Los Angeles, Don Clark, the former Whiteman saxophone player, had already invited the duo to make a record called "I've Got the Girl" with his Biltmore Hotel orchestra; it was cut on October 10, 1926, for Columbia.

Paul had two important business matters on his mind as he packed for New York—the opening of his own nightclub and an appearance in a Broadway musical. Vincent Lopez, Jimmy Durante, Texas Guinan, and other show business names had opened clubs along Broadway to cash in on the free-spending crowds out on the town. These night spots flourished by ignoring Prohibition and blatantly selling liquor. Raids by federal officers occurred regularly. A handful of employees, and sometimes an owner, would be arrested and spend a day or two in jail before being released on bail. It was pure ritual, a cynical nod in the direction of the law. Paul was willing to risk such notoriety in an effort to make big money as a showman-businessman.

The Whiteman Club opened on February 18, 1927, in the former Cinderella Ballroom at Forty-Eighth Street and Broadway. The hall where the Wolverines and other spirited jazz bands had played was renovated to accommodate nearly a thousand guests in an exotic black-and-gold setting. Paul held a 50 percent share in the venture, with several real estate entrepreneurs holding the other half. They hired the former head waiter at the Palais Royal to serve as the maitre d'.

A packed house of friends, admirers, celebrities, and even Prohibition agents welcomed Paul back to Broadway. Among the throng who paid the ten-dollar cover charge were Charlie Chaplin, conductor Nat Shilkret, music publisher Jack Robbins, Texas Guinan, songwriters Harry Warren and Lew Brown, and Jimmy Durante. Paul's band entertained and then played for dancing. A blues singer Paul had heard in Chicago was the featured attraction, but few people noticed Ruth Etting during her brief stint at the club. After a quick round of theater appearances back in Chicago, Ruth returned permanently to Manhattan, where her talent received the attention it deserved, both with Whiteman at the Paramount and with Ziegfeld in his new *Follies* starring Eddie Cantor.

Broadway's soothsayers predicted that Paul would make a small fortune in his new enterprise. A near capacity turnout the first month or so reinforced this belief. Notables from every field came through the front entrance. Even evangelist Aimee Semple McPherson walked in. She came to bring "greetings" from Paul's father whom she had just seen in Colorado. The Professor had come out of retirement to lead Aimee's large choir in Denver. When the crowd of patrons in the club recognized her, she fled in a burst of press camera flashes. But even men and women of the cloth could not save the large and costly Club Whiteman. When it was half full, it still looked like a barn. By late spring Paul backed out of the arrangement, taking his name and little profit with him. He suggested that he be replaced with a band he had heard in Cleveland which could be had for the sensible price of $1,000 a week. But Broadway was not interested in these unknowns. The band was Guy Lombardo and his Royal Canadians. Guy went instead to the

Granada Café in Chicago, where he built up a following that soon had New York chasing him on his own terms.

In order to appear in a Broadway show, Paul won a release from his Publix contract two weeks before the new production opened on March 22. Producer Charles Dillingham had offered the Whiteman orchestra $9,500 a week, a record high in 1927. *Lucky* proved to be misnamed. Though it had songs by Jerome Kern, Bert Kalmer, Harry Ruby, and Otto Harbach, and a cast led by Mary Eaton, Ruby Keeler, and Walter Catlett, the production generated little enthusiasm when it came into the New Amsterdam Theatre. There was not much Paul and his men could do with the lackluster score. In every direction, theater marquees beckoned with competing offerings: *The Desert Song, Oh, Kay!, Honeymoon Lane, Rio Rita,* and *Peggy Ann. Lucky* remained among them for only nine weeks.

Moreover, the show got Paul into hot water with Manhattan's Society for Prevention of Cruelty to Children. It discovered that Paul had hired a ten-year-old black boy to strum a banjo and dance with the band on stage. He had found the youngster, Edwin "Snowball" Harris, in St. Louis and offered him a job. Harris and his father came East. A few days after *Lucky* opened, Paul was handed a summons. In court a judge informed him that he was violating the law by permitting a minor to perform on a stage without proper supervision. The magistrate let Paul off when he agreed to send Snowball back to Missouri.

One of the few bright moments in *Lucky* came about because Paul insisted on giving Crosby and Rinker a feature spot. Because no number in the score seemed suitable for the duo, he picked up a Tin Pan Alley tune, "Sam, the Old Accordion Man," and added his band's Mario Perry on the accordion. The number went over big at a time when Paul was wondering what to do with the two musicians from Spokane.

A month before *Lucky* opened, the orchestra had bowed in the Paramount Theater. The men looked natty in their blue jackets and white trousers. To get the full effect of their striking outfits, Paul eliminated the music stands on stage.

Variety gave the show a rave review. Many members of the band came in for individual praise. The write-up lauded Paul's showmanship in putting together a miniature road show. "He knows what is wanted and goes after it with assurance. He has the smartest, quickest, and snappiest routine of his career." The paper particularly liked the first Broadway appearance of Crosby and Rinker, calling them "a smart two-man piano act, who sing pop ditties differently. After Whiteman gets through grooming the boys they'll be in the money."

Audiences at the Paramount thought otherwise. After an enthusiastic acceptance by Chicago theatergoers and a rave trade notice, Crosby and Rinker were dumbfounded. "They laid dinosaur eggs," Paul remarked of their flop. The Paramount manager demanded that they be dropped from the stage show. To keep them busy and out of trouble, Paul put them to work in the lobby entertaining the patrons waiting in line for the next show. But even there Bing and Al foundered. People offered them Cracker Jacks and taffy, but little applause.

Paul was perplexed. The team had wowed audiences in Los Angeles and Chicago. But on Broadway, they could not get to first base. The two thought of quitting. But after having headlined with the great Whiteman band, it would be tough facing their friends back West. It was easier to reach for a drink, then another, and forget about their failures.

By an odd quirk of fate, it was Paul's father who rescued Bing and Al. The Professor had urged one of his popular vocal students to go to New York for an audition with his son. The young man had demonstrated his talent in many musical productions in Denver. Wilberforce wrote Paul, "He can write songs. He is a quick and a very bright boy." Harry Barris arrived at Paul's office in March 1927, brim-full of ideas and suggestions.

"Tell me what you think I can do with Crosby and Rinker," asked Paul. "They've bombed nearly every place since we came back to Manhattan."

"I know one thing, I'd like to be on stage with you."

"I'm loaded with singers. I've a half-dozen in the band now. I've got more singers than a sewing-machine factory."

"I can do more than just sing. I write songs."

"Let's hear a few. Maybe you could bring some new life into those Walla Walla Indians. How would you warm up their hambone stew?"

"First," Harry replied, "I'd add myself and another piano to the act. Then I'd put in some slapdash humor. That would wake up the folks. I'm sure I can fix up the act."

Paul agreed to hire the confident newcomer from Denver. "You'll start at 75 bucks. If this trio flies, you get 150—the same as Al and Bing."

A new team was born. Harry wrote a jazzy tune called "Mississippi Mud" to launch the act. He rehearsed it thoroughly. As they worked together, his enthusiasm spread to Al and Bing, and they pushed harder than ever. Their verve and polish attracted everyone's attention. Bing and Al were back in the spotlight with a new partner. Calling themselves the Rhythm Boys, they used three-part harmony on the numbers that Bing and Al had been doing, added new songs, and brought in two pianos.

The trio scored when Paul and the band returned to the Paramount in June 1927 for six weeks—an unprecedentedly long run, to the tune of $10,500 a week. The movie being shown was a first-class comedy, *Running Wild* with W. C. Fields, but the stage attraction outlasted several Hollywood features. Ruth Etting, rejoining Paul, pleased New Yorkers with her modulated, almost crooning voice. Monologist Charles Irwin provided comic relief, and organist Jesse Crawford opened all the stops on his mighty instrument. Paul and the gang entertained a capacity house intent on enjoying the biggest and most highly acclaimed band in the country. Whiteman gave his audiences the best musical variety show in town, with such production numbers and musical finales as "Rushia," which put the Whiteman group in Russian dress, and "U.S.S. Syncopation," which had everyone wearing sailor suits. The costly presentations also included an "Ali Baba" segment featuring Vanda Hoff Whiteman in her dancing comeback. Working with Paul and the band on stage gave Vanda a chance to see more of her frequently absent husband. His never-ending public appearances meant that she could enjoy little or no home life. The marriage suffered as his million-dollar organization demanded more and more of Paul's time. And no doubt about it, Paul preferred the excitement of Broadway and the road to an easy chair in front of the fire.

In spite of the smashing success at the Paramount, Paul was still not satisfied with the band. He wanted to add more real jazz to the repertoire. For the next two years a contingent of hot sidemen climbed aboard the Whiteman bandwagon. These musicians changed the complexion of the organization as the Jazz Age roared to a climax. Most of the players stayed with Paul for only a year or so.

In 1924 Loring "Red" Nichols, at nineteen, had organized a band called the Redheads, with Miff Mole, Jimmy Dorsey, Arthur Shcutt, Joe Venuti, Eddie Lang, and Vic Berton. The following year Red and his cornet burst forth with his new band, Five Pennies, utilizing some of the same sidemen and introducing the kind of hot jazz that became his trademark. The Five Pennies' recording of "Ida" sold a million discs. It illustrated Red's method of taking a tune that had been popular years before and rearranging it, making it his own.

Red's approach to a song impressed Paul; for years he had been reworking old melodies himself. Shortly after Red became leader of another "hot" group, the Charleston Chasers, he joined Whiteman's trumpet section. Paul was pleased to add Nichols, and immediately made him feel that he was a very special member of his outfit. When Red married chorus girl Willa Stutsman, Paul served as his best man. But the honeymoon with Paul ended quickly. Red discovered that, as a member of the Whiteman band, he was restricted from carrying out the lucrative recording deals he had with a half-dozen independent companies. He had been accustomed to taking his own outfit to Vocalion, Banner, Okeh, Brunswick, and other labels, where he would cut the same tune for each, with only slight changes in the orchestrations. Red had lost a sizable income. He also began to feel that his style was cramped by the Whiteman mold.

Former Five Pennies drummer Vic Berton also found a place on Paul's bandstand when George Marsh left. According to Berton family lore, it was one of the worst things that ever happened to him. Vic apparently loved the limelight as much as did Paul. His flashy drumming rubbed Whiteman the wrong way; audiences paid more attention than the maestro liked to the band's latest member. Tension between the two grew, until one night it exploded into a nasty fist fight in the men's room. A short time later Vic was back on a bandstand, now playing for Roger Wolfe Kahn's Pennsylvania Hotel orchestra. Paul quickly rehired his original drummer Hal McDonald.

Red Nichols's reedman Jimmy Dorsey also entered the Whiteman ranks that spring. Born in the coal mining region of eastern Pennsylvania, Dorsey first played in a band organized by his father. By the early 1920s, he and his brother Tommy, a trombonist, became part of the Scranton Sirens, a popular jazz group in the area. Both went on to Jean Goldkette units based in Detroit. Paul liked the Dorsey boys' all-around musicianship on the bandstand. Soon after Jimmy joined Whiteman, Tommy followed. Paul was impressed with his new trombone player's straightforward delivery and tremendous drive. A certain integrity and decency placed him above many musicians.

Paul kept his eye on the Goldkette organization, recognized as the hottest commercial dance band in the country. Jean Goldkette dedicated himself to sponsoring and creating jazz. Born in France and trained as a concert pianist, Jean turned to the dance-band business, soon catching the attention of Edgar Benson, a Chicago orchestra leader. As a subleader of Benson's units, Goldkette was sent to Detroit. His first big job was at the Detroit Athletic Club, where his toe-tapping dance music attracted the younger set. When the Book-Cadillac Hotel opened, Jean organized a second outfit. He continued to branch out as more and more engagements came his way. The Greystone Ballroom was the third location to offer Goldkette's music in Detroit. He could now hire the best red-hot players, leaders, and arrangers. Among them were Paul Mertz, Doc Ryker, Don Murray, Danny Polo, Fuzzy Farrar, Bill Rank, and Chauncey Morehouse. A pioneer in the big-band field, Goldkette operated throughout the Midwest on such a large scale that he became the area's most important band booker and musical organizer of the 1920s.

Whiteman heard the Greystone aggregation when he was in Detroit on tour. The Goldkette line-up in this unit included sax player Frank Trumbauer, trombonist Bill Rank, trumpeter Bix Beiderbecke, and bassist Steve Brown. Paul held all of them in high favor, but refrained from making an offer to any one of them. He knew this great-sounding combo would suffer if even one member left. Goldkette's inventive and prolific arranger, Bill Challis, also caught his ear. But Paul, who had done so much to advance the band business, did not want to raid another band—especially of this caliber—and risk the break-up of an outfit. He would wait it out on the sidelines.

Bill Challis had been buying Whiteman records since his college days at Bucknell, where he organized an orchestra that helped to pay his way through school. Fred Waring offered him a job with his Pennsylvanians, but Bill wanted a degree first. He often wrote for his own outfit and other bands in and about his hometown of

Wilkes-Barre, Pennsylvania. Goldkette hired Bill when he delivered his arrangement of "Blue Room" to the band in 1926. He played piano adequately and saxophone well; but Goldkette's manager, Charlie Horvath, encouraged him to concentrate on arrangements for the three Goldkette units in Detroit. The most spirited of the three bands—the Greystone Ballroom unit—had a following among college students, jazz buffs, and young musicians. It lost money regularly, in spite of periodic record dates for Victor. Most of its players knew that the ax could fall at any time.

Whiteman had sent out feelers to Challis, letting him know that he would be welcome in Paul's organization if things did not work out in Detroit. Jimmy Dorsey, too, urged his boss to pick up Goldkette's star arranger. In late summer the Goldkette Greystone band appeared in Atlantic City. Dorsey and a handful of musicians, including Paul, traveled to the ocean resort to hear the band.

During the evening Challis suggested that Paul conduct a number. Paul agreed. He gave the downbeat on "St. Louis Blues" and the musicians struggled a bit to stay with him for the first sixteen bars or so. At the conclusion the band received a wild ovation. The men were thrilled with Paul's presence and showmanship. Many had secretly thought of making a play for a job in his highly acclaimed and well-paying band. Challis was the first to switch, just as the Goldkette unit started to fold. He joined up at the Paramount in New York in late September 1927.

Challis was itching to get into arrangements for a big orchestra with a full sound. On the first of his more than 200 orchestrations for Paul he put three baritone saxes in close harmony on the melody. Whiteman repeatedly told him to use any instruments he wanted, and he did so with superb results. Paul also suggested that he travel with the band for ten weeks to become familiar with the individual talents of its members. Challis roomed with Jimmy Dorsey, and he carried a small traveling pump organ for arranging on the road. Eager to write for the large Whiteman aggregation, in a few days Challis was turning out scores.

He soon talked Paul into hiring Steve Brown, a bass player with Goldkette. Brown was the first big-band musician to pluck the strings of a bass. That fall Goldkette's Greystone unit broke up; most of its players regrouped as Adrian Rollini's New Yorkers. But many of the bookings for this band did not pan out, and it, too, collapsed, playing its last date at a club in Greenwich Village with

Jack Benny. Paul now had no hesitation in offering jobs to Trumbauer and Beiderbecke. They joined for $200 a week each during a run at the Lyric Theatre in Indianapolis in November.

Trumbauer—nicknamed Trum and Tram—starred on the C melody sax. He frequently recorded with jazz combos under his own name. He made "Singin' the Blues" well known, and it became the theme of his own band in the late 1930s.

Tommy Dorsey felt lost among nearly thirty musicians. Freelance recordings and radio work were offering him many opportunities to be heard. Income from his independent nonstop work schedule provided even more money than a salary with Whiteman; Dorsey therefore decided to turn in his notice as 1927 drew to a close. His replacement, Bill Rank, caught up with his old buddies, Bix and Trum, in Pittsburgh. Rank had spent almost three years as a trombonist with Goldkette. The Whiteman bandstand became his home for the next ten years.

Briefly, at the end of 1927, the Whiteman aggregation, in addition to Tommy and Jimmy Dorsey, contained three brothers of the Mayhew family: Nye and Jack, on saxophone, and kid brother Bob, on trumpet.

Virtually all the newcomers were immediately overshadowed by trumpeter Bix Beiderbecke. Paul took a special liking to this remarkable horn player. He always became good pals with his newest band members, and for a short time, he did everything to make them feel welcome. Almost invariably Paul's enthusiasm would cool and he dropped them from his close circle of friends. With Bix, it was different. He remained a second son to Whiteman during his three erratic years on the bandstand.

Paul had come across few musicians with the playing ability and the exquisite tone Bix could produce. His was a great and spontaneous talent. He improvised with total ease, along a beat that sounded, in the words of Bill Challis, "like it came out of a precision-tooled machine gun." A musician's musician, for the first time he received widespread exposure when he became a member of the Whiteman orchestra. Nearly every new Challis arrangement offered a chorus or half a chorus for Bix, and he in turn delivered it with lightly styled spice and sparkle. His cornet solos became widely talked about and much imitated.

The jazz contingent of Paul's organization received a decided boost when Bix joined its ranks. He also upped the average alcoholic intake of the outfit considerably. Paul had learned to handle the Prohibition-era hooch. Although he suffered many hangovers, he kept to his full schedule with few cancellations. Bix, however, lost a growing battle with the bottle. That defeat came a year or two later. Meanwhile the band rushed into Victor's studio with a solid inventory of hot notes. Whiteman's latest thrust into jazz seemed complete and successful.

11

Columbia's Gem

President Calvin Coolidge chose not to run for reelection in 1928. His Commerce Secretary, Herbert Hoover, ran in his place, promising "two chickens in every pot and a car in every garage." Al Smith, the Democratic opponent, ran a tough campaign, but prosperity for which the Republicans took credit, impressed the majority of voters. Didn't Fifth Avenue jewelers Black Starr & Frost run an advertisement three days before the election for a pearl necklace priced at a staggering $685,000?

Americans were also buying some two and a half million cars, making the automotive industry the country's fastest-growing business. More and more people were driving, especially to the movies. People flocked to the first full-length sound motion pictures in 1928. Newsreels, travelogs, and cartoons added sound as well, and audiences laughed at Walt Disney's first Mickey Mouse "talkie" called *Steamboat Willie*.

Champion swimmer and future cinema Tarzan, Johnny Weissmuller, won the hundred-meter free-style Olympic event. World heavyweight boxing champion Gene Tunney retired after beating contender Tom Heeney. Just a year after Lindbergh's transatlantic flight Amelia Earhart was the first woman to repeat the feat.

Also in 1928, Mayor Jimmy Walker headed a committee that included hotel owner S. W. Straus and tea merchant Sir Thomas Lipton, to give Paul Whiteman a dinner celebrating his tenth anniversary in the city. Actually only eight years had passed since his arrival, but it was ten since he organized his first band. Jimmy

Walker was never very good at numbers. The more than 650 guests who gathered at the Hotel Astor included George Gershwin, Ben Bernie, Gene Buck, Jackie Coogan, Daniel Frohman, Major Edward Bowes, Bernard F. Gimbel, Senator Royal S. Copeland, O. O. McIntyre, and Leon Errol. The banquet saluted the "harmony and happiness" that Paul contributed to the people of New York.

Given Paul's schedule in 1928, it is a wonder he had time to attend dinners, read a daily paper, see a movie, or even vote. Beginning on January 4 and continuing to December 22, he spent sixty-eight days in recording studios. No other major artist has ever equaled that number of recording sessions in a single year.

By 1928 recording studios reverberated with the sounds of various dance bands. Many competed with Paul for the record-buyers' dollars. Jean Goldkette and Fred Waring continued to lead in foxtrots. Releases from Ben Bernie, George Olsen, Art Landry, Ray Miller, Ohman and Arden, King Oliver, and Miff Mole headed for many turntables. But more and more Victor's own Nathaniel Shilkret kept Paul on the run at "His Master's Voice."

Familiar with the symphony and opera repertoire from playing clarinet in several orchestras, Shilkret utilized his background well at Victor. The company appointed him a musical director at the age of thirty. He advanced to conductor on both popular works and semiclassical selections. Nat was increasingly involved with the type of recordings Paul had first advanced in a big way.

In April of 1927 Nat had stepped in to help the Whiteman orchestra when it met with Gershwin to rerecord *Rhapsody in Blue* with the new Victor electrical process. Paul arrived at the studio prepared to conduct, but the French horn players hired especially for the session did not show up on time. Paul argued with the studio managers over whether he or Victor had the responsibility to assure their presence. Paul left the studio in a huff. (Gershwin's disagreement that day with Whiteman over a point of interpretation may have been the real cause of the walk-out.) When Paul returned to the building, the two horn players had taken their places, and the recording session was under way—with Shilkret on the podium. Paul took one look and walked out again.

Three months later Paul was back in the studio to record "My Blue Heaven" in dance tempo. When Paul heard Nat's record of "Blue Heaven," he complained bitterly. "I'm the one who has first crack at the symphonic approach to popular stuff. What's going on? This is my territory!"

The Victor management tried to explain that the company usually aimed for as much mileage as possible on a single tune from several musical outfits, especially in-house. To add to Paul's annoyance, Victor explained that Shilkret was recording Gershwin's "The Man I Love" in concert form.

"Gershwin!" Paul shouted. "After all I've done with him on your label, you're now letting Nat get the best cut of the cake."

Paul's contract with Victor was due to run out in April 1928. His threat of leaving did not seem to worry the company. Actually the Whiteman records, which now had greater competition, were not selling as well as anticipated. As a result Victor gradually cut back on paying each of Whiteman's sidemen the usual $50 per side studio fee. To economize on recording such a large dance band, the company discussed setting a limit on payments. With checks of $50, $100, $150, or more going to some two dozen men at the end of each session, Victor was beginning to have second thoughts. These payments were, of course, an extra incentive to join Whiteman's outfit.

By 1928 the Whiteman organization had grown to thirty-four. It was inevitable that personnel changes occurred from time to time within that line-up. When, for example, heavy-drinking Harry Perrella missed an engagement or two, Paul looked to an experienced keyboard artist in Isham Jones's orchestra. He hired Roy Bargy, who had also served Edgar Benson in Chicago as pianist, arranger, and director for his Victor recordings. A distinctive Bargy device was the use of the "break," or interruption of the melody, incorporating it into his keyboard solos.

With Whiteman Roy Bargy took on even more. From 1928 to 1940 he was second in command on the podium, at the keyboard, and in the office.

Two months later, when arranger-pianist Tom Satterfield, who had been with the band for less than a year, gave notice, Paul acquired another pianist-arranger of a high caliber in Lennie Hayton. A native New Yorker, Hayton had studied classical piano, then turned to dance music, joining Cass Hagan's unit. He recorded with Red Nichols, Frankie Trumbauer, Don Voorhees, and Bix Beiderbecke. Lennie fit in well with Paul's sidemen, and the piano duo of Bargy and Hayton made a notable impression, especially on the dozens of records Whiteman made in the course of 1928.

Paul had already come to a decision: he would leave Victor that spring. His eight-year association produced scores of best-sellers. Four or five discs had sold in the millions, in an era when 100,000 copies meant a tremendous hit. Everyone connected with the band had made real money from studio work. Paul had recorded numbers in a wide variety of styles, ranging from snappy foxtrots and popular ballads to semiclassical suites and jazz-flavored nonsense songs. Many stayed in Victor's catalog for years.

Nat Shilkret's invasion of Whiteman's bailiwick bruised Paul's ego. And when Victor studio manager Eddie King left Victor for Columbia, Paul looked in that direction.

The Columbia Phonograph Company developed during the earliest days of record-making, before the turn of the century. Older than Victor, it had pioneered in lateral, or flat, discs—in contrast to cylinders—and in electrically made recordings. In 1927–1928 its line-up of dance-band maestros included Paul Ash, Cass Hagen, Fred Rich, Harry Reser, Don Voorhees, Jan Garber, and Ted Lewis. Columbia struggled to compete with high-powered Victor, which had built Irving Aaronson, Coon–Sanders, George Olsen, Jelly Roll Morton, Ben Pollack, and Whiteman into top-flight recording personalities.

Columbia eagerly accepted Paul. The firm guaranteed a yearly minimum of $50,000 against a two-year exclusive contract, to take effect immediately at the conclusion of Paul's Victor agreement in April. Paul signed and waited.

Victor faced the loss of its star ensemble by reacting in the only possible way: it practically barricaded Paul and his men in its studios for the remaining three or four months of his contract. The band worked long and hard. In January the musicians spent eight days there; in February, an unprecedented twelve days. From February 7 through 18, they broke away only three days. The output eventually totaled nearly sixty sides.

The results were impressive. Bing Crosby, Al Rinker, and Harry Barris—as Paul Whiteman's Rhythm Boys—had skyrocketed into the hottest trio in show business. Paul gave them solos on "From Monday On" and "Mississippi Mud." Bing soloed on "Make Believe" and "High Water." The jazz contingent blazed through "San," "Sugar," and "There Ain't No Sweet Man That's Worth

the Salt of My Tears.'' The Rhythm Boys and the ''sweet trio''—
Fulton, Young, and Gaylord—harmonized on ''Sunshine'' and
''When.'' The full orchestra immortalized Victor Herbert's *Suite
of Serenades* and Grofé's *Metropolis*. The old-timers and newcomers together rewaxed the original chestnuts ''Whispering,'' ''Japanese Sandman,'' and ''Avalon.''

Meanwhile Columbia bided its time, pleased at having captured
such big game. The company pledged cooperation, vowing to do
everything to make the new affiliation pleasant and profitable for
Paul. A company wag penned these lines to welcome him to Columbia's world of ''Magic Notes'':

He who leadeth a dog's life
Doth make the wisest choice
When he listeneth to ''Magic Notes''
And not ''His Master's Voice.''

Columbia spared no promotional and advertising effort to tell the
public that the ''King of Jazz'' was now exclusively on its label.
A special three-color record label of orange, blue, and green was
designed. The famous caricature of Paul's head appeared at the
center of each record as well as on the four-color record sleeve—
a novelty in the phonograph business.

To launch Whiteman in its catalog, Columbia brought out three
twelve-inch concert numbers, popularly priced at $1 against the
standard $1.25 tariff for this size. The selections were ''La Paloma''
and ''La Golondrina,'' ''The Merry Widow'' and ''My Hero,'' and
''My Melancholy Baby'' and ''The Man I Love,'' respectively. The
last side, sung by crooner Vaughn DeLeath, was a definite jab at
Shilkret and his Victor release of the Gershwin favorite.

In the dance series of ten-inch records selling for 75 cents, Columbia issued ''Last Night I Dreamed You Kissed Me'' (with Jack
Fulton on vocal) and ''Evening Star,'' and a second record with
''Constantinople'' and ''Get Out and Get Under the Moon'' (sung
by Crosby).

The Whiteman Columbia releases captured the band's prevailing
Victor ''sound.'' The only instrumental change occurred within the
brass section and could be said to result directly from the frantic
schedule Victor imposed.

On the next-to-last Victor session, the men gathered in Lieder-

kranz Hall to record "Do I Hear You Saying" and "Grieving."
They were irritable and weary after months of studio work and
anxious to get through the last two sessions as quickly as possible.
Among the visibly annoyed was Busse.

At preceding sessions Busse had not been given his usual featured
solos. He had only done bits on "Love Nest," "Mary," and several
other numbers. "This he found humiliation enough," wrote Richard
Sudhalter and Philip Evans in *Bix,* their biography of Beiderbecke,
"but to have to sit by and watch Bix, a technically unschooled
player, being given one solo plum after another by Challis, Malneck,
and Satterfield was worse yet. His resentment flared after the band
had finished a Satterfield score on 'Do I Hear You Saying,' with
a full chorus solo spot for Trumbauer."

Busse spoke angrily to Paul. Loud and bitter words were ex-
changed in front of the entire band. Paul was not reticent in re-
minding Busse who was boss. Drummer Hal McDonald, another
carry-over from the old days, immediately backed up Busse and
said so to Paul, drawing Whiteman's fire on himself. Both musicians
walked out on the spot, leaving two empty chairs with one number
still to be recorded.

Paul called the session off for the remainder of the day. He felt
crestfallen and numb over the loss of his old buddies. He pulled
himself together and told Jimmy Gillespie to scout the neighborhood
hangouts, including Plunkett's, to find substitutes. He needed re-
placements for the following morning. Gillespie tracked down a
former Whiteman player, George Marsh, for the drums. Harry
Goldfield, a onetime soloist with Jan Garber, came to take Busse's
place on trumpet. Goldie emerged as a dependable and frequently
featured brass player, and a well-known character in the band. A
look-alike of the rotund Busse, and of Paul as well, Goldfield stuck
with Whiteman for ten years.

The departure of Busse and McDonald dramatized the widening
split between the Palais Royal veterans and the jazz-trained newcomers. The division was in part personal. When Bix came in, Busse
didn't dig his kind of music. Resentment of the new men and the
new arrangements grew among the faction Malneck called the die-
hards. Challis had brought the two elements together musically in
a way that made good use of each one's capabilities. Nevertheless,
there was disagreement, in principle and in thought, and so there
was conflict.

Few Whiteman sidemen were completely surprised that Busse left. They were amazed, however, at the abrupt and heated manner of his leaving. Busse worshiped Paul. When Paul ordered tailor-made clothes from Benham's in Manhattan, Busse followed suit. When Paul showed off a new sporty roadster, Busse hurried to buy one like it. When Paul drank a dozen bottles of beer at one sitting, Busse kept pace. When Paul grew a moustache, Busse added one to his similarly round face. When Paul introduced Busse on stage, he'd quip, "Busse has been with me so long that he's beginning to look like me."

Paul paid Busse a generous $350 a week; only Grofé, at $375, earned more. Busse was Paul's pet, and everyone knew it. But the relationship fell apart when Bix came in and encroached on his turf. Now Bix could do no wrong; he could get drunk, come in late, miss engagements. Paul overlooked all failings. Some sidemen blamed Bix for causing the bad feelings. Yet he rarely, if ever, deliberately tried to secure favored status.

Busse was already freelancing in New York clubs, playing his distinctive growl on "Hot Lips" and "Wang Wang Blues" to good advantage. He had wanted his own band for a long time. He even asked Bill Challis to do an arrangement—an offer Challis declined. Busse's own band was slowly gathering steam by the summer of 1928. After working with the short-lived musical *Say When*, Busse opened at Risely's on the Lake in Saratoga in time for the August racing.

Meanwhile Jimmy Gillespie devised Whiteman's summer agenda: four weeks of one-nighters, three weeks on the Publix circuit, two weeks of vacation in New Hampshire. The bookings included Atlantic City's Steel Pier, where on a hot August 25 the one-day attendance mark was set when 35,000 people crowded the pier to dance to Paul's music.

Paul was once more in a quandary about Crosby, Rinker, and Barris. Paul had given them dozens of vocal bits on recordings, and Crosby had received solo work on many more. The money came in fast. For bachelors Bing and Al the income made chasing bootleggers, golf balls, and girls that much easier. More and more of their time, energy, and talent was spent in directions other than music. Paul, at least, felt that they could do better and be more reliable in their work. Their material became stale, and they rarely bothered to freshen up their act with new numbers. Years later, asked whether Bing was hard to handle, Paul said of his prodigal crooner, "No, he was never hard to handle. But sometimes he was hard to find." This period marked the beginning of a love-hate relationship that lasted for thirty years.

The escapades of Bing and his pals harassed Paul so much that in late 1927 he dropped the Rhythm Boys from his tour schedule. Instead, he farmed them out on the vaudeville circuit for nearly a year.

Bing's autobiography recalls that the Rhythm Boys got a little tired of each other. "We couldn't decide which of us was boss. Every three or four weeks we decided to break up, then the next day we would get back together again."

Paul sent them away to shape up and "find themselves." For their Keith–Orpheum tour he loaned them stage props and a big cardboard figure of himself which held a recording piped through a loudspeaker, "This is Paul Whiteman. I take great pleasure in presenting to you my Rhythm Boys." He also astutely wired the Rhythm Boys to return to New York whenever he had a recording date coming up that would benefit from their services.

En route the trio missed trains and forgot luggage; on stage the boys missed cues and forgot lines. Close to being fired by an irate theater manager, they finally realized where they were headed— and it wasn't the Palace! By mid-1928 they had shaped up. *Billboard* called their twelve-minute act at Keith's 81st Street Theatre in New York "worthy of big-time booking and a distinctive asset to any bill."

Columbia made no bones about utilizing Paul's musicians in every available way. His contract contained a clause—apparently overlooked by Paul at its signing—that permitted his men to be available to other Columbia conductors, not only for orchestral works, but also to accompany solo artists. Paul apparently failed to insist on artistic control of his material. He quickly found himself grinding out stacks of purely commercial tripe of dubious worth, such as "Felix the Cat," "Sorry for Me," and "Japanese Mammy." Victor, he complained, would have assigned this dribble to bandleaders of lesser stature.

The most challenging and noteworthy recording session of Paul's first year with Columbia reunited Whiteman with Gershwin's serious music—his 1925 follow-up to *Rhapsody in Blue*. Just before the 1928 fall tour Paul and his men gathered to record *Concerto in F*. Grofé reorchestrated the work to fit on three twelve-inch discs.

Roy Bargy learned the piano parts and Bix the trumpet segments. Both were thrilled at the prospect of recording Gershwin's sophisticated composition. Although there seem to have been some last-minute notations on the scores about which trumpeters would carry the solos, most musicologists, as well as Bargy himself, believe that Bix recorded the long, taxing part.

The other lingering mystery of the *Concerto in F* recording session focuses right on the podium. Paul had met a staggering workload during July, August, and September. With Columbia demanding more and more recordings, his schedule left little time for rehearsing the challenging Gershwin opus. As the studio date approached, Paul got a severe case of the jitters. He turned to a Gershwin associate, the conductor William Daly. A close friend, Daly lent his support and gave encouragement, and may have actually stood in during one or more of the five sessions it took to wax the composition. On the first two dates Paul failed to produce anything acceptable for release. Things went better on the next two sessions. Several weeks elapsed before the final session completed the work. Daly, of course, received no credit on the labels, which read "Paul Whiteman and His Orchestra"—a shading of the truth hardly unique in the industry.

Paul's unfamiliarity with the Gershwin composition could only be temporary. He had to master it by October 7. That night at Carnegie Hall he was going to use the piece as the highlight of his next concert in modern American music. This would be the third in his series of experimental concerts, and it brought together thirty-eight players, including a special battery of twelve violins. Twenty-six of the musicians represented Paul's current orchestra. They were:

VIOLIN: Kurt Dieterle, Charles Gaylord, Matty Malneck, Mischa Russell (a recent addition from the Ziegfeld Follies orchestra).

TROMBONE: Boyce Cullen, Wilber Hall, Bill Rank, Jack Fulton.

TRUMPET: Charlie Margulis, Bix Beiderbecke, Eddie Pinder, Harry Goldfield.

SAXOPHONE: Chester Hazlett, Frank Trumbauer, Charles Strickfaden, Red Maier, Rube Crozier, Izzy Friedman (who replaced Jimmy Dorsey in early 1928, when he joined brother Tommy as a freelance musician).

BANJO: Mike Pingitore.
GUITAR: Austin Young.
BASS: Mike Trafficante, Min Leibrook (Steve Brown had
          left in February 1928).
DRUMS: George Marsh
PIANO: Roy Bargy, Lennie Hayton.

The Carnegie Hall performance launched the band's customary
fall tour, comprising eighty concerts or dances in twenty-two states
and Canada. Paul's return to the Fifty-Seventh Street hall was sold
out a week in advance. On October 7 an eager audience of 7,000
gathered to hear Paul's latest concert program, with its anticipated
innovative works, colorful novelty numbers, and uniquely contrasting medleys. Overall the broad-based "experimental" program
did not hit the mark.

Gershwin's piano concerto, in fact, was brilliant only in spots.
In spite of special arrangements, it still was not up to the expectations of the crowd. The audience demanded his *Rhapsody* as an
encore, giving it a five-minute ovation. The public's allegiance remained with the earlier and still popular success. *Concerto in F*
simply did not approach the verve and spark of *Rhapsody*.

The first public performance of Ferde Grofé's *Metropolis* fared
badly as well. He had tried to interpret the musical cacophony of
a busy city. Olin Downes of *The New York Times* called it "high-
hat jazz." He further described it as "out of its own element, en-
deavoring to emulate the ways of its betters, to talk portentously
of deep and grave things . . . and loses all its naturalness and flavor
in the process."

Downes thought of the concert as chiefly an exhibition of the
remarkable virtuosity and precision of Whiteman's players. Willie
Hall, armed with trombone and bicycle pump, played a Grofé oddity
entitled "Free Air," or "Variation Based on Noises from a Garage." Chet Hazlett presented his own "Valse Inspiration." The
"sweet trio" vocalized on "Melody Out of the Sky." Mike signed
in with his banjo perennial, "Linger Awhile." An unusual twist
was the premiere of a keyboard work by Bix, whose singular talent
now began to focus on the piano. Bix joined Bargy and Hayton in
a three-piano rendition of Bix's own "In a Mist"; *Variety* called it
"so-so," and the *Times* ignored it, along with virtually all of Paul's
pretentious and greatly overdone musical vaudeville.

12

Old Gold and New

With Paul back in Carnegie Hall, Columbia Records rushed a mix of material onto records, including an arrangement of "Tchaikovskiana," traditional Christmas music, Gay Nineties medleys, and, of course, Gershwin's *Concerto in F*. Every type of record buyer could choose from the growing list of Whiteman-Columbia discs. The company gave its new maestro a real send-off. Full-page advertisements and large billboards appeared from coast to coast. Fox Movietone News shot footage of Paul and the band as it switched allegiance to Columbia from Victor and recorded "My Melancholy Baby" with Skin Young on vocal.

Columbia spent over $200,000 in 1928 to introduce Whiteman as the label's foremost dance-music artist. The countrywide launch was highlighted by a special one-hour radio broadcast of Whiteman's orchestra over thirty-eight stations of the NBC network. The Columbia promotion attracted much interest among radio listeners. For Paul it opened up a new performing area, one which he had only occasionally entered.

By 1928 radio was a fast-growing commercial enterprise. In November 1926 NBC had formed the first major chain of stations, linking most of the country with the leading entertainment centers. The flagship transmitters, WEAF and WJZ in New York, carried top talent to home audiences night after night. The days of irregular, static-filled broadcasting entertainment faded with the arrival of electrically powered receivers and well-built loudspeakers from the factories of Atwater Kent, Philco, Zenith, and Stromberg-Carlson.

Many dance bands of the 1920s now began to build a following through radio. Late-night pick-ups from hotel grillrooms, restaurants, and nightclubs gained enthusiastic fans for Vincent Lopez, Ted Weems, Jan Garber, Duke Ellington, Ben Bernie, and dozens of other young maestros.

Whiteman's overnight acclaim burst forth when radio was still in its radiotelephony stage. Most receivers were home-made novelties for ham operators willing to stay up half the night and wear earphones, hoping to catch snatches of voices and music from widely scattered outposts. Six weeks after Paul opened at the Palais Royal in 1920, station KDKA in Pittsburgh first went on the air. It and WWJ in Detroit inaugurated the start of commercially based broadcasting. Not until the summer of 1922 would New York have its own high-powered station, via AT&T's station WEAF.

Whiteman went on the air as early as February 1922. He journeyed over to the Westinghouse company outlet WJZ in Newark to broadcast a special long-distance birthday program for his mother. A year or so later, Paul returned to Newark and rival station WOR to beam the latest jazz hits overseas to the Prince of Wales, who was listening in London. Such novel events—aired at odd hours of the night and morning—publicized radio's far-reaching potential. And Paul received letters from distant listeners; a radio buff far across the Pacific in Tokyo even picked up the band playing at a WOR mike in 1923.

Paul claimed to have been the first to play "The Star-Spangled Banner" on radio. His appearances on the air were, nevertheless, infrequent. When he did perform, however, he was amply rewarded. For a single night's appearance in 1926 NBC's *Eveready Hour* paid him $5,500.

On the other hand, Victor discouraged "free as the air" offerings to a public who should pay for music on records. Paul's travel agenda also ruled out a weekly stint from a studio. When he broadcast, the performance often originated from a theater stage, an auditorium, a concert hall, or, as in the case of his program to thank New York for its warm welcome home from Europe in August 1926, a park.

Paul's first full-scale exposure on radio came about in early 1928, during the crunch to record the last sixty sides for Victor before he moved to Columbia Records. On the day of the broadcast the band recorded "Ramona," "Smile," and "Lonely Melody," then hurried to regroup at the NBC studios on Fifth Avenue for a forty-seven-station coast-to-coast program. The Dodge Brothers had requested Whiteman's services to help introduce their new Victory Six automobile. Will Rogers and Al Jolson shared star billing on what was described as the most widespread hookup ever attempted on radio.

Thirty-five million Americans heard Will Rogers open the show from his home in Beverly Hills. He chatted in his familiar folksy manner, telling about his movie-star neighbors who are "making New Year's resolutions and taking new wives. It's a question which they're going to drop first." Then he announced a great surprise: the program would switch to Washington and the White House. The comedian paused a second and proceeded to imitate the nasal twang of President Calvin Coolidge. "It gives me great pleasure to appear before you through the courtesy of Dodge Brothers to report on the state of the nation as a whole. You know the nation is in a hole, but I think that the nation is perfectly all right."

Rogers, as Coolidge, discussed foreign debts, farm legislation, and tax revenues. After he finished this comic bit—the first on-the-air imitation of a chief executive—he introduced Paul Whiteman, "the man who brought opera up to jazz and jazz down to opera, the man who got the most of music, but then tore up his music and started to play." Paul performed *Rhapsody in Blue*.

The hour-long broadcast special picked up Dorothy and Fred Stone before a microphone backstage at the Erlanger Theatre in Chicago, then switched to Detroit, where Dodge president Edward G. Wilmer described the company's latest motorcars, before piping in Al Jolson from the Hotel Roosevelt in New Orleans. Al sang "Mammy," "California, Here I Come," "Golden Gate," and "Back in Your Own Back Yard." The program ended in New York, where Whiteman contributed vocal arrangements of "Among My Souvenirs" and "Changes."

Every state in the Union was linked to the broadcast by 20,000 miles of wire. The show cost about $67,000, or more than $1,000 a minute. Some $35,000 went to the telephone and mechanical facilities that tied together the forty-seven stations and five remote settings; $25,000 paid for the talent (Paul received $5,000). It was big money for such a new medium, and it caused a tremendous stir. The following day mobs crowded Dodge showrooms to view the new car, priced at $1,095 for a low-slung sedan model.

The New York Times reported the broadcast on its front page under the headline, "All America Used As a Radio Studio." The event readily demonstrated to big industries how to utilize the charisma of stars to draw attention to commercial products. The press representative for Dodge, Edward L. Bernays, predicted that "big business in the immediate future will be glad to pay handsomely for such attractions as may justify the expenditure through definite results." Many others saw it as a new era in radio entertainment and advertising.

The *Dodge Victory Hour* worked out so successfully that the automaker planned a second broadcast to introduce the Dodge Standard Six in March. Once again Paul headlined the broadcast, along with an unsurpassed array of top Hollywood stars: Charlie Chaplin, Douglas Fairbanks, Norma Talmadge, John Barrymore, and Dolores Del Rio. Press coverage of the second Dodge show was even more extensive than for the first one. The audience also increased. With the cooperation of United Artists Pictures, many theaters installed loudspeakers, so that additional thousands could hear the stars they had only seen on the silent screen.

Large corporations and their advertising agencies hurried to NBC and to its new rival, the Columbia Broadcasting System, to buy air time. Palmolive, General Motors, Firestone, Sylvania, Cities Service, Maxwell House, and radio manufacturers Philco, Atwater Kent, Kolster, and Sonora reserved space on the radio for weekly broadcasts. A cigarette maker soon joined them; the American Tobacco Company and its flamboyant president, George Washington Hill, correctly estimated the public taste for music in 1928. As a result, the popular orchestra at the Palais D'Or in New York and its leader, B. A. Rolfe, were engaged.

A onetime cornet soloist, vaudeville bandmaster, and showman, Rolfe had flirted with motion pictures as a producer. But in 1920 he went broke and picked up his horn again. He played in vaudeville, taught music, and in 1924 joined Vincent Lopez. Rolfe's idol was Paul Whiteman. "Here was a kind of music I did not know and which must be learned," he wrote in *Etude*. His first break came when the Palais D'Or restaurant on Broadway hired his orchestra and allowed a radio remote seven times a week. The rotund conductor—like Paul Whiteman, flirting with 300 pounds on the scale—was on his way to becoming a national celebrity.

The initial broadcast of the Lucky Strike Dance Orchestra on

Saturday, September 15, 1928, inaugurated a long-running series of happily conceived but straightforward and loud dance music. Whether the band was playing a foxtrot or a waltz, the rhythm predominated. For vocals Rolfe brought in soprano Gladys Rice and contralto Elizabeth Lennox in a search for popular singers who had had rigorous voice training. From the start of the series Rolfe announced each program himself in a cool, clear, and persuasive voice. He soon became an established radio personality, backed by a large and talented aggregation. The fifty-five-piece orchestra included ex-Whiteman players Ross Gorman, Milton Rettenberg, and Tommy Dorsey.

A month or two after Rolfe's bow at NBC, P. Lorillard, makers of Old Gold cigarettes, approached Paul with the idea of mounting a similar show. Paul and Lorillard's advertising agency offered the Old Gold idea to NBC. The network turned them down: "We already have a cigarette account."

This was network policy at the time, and unalterable. Old Gold was a new product. Lorillard, which introduced the brand in 1926, adopted a package that had red lettering on a golden yellow background, showing scattered "pieces of eight" and the words, "The Treasure of Them All." Aiming to compete with the top three brands—Camel, Chesterfield, and Lucky Strike—the tobacco company publicized Old Gold as the cigarette with "Not a Cough in a Carload." Meanwhile Lucky Strike moved toward first place in sales when it blitzed the country with print ads and billboards urging Americans to "Reach for a Lucky Instead of a Sweet."

Lorillard readily found air time on the comparatively new radio chain, the Columbia Broadcasting System. William S. Paley, who had just been elected president of the network, aggressively sought to match sponsors and program ideas. With Old Gold and Whiteman he picked a ready-made radio package for his small line-up of stations; he knew that the great Whiteman aggregation could entice additional stations into his network.

Old Gold signed Paul at $5,000 per broadcast to outplay Rolfe's Lucky Strike orchestra. The cigarette maker seriously considered broadcasting Whiteman directly opposite Rolfe on Saturday nights. Clearer heads prevailed and placed Paul on Tuesdays from nine to ten in the evening. The company also urged its agency to turn Paul into an easily recognizable radio voice and personality. If Rolfe could talk well, why not Whiteman? But when Paul heard of this idea, he wanted no part of it. "Nope. I'll give up the contract. I just can't talk on the air at a mike. I won't do it."

The *Old Gold–Paul Whiteman Hour* bowed on February 5, 1929, from New York. CBS announcer-sportscaster Ted Husing introduced the orchestra, which played thirteen numbers, including several already available on Columbia Records. By the second or third broadcast Paul had built up enough courage to say a few words over the air. He never became totally at ease before a microphone, however, and he fluffed many lines during the long radio career that lay ahead.

Old Gold also wanted the Rhythm Boys on every program, especially Bing Crosby. Masculine voices—baritones—were rapidly becoming the vogue on popular tunes. Tenors or falsettos, the sponsor believed, had had their day. Paul sent an SOS to the trio to return to the fold. The boys agreed—at double their present weekly salary of $450.

Bing immediately pleased Old Gold. Week after week he sang arrangements of such current songs as "I'll Get By," "Louise," "I Kiss Your Hand, Madame," and "Sweet Georgia Brown." The program now had a rival to rapidly rising crooners Rudy Vallee and Will Osborne, and its producers felt confident that they were reaching the newest market for cigarettes: the flappers and collegians of 1929.

Thus the Whiteman sound became available to millions of people "live" and "free" at the turn of a switch. Some people in various parts of the country had long been able to enjoy Paul's brand of music in theaters, nightclubs, and concert halls. Now everyone all over could share in his music performances.

Old Gold and CBS brought Paul to radio with the understanding that his orchestra could take to the road; the network agreed to pick up the program from travel locations. CBS was also aware that Paul and his men had plans to head for the West Coast to conquer still another entertainment medium—talking pictures. Old Gold welcomed the travel; it gave the company an ideal opportunity to merchandise the new cigarettes in each of the towns and cities where Paul made theater appearances. Paley liked the road-show concept. There were scores of independent stations throughout the country that had no network hookup; Paul's regional broadcasts could stir up interest in an affiliation with CBS.

Paul had several commitments in New York in late 1928 and early

1929. The band had repeated the Carnegie Hall concert in late December as a benefit for the Northwoods Tuberculosis Sanatorium at Saranac Lake. It also filled in for George Olsen's orchestra in the new Eddie Cantor show, *Whoopee*. The Ziegfeld production opened with a medley of its outstanding score by Gus Kahn and Walter Donaldson ("Makin Whoopee," "I'm Bringing a Red, Red Rose," "Love Me or Leave Me," "My Baby Just Cares for Me"). When Ziegfeld and Olsen disagreed during the early days of the run, Flo called on Paul to take over for a brief spell.

The year-end bookings included a week at the Palace and an opening with the *Ziegfeld Midnight Frolics* on the New Amsterdam Roof. For many nights the men found themselves shuttling between the theater's ground floor and its top story. Engagements in Cincinnati, Cleveland, and Detroit filled several weeks in January.

The new year brought some changes in personnel. In Cleveland, Bix suffered a devastating mental and physical breakdown, triggered by his growing dependence on alcohol. A month earlier he had been hospitalized in New York with pneumonia, but he rejoined the band for its opening at the Palace on December 30. The combination of physical weakness from the pneumonia, fatigue, and alcohol withdrawal led to a massive attack of delirium tremers. Paul helped to arrange for his recovery at the Beiderbecke home in Iowa in late January. However, Bix escaped from his male nurse and was found on a New York street, beaten up and badly cut. Paul immediately sent him home on full salary. To take Bix's place he brought in a cornet player from a Goldkette unit in Kansas City—Andy Secrest; well into the 1930s he emulated Bix's hot style.

A few days later, vocalist-guitarist Skin Young left the band, and as a replacement, eighteen-year-old Ray Heatherton signed on as vocalist, chiefly for the Old Gold series. Ray's brief association with Whiteman launched a long professional career that led to Broadway's *Babes in Arms*, his own dance orchestra, and an early television role as the Merry Mailman. In the 1960s daughter Joey became a popular television and film singer and dancer.

Bix returned to the trumpet section in March, replacing Eddie Pinder, in time to rehearse for the following day's Old Gold broadcast. In May two of Bix's buddies from the Goldkette days joined Whiteman-violinist Joe Venuti and guitarist Eddie Lang. The Venuti–Lang partnership was a prolific one on records, and the two musicians worked with Bix and Trumbauer, as well as with Goldkette, Red Nichols, and Roger Wolfe Kahn. Venuti, a gifted jazz violinist, was a pioneer in the field of translating jazz to a string instrument. In league with Lang, who was a profound musician and stylist with an elegant rhythmic texture, Joe dazzled audiences. The two complemented each other and enhanced the Whiteman orchestra. Lang, with Venuti at his elbow, charmed fellow musicians and legions of fans during an all-too-brief coupling that ended with Eddie's untimely death in 1933 at the age of twenty-nine.

On May 24, Paul bid good-bye to Vanda and five-year-old Paul, Jr. They seemed less and less a part of his life as he prepared to meet the band for yet another road tour. The men gathered at New York's Pennsylvania Station for one of the most unusual and memorable trips in the entire saga of the Whiteman aggregation. Over fifty people, including Paul's valet Bill Black, boarded a private train. Their final destination: Hollywood.

Film producers of the 1920s recognized the box-office draw of Paul's name on a marquee, but until moving pictures began to talk, it made little sense to feature Whiteman and his band in a screen feature. Even in silent days Paul and his men had appeared in many news clips. During the 1923 European tour he was featured in a Fox British short. Again, in 1926, he and Vanda were shot at the Kit Kat Club for a sequence in the feature *London*. When Fox Movietone and other studios added sound tracks to their newsreels, the band played for several, particularly when it switched recording companies in 1928. Now Universal Pictures wanted Paul and the band to star in a full-length musical. The studio agreed to pay a total of $440,000 for their part in the forthcoming *The King of Jazz*. It was an experience that Paul often wished he had avoided.

The Old Gold Special ballyhooed Paul's radio sponsor as it moved westward. A train of eight coaches—including three baggage cars (one contained Paul's Duesenberg), a dining car, and a club car—it had been repainted a bright gold and lettered with the names of its occupants at a cost of nearly $20,000. At the tail end of the train an observation car with an open platform provided space for Paul to greet fans and dignitaries. A specially built folding extension allowed the band to stand out there and play. Each day as the train wound its way to California, it stopped for an hour or two to give a short program on a station platform. Many local radio stations thrust a microphone in front of the band and picked up the entertainment. The mobile plug for Old Gold gained enormous goodwill for all parties during the twelve-day trip.

On the second day of the journey—May 25—the band performed at a special broadcast at the Syria Mosque in Pittsburgh. Cosponsored by Old Gold and the Pickerings Furniture Company, the Saturday program featured selections from *Showboat* by Bing and the Rhythm Boys and *Rhapsody in Blue* with Bargy. The following day Paul broadcast from station WHK in Cleveland in the morning, played at Toledo Armory in the afternoon, and performed in Detroit in the evening. In spite of a heavy rain on Monday, an enormous crown greeted the train in Fort Wayne and listened to the men play, huddled beneath the station arcade.

The regular Old Gold Tuesday night broadcast announced by Ted Husing went over the air from the WBBM studios in Chicago on May 28 without a hitch. It marked the first stage in an innovative attempt to move a radio series from one side of the continent to the other without any interruption in its broadcasting schedule.

Later that same week the band arrived in Indianapolis for the annual Memorial Day Indy 500 race. The musicians boarded buses to take them to the track, where they played from the platform of a huge truck that slowly circled the racing area. At the conclusion of the concert the vehicle wheeled onto the track's center area, where the men watched Ray Keech win the 1929 event. Paul and the band spent nearly five hours unsheltered in the ninety-seven-degree heat. At least no concert or broadcast was scheduled for that night.

Omaha rolled out the red carpet for the Whiteman special. The entire troupe was taken on a tour of the city, then to lunch at the Hotel Chieftain, by municipal leaders and executives of Mona Motor Oil Company. More than 4,500 people attended the afternoon concert at City Auditorium—500 over capacity—while thousands listened at home over KOIL. Immediately following the performance, the band departed for Lincoln. At seven o'clock that night an audience of 1,500 waited at the station, where bleachers and a platform had been built. An hour later, after the crowds had cheered the final number, the train headed for the Rocky Mountains and Paul's hometown, Denver.

On Monday, June 3, a group of old friends, Paul's parents, and his onetime boss, the orchestra leader Raffaelo Cavallo, welcomed the troupe in the crisp early-morning sunshine. Wearing a knit yellow jersey and a tweed suit, Paul jumped from the Pullman and hurried toward his mother and father. Newspaper reporters and photographers clustered about the group. Harry Barris and Matty Malneck—both former Denverites who had studied music under Wilberforce—posed for pictures.

"I want the boys to see what my home state has to offer in the way of scenery," Paul told the gathering. "We're going to go up into the mountains, then have lunch at Idaho Springs, a short distance from the spot where gold was first discovered in Colorado. Mother is cooking a big spread for the entire outfit tonight at the ranch, and you all know what that means—baked ham, fried chicken, biscuits, pie, and all the fixings. Tomorrow we go back to the mines. We're giving a free show at the Auditorium and then a broadcast for Old Gold over CBS station KLZ."

Helen Black of *The Rocky Mountain News* cornered Paul for a hometown interview that day. In answer to her question, he explained how he had managed to stay on top for nearly a decade.

I am not a fad, and what I have to offer is not a fragile vogue of the moment. We are always one jump ahead of every fashion; we are the first to present new things. We progress and, in short, I am just a good band manager although some folks call me lucky.

To keep at the top means you must always be thinking of something new. There must always be an interesting trick up your sleeve. I have always had a good band and I believe my success has been due to that fact. I don't kid myself or get the swell head. I know that some of the boys in the band are better musicians than I am. It's the fellows with the inflated domes that take the falls, and I steer clear of anything like that.

He was asked about the motion picture he was to make in Hollywood that summer. "The picture is built about the story of my life. Not authentic dates and such details, but a pretty general outline of my career. I'll be interested to find out how it ends."

The cross-country trip had only one more stop—Salt Lake City. The undertaking had been arduous and rugged for everyone, but especially for Bix. His health remained a matter of serious concern. The regimented stops and starts, the strict arrangements for the radio, and the almost unbearable workload were stifling the young trumpet player. His jug of booze was carried along as carefully as his brass instrument.

At least on this trip, thought Paul, Bix never missed the train. The year before, Bix had disappeared in Oklahoma City when some of the men went for coffee and drinks. He returned alone to the station and boarded the wrong train.

The conductor asked for a ticket. "I'm with the boys," he replied.

"What boys?" asked the trainman.

"The Whiteman band boys."

"You're going in the opposite direction! Get off at the next stop."

Bix scrambled off the train as soon as he could and hired a crop-duster to fly him to the troupe's next stop. Arriving at the auditorium before the rest of the band, he went backstage and curled up in a roll of scenery. He ended up sleeping through the first half of the show, only yards from the full brass section.

The Old Gold Special arrived in Los Angeles on June 15 after several bookings in San Francisco, where Paul had also done the weekly radio broadcast over KYA. The film capital welcomed the band with a parade to the Pantages Theatre. Whiteman played a week's engagement there before reporting for work at Universal Studios on June 28.

Although the film industry had accepted the arrival of talking pictures in 1928, it was not until 1929 that the total impact of sound was felt. MGM's all-talkie *The Broadway Melody* opened in February at Grauman's Chinese Theatre in Hollywood. The 1929 Oscar winner for best picture, it set the pattern for the rest of the year. Every studio turned out one musical after another—all-talking, all-singing, all-dancing.

Fox produced a comic musical, *Hearts in Dixie,* and a dazzling *Movietone Follies.* Warner Brothers, which had first brought sound successfully to the screen with *The Jazz Singer* in 1927, moved ahead with the operetta *The Desert Song* and a tuneful *On with the Show.* MGM prepared its all-star *Hollywood Revue of 1929* and a Negro epic, *Hallelujah.* RKO Radio cast Ziegfeld's production of *Rio Rita* and Vincent Youmans's *Hit the Deck.* Universal was more cautious, not releasing its first major talking and singing production—*Showboat*—until June. The studio now hoped to get into the movie musical sweepstakes with a colorful, tune-filled musical with Paul Whiteman's name above the title.

Carl Laemmle, president of Universal, greeted Paul as he came on the lot. Anxious to complete the film by the end of the summer, the studio guaranteed $200 per week for each of the band's members for a period of eight weeks. The group now stood at thirty-five men—its maximum size. Paul, who picked up $50,000 on signing the contract, received another $50,000 on his first day at Universal. Additional payments of $50,000 were made at the completion of the film and upon national release. Paul was also guaranteed 40 percent of the picture's net profits above his fee of $200,000.

Once inside the studio gates, Paul discovered that no screenplay had yet been completed. The writers seemed unable to develop the film biography. The events of Paul's life appeared almost contrived. Furthermore, he had ruled out a romantic role for himself. His music would have to carry the plot, if any. Paul and his men waited for a script and a shooting schedule.

To house the band and make it feel at home, Universal built a big lodge on the back lot. It was complete with rehearsal rooms, lockers, showers, and a recreation area with pool and billiard tables. During the first week or so the men gathered there to await word on the picture. Soon they merely picked up their checks and went off to relax, sightsee, or drink. For most, this was a paid vacation.

The only day they worked was on Tuesday, for the Old Gold show. When Ted Husing was reassigned to broadcast the Poughkeepsie Regatta back East, no temporary replacement to work with Whiteman could be found. Paul had auditioned a young baritone, Harry Von Zell. Certainly he was no threat to Bing, who began looking for work outside the Whiteman organization as soon as he arrived in Los Angeles. Husing suggested that Von Zell serve as the West Coast Old Gold fill-in announcer and actually coached him. Von Zell had had some experience talking into a mike, but this was his first break. After the stand-in broadcasts, Paul urged him to go to New York, where he was taken on as a staff announcer by CBS. He quickly became associated with the major stars of radio—Eddie Cantor, Will Rogers, Jack Benny, Ed Wynn, and Burns and Allen.

As the summer passed, Bing Crosby, Kurt Dieterle, and Mischa Russell rented a house on Fairfax Avenue, with a houseman to cook and clean. They joined the Lakeside Country Club at a special golfing fee of $500. Rinker, Bargy, and Hazlett also became members of the club near the Universal lot. The six played golf mornings and afternoons. Hazlett even won the Hollywood Open tournament with a score of 72–76.

Trum, Hall, and Rank took flying lessons to pass the time. Transportation to airports and golf courses—and to occasional rehearsals and broadcasts—was solved by a local Ford dealer. He gave each musician a special deal on the new Model A. As an advertising gimmick he added the eye-catching Paul Whiteman logo to the rear spare-tire covers.

By midsummer the studio heads had agreed on nothing more than the film's title, *The King of Jazz*. Production remained in limbo. The men no longer even stopped by the studio to pick up their weekly checks; they hired a young guy to do it. Paul tried to keep the gang busy and productive. He offered to play for an Actor's Equity benefit, but Universal informed him that he would be in breach of contract if he performed without pay.

The leisure and the Ford cars began to cause headaches for Paul and Jimmy Gillespie. One day Mischa Russell was picked up for reckless driving and sentenced to fifteen days in jail. Paul managed to get him temporarily released in time for the weekly radio broadcast. He came accompanied by a vigilant police officer who stood by as Mischa rehearsed and did the show. His friends spent a good deal of their time visiting his jail cell and bringing him such goodies as broiled trout for breakfast.

Then on July 31, tragedy struck. Members of the band were headed for an engagement in Santa Barbara. Paul suggested hiring a bus, but some of the men wanted to bring their wives and decided to drive their own cars. Joe Venuti and Mario Perry shared an auto, Mischa Russell and Charlie Margulis drove together, and Eddie Lang and his wife Kitty followed in their vehicle. The fleet of cars stopped for gas near Carpinteria. Venuti pulled out of the station first and sped on ahead. The Langs followed close behind. For some reason Venuti suddenly decided to pass the automobile in front of his as they were negotiating a turn in the two-lane coastal highway. An oncoming car loomed in the opposite lane, and Venuti swerved to avoid hitting it. He skidded on the gravel at the edge of the road, and his car turned over several times.

Eddie and Kitty Lang quickly pulled off to the side and ran to help. Mario Perry had been thrown out of the car, and Joe Venuti was caught inside, unconscious. Lang and several others from the band dragged him out of the vehicle. Someone summoned an ambulance to take both victims to the hospital. The Langs followed in their car.

Kitty Lang recalled the incident in a letter to the author.

I went over to Mario and tried to comfort him as he was screaming, "My God! My stomach." The blood was pouring out of his nose. I wiped it as much as I could, and then two doctors rushed him to the operating room. Poor Mario died shortly after.

Joe had several bad cuts on his face, but his wrist looked the worst. Two bones were sticking right out of the flesh. I thought to myself: He'll never play again. After four weeks Joe, against his doctor's orders, took the cast off of his bowing arm and started to try to play his violin. Amazingly, he did very well, and I swear, as time went by, he played better than ever, although his wrist remained misshapen.

In the somber aftermath Paul and several of the men gathered at the house of Al Rinker's sister, Mildred Bailey. Plenty of food, liquor, and music eased the pain of losing the band's well-liked violin player and accordionist. As the evening wore on, Paul settled in Mildred's kitchen, where mountains of delicacies were in easy reach. Bing and Al asked Mildred to sing. Her well-phrased blues laments and effortless jazz solos brought Paul out of the kitchen and into the living room.

"You've got to join the boys, Mildred. You can handle anything."

The next day, Paul signed up Mildred Bailey. She was probably the first female solo vocalist with a major orchestra in the country. Paul introduced her nationwide the following evening. Mildred's radio debut with Whiteman was a Bargy arrangement of "Moanin' Low" and featured Bix and Trum. Before the end of the program Paul announced that a fan had telephoned the station to say that Mildred's song was the best number he had ever heard the group perform.

Radio audiences heard Whiteman again the next night, when he participated in the Hollywood Midsummer Jubilee aired over KFWB from the Hollywood Bowl. The two-hour gala included Jack

Benny, Clara Bow, Belle Baker, Moran and Mack, Benny Rubin, Fannie Brice, and George Jessel, most of whom were busily making their first talking picture.

With so much leisure time, Paul accepted Hollywood party invitations for every night. He knew dozens of screen stars; some had been starting out in the business when Paul had organized his early band in Los Angeles nearly ten years before. Tom Mix, Gloria Swanson, Chaplin, and Douglas Fairbanks remained big box-office names as the decade drew to a close. Scores of new faces, especially if they had good microphone voices, were appearing on the screen every week.

And he had plenty of time, too, to renew and pursue an old acquaintance. Paul Whiteman had first become aware of Margaret Livingston, a young actress making the transition from silent pictures to talkies most successfully, long before he knew her name.

As sound pictures began to become established, Whiteman's advice was asked from time to time on the selection of music for motion pictures. He acted as a consultant to Leo Feist, the music publisher, and in this capacity he gave his opinion on what tunes had possibilities and what melodies might work in a particular film.

In 1928 Paul was shown a recently completed Fox film—*Sunrise,* directed by F. W. Murnau and starring Janet Gaynor and George O'Brien. Filmed as a silent, by the time it was released Fox had added a musical soundtrack. Paul watched the movie over and over, each time more fascinated by an actress who played a scheming vamp; in one memorable scene she could be glimpsed through a thicket of bulrushes, bathing in the altogether.

It was not until early 1929 that Paul learned the seductress's name and met her in the flesh. Margaret was among the guests at a press party for Maurice Chevalier, in New York to plug his first American talking picture, *Innocents of Paris*. Ziegfeld was throwing the party to publicize the fact that he had hired the French singer-actor for a brief run in the *Midnight Frolics,* and he asked Paul to provide the music for the gathering.

Paul gave one look at the well-remembered face and blurted out, "Why—why, you're old bulrushes!" Paul spent a good part of the afternoon with Margaret Livingston and they went out to dinner together with friends.

They seemed to enjoy each other's company in equal measure, but when Paul telephoned her hotel the next afternoon, he was told that she had checked out, leaving no message. They met again when Paul came to Hollywood; when producer Carl Laemmle, Jr., gave him a tour of the Universal Studio, she was working on the set of *Tonight at Twelve*. Some nights later Paul gave a gala party at the studio, and there she was again, dancing by the bandstand in the arms of her escort.

During the evening Paul joined the popular actress at her table and rarely left her side until the party ended. The following day they shared a meal at the studio commissary. In the days and weeks that followed, they were seldom apart.

As an actress not under contract to any one studio, thirty-three-year-old Margaret had set some sort of record; no other performer had come close to the number of roles she had taken on in a single year. By her count, they totaled nineteen in 1929. She was proud of her professional skills, and equally proud of her acumen in earning and investing money. By the time Paul came to Hollywood, her holdings included part ownership of an elegant, brand-new, seven-story apartment building, where Hollywood luminaries were rushing to rent.

Margaret had learned the value of money early in life. Though she had been brought up to believe that she would inherit a mining and real estate fortune, she was in fact nearly penniless when she left Salt Lake City for Hollywood during the First World War. After struggling as an inexperienced extra and bit player, she was lucky enough to land a series of small parts in serials and feature pictures. Soon she was under contract to Thomas Ince, at a salary that grew to $300 a week. In 1924 she accompanied Ince on a cruise aboard William Randolph Hearst's yacht, along with such other notables as the novelist Elinor Glyn, the columnist Louella Parsons, Charlie Chaplin, and Marion Davies, Hearst's companion. The cruise came to an abrupt end when Ince had to be rushed off the ship and back to his home, where he died under mysterious circumstances.

The official explanation blamed a sudden attack of acute indigestion, but rumors insisted that he had been shot by Hearst, an extremely jealous man, who may have been aiming at Chaplin, whom he suspected of seducing Marion Davies. Whatever the truth of the story, Hearst was eager to ensure everyone's cooperation. Mrs. Ince received a lifetime trust fund, Louella Parsons landed an iron-clad contract with the Hearst chain of newspapers, and Margaret Livingston's career took a dramatic upswing. In 1925 she signed a contract with Fox at $1,000 a week, and thereafter she was never out of the money again. Her screen specialty—vamp and "other woman" roles—kept her very much in demand playing opposite Edmund Lowe, Adolphe Menjou, Warner Baxter, Ralph Graves, and other leading men.

Now, as Paul and his men waited in vain for the studio to produce a viable script, Paul pressed his courtship of the beautiful, shrewd actress. Of course he sent her American Beauty roses almost daily; but such a gesture was not enough for lavish Paul. Impulsively he went out and bought a sporty little LaSalle convertible, which he had delivered to her front door without any explanation.

It took three days before Margaret realized that the car was meant for her and came from Whiteman. When she finally understood, she had some qualms. "Don't you think," she asked, "it's a little early to get so serious?"

But Paul had a ready answer. "It may be early for you. But for me it's getting kinda late, and I'm going to do something about that, too."

There was not very much he could do then and there. As Universal continued having trouble coming up with a script that would fit Whiteman's talents, he became increasingly concerned about the band's relative inactivity and the possible effect on its popularity. He and the studio agreed to an eight-week moratorium, during which time the band could do concert bookings and the studio would finish a script. Paul promised Universal and Margaret that he would be back in October.

Exactly two months after reporting to the studio the band left for the East. The train made few stops en route. The outfit had lost Mario Perry and gained Mildred Bailey. It also had acquired a "stowaway," who was eager to make a success as a pianist and songwriter in New York. With stardust on his mind, Hoagy Carmichael hitched a ride on the train. The onetime Jean Goldkette sideman shared an upper berth with Bing Crosby.

No one was more relieved to depart California than Jimmy Gillespie. "Just in time to save my sanity, if any," he later exclaimed in his story "Hot Music" for *The Saturday Evening Post*. "Thirty-six young men with full pockets and idle hands to chaperone! I could sympathize with Lightnin' Bill Jones who drove a herd of bees across the desert to California."

The band regrouped only hours after the train pulled into Manhattan to rehearse for opening at the Pavilion Royale in Valley Stream, Long Island. The nightclub had originally been built to accommodate the Whiteman band during the summer following the first trip to Europe in 1923. Back then Paul and Vanda were still acting like honeymooners. Now, six years later, the first hint of domestic trouble surfaced as the couple quarreled publicly. Vanda became incensed when Paul stopped at various tables to visit with friends. She walked out, asking another man to escort her home. Vanda and Paul would soon be very far apart indeed.

In October the band packed up once more for Hollywood. Before leaving, the gang bid Bix farewell. He had become ill during a recording session of "Waiting at the End of the Road" and "When You're Counting the Stars Alone." Paul urged that Bix take another extended rest at home on full salary. On September 15 Whiteman and Kurt Dieterle put Bix on a train for Davenport. He was to miss out on the second trip to California and a chance for a measure of celluloid immortality in *The King of Jazz*. Frank Siegrist took his place.

Universal Pictures had decided to turn the planned Whiteman film into a supercolossal revue. The studio wanted Ziegfeld to mount a big screen extravaganza, but Flo was unavailable. Paul suggested that stage director John Murray Anderson, with whom he had worked on the Publix circuit, be used instead. Universal hired Anderson for the formidable fee of $50,000—and he would earn every penny of it during the following seven months.

Herman Rosse, his set designer, followed him to the West Coast. Soon Murray brought the Roxy Theatre dance director, Russell Markert, and a group of sixteen chorus girls from various Broadway shows. The unit producer, Carl Laemmle, Jr., asked Anderson to consult with Paul Feyos, the inventor of the first "boom" camera, so that his equipment could be used. Jerry Ash, a trick cameraman, joined the planning stages of the film. He suggested that Paul make his entrance carrying a small suitcase, out of which his entire orchestra would emerge, one by one. The tiny figures took their places on a seemingly miniature bandstand, which grew to huge proportions, the men assuming their normal size in full view of the audience.

Next it was decided to shoot the entire production in Technicolor—making it the second all-talking, all-color picture to emerge from Hollywood. Warner's *On with the Show* was the first. *The*

King of Jazz also included the first color cartoon. Whiteman's film became the first Technicolor feature to win an Academy Award—for best set decoration by Herman Rosse. The colors were rudimentary, at best, since at that time Technicolor was able to print only in red and green. The third color was developed several years later for *Becky Sharp,* the first full-length three-color picture.

John Murray Anderson devised ways to enhance the existing two colors. He used lamps with colored projection, chiefly side lighting through red and green gelatin spots. To create the illusion of blue for *Rhapsody in Blue,* he used a gray and silver background with a touch of green shading. "It took twelve weeks to photograph *The King of Jazz* and it was entrusted entirely to me," he stated in his autobiography *Out Without My Rubbers.* "A procedure unique in motion picture technique was followed. The script was written, not before, but after the shooting of each sequence."

Paul was chiefly responsible for an innovation that changed the method of recording music in talking pictures. In 1929 there were few professional recording engineers on the West Coast; consequently radio technicians filled the void whenever possible.

One day on the set, after listening to the endless discussion on how to record the band and the singers as the cameras rolled, Paul made a suggestion that startled the audio experts. "Let's prerecord it."

The sound engineers turned thumbs down. It had never been done before. They were certain that it just would not work.

"I've been making phonograph records before Rin Tin Tin could bark and worked out more problems than you guys could invent. It's no good hanging a clothesline full of microphones overhead and assuming you'll get the right balance between the band and the singers."

The studio engineers explained that direct recording on film had already produced soundtracks for a number of musicals. The public accepted them and made few, if any, comparisons with phonograph discs.

"Let's do their ears a favor. We'll build a studio right on the sound stage and prerecord the whole business and then play it back as the band 'fakes' it. It's bound to be an improvement." And so the method of making soundtracks independently of the actual filming of a scene or song was devised and used for the first time.

In contrast to their first trip to Hollywood, Paul and his men rarely had a day off. But most of them got their Fords out of storage and dusted off the easily recognized Whiteman caricature on the spare tire cover. Some of the gang—including Kurt Dieterle and Bing Crosby and Roy Bargy and his family—rented houses or apartments. On Saturday nights all of them let off steam.

Following hours and hours of rehearsal, a party got started at the studio recreation lodge. Some women joined the fun, and after a number of drinks, Bing offered to take a particularly attractive lady home in his Ford convertible. As they drove along Hollywood Boulevard, another motorist slammed into the rear of Bing's car. He and his date were thrown out of the convertible. Both were badly shaken up but not seriously hurt. The police quickly arrived and took Bing and the other driver to a nearby precinct. They were booked on charges of reckless driving and suspicion of drinking. Bing spent the night in jail before Paul bailed him out. Bing later appeared in court before a militantly anti-drinking judge, who sentenced him to sixty days in the Hollywood jail.

Bing had been rehearsing a big number, "Song of the Dawn." Paul tried to hold up production, but Universal would not agree. The studio instead brought in John Boles, who advanced his singing career several notches by filling in for the jailed Bing.

Whiteman was furious about the incident but soon arranged to have Bing released from his cell and on a sound stage during the day. Thus Crosby, with Rinker and Barris, made his film debut singing "Mississippi Mud," "Happy Feet," and "A Bench in the Park" with the Brox Sisters. Each evening Bing returned to the local jail in the custody of a policeman. He served forty days before his sentence was commuted.

While filming on *The King of Jazz* progressed, Paul and the band still did the weekly Old Gold show. Such Hollywood stars as Blanche Sweet, Harry Richman, Richard Arlen, Jack Oakie, Lillian Roth, Lew Cody, and June Clyde were guests on the show. Charles King, star of MGM's *Broadway Melody,* was scheduled to sing a solo; as he stood up at the mike, Joe Venuti opened his violin case and pulled out an old shotgun and drew a bead on King. The band started to laugh, wondering if Joe would be crazy enough to shoot. Paul exploded and lost control of the band in the uproar going out "live" from coast to coast. "Undoubtedly, Venuti helped age Whiteman," Bing once wrote of the jazz violinist.

Gray hairs were certainly added the day Joe borrowed Paul's

(Left) Paul and the boys help sell Florida real estate in the halcyon 1920s. Here they are seen at a pool in Coral Gables. *(Courtesy of Margaret L. Whiteman)*

(Middle) Violinist Fritz Kreisler and his wife visit the orchestra during a rehearsal in Berlin's Schauspielhaus. *(Courtesy of Leslie Lieber)*

(Bottom) Paul braves an air trip in a trimotor plane over Berlin during the 1926 tour. Teddy Bartell on trumpet leads a handful of Whiteman's men in an impromptu send-off. *(Whiteman Collection, Williams College)*

During a brief family vacation Vanda and Paul pose with two-year-old Paul, Jr. *(Whiteman Collection, Williams College)*

After his second European trip in 1926, Whiteman played for patients at an Adirondack sanatorium. Then, with comedian Benny Rubin (right), he meets with President Coolidge at the nearby summer White House. *(Courtesy of Benny Rubin)*

For the Old Gold radio series in 1929 Paul hired William Grant Still as a staff arranger. Whiteman was the first major orchestra leader to add a black musician to the staff. *(Courtesy of Judy Anne Still Headlee)*

To promote his vaudeville tour for the Paramount-Publix chain, one-time sailor Paul appears dressed as a gob, peeling potatoes. *(Courtesy of Margaret L. Whiteman)*

During his 1927 Los Angeles engagement Pops visits Hollywood cronies at the United Artists studio. Accompanied by manager Jimmy Gillespie (right) and tour director William Morris, Jr. (2nd from right), the King of Jazz poses with Charlie Chaplin, Douglas Fairbanks, Sr. and Jr., and comedian Charlie Murray. *(Whiteman Collection, Williams College)*

Paul and the gang, including Bing Crosby (holding trumpet in front of tuba), appear on Broadway in the 1927 production, *Lucky.* The cast of the short-lived musical included Mary Eaton, Walter Catlett, and Ruby Keeler. *(Whiteman Collection, Williams College)*

Vaudeville and movie audiences flocked to hear Whiteman's band in 1927. Rhythm Boys Harry Barris and Al Rinker play miniature pianos. The trio's Bing Crosby holds a guitar in the back row. *(Courtesy of Margaret L. Whiteman)*

The best song to emerge from *The King of Jazz* was "It Happened in Monterey" by Mabel Wayne and Billy Rose. *(Courtesy of Louise F. Clark)*

Not even the *Rhapsody in Blue* could save Universal's *T... King of Jazz* from a box-office slump. *(Whiteman Colle... tion, Williams College)*

Pops beams over shedding nearly a hund... pounds as part of his wooing of Margar... Livingston. *(Courtesy of Margaret L. W... man)*

violin for the "Caprice Viennois" number. The Technicolor lights were so hot that the varnish on the expensive instrument bubbled and peeled.

At the end of each day Paul looked forward to escaping the long and trying hours on the set by spending some time with Margaret Livingston. Now that Paul's marriage was headed for the rocks, Paul and Margaret appeared together publicly at dinner parties, dances, and movie previews. As the year drew to a close Paul proposed to Margaret, repeatedly and ever more urgently.

But Margaret felt uncomfortable about Paul's lavish ways with money and especially with his gargantuan appetite. When she suggested that he reduce, he stormed out in a rage. After a few days, during which she realized how much she missed him, Margaret made sure that the stage could be set for a reconciliation. By now Paul was also ready to admit that he had a weight problem and promised to diet. Margaret set a goal: if he would lose 100 pounds, she would become Mrs. Paul Whiteman.

The King of Jazz was completed in March 1930 at a record cost of nearly two million dollars. Paul wasted no time in arranging a short tour to get his band before live audiences once more. It started in San Diego and continued up the coast to Portland and Seattle. Margaret saw Paul off on the train for Seattle, the first step on his return trip to the East. The parting was sad, but both Paul and Margaret knew that it would not be for long.

The Rhythm Boys left Paul in Seattle. Bing had been anxious for some time to break away and be on his own. His solo records proved that he had ample talent as a single. With sound movies flourishing, he wanted to stay in Hollywood and advance his own career. He and Paul were never close friends, as Busse and Bix had been. Bing relished his independence and freedom, and he did his own thing—even if the outcome led to a courtroom. All in all, a parting seemed in the cards sooner or later anyway.

Paul had hoped that the trio would stay with his organization. But Bing wanted more money, and although the Rhythm Boys had about eighteen months left on their contract and could have been held to it without a pay increase, there seemed little advantage in keeping three disgruntled employees on the payroll. Bing's autobiographical version of the story claims that he was fired when a bootlegger trailed the band and made threats over Bing's failure to pay his debt. Al Rinker often stated that there was no truth to this curious tale. The trio left because they believed that the film capital held more promise for the future of their act.

Bing summarized his leave-taking of Paul. "When I was younger and more hot-headed, I used to think he should line my pockets with more gold. But I confess he owes me nothing. It's the other way around."

13

The End of the Gold Rush

On May 2, 1930, backstage at the Roxy Theatre, Paul waited for his entrance cue. The familiar notes of *Rhapsody in Blue* played by his orchestra and led by concertmaster Kurt Dieterle came from the pit and up into the far reaches of the large movie palace on Broadway. Heavier and more cherubic-looking than ever, Paul pushed aside the velvet drop and stepped into view of the several thousand people in the audience. A few moments earlier, in *The King of Jazz,* Paul had conducted and appeared on the screen during the course of a dozen musical skits. Now he prepared to lead the orchestra and George Gershwin at the piano in his popular composition.

Before going on, he carefully rubbed wax into his pencil-thin moustache, drawing out the ends to needlelike points. He conferred with his valet on the advisability of wearing a collar pin. The collar pin was decided upon, and several other sartorial adjustments were attended to.

Paul walked to center stage and raised his long baton before his own band and the Roxy Symphony orchestra, a grand total of nearly 130 musicians. He conducted several jazz pieces and a Spanish song, and then the opening bars of the *Rhapsody in Blue* were again sounded.

Backstage Gershwin placed the stump of a cigar on the floor and then danced around it in a tap routine while a girl looked on and laughed. The orchestra out front was accenting the piece with beats on the tympani. Gershwin stopped and began to massage his long

147

fingers. He listened and then walked out on stage to the grand piano amid waves of applause.

Gershwin and Whiteman and *Rhapsody in Blue*—together again. Whiteman and his orchestra—both on the screen and on the stage, five performances a day. A bigger-than-life *King of Jazz,* all-singing, all-dancing, all-music-making, and in Technicolor.

Universal Pictures and the maestro eagerly waited for enthusiastic newspaper reviews and throngs of ticket buyers. But neither materialized to the degree hoped for.

Nevertheless, *The New York Times's* Mordaunt Hall had a positive reaction. He called *The King of Jazz* a "marvel of camera wizardry, joyous color schemes, charming costumes, and seductive lighting effects." He praised its originality, predicting that the film would appeal to all types of audiences. Hall singled out one segment—a Walter Lantz cartoon—which showed Whiteman being crowned king of jazz in the African jungle. Hall also liked the film's conception of the *Rhapsody.* "There is no sequence that isn't worth witnessing and no performance that is not capable in this fast-paced picture."

Variety, which on the whole sided with the majority opinion, took issue with the film's overpeopled production numbers, poorly edited camera angles, barren comedy bits, and excessive running time. Only in its songs and through Whiteman himself did the picture hold up. "Paul Whiteman does admirably, whether talking, kidding, or leading. His voice is A-1 for the screen, while the recording is exceptional. As Whiteman is well known as an expert on sound, he reserving for himself the privilege of always being in the recording room when his band is making phonograph records, an unusual demand with the disc makers, the recording here may go to the Whiteman credit." The paper praised the film's two ballads— "Dawn" by Milton Ager and Jack Yellen and "It Happened in Monterey" by Mabel Wayne and Billy Rose—both sung by John Boles. It felt that the *Rhapsody* segment with Roy Bargy at the piano (looking strikingly like Gershwin) was a big disappointment. "The director has seen fit to scramble it up with 'production.' It's all busted to pieces, and while it's all there, it's not the Whiteman number it would have been had it been played simply straight as a musical composition by the jazzing orchestra that does it so well and as it should have been." *Variety*'s critic signed off with the remarks, "What this picture muffed is a pity."

Years later John Murray Anderson thought that the movie was

far in advance of its time and too highbrow. His aged uncle, who saw *The King of Jazz* in London in 1930, commented, "I like the color and the music. But the comedy, well damn it, I heard those same old jokes fifty years ago."

Even Paul Whiteman and Technicolor could not save the picture at the box office. By 1930, audiences had had their fill of musicals, especially the plotless, all-star revues. Every major studio had beaten Universal to the screen with such diverting novelties in 1929. Singing and dancing had quickly lost their appeal. People were turning to dramatic and suspenseful talkies. Indeed, the studio's chief competition stemmed from its own overwhelming success in that area. The grim battlefield story, *All Quiet on the Western Front,* attracted moviegoers day after day as the movie was held over in theaters. In addition, audiences of stage performances had elected a new favorite during Paul's long sojourn in California. Crooner Rudy Vallee was packing them in at the Brooklyn Paramount.

Whiteman and Gershwin anticipated a three-week engagement on stage at the Roxy at $12,500 and $3,000 per week, respectively. By the end of the first week box office receipts fell within a few thousand dollars of the previous record low for the house. The Roxy dropped Whiteman and the stage show and kept the film running for only another week. During its national release the picture cleared less than $900,000. Overseas it fared better and eventually made a profit. During the 1930s the film found its best audience in Cape Town, South Africa, of all places, where, oddly enough, it played seventeen return engagements.

The era of good times and endless nights out on the town had ended while the band was staying on the West Coast. The effects of the stockmarket crash of October 1929 became more visible every day, especially in New York. Business failures, unemployment, bread lines, and stockmarket declines signaled bad times ahead. The White House predicted a recovery just around the corner, but it had not materialized by mid-1930. As the highest-paid group of musicians in the country, the Whiteman band felt the downward spiral acutely. Paul had been king from the very beginning of the Jazz Age, and in 1929 alone he took in over $640,000. The youngsters who had danced to "Whispering" and "Avalon" had married and were now home with children, desperately trying to make ends meet. Moreover, a new wave of young people were looking elsewhere for new musical idols.

At the end of the run of *The King of Jazz* at the Roxy, Paul could not meet his large payroll; he had no choice but to cut personnel. He did so immediately, shaving ten musicians and arrangers from his organization of nearly thirty people. Many of the highest-paid members of his group were dropped to keep the band out of the red. They included some of the best and most talented men any band had ever embraced: Eddie Lang, Joe Venuti, Lennie Hayton, Boyce Cullen, Bill Challis, Charlie Margulis, and Min Leibrook. The remaining players had to take a 15 percent reduction in salary. And arranger Ferde Grofé went back again to the piano as the outfit regrouped for the lean days ahead.

The retrenchment greatly depressed Paul in the weeks following the disappointment at the Roxy. Everything seemed to be going against him. Everywhere he turned, there was an impasse. Had his incredible streak of good fortune run out? Could he keep his orchestra going? Was his music old hat? Had his reign ended? Day after day he worried that he would soon be back in the fiddle section of somebody else's orchestra.

Paul's personal finances had gotten a jolt. He had spent, loaned, and given away thousands of dollars a week in the belief that the flow of money would never end. Most of his purchases were king-size and custom-made, whether an automobile, a suit, or a shotgun. Now he faced cutbacks in every direction. When Mike Pingitore heard about his depleted resources, he came to Paul, and offered him all his savings and assets. Paul would take none of it. Perhaps he should have; when more and more banks and businesses failed at the depths of the Depression, Mike lost the large segment of his nest egg—a sizeable real estate investment in the Straus Building in New York.

Any hopes that Paul had of repeating his Hollywood windfall at Universal were dashed when the studio declined to pick up his option. And no other film maker showed any interest in bringing Paul back to the screen. Moreover, Universal was threatening to sue Whiteman for certain expenses he had incurred during the filming. Paul, the front office claimed, had ordered twenty-two blue tuxedos for his orchestra and charged them to the studio, along with numerous telegrams and food bills. Now cost-conscious Universal wanted to collect some $1,500 for what it had paid out on Paul's behalf.

Aggravation stemming from *The King of Jazz* increased when an Albany orchestra leader named Frank Graves brought an action to restrain Paul from using the jazz title. The Albany maestro, who called himself King Jazz, obviously hoped to focus attention on his band by using the courts. Several years later Graves was continuing to link his title to Whiteman. Paul finally countersued and won a $10,056 judgment against Graves.

Record royalties, too, had slumped. Tunes from *The King of Jazz,* recorded in Los Angeles at the conclusion of filming, found little success. As record sales dropped significantly throughout the country, Columbia offered little hope that Paul's contract with the phonograph company would be extended beyond 1930. Indeed, after Paul's return to New York, Columbia arranged only three sessions, the last on September 10.

Paul's road bookings also diminished. His short tour in the Northwest in April 1930 just prior to the Roxy opening had ended in a roadblock. For the first time in his ten years of travel a foreign country barred his band's appearance. Without one word of advance notification Canadian immigration authorities ruled out Paul's engagement in Vancouver. Paul was amazed at the unexpected action, which was endorsed by the local musicians' union. He offered to pay thirty-five local musicians—the equivalent of his outfit—if he could fulfill the dance booking. Immigration officials allowed his concert in Vancouver, but not the dance date. Other countries instituted similar restrictions. Even far-off Romania barred foreign musicians in an effort to ease the unemployment situation as far as musicians were concerned because of the advent of sound pictures in theaters. In retaliation, Paul traveled to Washington in 1937 to urge the House Immigration Committee to report favorably on the Dickstein bill to restrict the entrance of alien stage artists into the United States.

Without question, the roughest economic blow to Paul and his men came during the Roxy booking. Lorillard dropped the Paul Whiteman–Old Gold show from the air. The weekly radio stint had swelled Whiteman's coffers by more than $5,000 each and every week. The popular series had brought in a total of $350,000 for Paul over a period of sixteen months. By early 1930 it was the largest single source of revenue for the band. No one else came forward to sponsor the band on radio. Paul quickly faded from the air.

Jimmy Gillespie scurried around New York trying to keep the band together. He found a booking in the Bronx at a new roadhouse. On June 12 the band played at the opening of the Hollywood Road

Resort near Pelham Park. Charging no cover, the open-air pavilion had a capacity of over 3,000 and a weekly overhead of $20,000. "We had a contract at $5,000 to open this outdoor pavilion," Gillespie recalled in an article in *The Saturday Evening Post* in 1932. "A year earlier we wouldn't have listened to less than $10,000 per week. Saratoga during the race meeting followed, and again $5,000 was the top figure. It meant no better than breaking even."

Paul struggled to keep up a solid front and keep up the quality of the music. He was heartsick at the thought of losing any additional musicians. Many had been with him for years, and he knew some would have difficulty finding new jobs as the Depression worsened.

In the midst of these doldrums Paul recalled the happy times in Hollywood with a vivacious and attractive Margaret Livingston. So much had happened in less than a year. He longed for her company, her sympathy, her advice. If anyone could bring some cheer and direction into his life, it was Margaret. Yes, he was ready to give up eating and drinking so much if she were to be by his side. There was only one woman who could turn the tide in his favor, but she was 3,000 miles away. Somehow he would find a way to bring her closer.

14

On the Comeback Trail

In August 1930 the country lumbered into the early stages of the Great Depression. In spite of the growing economic malaise, the big spenders and sporty socialites flocked to Saratoga for the summer horse-racing season. The resort's Arrowhead Hotel hired the largest and most famous band in the business—Paul Whiteman's.

Paul was grateful for the booking. His orchestra now consisted of eighteen men, supplemented by vocalist Mildred Bailey and the King's Jesters, a quartet. Among the most recent departures were those of clarinetist Izzy Friedman, trumpeter Frank Siegrist, and trombonist Wilbur Hall. They were replaced by Fud Livingston, Nat Natoli, and Herb Winfield, respectively.

Bix Beiderbecke did not rejoin the band. After several months of rest in the fall of 1929, he had resumed his playing in and about his hometown, moving on to Chicago. When Whiteman returned to New York in the late spring, Bix also came back to the city. Preparing for the Roxy engagement, Paul worried whether Bix had the stability and stamina to do five theater shows a day as well as radio broadcasts. Bix, too, was uncertain; finally he told Paul that he did not feel ready. Meanwhile he intensified his work on a piano piece he called "Candlelights" and brought it to Whiteman's music publishers. They encouraged him, hoping to discover another *Rhapsody*.

By then Bix was making overtures to Paul about getting back in the band. But Paul had cut his personnel drastically, eliminating many of his jazz contingent. Paul and Roy Bargy knew that Bix would not be satisfied with the changed makeup and direction of the band. His days on the Whiteman bandstand were over. Heavy-drinking Bix floundered in freelance jobs on radio, in hotel bands, and at college proms for a year. A very real and gifted musician, he died of pneumonia in New York in August 1931.

Paul was sick over the loss of Bix and worried about having to let so many of his men go. What would they do, and how would he keep going? He took the podium with a vengeance. He rehearsed the smaller outfit every afternoon. Gradually he shaped the unit into a fine-tuned musical aggregation that sounded like the solid Whiteman band of yore.

He was certainly spending more time on the bandstand and a little less at the dinner table. Nearly every day a letter postmarked Hollywood came to his hotel room. Margaret wrote suggestions for a daily diet, interspersed with lots of humor and gossip and affection. She had agreed to keep in touch. Paul, in turn, swore to lose 100 pounds from the 300 he was carrying around. "I'm going to miss you a hundred times more than you are going to miss those hundred pounds," she reminded him.

Paul was as touchy about his band's financial straits as he was about his weight-losing regimen. At Saratoga's Arrowhead Hotel concertmaster Kurt Dieterle was handed a $200 tip from a patron between dance sets. He walked to the cashier's office to break the two large bills into smaller denominations in order to divide the windfall among the men. As he passed a table where Paul and the owner of the hotel were seated, Paul asked where he was going.

"I just got a large tip and want to split the money among the band," Kurt replied.

"You don't mean you're going to accept tips! Times are tough, but they're not that bad."

Paul's thoughts focused on Margaret more and more. Finally he decided to call and invite her and her family to Saratoga. He insisted that they come East; he had already rented a cottage and planned to send money for train tickets. Paul had made only a slight dent in his forty-five-inch waistline. Margaret's presence might inspire a real effort on thinning down. The Livingston family spent the month of August with Paul, who barely passed the weight-reducing test before seeing Margaret off again on a Los Angeles-bound train.

Gillespie next booked the band for three weeks into the Gibson Hotel in Cincinnati, where business was bad. Chicago's Granada Café evidenced interest in Whiteman. Jimmy grabbed at the offer—

a solid $6,000 a week. Everyone in the band believed that the Whiteman outfit would be back in New York in no time. Chicago held the promise of a new beginning, and it was there that Whiteman truly began his climb back into the mainstream of the big band business.

Paul had always done well in that city. From his very first visit in 1922, when he played at the Trianon for a full week, Chicago embraced Whiteman warmly and generously. Both audiences and critics loved Paul during his appearances at downtown theaters and concert halls. "I doubt if we ever played better in San Francisco or Denver, both of which were home, than we did on our first visit to Chicago," Paul had written in the mid-1920s. "That warm glow that came across the footlights started out front and ran right back-stage. Since then, I have thought of Chicago as the jolly, friendly, self-made millionaire of cities, with the heartiest hand clasp of all."

Chicago was a leading site for creating and appreciating the best in popular music. Its musicians of the 1920s produced a jazz dance music that became known as Chicago Style—a rhythmic, strident, and vigorous sound. Many Chicago bands also borrowed and adapted the Whiteman instrumentation of the early jazz era. And the city's ballrooms and hotels offered the best musicians they could find, both hot, like the Benson Orchestra, and sweet, like Wayne King.

The Prohibition era supported activity on bandstands in the Windy City. Night life flourished, stimulated by gamblers, boot-leggers, and racketeers who controlled most of the places where bands played and people drank. For many musicians, it was a hard existence. They had to play the music the bosses demanded, with no questions asked. Moreover, most entertainers in some way or another were shaken down under threats of bodily or financial harm. Yet the money that came in to musicians was both substantial and steady—if you only played along on the bandstand and off.

The Granada Café on the South Side of Chicago was not the most flagrant lawbreaker, but on the other hand, it was not the safest place for letting off steam after sundown. In 1927 Guy Lombardo and his Royal Canadians experienced a taste of big-city gang warfare there one night, when shooting broke out during a dance tune. A gunman was killed to Lombardo's saccharine strains. The gunfire was heard all over town, since the band was being broadcast live.

Paul apparently came into the Granada knowing he was in the

hands of Chicago's toughest gangster, Al Capone. His henchmen were never very far away. They provided protection from rival gangs, and Paul found them friendly and considerate. Their presence led to a brief indulgence with cocaine; Paul believed that the drug would curb his cravings for food and take his mind off his rigorous diet.

Friendly shooting contests also helped to keep him from the dinner table. One night Paul was dining in a restaurant owned by one of Capone's former chief lieutenants noted for his deadly aim. "I'll bet you," Paul bantered, "I'm a better shot than you."

The gangster eyed Paul with amused incredulity. "Come on. We'll go to a shooting gallery and see."

The years of hunting in Colorado and target practice with Tom Mix paid off in spades. Paul was so much better than the gangster that he tossed the expensive pearl-handled .38 caliber revolver he was carrying on the table.

"Take it," he said disgustedly to Paul. "You won it fairly."

The manager of the Granada brought Paul back to radio on a modest scale. He contracted with station WBBM to carry nightly pickups from his café. Whiteman, who had been off the air for over six months, hoped that the exposure would attract a major sponsor for a regular series. A pianist at the station, Harry Sosnik, supplied arrangements. Later he formed his own band at Chicago's Edgewater Beach Hotel and played at the Century of Progress Exposition. In 1936 he conducted on *Your Hit Parade,* joining the lineup of top radio bands.

Paul was soon approached by the National Broadcasting Company's Chicago vice president, Niles Trammell, about greater participation in NBC programs. The discussions led to the job as musical supervisor for network midwestern operations. NBC had recently expanded its headquarters in the city, with plans for more Chicago-originated programs, particularly band remotes. With Paul's NBC affiliation came a weekly network show for the Allied Quality Paint Company. But to make ends meet, Paul still had to accept every available dance, concert, and theater date.

Daily menus and edicts from Margaret arrived regularly at Paul's quarters at the Flamingo Hotel. She addressed him as "Dearest Pig o' My Heart" or "Darling Sweetness and Light Weight," and signed off as "The Old Medico" or "Red-headed Cross Nurse."

When Paul appealed for baked potatoes and chocolate cake, Margaret countered with spinach and lemon Jello and with lettuce and watercress salads. She urged lots of water. "Have a glass of it every hour or so . . . I'm delighted you have bought a bathroom scale and weigh in each morning. Let me know the staggering sum total each day or so that I may be guided accordingly. You mustn't lose too quickly for we're trying to lose weight to gain health, and two pounds a week must be your maximum reduction for a time. Later on we'll do better for you."

Margaret's letters frequently injected bits of Hollywood news. "Guess whom I worked with today?" she wrote. "That honey with the eyes that have it—Dick Barthelmess. He made love to me all day (on the set, I mean)."

The next day, she began, "Am I a-twitter today! Clark Gable is moving into Colonial House, which automatically makes me his landlady. I just knew something good would come of my saving my pennies and buying that shack."

A week later, "I can scarcely contain myself for joy! Mary Pickford sent for me to make a test for her picture." Margaret won the part in *Kiki* at United Artists. "As usual, I play old Nastyface and knock Mary around something fierce. We have the time of our lives doing our dance routine."

Between movie making and menu planning, Margaret kept in the social whirl and got around. She attended prize fights and polo matches and nightclub parties. It was at one such gala that a press photographer snapped Margaret and New York socialite Whitney de Rham as the winners of a dance contest. The picture made the wire services and appeared in a Chicago paper. Paul, who had shed over forty pounds by closely following Margaret's letters and menus, took the photograph badly; he wasted no time in phoning Hollywood and venting his displeasure.

The relationship seemed doomed when Paul received a package containing all the expensive jewelry he had given Margaret during the past year. When he failed to reach her by phone, he instructed Gillespie to make train reservations for two on the Santa Fe Chief to Los Angeles. He ordered Mischa Russell to go along as all-round major domo.

Mischa arrived at the station ahead of time with all the luggage. A very drunk Paul followed at the very last minute in the care of a Granada Café henchman. The two maneuvered Paul into a drawing room, where he slept it off for the three days of the cross-country trip. Two weeks in California turned the tide in his favor. By the time Paul left again, Margaret Livingston was wearing a ten-carat diamond ring. The two were officially engaged, though Paul was still legally married to Vanda.

In a front-page story on February 28, 1931, *The New York Times* informed Margaret and the rest of the country that Paul had filed for divorce. The action was "friendly," both sides being in accord, noted the newspaper, and the formal charge was desertion. Vanda had left Paul over two years previously, but she continued to occupy the Whiteman apartment on Riverside Drive in New York. Vanda had accused Paul of being married to his dance band, and he agreed. Since 1928 he had spent only three months a year with Vanda and young Paul and had virtually lived out of a trunk or in Hollywood. "We tried married life on the road seven years and found it's no go," Paul commented. "It certainly was no place to bring up a baby."

Vanda's settlement in the divorce was a sizable lump sum for her and Paul, Jr., and an allowance of $600 a week. "I'll have the boy, Paul, Jr., three months out of the year," Paul explained. "His mother was very generous about that. He will be with me when I'm not playing one-night stands."

Paul's progress on the comeback trail was hampered by this heavy financial burden, an on-going obligation he would carry for many years. But he was pleased that his son would spend school vacations with him or at the Whiteman ranch in Colorado.

Gillespie negotiated with several Chicago hotels for Paul's services, hoping to up his weekly take. But none offered more than $3,000. It took months before Gillespie could line up a choice spot for the band at the Edgewater Beach Hotel on Lake Michigan. A metropolitan hotel in a country-club setting less than twenty minutes from downtown Chicago, the Edgewater Beach offered an ideal setting for the Whiteman group. Its Marine Room accommodated 1,000 people and provided entertainers with a spacious stage, good lighting, and perfect acoustics. Surrounding the large thousand-room hotel were tennis courts, a nine-hole putting course, a private beach and promenade, and an outdoor dance pavilion. Paul was engaged to succeed Phil Spitalny's orchestra to play nightly and for special Sunday evening concerts. (Spitalny had not yet reorganized his band into an all-girl orchestra.) Frequent radio remotes from the Marine Room were also included in the deal that was to begin in May.

The engagement was the start of a rejuvenation for the band. Mildred Bailey, especially, came into her own during this period. Bails, as Paul called her, had been hired for $75 a week in 1929. Within a year Paul was paying her $250. An anecdote claims that she asked for $1,250 to which Whiteman made a counter offer. "I'll tell you what. You give me $1,250 a week, and I'll give you the band." But in 1931 he upped her take to $300 when she threatened to walk out. It proved a good investment for all hands. According to several musicians, Mildred almost single-handedly saved the orchestra from breaking up. Paul knew that he could not keep her under his wing for too long, and after she introduced a number called "Ol' Rockin' Chair's Got Me," it was only a matter of time before she was a big star in her own right.

Hoagy Carmichael had been inspired to write this song after spending time with the blues singer during the filming of *The King of Jazz*. Mildred, who suffered from a thyroid condition and weight problems, struck Hoagy as well suited to an unfettered loll in a rocking chair. In 1931 he sent Mildred his tune in the hope that she could sing it with Whiteman's band. Matty Malneck worked up an arrangement. Mildred tried it out during a broadcast from the Edgewater Beach. The response from listeners was phenomenal. Western Union received so many enthusiastic messages for Mildred that the company was unable to deliver all the telegrams. The publicity helped Paul and earned Mildred her nickname, the Rockin' Chair Lady. Hoagy's melody became her theme song.

Red Norvo, who worked as a staff musician at NBC in Chicago and occasionally backed Mildred with his vibraharp on broadcasts, became one of her biggest fans. He arranged to play more and more shows with Whiteman. "She gassed me as a singer." Red said. "I really dug her, and we started having a bite together now and then. The first thing, we were going together." Red soon joined Whiteman as a xylophone player, and he and Mildred were secretly married. Later they teamed up, billing themselves as Mr. and Mrs. Swing, backed up by a thirteen-piece combo.

When Paul called Mildred "Bails," she countered by calling him "Old Father Whiteman" or "Fatho" for short. That tag quickly evolved into "Pops"—a name that stuck and was picked up by just about everyone in the band and all who had any dealings with Paul.

During this period Whiteman heard a young, attractive singer from Columbia, Missouri, who was on staff at WLW in Cincinnati;

she was a graduate of the Music Conservatory. Paul sent her a wire: "Opening a two-week engagement and staying at Sinton Hotel, Cincinnati. Please contact me." Jane Froman never got to see him. She had a sore throat and was sent by WLW to recuperate at a nearby resort. When she returned, Paul and the band had already left.

While at WLW she met and married Don Ross, another staff singer. Soon after, the two decided to try their luck in Chicago. Ross was hired by WBBM, the CBS affiliate, and Jane arranged an audition with Whiteman at the NBC outlet.

On the day she was to sing for him, in her excitement Jane caught her heel and fell down a flight of stairs at the Three Arts Club, where she was staying. "I went on and sang without knowing how badly I was hurt," she later told an interviewer. "I sang song after song, and at the end of the session, was told I had the job. I realized I had broken my ankle and promptly fainted from the pain, but not before Whiteman congratulated me. He said, 'I've been trying to get hold of you for a long time.' Before I knew it, I was off to a hospital."

Listening over a loudspeaker in an adjoining room were potential radio sponsors Paul had invited. One of them, Florsheim Shoes, signed Jane for a weekly series. Paul acted as her manager, and also signed her to a three-year contract. She began a daily fifteen-minute show of light music following *Amos 'n' Andy*. Consequently Jane Froman was heard in millions of homes throughout the country for at least a minute or two. Her career was well on its way.

After six months with the Whiteman organization Jane realized that she was not cut out to be a band vocalist. "If you want to get someplace, you have to be out by yourself," she observed. Apparently Paul agreed. He tore up her contract, and they parted friends. In early 1933 Jane left Chicago for radio work in New York and a part in the *Ziegfeld Follies* produced by the Shuberts. Within a year every broadcast poll rated her the number-one female vocalist on the air. And in spite of a bad stutter—which never surfaced when she was singing—she signed a movie contract for featured roles at Warner Brothers.

Another Jane came on the bandstand at the Edgewater Beach. Jane Vance, a freshman at Northwestern University, ended up a band vocalist as the result of a sorority initiation stunt. She was instructed to appear at Paul's weekly College Night to sing with the band. Terrified of appearing alone, she persuaded two other girls to join her act. They memorized a Boswell Sisters' recording and practiced it with a piano accompaniment. The trio attracted a large numbr of local undergraduates to cheer them on at the Friday night college salute. After a few bars Jane's companions froze at the microphone, but she kept right on singing. Afterward Paul said to her, "Be at NBC tomorrow morning at nine. I wanna hear you in a studio with a proper mike."

Paul, who had spotted a natural talent, offered Jane Vance a five-year contract at $50 a week, turning her from student to singer virtually overnight. So that she might gain on-the-job experience, Paul had her work with every back-up band that came into the Edgewater Beach Hotel.

In spite of low salaries, pay cuts, and fewer bookings, the Whiteman gang's sense of humor had not suffered. Practical jokes continued on and off the bandstand. The most memorable gag during the Edgewater Beach stint was Kurt Dieterle's inspiration. The butt of his prank was John "Bullet" Cordaro, an exceptionally able clarinetist and sax player but extremely naive and trusting.

Paul's Sunday evening concerts at the hotel always had a theme—Spanish or French music, or regional American melodies, for example. The morning of the program on songs of the South, Kurt ran into Cordaro near the hotel. Kurt called out, "Hey Bullet, don't forget your makeup for tonight."

Cordaro stopped abruptly. "Makeup? What makeup?"

"Haven't you heard? Paul's ordered everyone in blackface for tonight's concert."

"Why blackface?"

"Don't you remember? We're doing music about the South."

"Sure. But nobody told me about makeup."

"I don't know how you missed out on hearing it. Paul says anyone who shows up without blackface gets fined twenty-five dollars."

"What'll I use?"

"Go to a drugstore and get some burnt cork like they use in minstrel shows. Or find some black greasepaint."

At concert time the musicians dressed in tuxedos, straggled into the ballroom, and took their places. Bullet had not shown up by the time Paul arrived. Kurt thought it wise to let his boss in on the joke. The scheme so amused Paul that he decided to go along with the gag.

By the time Bullet was spotted at the ballroom's main entrance, the rest of the men had taken their seats. Scattered laughs broke out among such members of the audience as had already gathered. They laughed as Bullet walked toward the bandstand—in black tie and blackface.

Paul smiled as his reed player approached. When he got a full look at Bullet, he nearly lost his composure. The rest of the band broke out in guffaws at the sight of the perplexed Cordaro. Paul rapped his baton on the music stand for attention, glancing quickly at his bemused concertmaster.

"You all knew that this evening is our tribute to Southern music. Bullet is the only guy who followed instructions. I'm fining the rest of you characters twenty-five dollars each for not being in black-face."

Paul's obligations to the Edgewater Beach and NBC Chicago kept him in the city, with only an occasional day off. There was no chance to break away for a visit to California and Margaret. Because Paul could not bear to be alone, he asked Matty Malneck to move into Paul's suite at the Edgewater Beach Apartments.

As Paul lost weight by following what he called the grapefruit diet, skinny Malneck gained. Paul also found that he was sleeping only four hours a night and felt much more energetic. He composed the melody for a song that became known as "Our Little Kingdom of Love," and he told everyone that the tune was inspired by the grapefruit regimen.

Malneck remembered Paul's cavalier way with money. When he emptied his pockets at night, he dumped crumpled up $20 and $50 bills on the bureau. Sometimes a dogeared check for several thousand dollars would go from his suit to a drawer, and be forgotten for weeks. Paul never seemed to know how much money he was carrying or how much he spent.

His long-distance telephone charges added up as summer came to Chicago. He phoned Margaret every day; if for some reason he could not reach her, he was miserable. He decided to bring Margaret and her family to Chicago and to bring his relatives in from Denver so they might all meet. Margaret's mother Eda, her sister Ivy, Paul's parents, his sister Ferne, and her husband, Paul Smith, gathered at the Edgewater Beach in June. Margaret immediately noticed that Paul had lost about thirty pounds since their last meeting. He was, indeed, coming close to dropping off the 100 pounds he had to shed before he could stand at the altar. The wedding date was set for Tuesday, August 18, the ceremony to take place at the Whiteman ranch in Colorado.

The day before the wedding members of both families began to arrive in Denver, where the "king" was about to take his fourth "queen." In a household where music had always been paramount, not a note was played before or during the wedding. Lack of space in the living room ruled the possibility out. Wilberforce also ruled out liquor at the indoor reception; no alcohol had ever been served in the Whiteman home. He compromised on an outdoor bar.

The immediate family gathered around Dr. George B. Vosbaugh, who had officiated at the marriage of Ferne and Paul Smith in 1908. On this occasion Ferne and Paul attended the couple. Following the brief ceremony they posed for numerous pictures. "If we are not happy," Paul commented, "it will be all my fault."

Paul and Margaret began married life at the rustic Whiteman cottage at the foot of nearby Mount Evans in Estes Park. The following day they boarded a train for Chicago. "Wear your bullet-proof vest," Paul told his bride, "because we're going to live in Chicago."

Paul had wanted Jimmy Gillespie as his best man, but after his boss's engagement became official, Gillespie clearly and emphatically announced, "If you marry that woman, you can start looking for a new manager." Jimmy knew band wives; he had pacified many of the orchestra's mates. He had settled arguments, patched together split households, and soothed flaring jealousies up and down the land and a couple of times in Europe.

But when Margaret came on the scene, he was powerless. She and Jimmy clashed from the outset, pulling at each other like a couple of strange and angry bulldogs. Margaret felt capable of running the business and accounting part of Paul's operations herself. Hadn't she parlayed a modest Hollywood income into a sizable nest egg? Jimmy resigned as Whiteman's manager on September 1, twelve days after the wedding.

Jimmy had harbored hopes that Margaret—now Maggie to Paul and the boys—would continue her acting career and be out of the way much of the time. She did return to Columbia Pictures and a part in *Blonde Baby* in late September. But Maggie's work at Columbia marked the end of her film activity. She rented her apartment to actor Walter Huston and rejoined Paul as full-time wife and part-time manager, all the while keeping a close eye on hubby's waistline. Her concern over proper diet and nutrition, especially daily weight-losing schedules, sparked the interest of many people. Soon her expertise in reducing diets was shared in a series of articles in such newspapers as New York's *Daily News*. In 1933 a book dedicated to the twenty-four million overweight people in the country came off the press. Published by Viking and coauthored by Isabel Leighton, it bore the title *Whiteman's Burden*. The book, a compendium of recipes and personal anecdotes, delighted readers.

During the economic slump, music lovers listened to their radios and stopped buying records. Even the release of low-priced discs, at 35 cents or less, could not boost the record industry sufficiently in the early 1930s. Sales of records fell to six million from tens of millions before the crash. For a full year Whiteman stayed out of recording studios while Columbia guaranteed Paul $50,000 for those twelve months. The fee allowed Paul to keep his eighteen-piece band together and to meet Mildred Bailey's rising salary.

Then, in September 1931, Victor slipped Columbia $60,000 for the right to record Whiteman again. The buy-out deal placed Paul under the aegis of RCA, which now owned both NBC and Victor, and which ran the NBC Artists Bureau for the exclusive services of its broadcast musicians and singers. The new record contract specified $25 a side per musician for dance numbers and $50 for concert selections—a considerable dip from fees during the high-rolling 1920s.

Paul and his men anxiously gathered at Victor's Chicago studio on September 30. It was the first recording session with Pops Whiteman for newcomers Ray McDermott on clarinet, Fritz Hummel on trombone, Pierre Olker on string bass, and Nat Natoli on trumpet. Jack Fulton, Mildred Bailey, and the newly formed trio called the Romancers (Fulton, Bill Seckler, and Craig Leitch) handled the vocals for most of the band's seven recording dates that year. But it was Mildred's uniquely high-pitched tone and rhythmic phrasing on "All of Me," "When It's Sleepy Time Down South," and "Can't You See" that caught the attention of the country's few remaining record buyers.

After the band had moved to Chicago in September 1930, Ferde Grofé played a steadily diminishing role in the day-to-day affairs of the organization. Once a mainstay in the recording studios as arranger, rehearsal conductor, and pianist—at $50 per side for *each* of these functions—he now lost a great deal of income. Roy Bargy took over more and more of his chores while Ferde remained back at his home in New Jersey. As chief arranger, he still contributed to the band regularly. But other orchestras, especially the growing number on radio in New York, wanted his services as composer and orchestrator. Several radio stations and sponsors asked him to conduct over the air. His career seemed headed in a new direction away from Paul.

During the summer of Paul's marriage Ferde came to Chicago. Paul wanted him to start work on a new orchestral piece, a big modern number that would help to send the Whiteman outfit back to the concert stage. Ferde agreed to try.

His vivid memory of a vacation in Arizona, when he had gazed on the magnificent Grand Canyon, inspired a new composition similar to the *Mississippi Suite*. Sounds in and about the Edgewater Beach stimulated him. A cowboy sequence came from the gentle rocking of Ferde, Jr.'s baby carriage. The rhythm for "On the Trail" stemmed from the sound of pile drivers outside the hotel. But the country-club atmosphere of the Edgewater Beach began to distract Grofé. Paul suggested that he go to a secluded lakeside cottage in Wisconsin to complete the piece. There Ferde proceeded to finish his best-remembered composition, a suite he called "Five Pictures of the Grand Canyon" but which was always referred to as The *Grand Canyon Suite*.

At its premiere in Chicago's Studebaker Theatre in late 1931, it won overwhelming praise, and "On the Trail" immediately entered the vernacular. The Philip Morris cigarette firm picked it up as the long-lasting signature for its radio programs. Grofé's popularity soared. At the age of forty he felt that his old association with Whiteman could only hamper his chances. When he spoke to his old pal about his decision to leave, Paul begged him to wait. The band, on the comeback trail, needed him. But Grofé wanted to get the spotlight and hear a little applause for himself. He could not be persuaded to stay.

Ferde returned East, where he started to rehearse a concert orchestra for the New York premiere of the *Grand Canyon Suite* at a benefit performance for unemployed musicians. But Paul had also made plans to present the work at a similar concert in New York, and he felt strongly that Ferde had not only run off with the new composition but had also invaded Paul's turf. Grofé's plans killed the Whiteman concert, announced for the same month. There were harsh words and bad feelings, and neither spoke to the other for a year or so. When Jimmy Gillespie became Grofé's manager, oil was really added to troubled waters. In spite of the break, Ferde provided orchestrations to his old aggregation on a fairly regular basis, and Paul considered him an ex officio staff arranger.

With Grofé's departure, Paul lost a vital and dependable element of the organization. Ferde Grofé joined the growing body of Pops alumni—which included Ross Gorman, Henry Busse, Bing Crosby, Red Nichols, and the Dorsey brothers—who moved on to greater success and popularity.

15

Back to Broadway

During his time in Chicago at the Granada and the Edgewater Beach, Paul mapped out plans to build his band into the best of its kind, at the same time taking his men back to Manhattan, where greater and more lucrative opportunities had always existed. In 1931 radio broadcasting, which gave the vast listening audience what it wanted to hear week after week, was the road to the center ring of show business. First Paul had to prove that the band could draw millions of listeners across the country; then he had to convince major sponsors that he could successfully promote and stimulate sales of their goods from coast to coast.

When Paul signed a radio contract with Allied Quality Paints, a moderately large manufacturer of paints and varnishes, he viewed the arrangement as a step in the right direction. But he believed that the next move required him to affiliate with a bigger company, one with a well-known name and product.

Along with a strong emphasis on radio work, Whiteman believed that the band should seek out new young entertainers and bring them into the organization. It had to take on the complexion of youth and energy if it was to continue to please the public and stay on or near the top. Once he had solid network radio commitments in his pocket and a handful of fresh, new performers in the fold, Paul would not lack well-paying recording sessions, dance and theater bookings, concert dates, hotel engagements, and special performances, perhaps in a Broadway show or a Hollywood film.

Paul's new manager played an important role in implementing

the strategy. Jack Lavin, who had worked as a Chicago song plugger, joined Whiteman soon after Gillespie left. A resourceful and determined organizer, he brought new ideas and direction to the band. He also had the approval and backing of Margaret, who spent much time working with him on strategy and money management.

Lavin's first big coup linked Paul with General Motors on the radio. In January 1932, Paul Whiteman (with his band now billed as the "Chieftains" by his new sponsor) went on the air for GM's Pontiac Division, which had been named for the Indian, Chief Pontiac. The association with General Motors for its various divisions, which lasted for fourteen months, allowed Paul to achieve several of his goals in a shorter period than he had hoped.

A major drawing card of the Pontiac broadcast was a segment built on Paul's search for new talent. At the Edgewater Beach Hotel he had featured weekly college nights as well as an undergraduate talent contest to choose a promising young performer. Participants from schools throughout the Chicago area flocked to the hotel, boosting business and patronage at a particularly low point in the economy.

The success of those competitions resulted in a similar scouting expedition on the Pontiac shows. Billed as the "Youth of America" segment, it took the band on the road once again to movie houses and to weekly broadcasts from different cities. Contestants who registered at a local radio station four or five days ahead of the band's arrival were auditioned and selected for a final hearing by Paul. The winner, of course, appeared with Paul's Chieftains. Local Pontiac dealers and newspaper space salesmen benefited from the flurry of publicity and advertising. Town fathers beamed in the national limelight. And Paul was gaining a new following of young fans.

His "best" fan tuned in, too. "Last night's broadcast was very good," wrote his mother. Wilberforce also dashed off letters suggesting music for Paul's broadcasts, which were featuring native American melodies. The professor urged his son to consider the lesser-known works of Stephen Foster, Henry Clay Work, George F. Root, and Daniel Emmett.

In early 1932 the radio series finally brought Paul and his men back to New York. Margaret was pleased; she always had misgivings about traveling. At some time during Paul's appearance at the Stanley Theatre in Pittsburgh she lost a diamond-and-sapphire pin valued at $7,000.

Paul's radio popularity and his ratings carried the band to Broadway. It played the Palace in what tabloid journalists described as "one of the grandest comeback efforts ever applauded on a fickle boulevard." Sharing a bill with fast-rising crooner Russ Columbo and veteran comics Weber and Fields, Whiteman emerged the favorite on the Palace stage with a solid forty-eight-minute revue. His band seemed better suited to stage work than ever before. Mildred Bailey, Jack Fulton, Red Norvo, Goldie, and Mike contributed specialty acts the audience recognized from Paul's frequent broadcasts. Baritone Red McKenzie, a newcomer to the outfit, had already built a following with his solos on radio.

Paul was also given raves in the looks department. Down to 197 pounds and looking like a matinee idol from the rear, with his suits nipped in at the waist instead of hanging straight down, he caused audiences to murmur on his entrance.

Variety sized up the new Whiteman band perhaps better than any other observer. "In the line of syncopation for dancing and listening," its review noted, "Whiteman probably went as far as a bandsman possibly could go, which was further than any other leader had gone. That takes in fame, musical excellence, and salary. It's remarkable how he has changed over into an entirely new band field for him without losing an inch of ground. It's more likely Whiteman has gained by the change."

Paul and the gang brightened the proscenium during vaudeville's last days. Along with Bing Crosby, the Boswell Sisters, Kate Smith, Morton Downey, the Mills Brothers, and Arthur Tracy, "The Street Singer"—all headliners "made" by radio—Pops helped to close an era of all-around family entertainment for millions of Americans.

Back on Broadway in 1932, the band contained many familiar Whiteman musicians from the 1920s. Trum, Dieterle, Mike, Hazlett, and Goldie were still on the payroll, although new faces had appeared. The Whiteman aggregation now consisted of nineteen instrumentalists:

VIOLIN: Kurt Dieterle, Mischa Russell, Matt Malneck, John
          Bowman.
TROMBONE: Jack Fulton, Hal Matthews, Bill Rank.
TRUMPET: Andy Secrest, Harry Goldfield, Nat Natoli.
SAXOPHONE: Chester Hazlett, Charles Strickfaden,
             Frankie Trumbauer, John Cordaro.
BANJO: Mike Pingitore.

BASS: Pierre Olker.
DRUMS: Herb Quigley.
PIANO: Roy Bargy.
XYLOPHONE: Red Norvo.

During his run at the Palace, Paul's talent search attracted hundreds of performers to the contest at NBC's Times Square studio, which had been the New Amsterdam Roof theater and the late-night showplace for Whiteman only a few years earlier. The Pontiac auditions advanced a weekly winner to the microphone for a one-shot engagement with Whiteman. A young instrumentalist and vocalist named Peter Dean entered one week but lost out in the semi-finals. Twenty years later the onetime singer became Paul's manager.

The greatest talent to emerge in the New York auditions was a twenty-three-year-old songwriter and singer. A native of Savannah, Georgia, Johnny Mercer was working at Charlie Miller's musical publishing firm and living in Brooklyn with his wife, Ginger. Paul spotted Mercer's talent among the 300 entrants that week. He had just written "Lazybones" with Hoagy Carmichael. Paul signed him at $75 a week to sing and to write special song material and comedy sketches.

The band's growing radio popularity and Paul's skill at attracting young talent and, in turn, young audiences paid off in still another crucial area. New York's Biltmore Hotel asked him to open the summer season on its rooftop Cascades Room. Near Grand Central Station, the Biltmore drew a cross-section of prospering New Yorkers and visiting guests, including businessmen, collegians, socialites, bankers, and artists.

Paul's Biltmore debut—a formal affair—attracted 600 people. Whiteman conducted on a colorful bandstand in front of a simulated waterfall, moon, and orchard. The room was jammed with many old New York friends: Jimmy Walker, Bert Wheeler, Harry Richman, Admiral Richard E. Byrd, O. O. McIntyre, and George Gershwin, who joined in at the piano. Margaret's talents as a New York hostess soon brought together Broadway, Park Avenue, and Radio City at parties where such guests as Deems Taylor, Mrs. Marshall Field, Blanche Sweet, Jules Glaenzer, Cobina Wright, Mario Braggiotti, William Rhinelander Stewart, Phyllis Haver, and Jacques Fray mingled.

By midsummer of 1932 all was going well with Whiteman. He was back in New York to stay. The band was busier than ever on radio and at the Biltmore. Recording sessions for RCA Victor were coming along about once a month (and they included *A Night with Paul Whiteman at the Biltmore,* a December 3, 1932, recording for one of the very earliest forerunners of the long-playing records). Plans were under way for more concerts of modern music. Paul was particularly pleased that he had been able to commission John Green to write a piece for his next concert at Carnegie Hall.

In a few short years the Harvard-educated economist-turned-musician stood out as one of the youngest and most talented composers in New York. As an undergraduate in the 1920s, Green had contributed arrangements to Harvard's Gold Coast Dance Orchestra and written "Coquette" with Carmen Lombardo during one summer vacation. Other songs flowed from his keyboard after he left Cambridge in 1928: "I'm Yours," "Living in Dreams," and the immortal "Body and Soul."

After a brief stint on Wall Street, Green served an apprenticeship as a rehearsal pianist at the Paramount Studios on Long Island. Frank Tours, a conductor for Paramount, asked him to orchestrate the 1930 Maurice Chevalier film, *Big Pond,* which introduced the song "You Brought a New Kind of Love to Me." John soon found additional work arranging for Lopez and for Victor Young on the *Atwater Kent Radio Hour*. Whiteman had watched John Green's progress and wondered if a talent similar to Gershwin's would develop.

With Paul's newly announced plans and ever-increasing activities in the music world, the press still found Whiteman good copy. Ring Lardner, for one, contacted Paul for a *New Yorker* profile, and on July 20 Paul himself replied. It was a rare occasion that Pops picked up a pen, but Ring's colorful, zany letter triggered a response directly from the "slim fiddler." His letter read:

Dear Ring,
    Having derived such pleasure out of reading your letter of Bastille Day, I became enhanced with the idea of answering it myself, and sitting down to the typewriter, I am amazed to learn that I can write very well—having never tried it before, I am doubly amazed. . . . I am enclosing a personnel sheet of my entire organization . . . that takes care of a couple of ques-

tions all in one. I'll answer the other ones in the order in which they hit me. Ferde Grofé, Roy Bargy, and Matt Malneck take care of most of my arranging, but I do have several odd persons to work from time to time. Ferde Grofé at the present time is not active as a musician, confining himself to composing and arranging.

Regarding broadcasts: we do a rhythmic concert every Sunday night from 6:00 to 7:00 featuring the works of Grofé, Gershwin, or some new modern composition by some new modern composer—the point being to introduce modern American music to the public. We also feature classical vocalists at these concerts such as Jimmy Melton, Gladys Rice, and in the future such artists as Virginia Rea . . . will be featured.

Then I have my regular sponsored broadcasts (Allah be praised) each Friday night from 10:00 to 10:30—Buick–Olds–Pontiac . . . then we are on the air every night from the Cascades at the Biltmore at any old time when the NBC happens to run out of funds for more artists.

Now as to my functions . . . What I do outside of leading the band? First of all, we play in the beautiful Cascades atop the Biltmore—forgive me—I thought I was a radio announcer—from 7:00 P.M. to 3:00 A.M. The evening is comprised of leading the band, and making a circle of sitting at tables talking to my friends; then each Wednesday morning from 10:00 to 12:00 I am continuing the auditions for the Youth of America. You probably have heard of these auditions. Since the first of the year, I have auditioned about 7,000 young people in various cities of the U.S.A. and many of these kids have pretty good jobs as a result of being winners of these contests. The afternoon of the same day is devoted to song publishers—selecting tunes appropriate for my individual singers.

Between times I listen to a tango band, an accordion quartet, or a harmony trio. The rest of the time is spent in rehearsals for my Sunday concerts, and my commercial broadcasts. I try to squeeze in a meeting with my business organization every morning at 11:00 but most of the time I am out before they ever get there. Then again, I find myself running around trying to locate a spot for my band to play after this engagement is completed . . . which is fairly important.

Also do a certain amount of recording, as well as climbing
around in different poses to suit the whims of newspaper men
who want different poses for publicity work. I also have to
take a little time to listen to the complaints of whatever em-
ployer I may happen to have. And then, as a result of certain
"finds" in my auditions, I am faced with the "now-that-I-got-
em-what-am-I-gonna-do-with-em" problem.

I think your selection of All-American bands is swell—only
don't forget mine. [Gus] Haenschen's all-string orchestra
which was on Coca Cola was originally started by Leonard
Joy. I can't think of any outstanding band you are overlooking,
but I do think [Jack] Denny's band deserves mention . . . Well,
my good man, for one who asks so many questions as you
did, I think you got what you deserve. I dare you to print all
of it.

Paul's long letter conveyed more insight into the Whiteman organization of 1932 than Ring Lardner's actual story, which appeared
that summer. The importance of radio time—especially sponsored
time—grew as vaudeville died and record and sheet-music sales
slumped. In the fall, General Motors signed Paul to a full season
on its Buick show on Monday evenings over NBC. The beginning
broadcasts starred two radio favorites from the recent *Palmolive
Hour:* soprano Virginia Rea and tenor Frank Munn. They brought
a repertoire of more traditional music to the program with such
selections as "Songs My Mother Taught Me" by Dvorak, "Maidens
of Cadiz," and "El Relicario." Short and stocky Frank Munn,
weighing over 250 pounds as he sang at the mike, may have led
Pops to wonder if leanness was really so important.

The Buick show changed direction by the end of the year. It
brought back Whiteman's regular singers and augmented them with
guest performers—blues singer Lee Wiley, Phil Duey, and the
Pickens Sisters. The emphasis shifted to Broadway medleys and
current tunes and novelty numbers. It seemed that Paul was saving
the innovative, attention-getting numbers for the concert stage program he was arranging for November. And should another young
Gershwin emerge to make February 12, 1924, happen all over again,
so much the better.

Music publishers heard of Paul's forthcoming experiment in music
and began parading the works of their young staff writers before

him. Famous Music Corporation interested Paul in a highly talented twenty-year-old composer and pianist from Kansas City. A musical prodigy at the age of eight, Dana Suesse had been writing piano pieces and popular songs for several years. Her first big hit, in 1932, was "My Silent Love," based on her own "Jazz Nocturne." She occasionally made guest appearances on such radio variety shows as Rudy Vallee's *Fleischmann Hour.* In the eyes of Pops she had all the qualities of Gershwin—youth, creativity, genius, flair.

For Whiteman's Fourth Experiment in Modern American Music at Carnegie Hall, he commissioned Dana's *Concerto in Three Rhythms,* with the provision that the composer would also appear as the piano soloist. The program for this first major concert since 1928 was to include Grofé's *Grand Canyon Suite,* which Victor had recorded with Whiteman earlier in 1932; Ravel's *Bolero*; Roy Bargy's "Waltz Caprice"; three recent works by Gershwin—"I Got Rhythm," *An American in Paris,* and *Second Rhapsody*—and *American Concerto* by Michael Gusikoff, concertmaster of the New York Symphony.

Many in the audience considered Dana Suesse's concerto the most significant and worthwhile new work of the program. "Ideas abound in the composition," stated the New York *American,* "vital unique ideas—treated with unconventionality, shaped with tasteful form and saying something distinctive." Dana's work had life, held interest, and represented the best type of jazz writing. As a composer and pianist, she would be heard from again. Concertgoers and critics alike praised the courage and daring such concerts required from Paul. It was noted that his orchestra was the only current forum for new American concert music and that he was bringing a new sound to concert stages.

Whiteman and his orchestra returned to Carnegie Hall two and a half months later, on January 25, 1933, for his Fifth Experiment in Modern American Music. "One feature which should not be considered lightly," the program notes stated, "is the use of a new instrumentation and orchestration. . . . Change, addition, and improvement have come only as a result of innovation prompted by such efforts as these concerts."

John Green, with his commission to work on an important piece for the midwinter concert, mulled over what to compose. Several months earlier Whiteman had introduced his *Poem* concerto for piano and symphony. Now Green came up with the idea of using three pianos. Paul loved the suggestion.

"Don't you want to hear the rest?" he said to Pops. "Is it enough, it's going to be three pianos?"

"Let's just put the three pianos out in front of the orchestra," Whiteman replied, "and all take a bow. That'll be enough entertainment for them!"

Green proceeded to describe his new composition titled *Night Club*. It consisted of six impressions of a cabaret, from setting up the tables at 7:00 P.M. ("Linen and Silver"), through the arrival of patrons at 9:30 ("Ladies and Gentlemen") and the smoke-filled corner for two lovers at 10:00 ("Table for Two") to the champagne toast at 2:00 A.M. ("Corks and Bubbles"). Paul liked the theme and the blatantly programmatic music. It had flair, spontaneity, and rhythmic effects worthy of a Gershwin. The strident "Dance on a Dime," capturing the packed dance floor as the young lovers swayed with the crowd, even had possibilities as a song hit.

Ferde Grofé put together an equally ambitious work. *Tabloid— Four Pictures of a Modern Newspaper* attempted to capture the sounds associated with the newsroom and printing plant of a big-city paper. Grofé used a battery of actual typewriters and other real props, including revolvers, to carry off his novel and very modern composition. The audience, however, gave greater approval to a number earlier on the program—Ferde's increasingly familiar "On the Trail" from his *Grand Canyon Suite*.

Paul rounded his fifth venture into Carnegie Hall with Roy Bargy's arrangements of "Peanut Vendor" and "Liebestraum," Richard Rodgers's waltz interpretation of "Lover," and Victor Young's orchestration of "Valencia," along with the third movement of William Grant Still's *Africa* and Robert Braine's *Concerto in Jazz,* which had a violin solo by Josef Stopak. Nearly all the selections contained provocative segments and reaffirmed Whiteman's place as an innovator in American music and a showman with verve. Three pianos and a row of typewriters, no less!

The program, with some omissions, was repeated the following summer at an outdoor concert in New York's Lewisohn Stadium. Paul appeared as guest conductor with the New York Philharmonic, augmented by his own orchestra. New selections on the program included Duke Ellington's "Mood Indigo," Don Redman's "Chant of the Weed," and John Jacob Loeb's "Jazz Bolero." Once again the three pianos for John Green's *Night Club* surprised and delighted the audience.

What especially pleased Paul was the invitation to lead the famous Philharmonic. When he first saw the souvenir of the occasion—a large panoramic photograph of the orchestra and the record turnout of 18,000 people in the stadium—he immediately thought of the Professor back in Denver. He ordered a framed copy of the photo for the sunroom back at the Whiteman ranch.

Whiteman had much to celebrate by the end of 1933. Whereas many millions of Americans remained unemployed and business fell deeper in the doldrums, he and the band worked and made money.

In April the William Morris Agency had booked them into a variety road show, called *Nuts to You* with Jack Pearl, Cliff Hall, and the Boswell Sisters. It played one-nighters in Texas, Louisiana, Oklahoma, and Missouri. The revue settled into Chicago's Oriental Theatre for two weeks, where George Burns and Gracie Allen joined the line-up. In September Paul conducted the Metropolitan Opera Orchestra and his own at Madison Square Garden in a repeat of the Lewisohn Stadium concert. Pianist Dana Suesse and her *Concerto in Three Rhythms* replaced John Green's *Night Club* in the program, which consisted for the most part of works by Gershwin and Grofé.

In November, Paul assisted in the dedication of RCA's Radio City complex at Rockefeller Center. He conducted for Rudy Vallee, who sang "Under the Campus Moon," on an all-star broadcast from what was the world's largest radio auditorium, NBC's Studio 8-H. Listeners all over North America shared in the celebration of music and song led by Walter Damrosch, John McCormack, Maria Jeritza, Jessica Dragonette, Frank Munn, and the Schola Cantorum choir.

In December Paul and an augmented orchestra of seventy-five players gathered in the Metropolitan Opera House for the Sixth Experiment in Modern American Music. Four new compositions highlighted the program, a benefit for the Episcopal Church Mission of Help. Dana Suesse's *Eight Valses* for piano and orchestra again demonstrated her considerable accomplishments as a pianist and her valuable gifts as an extremely clever composer. One of the youngest members of the American Society of Composers, Authors, and Publishers (ASCAP), Dana contributed to the Whiteman repertoire throughout the 1930s.

William Grant Still created a suite of five pieces bound together by interludes of solo piano. *A Deserted Plantation* reaffirmed the Mississippi-born composer's skill in longer works and revealed the influence of Grofé's musical-picture approach.

The other two new numbers came from musicians—"Park Avenue Fantasy" by Matty Malneck and "Peter, Peter, Pumpkin Eater" by Al Rinker, who had gone back to vaudeville, where he developed an act with a young female singer. Both pieces had already been heard on the radio, but this was their first concert performance.

The greatest stroke of good fortune came in the form of Miracle Whip salad dressing. Kraft Phenix Cheese Company introduced the new product nationally in June. To bring it to the attention of millions of households, the company signed two of the biggest entertainers in show business—Al Jolson and Paul Whiteman. The program, soon to be known as the *Kraft Music Hall,* bowed with a two-hour broadcast from NBC's Times Square studio.

On radio for Kraft Paul played the father figure to a versatile stock company of performers. He was the man in the middle of the tremendously popular group and gave the show cohesiveness and direction. Naturally Jolson "stole" much of the premiere, contributing an emotional wallop and quality rarely heard on the air. He hit home with a narrative and dramatization knit around "Sonny Boy" and "A Singer on the Sabbath."

Pops was in fast company that night as he stood shoulder to shoulder with Jolson reading lines from a script. Every once in a while Paul would look up with a surprised grin, as if to say, "You son-of-a-gun, that's not on the paper!" Paul was slightly tense when he spoke his lines to introduce members of his orchestra. Deems Taylor, the musicologist and composer, assisted in describing such Whiteman concert selections as *Bolero, An American in Paris,* and "The Toreador Song" from *Carmen.* His annotations were brief, humorous, and quietly enlightening.

Paul's verbal stints at the mike did not come easy. Although he was an engaging and relaxed storyteller in private, a piece of paper in his hand tended to turn him into a mummy. The man who wrote the scripts, Carroll Carroll, whom Paul tagged "Mousie," coached him after every dress rehearsal. "He just was never comfortable with a script," Carroll observed. "Sometimes at the mike he sounded as if he had never seen the words before.

"After one broadcast in which he felt he'd 'acted' (that's what reading from a paper meant to Whiteman), after he'd talked better than usual and people were telling him what a good show he'd just put on, he threw his arm around my shoulders—which wasn't easy to do because my shoulders were about level with the middle stud on his dress shirt—and said, 'Mousie here taught me to talk.' "

Jolson made frequent guest appearances on the show during his first season before heading into his own series, *Shell Chateau*. After he left, vaudeville comedian Lou Holtz became a regular to give balance to the musical outpouring of Pops's featured vocalists and instrumentalists. By January 1934 the one-hour program ranked seventh in the comedy-variety line-up, the first three places going to Eddie Cantor and Rubinoff's orchestra, *Maxwell House Show Boat* with Lanny Ross and Don Voorhees's orchestra, and Rudy Vallee and his *Fleischmann Hour*, respectively.

The wide acceptance given to Whiteman's broad spectrum of music, from popular tunes and folk melodies to operetta favorites and concerto movements, allowed Paul to innovate and experiment. He could even successfully integrate operatic arias into the format of the *Kraft Music Hall*. When Madame Yvonne Gall of the Paris Opera visited the United States, he engaged her for many appearances; on most shows she sang not one selection, but two or three from such operas as *Manon* and *Madame Butterfly*.

In 1934 and 1935 Paul became more familiar with the pronunciation of operatic arias and composers. His discovery of a young and well-trained soprano with aspirations for a career in opera launched a Metropolitan Opera star.

Educated at the Curtis Institute in Philadelphia, Helen Jepson came to New York with her husband, George Possell, a flutist with several symphony and radio orchestras. She took voice lessons with Queena Mario, a well-known Met singer. But except for studio recitals, Helen had no opportunities to work at her profession. One day Possell asked Philip James, a conductor at station WOR, to give Helen a chance. James invited her to sing with the Bamberger Little Symphony, which he led. As a result NBC asked her to join the network as a staff singer on sustaining shows. But before the contract was actually signed, the radio department of the J. Walter Thompson advertising agency called her. Whiteman's guest soprano had laryngitis; did Helen know the well-known aria from *Butterfly?*

"I not only know it," Helen Jepson answered, "I'm on my way over."

Though she appeared on only one segment of one show, letters and telegrams immediately flooded the mail room. "I have never heard a soprano like her," Paul told everyone. "Her diction is perfect. She sings words as if she meant them. She has such warmth."

He immediately signed her to an eighteen-month contract to sing both serious and light music on his broadcasts.

"I was paid well and had lots of fun with Pops," Jepson remembered, "and every week we received plenty of cheese from the sponsor. Soon someone from the Met heard me on Paul's show and called Queena Mario to ask if I were up to Met standards. She insisted I was ready."

In January 1935 Helen made her debut at the Metropolitan Opera in the premiere of *In the Pasha's Garden* by American composer John Laurence Seymour. Seated in the balcony was the entire Whiteman orchestra, giving her the biggest ovation any new singer at the opera house had ever gotten. The work was poorly received, but Helen received good notices and went on to better-known operatic roles and a Met career that lasted into the 1940s.

The Whiteman "stock company" of players took its place as the foremost musical group of the 1930s. Only Fred Waring and his Pennsylvanians and Horace Heidt and his Musical Knights provided serious competition. Paul's ability to recognize outstanding talent and bring it into his organization was demonstrated time after time. He rarely missed with his discoveries, and he enjoyed finding and developing a new voice, a special instrumentalist, an unusual combo. The public, too, always seemed pleased and rewarded his latest choice with acclaim and a swift elevation up the ladder to stardom. Youth was a requisite, so that Paul might present the modern music to a young generation. Its interpretation required a young ensemble that brought youthful exuberance to the bandstand.

Paul found twenty-year-old Ramona Davies in Cincinnati in the spring of 1932. A tall and very attractive pianist with a good voice, she worked at station KDKA in Pittsburgh and with Don Bestor's orchestra. At seventeen she had married Howard Davies, a musician with Bestor. They were often apart when the band went on the road.

Paul immediately spotted Ramona's tremendous singing-pianist potential as he listened to her audition. He signed her to a two-year contract at $125 a week intending to team her with baritone Red McKenzie, billing them as Red and Ramona. A versatile stylist, she knew her way around the keys and was particularly adept at injecting distinctive "tricks" in the melody. What radio listeners missed, theater and nightclub audiences enjoyed—she was the most glamorous member of the troupe—and among the best liked. Ramona became one of the boys, clowning around, playing the baby grand and singing, and occasionally doubling on the celeste.

Jack Fulton acquired a singing partner when Peggy Healy joined in mid-1932. The new Rhythm Boys—George MacDonald, Al Dary, Ray Kulz, and Jimmy Noel—hardly measured up to the original trio. Baritone Bob Lawrence joined Paul after a Radio City audition. A petroleum technologist, he turned to singing at a Hartford, Connecticut, station when the Depression hit the construction field. Likable and attractive, with a distinctive, fine voice, Bob handled well the contrasting requirements of "The Last Roundup" and "The Toreador Song."

Pop singer John Hauser contributed a contemporary sound and look. A successful audition with Pops paid off with a contract at $75 a week. During his three years with Whiteman the young baritone worked the *Hit Parade* when Lucky Strike first offered radio listeners a run-through of the weekly top tunes.

Paul's troupe of vocalists worked well in various combinations on radio, recordings, and on the road.

Headstrong Mildred Bailey, however, had become sand in Pops's well-oiled machinery. Every three or four months Mildred and her manager came to Paul for more money. She was good for the band, and everyone knew it. But her demands never ceased. By 1932 Paul was paying her $350 a week, with NBC contributing an additional $600. At a time when a new car sold for $800 or less, Mildred wanted $2,000 a week. And when Paul was booked at the Paramount Theater for June, she wanted a big share of his take of $8,500. She believed that Pops's generous pay was in large part due to her show-stopping numbers.

Whiteman held firm and brought in young Sylvia Froos in place of the determined Bailey, and he hired Chicago blues singer Irene Taylor as backup. The Rockin' Chair Lady left Pops in a flurry of lawsuits against his organization and NBC. In 1933 she joined CBS as a sustaining performer.

"I didn't feud with Bails," Pops pointed out, "but she feuded with me. She didn't achieve success at first, but when she did, her demands were crazy."

Paul decided to put Lee Wiley on his program. She had had her own popular show with Leo Reisman's orchestra, but it lasted for only a season. The jazz-influenced vocalist contributed a distinctive sound to the Whiteman broadcasts.

In 1931, as a youngster in California, Durelle Alexander had tuned in Mildred Bailey and Whiteman. She never dreamed that four years later, on her sixteenth birthday, she would be singing with Pops in New York. With a natural voice with the texture and technique of the boop-boop-a-doop girl Helen Kane and little Shirley Temple, and the looks to match a Ginger Rogers and an Alice Faye, Durelle was very much the baby of the band.

While she was singing at the Park Central Hotel in New York during a spring recess from school, Archie Bleyer heard her and offered her a job with his orchestra. Though she wanted to finish high school back home, Bleyer suggested an audition for Pops, who was looking for a replacement for Peggy Healy. Paul liked her immediately and offered the usual $75 per week. The contract included appearances on the *Kraft Music Hall*. A spot on that coast-to-coast show convinced young Durelle Alexander to stay in Manhattan. Her mother remained with her—and she got her diploma by mail.

Paul had a very protective feeling for Durelle. Most of the band did, too. She wanted to reciprocate by sharing her good fortune. She was often willing to give up some of her own air time and numbers to others. When Paul heard this, he took her aside.

"You're too nice," he said. "You're not going to get anywhere in this business. You should fight to get all the songs you can get."

"So maybe I'll never go to the top," Durelle replied.

"Well, maybe you've got the right idea after all," Paul concluded. He'd seen how an obsession with success could affect a young performer's life for the worse.

In 1934, Paul picked up a foursome, sight unseen. His onetime saxophone player Don Clark had suggested that the quartet send a transcription of songs to Paul. Ken Darby, Bud Linn, Rad Robinson, and Jon Dodson, Californians all, had met in college, and joined together for campus shows, club dates, and movie roles. In 1930 they were staff singers at station KFWB on the old Warner Brothers lot and working with the Boswell Sisters. They called themselves the King's Men after station manager Jerry King.

Whiteman liked the transcription, and he told Jack Lavin to go to work and handle the rest. Lavin wrote to Ken Darby, explaining

the heavy overhead the band carried. "You, of course, know that
as far as the East is concerned, no one is in a better position than
Whiteman to get your organization into important money." A telephone call cemented a five-year agreement for a weekly $100 per
man and allowing for additional outside fees from recording dates
and radio appearances.

On July 28 the cross-country travelers arrived in New York at
the doorstep of Donald Novis, a fellow Californian and radio tenor.
The next morning Paul's secretary called to tell them to be downtown at Radio City where Paul was rehearsing for his Kraft show.
As they entered the large studio, he and his new staff arranger and
composer, Adolph Deutsch, were arguing about a certain bar with
five beats in it.

"Who's there?" Paul asked, turning toward the back of the studio.

"Here's the quartet you bought, Mr. Whiteman," Ken replied.

"Come on. Let's hear what you can do."

Paul escorted them into a tiny studio across the hall. Deutsch
and Ramona listened from the control booth. Paul also alerted the
head of NBC and had the quartet's vocalizing piped into all the
business offices in the network headquarters. They sang popular
tunes, folk songs, old favorites, some of which they had not planned
on. At the end of forty minutes the door opened and Whiteman
came in whistling, then said, "You aint' much to look at, but you
cowpokes can put it together with the notes. We'll get you on the
Music Hall next week and a sustainer, too. But right now run over
to Saks Fifth Avenue and buy white suits for the summer. Stop by
the Biltmore Roof tonight for dinner. You all need to be fattened
up."

That night Paul introduced the King's Men to his audience at the
Biltmore, and they sang a couple of songs. The crowd stomped and
cheered for an encore. Paul beamed, and there was a flicker of
pride in his eyes. All Ken Darby could say to his companions was,
"This must be some crazy, beautiful dream."

In short order Darby—alias Joe Lyrics to Paul—organized an
octet to back baritone Bob Lawrence, assisted Bargy at the piano,
substituted for Goldie on the trumpet, and arranged and wrote music
for his foursome. The quartet also popped up on three other radio
programs—as the Red Norsemen on the *Flying Red Horse Tavern*,
King's Guard on the *Asporub Show,* and King's Merry Men with

Ed Wynn. Their flair for pure harmony in a subdued manner gave their listeners a pleasant interlude.

Working for Paul often meant getting only five hours' sleep a night for months at a time. The band played far into the night and sometimes continued playing until the next day. There was lots to do beside the regular job—radio programs, guest appearances, record sessions, charity events, private parties, and any number of unscheduled appearances here and there. In summer the pace often increased. One July, Paul signed up the gang to work three hours a day, seven days a week in Manhattan Beach, with a tiresome journey back and forth from the city. In the depth of the Depression, the extra bucks for a full week at the beach pavilion did not equal the amount they were formerly paid for recording one side of a record, which often required no more than one hour to cut.

In spite of hard work, plenty of sidemen vied for a chair with Pops. Instrumentalists kept an ear tuned to personnel changes. When Andy Secrest left in 1933, trumpeter Bunny Berigan stepped in. He flourished, albeit briefly, on the Whiteman bandstand as a high-powered brass soloist. A first-class technician, he left for Abe Lyman's orchestra and staff jobs at CBS before joining Benny Goodman. Berigan organized his own band in 1937, scoring big with the enduring "I Can't Get Started with You."

Harpist Casper Reardon made frequent appearances with Whiteman, most notably on recordings of "Deep Forest" and "Serenade to a Wealthy Widow." A pioneer to bringing jazz and the harp together, Reardon had been with the Cincinnati Symphony and taught at the Cincinnati Conservatory of Music. He recorded with an all-star jazz group led by Jack Teagarden, another one of Pops's recruits in late 1933.

One of the greatest trombone soloists in the jazz field, Teagarden joined Bill Rank and Jack Fulton in that section of the brasses. Paul wanted Big T in his outfit, and Jack Lavin drew up a contract at $150 a week. Teagarden was tired of playing on the road with Mal Hallett, and his bank account was nearly depleted. Whiteman's offer was tempting. "I'll get my horn," he said to Lavin. "Tell Rank to warm a seat for me."

His wife Claire spoke up. "Let's see the contract first."

At Lavin's office at the Park Central Hotel, Teagarden studied the contract. Then his wife read it through. "It's tighter than a new pair of shoes," she said. "And it's for five years."

"Paul wants it that way," Lavin injected. "Says it takes that long to break a man in."

"Five years," Jack muttered. "That's a future."

"So's the salary," said Lavin.

A month after Big T's arrival, another Teagarden from Vernon, Texas, was signed up. Twenty-year-old Charlie Teagarden, known as Little T, left the orchestra pit of Broadway's *As Thousands Cheer* and took Bunny Berigan's chair on trumpet. The brothers added significantly to the jazz vernacular of the Whiteman organization, and Pops, who had managed to retain Trumbauer from the Bix days, once more had the nucleus of a real jazz unit. The band featured Jack on Fats Waller's "Ain't Misbehavin' " and Johnny Mercer's "Fare Thee Well to Harlem," on both of which he also sang. Charlie performed a Bix-like trumpet solo on "Announcer's Blues" and held his own on "Pardon My Southern Accent," another Mercer tune. As the Three Ts, Charlie, Jack, and Trumbauer blew their hot licks within the Whiteman aggregation and especially after hours in such New York clubs as the Hickory House.

The addition of these singers and instrumentalists, most of whom Paul had signed to contracts with management clauses to farm them out for extra engagements and bookings, required an increase in Paul's staff. Margaret exerted a growing influence in the business affairs of the organization, working closely with Jack Lavin. Together with Paul, the two officially formed an artists' management firm to handle as many of the Whiteman performers as would agree to it. Paul had noted before their marriage that Maggie knew how to make money grow; now she could do her magic for Pops.

Paul disliked paperwork and record keeping. Margaret seemed well-suited to this chore, and Paul gladly turned over the books, files, and payroll to his business-minded wife. She relished the role, bringing a much-needed measure of efficiency to the organization. Margaret's streamlining changes eliminated a job-by-job breakdown of payments for each band member. Each now received a blanket check for his or her services for a set period. A few musicians complained, and some felt cheated by Margaret and her methods, but Paul backed her down the line, and he was still the boss. Several musicians questioned his authority and went to court over the matter. They won. Whiteman was ordered to pay out approximately $10,000 to his musicians for past services.

Trumpet player Teddy Bartell and Margaret clashed frequently, yet at one point Paul assigned him the key post of payroll assistant. One day in the late 1930s Bartell went to the office to pick up the checks for distribution. A secretary told him, "Mrs. Whiteman hasn't signed them yet; she's at the beauty parlor."

"Listen," Bartell answered, "when Mr. Whiteman gives a downbeat, we don't go out to the barber shop!"

Not long after, when Bartell reminded Paul of his promise to double Bartell's salary, Margaret had the last word. She had him fired.

16

Podiums, Premieres, and Pullmans

At the end of 1933 Wilberforce and Elfrida Whiteman celebrated their fiftieth wedding anniversary. To mark this great occasion, Paul persuaded his parents to come to New York for a holiday and family reunion. He arranged their visit to coincide with his concert of modern American music at the Metropolitan Opera House on December 15. The Professor and his wife spent a leisurely vacation in the city. At the special Whiteman program the couple was seated in a box in the Met's fabled Diamond Horseshoe as Paul conducted.

Following the concert, Wilberforce joined his son at the new Paradise Restaurant, where Paul had recently opened. Anticipating the repeal of Prohibition, the nightclub booked a lavish floor show with Paul's band. To create a continental atmosphere emphasizing female beauty, producer N. T. Granlund was hired. He spent $8,000 a week on showgirls and musicians. He presented Miss America of 1931 and the dramatic dancer Felicia Sorel. One of the most startling acts featured a sylphlike nude dancing behind a translucent scrim as Paul and the boys played "Zigeuner" or "Love for Sale." From a glittering auditorium of sedate musicians to a smoke-filled pleasure dome of exotic dancers, it was a night to remember for the old Professor.

Before the Whitemans boarded the train back to Denver, Paul told them of his plans for more special concert programs and a competition for young composers in 1934. He and the orchestra would also be appearing at the Brooklyn Academy of Music in an Enjoyment of Music series with commentary by Olin Downes, music critic of *The New York Times*. Paul and the orchestra would illustrate the theme, "The Significance of American Popular Music." The lecture with music scheduled for January 7, marked the first time jazz had been presented on the Academy stage and marked the tenth anniversary of the first presentation of jazz as an art form in a concert hall—Paul's 1924 Aeolian Hall concert.

Following his acclaimed appearance with the Philharmonic Orchestra in New York, other major symphonies approached Paul to appear with their musicians. He agreed to travel to Cincinnati for a huge benefit concert for the relief of unemployed Cincinnati musicians. On March 6, 1934, eleven members of the band and Paul joined several hundred musicians under the direction of Eugene Goossens, the conductor. Paul led the third part of the program, when his men joined the 125 members of the Cincinnati Symphony in the familiar line-up of selections—"Park Avenue Fantasy," "Valencia," "I Got Rhythm," "A Deserted Plantation," "Wabash Blues," *Rhapsody in Blue,* and a movement from Grofé's *Tabloid.* The newer pieces included Frank Trumbauer's "Bouncing Ball" and "Waltzing Through the Ages," arranged by Adolph Deutsch.

At one of the rehearsals a string bass player from the Cincinnati Orchestra was requested to "slap" the strings, a method called for in one of the syncopated scores. Job or no job, he walked off the stage, refusing to prostitute his art by inflicting such an indignity on his instrument. When the incident received widespread publicity, his professional life took a decidedly commercial twist, and he ended up happily slapping his bass in a New York nightclub.

Paul's search for new young American composers made headlines when he announced the Whiteman Scholarship for the best musical composition in a modern form. Professional or amateur musicians who were American citizens and under thirty were invited to submit works. Each entry had to be scored for orchestra; piano copies were not accepted. The award was a year's study at a musical conservatory. Paul explained his reasons.

I have tried for many years to put American music on a definite plane—one apart from the raucous and blatant jazz that characterized the Tin Pan Alley product of the period.

I believe that an orchestra is no greater than the material it plays. Many symphony conductors can attain prominence because they are able to express themselves by their selections.

Their libraries are huge and go back some centuries, but we in modern music have been handicapped because of the scarcity of available material. Perhaps it has been our fault; perhaps the rewards have been too slim and the possibility of fame too slight to encourage the composer to labor long over a musical brainchild that could do nothing but bring him inspirational and emotional satisfaction. We have done nothing to insure a future for American music.

Paul hoped to endow the scholarship fund for at least five years. When he made the announcement, he had no idea that the prize would be linked with his mother and her influence on his career.

Three weeks after Paul's engagement with the Cincinnati Symphony, Elfrida suffered a paralytic stroke. Seriously ill for days, she had regained some strength by mid-April. Paul and Margaret flew to Denver to visit her on her sixty-eighth birthday. But a week later her condition took an unfavorable turn; she remained in critical condition as spring turned to summer. On Sunday, June 24, the Professor telephoned both Ferne and Paul to tell them that the end was near. Ferne arrived from St. Louis late the following day. Paul, accompanied by Margaret and Paul, Jr., was stopping briefly in Chicago on Tuesday morning. There word reached him of Elfrida's death at Denver's Presbyterian Hospital.

To honor his mother's memory, Paul called his new musical award the Elfrida Whiteman Scholarship. During 1934 hundreds of young composers began working on entries for submission early the following year.

Paul's summer engagement at the Biltmore and his weekly broadcast at Radio City did not allow for an extended period of mourning. It was work as usual and as soon as possible. Paul also had agreed to join other leading radio conductors in an effort to keep songs with suggestive titles and lyrics off the air. Rudy Vallee, Richard Himber, Guy Lombardo, Abe Lyman, and Paul formed the Committee of Five for the Betterment of Radio. The self-imposed review board was chiefly intent on avoiding possible censorship from outside and preventing any extension to radio of the "clean film" crusade against sexually suggestive and morally repugnant segments in motion pictures. The group met each Friday to monitor all the songs published during the week. When a song was found objectionable, the publisher was asked to revise it. If he refused, the number was included in a list of black-balled songs that was mailed to orchestra leaders who were broadcasting throughout the country. The committee expected a national change in the quality and decency of songs on the air within two or three months.

Paul felt that there was an urgent need for improvement of radio by broadcasters themselves before the FCC or other agencies came in and restricted material. "It has been proven in the theater and motion picture business that clean shows have always attained a greater success from a box-office standpoint and have survived longer in popular favor than anything that has been off-color," he stated. "Radio has been quite strict during its young life about the quality of broadcasting, but now and then obnoxious things creep in. I feel it is to the advantage of all concerned in the radio world that a committee of this sort function to maintain high standards consistently." Of course very few radio listeners had heard Paul's creative use of four-letter words or his off-color stories. If they had, his role as a monitor of objectionable songs would have ended right there.

Whenever the New York commitments of the Whiteman organization eased, Jack Lavin and Paul mapped out a short road tour. For the most part the days of extended travel across the country had ended when the band's radio shows anchored them in Manhattan. But a week or two of traveling on trains and buses to the hinterlands kept Whiteman before a "live" audience. Movie theaters continued to book Paul and several acts for presentation between film showings. Dance halls and auditoriums sought the band for one-nighters, and business and trade conventions lined up the band for special dates. Most of the time Paul played to a full or nearly full house. When the audience failed to materialize, it was unusual enough to stick in everyone's mind. A dance at a lakeside inn in Wisconsin on a cool summer night attracted only three couples. The manager wanted his money back, but Paul insisted on playing for the full tariff.

Chair cars and Pullmans provided accommodations for the long jumps from city to city, but not much sleep for the gang. "Survival became the primary pursuit," recalled Charlie Strickfaden of his twelve years on the road with Paul, when more than five hours' sleep a night seemed luxurious. "Oddly enough, everyone held up remarkably well. Even if a serious fever or a chest cold developed, we still managed to play the shows. Paul was concerned, but he pointed out that each individual part of every arrangement was unique and indispensable to the whole, and that one missing voice marred the entire performance. He also made it clear that no other musician (without adequate rehearsal) could step in and fill any chair properly, even though the notes were there to read. So the show went on.''

The complexion of the traveling musician—Pullman pallor—was identifiable at a hundred yards. Usually these travelers found themselves next to a window at a time when the passing scene was lit, not by sunlight, but by the moon. Night after night the view revealed scattered farmhouses, dew-mantled fields, and, in winter, glimmering snowdrifts. It was a haunting frustration to Strickfaden in the 1930s to be constantly reminded that people out there in the night were remaining in one place, sleeping in beds, staying close to home and fireside with wives and children, and never having to catch a train or leap from city to city and scramble after luggage. Strickfaden expressed this one night to Paul, who replied, "Think, Charlie: don't you suppose those farmers watch the trains go by and envy the travelers? It's just as frustrating to them to be stuck in one spot when everybody around is going someplace. Frustration, like money, has no home.''

Mischief tended to brighten the gloom of night. Sleeping colleagues were often the prime target. Their shoelaces would be set on fire, a red-hot penny would be placed where the leather was thin. Both yanked the snoozer out of sleep with a yelp. A feather attached to a strand of hair would sooner or later block a snorer's nose, and bets would be laid on the length of time it would take to bring on the inevitable sneeze. Others would find slices of rubber in their ham sandwich or a trick violin smashed to splinters inside an expensive case.

One night Norman McPherson, a tuba player, fell asleep in a chair seat, and with the help of Jack Teagarden, Paul proceeded to dismantle the large instrument resting next to Mac. Piece by piece, tube by tube, the tuba was scattered all over the railroad car. Many parts were tossed from player to player in a zany game of catch. When McPherson woke up and spotted the wreckage, he nearly went into shock; many of the pieces were lost or bent beyond repair. The horseplay cost Paul the price of one new tuba.

Mike Pingitore always favored an upper berth—his lucky number five—in spite of the fact that he was very short and had a crippled leg. Night after night the boys boosted him up into his sleeping accommodations. During one Pullman trip Mike decided not to bother his companions, who were in the club car. Instead he crawled into an empty and unreserved lower berth in the band car. As the train sped through the darkness, it plowed into a horse-drawn dray. In the course of the two-hour delay during which railroad crews, police officers, and medical aides cleared the tracks, someone noticed that Mike was not in his customary berth. The gang later attributed the accident to Mike's switch in sleeping arrangements; if he had been in his usual berth, everyone agreed, the accident would not have happened. More superstitious than ever, Mike never again deviated from his magic Pullman berth.

On another occasion the train was slowly crossing an inundated bridge, where even the rails were submerged. Paul's train made it, but the very next train broke through the bridge and plunged into the raging waters.

Several musicians had a tendency to create instant relationships with local people, and they attempted to bring them along on a train. Paul had repeatedly announced that anybody who brought a woman on the train was out of the band.

But Jack Teagarden, for one, often trod on thin ice with his antics. At bedcheck one night Paul discovered him in the last car with a young woman.

"Jack, get her off the train at the next stop," he ordered.

Teagarden did so.

"Haven't I told you again and again not to bring women into the train? What happened this time?"

"It was an accident, Pops. She came down to see me off. I waved good-bye but just happened to turn my hand around, and it signaled a 'come aboard.' "

A 1934 New Year's Eve booking at the Mount Royal Hotel took the troupe to Montreal. Charlie Strickfaden, indefatigable chronicler of the organization, compared the train trip with an earlier one in 1924. He provided this and other unusual insights into the orchestra in a regular column, "The Whiteman Bandwagon," published in *Orchestra World* during the mid-1930s.

In 1924, Charlie observed, "parched throats thirstily looked forward to Montreal as an oasis in a desert of prohibition." Before the last curtain call there would be a stampede for hats and coats, leading to a hasty exit and speedy advance upon those establishments dispensing bottled goods. "Big beer busts marked the after-concert recreation hours. Ale flowed from large bottles and kindled the fires of alcoholic friendship."

On the return train nearly everyone cleverly deposited choice bottles of liquor in those parts of the car least likely to be searched. "The ventilators near the ceiling were crammed full, the springs under the seats were sagging, and even the water coolers hid bottles. No one risked hiding anything in his luggage. Smug smiles of innocence greeted the customs agents as all obligingly stood up with opened luggage."

The luggage, of course, was disregarded, but the hiding places unerringly drew the agents. Seats gave up their costly bottles, ventilators once more allowed the passage of air, and even water flowed freely in the coolers. "Not a bottle remained undiscovered, not a suitcase was inspected, and not a smile remained."

A decade later the art of large-scale elbow bending had been lost; worship of Bacchus was confined to a small cult in the band. Instead, the musicians of 1934 spent their free moments in sports of all kinds. In Montreal, with the temperature ten degrees below zero, Paul hired a horse-drawn sleigh to carry him, Santa Claus-style, up Mount Royal. Most of the performers climbed up under their own power. Skiing, skating, and romping on snow and ice triumphed over the earlier emphasis on elbow bending. "Another remarkable comparison between the old times and the new lies in the choice of merchandise brought back to the States. Nearly everyone bought heavy woolen blankets, perhaps anticipating a poor year in the music business."

By the mid-1930s, when the more direct and less expensive buses had increasingly taken the place of trains, a good bit of glamour fell by the wayside. The gang piled into the vehicle at a very late hour of the night. Most were tired and quickly fell asleep. A choice bed was the luggage shelf that ran around the ceiling, offering the distinct advantage of six feet of unblocked horizontal space for the lucky one who claimed it first. But often a pair of wide-awake talkers kept everyone from anything more than fitful dozing.

During a particular post-midnight trip someone walked down the bus aisle for a bit of exercise, then swore and turned around and walked back toward his seat. As he passed Charlie Teagarden, he said, "Hey, Charlie, you better go look at your brother."

"What for?"

"Jack's down in the stairwell by the driver. He was in the front seat and slid down toward the door and rolled into a ball. No one can open the door to get in or out."

Charlie went up front, then came back and sat down.

"Aren't you goin' to pick him up?"

"Hell, no! He's comfortable there."

During another journey in the middle of the night Mike, who always sat right behind the bus driver and rarely ever closed his eyes, saved the entire troupe from possible injury. The driver fell asleep at the wheel, and the bus drifted off the dark mountain road. Mike, who instantly realized what was happening, grabbed the wheel. He turned the bus back on the roadway, jolting the driver out of his slumber and back to his job.

Competition on the road had also grown keener by the mid-1930s. Other bands took to traveling, acquiring reputations and audiences that nibbled at Paul's popularity.

These groups generally were led by men younger than Whiteman. Some of these newcomers, such as the Mike Riley–Eddie Farley band, mounted the bandstand full of tricks and gimmicks. In full view of the audience they juggled their instruments, flourished in unison to the left and right, and performed dance steps while playing. Paul maintained his status quo, but after several concerts in the Midwest, where audiences reacted with disappointment and surliness to the excess dignity of the Whiteman orchestra, he gave these gimmicks a try. If some popular traveling outfits were making "the music go round and round" in a display of gymnastics, he would also go with it.

The band swung to the left, jogged to the right, tipped back and forth playing to the ceiling, and tossed its instruments back and forth in time to the beat. But when Paul earned laughs instead of applause, he realized that he was making a fool of himself and of the entire outfit. Audiences were offended, too; they did not expect acrobatics at Whiteman concerts. Since Pops could not imitate the flashier bands in this manner, he gave up trying. And he was rewarded by the realization that none of the others could imitate him.

While casting about for new ideas and talents, he stayed in his groove as a founder of a certain established style and approach. Through countless changes in musical trends his orchestra remained busy and popular. Yet he never allowed the groove to become a rut. And one way to keep out of the rut was to expose his organization to both the farflung hinterlands and the metropolitan mainstream.

To keep the customers coming back to the Biltmore, Paul and the band held special weekly events. During 1934 he invited guest entertainers to come on the bandstand. When Latin American music caught the attention of dancers, he brought in bandleader-composer Enric Madriguera. He also welcomed his former rival, Vincent Lopez. Numerous guest artists appeared that year. Pops next organized a homecoming gathering for those who had worked under his baton and were in New York. Lennie Hayton, Willie Hall, and Fud Livingston returned to pay their respects to Pops. It was the beginning of a popular and nostalgic feature of countless Whiteman programs on the bandstand, on radio, and later on television.

Paul made a great effort to introduce his latest recordings at the Biltmore and on the *Kraft Music Hall*. The band maintained its popularity among record buyers, although sales came nowhere near the pre-1930 totals. Nevertheless, the results of the nine sessions Victor scheduled during 1934 were impressive.

The orchestra, augmented by Dana Suesse, recorded Peter De Rose's "Deep Purple" after Whiteman had introduced the instrumental. Its popularity led Mitchell Parish to write lyrics for the melody, which was continuously requested. Paul devoted a twelve-inch disc to selections from Cole Porter's *Anything Goes*. In the absence of original cast albums, this programming sold well for years. Paul's versions of "Smoke Gets in Your Eyes" and "Wagon Wheels," with vocals by Bob Lawrence, hit the best-seller charts in the winter of 1934 during a bitterly cold spell, when temperatures in New York dipped to a record eighteen degrees below zero. In all, Paul recorded over forty sides from January to December 1934. Among the big bandleaders, not even Rudy Vallee and his Connecticut Yankees surpassed Whiteman's output that year.

In December 1934 Paul's friends in the music business met to plan a special week-long celebration in March to mark the twentieth anniversary of Paul's debut as a bandleader. Actually he had been conducting for eighteen or nineteen years, but Richard Himber, whose orchestra was playing at the Ritz Carlton and on radio as the Studebaker Champions, wanted to organize the Whiteman week for 1935. The unusual tribute ended with a banquet at prize fighter Jack Dempsey's new restaurant on Broadway. Rudy Vallee, acting as toastmaster, presented Paul with a gold crown to symbolize his long reign as "King of Jazz." Such fellow artists as Dempsey, Fred Waring, Lou Holtz, Ray Noble, Ozzie Nelson, and Helen Jepson participated. During the celebration Chicago bandleaders Wayne King, Jan Garber, and Kay Kyser broadcast special tributes to the durable Pops. That city's acclaim during Whiteman week encouraged Paul to return there for two concerts with his radio troupe at the Auditorium Theatre.

That spring hundreds of entries in the Whiteman scholarship competition piled up in Jack Lavin's office. Dozens and dozens of compositions were weeded out, but stacks of scores remained for the judges to hear. Adolph Deutsch ran through them and played excerpts before the selection committee of Deems Taylor, George Gershwin, Edwin Franko Goldman, and Robert A. Simon, Jr.

"I never heard so much shit in my life," Gershwin later remarked. "Then suddenly there came that opening sound of the 'Sinfonietta,' and we couldn't believe our ears. We wanted to know immediately who wrote it, and in anticipation we tore off the envelope to reveal the name."

On June 13 the judges announced that nineteen-year-old David Diamond, a native of Rochester, New York, and a student of Roger Sessions in Manhattan, had won the coveted prize for *Sinfonietta,* a twenty-minute work inspired by Carl Sandburg's poem, "Good Morning, America." Few young composers needed the tuition and weekly stipend more than Diamond. He attended classes eight hours a day at the Dalcroze Institute, where he also mopped floors every morning, and he worked at a drugstore on Ninety-Sixth Street and Broadway from ten-thirty to three every night. He was near a physical breakdown. The Whiteman scholarship and gold medal brought him widespread recognition in the music world and sorely needed money for living expenses. He continued his studies with Sessions, quit his tedious jobs, and moved from a room at the YMHA to an apartment in Greenwich Village.

"I could not have gone on with further study in 1935 without winning the competition," Diamond stated. "The scholarship continued for over a year, and led to collaborating with E. E. Cummings on a ballet in Paris and study there with Nadia Boulanger. Being a recipient of the Whiteman award was a happy experience. I met many fascinating people, including George Gershwin and Oscar Levant. I never knew until I became friends with George that composers did not have to orchestrate their own works."

David Diamond's career progressed quickly. But he came to view his *Sinfonietta* as juvenile and withdrew it from public performances in the late 1930s. He later won a Guggenheim Fellowship, worked on films and radio, and taught at the Manhattan School of Music and Juilliard while writing dozens of important instrumental works.

Whiteman premiered *Sinfonietta* at Philadelphia's Robin Hood Dell in June 1935. Diamond did not actually hear the first performance, only a final rehearsal. "I was amazed at how well Paul would read new compositions," he remembered. "I observed him at work with a Roy Harris piece years later and was impressed at how he handled such works. He knew music."

The Robin Hood Dell concert aided the pension fund of the Philadelphia Orchestra, and once again Paul conducted the combined groups of musicians. Most musicologists consider this joint concert the seventh in Paul's series of experiments in modern American music. Many of the numbers were new and were selected for musical innovation and importance. At one time or another Paul supported benefits by donating the services of his men and conducting without a fee in Boston, New York, Washington, St. Louis, and Cleveland.

Along with David Diamond's prize-winning piece, Paul conducted the first performance of Ken Darby's *Ebony Suite* (in the retrospective words of Darby, "a synthetic piece of jungle nonsense") and Walter Freed's *Impressions* (which had taken second place in the Elfrida Whiteman competition). Other lively and novel selections included Adolph Deutsch's arrangement of "Tales from the Vienna Woods," Clay Boland's "Havana," Ken Hopkins's "Chinatown," and Van Phillips's "Thank You, Mr. Bach." The concert, which shattered all previous attendance records at the Dell, led to a return engagement that same summer.

On July 29, Whiteman set a record when 9,100 Philadelphians heard one of his longest programs—twenty-six selections, plus an encore. Paul was breezily at home at the amphitheater with an audience that was obviously all his even before he appeared on stage. The first half of the concert featured works by Grofé, Malneck, Still, and De Rose. The second part spotlighted the Whiteman troupe. Outstanding were the King's Men, harmonizing on "Old MacDonald Had a Farm" and a parody of the quartet from *Rigoletto*; Ramona, accompanying herself on "You're a Builder Upper"; Jack Teagarden and Johnny Hauser, joining forces on "Fare Thee Well to Harlem"; and Durelle Alexander, chirping "You're the Top."

Pops's long-range hope of returning to the movies also became a reality that summer. Five years after *The King of Jazz,* he signed a contract with Fox to appear with the band in a Dick Powell musical. The agreement called for a specialty number as well as recording and plugging the entire score by Arthur Johnston and Gus Kahn. No lengthy and lucrative junket to Hollywood this time around; the band crossed the Queensboro Bridge to the Astoria, Long Island, studios, where Fox shot the number "Belle of New Orleans" for the Darryl F. Zanuck film titled *Thanks a Million.* One of fifty-two musicals filmed that year, the production matched crooner Dick Powell with humorist Fred Allen, violinist David Rubinoff, actress Ann Dvorak, and comedienne Patsy Kelly.

Paul and the band appeared as themselves, strikingly dressed in white tails with black shirts. Ramona at the baby grand and the King's Men were on camera to their best advantage. On the film's release in November, *The New York Times* tagged it "superior fun." An amusing political lampoon in which Powell, an unknown singer, seeks a radio career by running for governor, *Thanks a Million* easily emerged as a "happy success for Fred Allen as the campaign manager in this, his movie, debut."

In early 1935 Billy Rose, the Broadway producer and lyricist, returned to New York after a trip to Europe. His Music Hall restaurant-nightclub had recently failed, and he was poking around for new ideas to embody his theatrical showmanship. A musical play about a circus he had seen in Europe gave the onetime stenographer and songwriter the impetus for a New York production— *Jumbo,* one of the most elaborate shows ever produced on Broadway.

Rose hired Ben Hecht and Charles MacArthur to write "the biggest musical extravaganza in the history of the world." John Murray Anderson and George Abbott came in as directors. Richard Rodgers and Larry Hart were engaged to write the music and lyrics, Raoul Pène du Bois was asked to design the costumes, and Albert Johnson did the scenery. Only New York's biggest theater could hold the grandiose and expensive production Billy Rose had in mind. The old Hippodrome on Forty-Third Street and Sixth Avenue was leased, and its interior was transformed into an amphitheater. A large circus ring took the place of the orchestra seats, and seating was terraced in a circle around it. A runway was constructed to bring circus equipment and animals up from the basement into the ring.

The planning and preparation took many months and scads of money. One evening all the backstage key people met in Rose's office, where they went over the entire show for a young man and his sister. Thus, in one audition only, John Hay Whitney and his sister, Mrs. Joan Payson, became the principal angels of *Jumbo*.

With unbounded energy and enthusiasm and plenty of bucks, Rose lined up an enormous cast of show people and animals led by Jimmy Durante. For a romantic vocal duo he signed Donald Novis and Gloria Grafton. And for circus bandmaster he brought in the jumbo of jazz, Paul Whiteman.

The cast and crew rehearsed all through the summer of 1935. The many setbacks and mishaps at rehearsals postponed the opening several times. Aerial artists practiced on high wires while, below, animal trainers put a small menagerie through its paces. A chorus of thirty-six men, coached by Charles Henderson, worked through arrangements and then played roles as circus roustabouts. Clowns and bareback riders practiced their acts while Whiteman's musicians studied Rodgers and Hart's "My Romance," "The Most Beautiful Girl in the World," "Little Girl Blue," and "The Circus Is on Parade." And, of course, the biggest star of the show, Jumbo the elephant, had to be primed and rehearsed.

Finally, after ten weeks of dress rehearsals, *Jumbo* opened on November 16 as a benefit for Mrs. William Randolph Hearst's Milk Fund. A dazzling endeavor, the show became the talk of all New York overnight and settled in for a six-month run with daily matinees and evening performances at a top of $4.40.

Paul was an integral part of the show from the opening fanfare to the grand finale. A circus parade jolted the audience to attention. Led by the Whiteman musicians dressed in blue and gold uniforms and a calliope wagon drawn by four white horses, the procession weaved its way into the center arena. Wearing a white uniform and boots and a shako trimmed in gold, Paul rode on stage astride a high-stepping white stallion named Popcorn. Wielding a drum major's baton, he circled the ring and came to a halt in the center spotlight. As the audience applauded, Popcorn kneeled, took a bow, and struggled hesitantly to rise up under the extra weight of Paul's costume. The formally attired first-night audience witnessed an extra added attraction from Popcorn. After the bow at center stage, Popcorn slowly turned his back to the audience, lifted his tail, and committed a nuisance.

During the early weeks of the show Popcorn followed the script.

As Paul and the animal became more secure in the routine, they would accelerate the pace of the first-act retreating procession toward the exit. Paul became adept enough to thump his heels into Popcorn's ribs, encouraging the horse to move just fast enough to spur the musicians into a quickstep. Many times Paul's men and the rest of the cast ended up running off in an undignified fashion.

Paul liked to show off whenever some of his old pals were in the audience. For William S. Hart, the cowboy movie star, Paul made a couple of extra loops around the ring before discovering that the stage manager had closed the exit gate. Paul had to keep on looping a half-dozen times more. Hart, who thought the circling was all enthusiastically part of the show, yelled out "Ride 'em cowboy!"

Jumbo was fun for everyone. Durante and Paul carried on a friendly feud as to which one was the true star of the show. One day Paul persuaded the painters to redo his dressing room with twenty or more big stars dotting the walls. "Hey, Jimmy, get a load of this! Now we know who's the star of the show."

Jimmy refused to give in. When Paul went on stage that night, Durante added photographs of himself staring from the center of every star in Paul's dressing room.

To many people the real star of the show was Rosie, the elephant. Paul developed an affection for the animal and regularly fed her Cracker Jacks. "She'd eat the whole box, prize and all," Paul recalled. "She'd lift me up onto her back, and sometimes we'd snooze together. We were great buddies."

Paul's childlike and impudent antics were encouraged by the circus atmosphere. Between appearances Paul would pass a caged lion, and almost every time he would indulge in a game to prove that he was quicker than the big beast. To attract the attention of those standing about, Paul would reach in and slap the lion's rump. The big cat would turn angrily to swat Paul's hastily withdrawn hand. Fools and children emerge unscathed. Paul never once suffered a scratch. When one of his musicians tried the same trick by poking the full length of his saxophone between the bars, the lion succeeded in crushing the shiny instrument beyond recognition.

One night the entire band lost its instruments in another incident. While the musicians were parading around the ring, several men climbed twelve feet up the ladder leading to their stand and made a clean haul of the musical instruments. Luckily, most of them were recovered at pawn shops later.

For 233 peformances Whiteman and the gang participated in an unprecedented and exciting mixture of carnival, circus, and spectacle. Billy Rose, a pint-sized Barnum, gave New Yorkers the biggest extravaganza in the city's history. *Jumbo* had no successors along Broadway or in the Hippodrome. When the show closed in 1936, the wreckers moved in to demolish the mammoth theater. The show ended an era of large-scale entertainment for millions of theatergoers.

A month before *Jumbo* rode into town, Gershwin's *Porgy and Bess* bowed to mixed notices, ultiately chalking up a run only half as long as the Billy Rose production. An opening-night party given by composer Kay Swift and publisher Condé Nast at his New York penthouse attracted the cream of business and society. Paul and the orchestra played for the 410 guests, many of whom stayed into the early morning hours to listen to the *Porgy* score played by Gershwin on the piano.

Paul's organization lost two veteran players before its return to Broadway. After more than eight years Jack Fulton wanted to put down roots and cut down on travel. It was a tough decision for him. "I would have stayed with Paul till it was all over," Fulton recalled in a letter to the author. "We cried a lot over the thought of missing our wonderful friends." But he and his wife, Thelma, had two small children to whom they wanted to give a real home.

When Jack left, the band gave him a watch on which everyone's signature was engraved. He soon starred on his own radio series, *Penthouse Serenade,* sponsored by Maybelline. The weekly NBC broadcast featured another Whiteman alumnus, Charles Gaylord, who conducted. Fulton sang for another twenty years, chiefly as a staff vocalist-musician on radio, and wrote a number of very popular tunes, including "Until" and "Wanted."

Concertmaster Kurt Dieterle was also weary of travel and tempted by additional radio jobs. He approached Paul at the start of a recording sessing in 1935. The violinist, who had been with the group for over eleven years, suggested to Paul that he do merely Pops's weekly broadcast for Kraft, leaving the rest of his time free. He suspected that the plan was impractical, since it would mean Paul's revamping the entire violin section each time Kurt came and went.

Paul was amenable, but then had second thoughts. He did not believe such an arrangement would work out, and looked so downcast that Kurt hurriedly added, "If you really feel that badly about my leaving, I'll stay."

"No," Paul replied sadly, "everyone eventually has to go out on his own."

Dieterle soon joined radio orchestras led by André Kostelanetz, Don Voorhees, Victor Arden, and Mark Warnow on such programs as *The Bell Telephone Hour, Your Hit Parade,* and *Waltz Time.* In the long run both Paul and his friend agreed that things had worked out for the best.

In the meantime Whiteman's association with the *Kraft Music Hall* neared an end. The sponsor wanted a variety show with music, while Paul favored a musical variety program that carried on the Whiteman tradition of establishing unknown but good artists. Moreover, Kraft barely covered Paul's expenses, even at the bulky sum of $7,000 a week.

On December 5, 1935, Kraft announced that Bing Crosby would be the new star of the *Music Hall.* For four weeks the producers featured both Whiteman and his orchestra from New York and Bing with Jimmy Dorsey's band from Hollywood. Paul was pleased that two of his alumni were taking over the series. In fact, Bing had telephoned Paul to make sure that Whiteman did not mind his taking over the series. Then, in a not uncommon radio switch, Bing's earlier sponsor, Woodbury Soap and Cosmetics, asked Whiteman to take over the former Rhythm Boy's program. Apparently both performers got what they wanted—different shows more to their liking, new sponsors, and more money.

Thus Paul began a new year with a new series. The forty-five-minute Sunday program, *Paul Whiteman's Musical Varieties,* featured Bob Lawrence, Ramona, Durelle Alexander, Johnny Hauser, the King's Men, and NBC announcer Alois Havrilla. Pops was back selling music in the modern manner, without comics, diverse celebrities, or freak acts to distort the mood. The results proved that Whiteman had a flair that turned many of the country's radio fans into regular listeners.

Another new wave in popular music was sweeping the country when Paul inaugurated his new Woodbury series in 1936. Soon Whiteman would be part of it, but first he had his eyes on Texas.

17

Trek to Texas

It was a hot July evening in 1936 when during dinner Paul began complaining to Margaret about taking a train from New York to Texas to fulfill a contract. He did not relish the thought of traveling for several days in the heat that was blanketing much of the country and particularly the Southwest.

"I hate to go down there on a train, especially alone. The band has to stay in town to play a couple of more nights. But I'd like to get to Texas before they do. I think I'm going to fly."

"You're a big sissy about flying." Margaret knew all about his fears. "You know you're not about to take a plane."

Paul got up from the table muttering, "We'll see about that!"

He walked out of their new apartment in the Essex House Hotel and took the elevator down to the lobby. "I need a little reinforcement," he thought. "First I'll have a few drinks and then go to the airport." After an hour of reinforcements, he hailed a taxi which dropped him at the airport terminal. He carried no luggage since his trunks had already been shipped ahead. Paul bought a ticket to Chicago and boarded the plane. By the time it touched down, he needed a few more drinks to take his mind off flying the last leg of his trip. He went into town to one of his favorite bars at the Blackstone Hotel.

A fellow across the room called to him as he ordered a scotch and soda. "Paul, how are you? I'm Fowler McCormick. Remember me from the Edgewater Beach? What brings you to this God-forsaken town in the middle of the summer?"

"I'm on my way to Fort Worth."

"I'll fly to Texas with you. Let's save time and hire a plane and pilot. I hear there's a big centennial celebration about to begin down there."

"That's right. And I'm part of it. Say, that's a great idea. Let's get our own wings."

The two Texas-bound buddies chartered a small airplane.

"As long as you're paying for the plane, Paul," Fowler offered, "let me pick up the rest of the expenses. If there's no rush, why don't we stop off at Memphis on the way down? There are some great bars in that town."

Paul's companion cashed some large checks en route to Fort Worth. Although the name of Chicago financier Fowler McCormick was well known, his face was not. Paul readily agreed to cosign McCormick's vouchers. No one could mistake the cherubic Whiteman face.

Paul landed at Fort Worth in a sorry state. His clothes were soiled and rumpled, his face was pale and unshaven, his stomach hurt and growled, and his breath would have melted the thorns on the toughest desert cactus.

He made a beeline to the nearest phone to call Jack Lavin who was already in town. He described the aerial adventure and his colorful companion.

"Fowler McCormick?" Lavin shouted. "That sounds out of character. Wait a minute! I've got to make a call."

He placed a call to Chicago to Fowler McCormick to ask about his trip with Whiteman.

"Sure, I've met Paul Whiteman, but I've never traveled with him. And I'm certainly not in Texas and haven't been for some time."

When Lavin told Paul of the call Whiteman was flabbergasted.

"Jack, I really don't know Fowler McCormick, but this fellow had lots of class. I thought he was one of those well-heeled regulars at the Edgewater Beach."

The escapade cost Paul about $4,000, not including the price of the chartered plane. He'd been taken by a clever impostor. But at least it was a big step toward overcoming Paul's fear of flying.

Certainly Paul's arrival in Fort Worth was less than auspicious. He did beat the band by twelve hours. But he needed every moment of that time to get cleaned up and find medical help. A local physician treated Paul's stomach cramps and nausea. The doctor got Paul on his feet in time to rehearse for his Woodbury radio broadcast the following day.

If Paul initially had second thoughts about his agreement to spend the summer and early fall in Texas, they were soon dispelled. He came to consider the months of work in Fort Worth and at its fair the most agreeable he ever spent. The reasons were easy to understand. Paul was returning to the West and the great outdoors where he had grown up, where he had gone riding, hunting, camping, and carousing. Now he was being paid a princely sum to do all that and make a little music every night. Paul's great affection for Fort Worth continued long beyond the two summers he lived and worked there. He returned time after time to spend many months, sometimes even a year or more at a stretch, among friends and family there.

But in 1936 the trek to Texas started as merely another big booking for Paul and the gang. He'd been given the assignment by Billy Rose after *Jumbo* closed.

Amon G. Carter, publisher and owner of the Fort Worth Star–Telegram, had seen the show and wasted no time in telling Rose that it would be ideal for Texas and the upcoming Fort Worth Frontier Centennial. This celebration, he pointed out, would show the rest of the state and especially neighboring Dallas, with its official Texas Centennial Exposition, that his city could provide a real good time for everybody. A musical circus had all the elements Texans enjoyed. Carter, the mayor of Fort Worth, and the city fathers soon made a deal with Billy Rose. He would produce an extravaganza for the residents and the tens of thousands of visitors expected in the Lone Star State. Rose asked for and got $1,000 a day for 100 days to stage a musical revue in the huge new outdoor theater-restaurant called the Casa Mañana and to produce a handful of other audience-grabbing attractions on the 162-acre site. Rose ultimately spent $1,500,000 on a half-dozen productions.

As director general of the Frontier Centennial, the thirty-seven-year-old Rose assembled a bevy of beautiful tall chorus girls and a group of talented singers and dancers. Many were recruited from the *Jumbo* spectacle. John Murray Anderson joined Rose as director; Raoul Pène du Bois and Albert Johnson were again signed up for stage design and costumes. Baritone Everett Marshall and dancer Ann Pennington, both headliners with the *Ziegfeld Follies,* sang and danced to the music of young Dana Suesse, now established as one of the most successful songwriters. Exotic fan dancer Sally Rand costarred, adding to her fame after a sensational appearance at the recent Chicago Century of Progress Exposition.

Rose and Carter agreed that no mammoth pageantry for Texas would be complete without Paul Whiteman. He and the band fit in perfectly with the oversized, eye-stunning, and melodically lavish proceedings. Paul often remarked that it was by far the best show he was ever connected with.

The Casa Mañana Revue became the big hit of the Centennial summer. Before long, audiences were singing and humming the most popular song of the show, "The Night Is Young and You're So Beautiful," composed by Dana Suesse with lyrics by Billy Rose and Irving Kahal. The theater-cabaret production highlighted the twentieth century's earlier world's fairs in St. Louis, Paris, and Chicago. But the real visual drawing cards were Rose's hand-picked statuesque showgirls, 100 of his special choices, including beauty queen Faye Cotton. "You never saw such beautiful girls," the showman recalled. "They grow them in Texas like nowhere else in the world. Stars in their eyes and corn tassels in their hair."

When it came to picking showgirls, dancers, and vocalists, Rose admitted, he was just as big a dope as any other smart producer on Broadway. "Most producers are as blind as Justice, and I'm standing right there with them, with that nice black blindfold covering my all-seeing eyes." When, for example, a young singer and dancer named Mary Martin applied for a job in the revue, he advised her to go back to her dancing school and settle down with a cowpoke in her hometown. Two years later she was a star on Broadway in Cole Porter's long-running *Leave It to Me,* singing "My Heart Belongs to Daddy."

The Frontier Centennial of 1936 opened on July 18 as 25,000 spectators crowded the entrance to the grounds, where the dedication ceremonies were held. Amon Carter arrived in cowboy costume, driving a Wells Fargo stagecoach and firing two pistols. Seated beside him were Governor James Allred and Senator Tom Connally. Over 1,000 newspaper reporters and columnists witnessed the fanfare. Later, Carter gathered them all for a champagne and chili cookout at his Shady Oaks Farm. The special press party was preceded by an hour-long eighty-five-station hookup on NBC, allowing the entire country to sample the Centennial festivities. The press soon blanketed the nation with stories. Robert Garland of the New York *World–Telegram* described the spectacle as "gargantuan, fantastic, and incredible . . . they have merged the dreams of Buffalo Bill with Broadway Billy."

Along with the Casa Mañana Revue, Rose offered a handful of other attractions for daytime and nighttime visitors: Jumbo (the least successful of the lot), the Last Frontier (with cowboys and Indians doing battle), Sally Rand's Nude Ranch (her picture appeared 947 times in Texas newspapers during her three-month stay in Fort Worth), and Pioneer Palace (a honkytonk with ten-cent beer and a chorus line of hefty women called the Rosebuds).

Night after night, under the Texas moon, the Casa Mañana show played to standing-room-only performances. A revolving stage a block long allowed fast scene changes and tableaus; a lagoon with a curtain of jet spray separated the proscenium from the audience. At the close of the second performance the huge circular stage converted to a dance floor. Paul's band regrouped to provide the music into the early hours of the morning. On Thursday at midnight the Casa Mañana held Jamborees with all the performers from all the shows at the fairgrounds.

Billy Rose wanted two bands at the Casa. Paul suggested that his old pal Joe Venuti would be a good choice for the alternating group. The fiddler and his band of a dozen men were hired to split the dance music with Pops. The Whiteman bandstand was placed opposite the smaller platform holding Venuti and his players. As the open-air theater was generally dark, Paul decided to use a lighted baton so that both bands could see him directing them when they played together. The next night Venuti stepped onto his bandstand with a baton in the form of a long broomstick with a flashlight tied to the end.

Amon Carter boasted that he visited the Casa sixty times in less than four months. He haunted all the shows, occasionally even narrating at the Last Frontier or singing his favorite tune of the celebration at the Pioneer Palace, "I'm in Love with a Handlebar Moustache." Carter greeted scores of famous visitors from such government luminaries as J. Edgar Hoover and Patrick J. Hurley to Ernest Hemingway and Max Baer, the boxer. He made them all welcome, Texas-style.

The Whiteman aggregation had arrived by train, bus, and car. The four King's Men drove their autos in a caravan, stopping to cool off at roadside stands and country stores with ice cream, sodas, and watermelon. In Texas they rented a house on Lake Worth, including a maid-cook, for $75 a month. The quartet only worked on the weekly radio show. Because the rest of the time was the men's own, they and their wives—all but Jon Dobson were married—had a summer to remember. Swimming, croquet games, and photography filled the long days.

All the Whiteman troupe settled in with the help and hospitality of Amon Carter and his friends. They quickly came to love Texas, and the state adopted them. At a lavish barbecue, the members of the band were named Texas Rangers by an edict of Governor Allred. They came away with ten-gallon Stetsons, hand-tooled Justin boots, and in some cases a broad Texas drawl.

Paul "went Texas" in a big way. When Carter gave him a dazzling white Stetson, he immediately acquired an all-black cowboy outfit, complete with cartridge belt and a pair of holsters. He added the three-inch-high letters "Mr. P.W." on his black leather chaps, and the name stuck with him throughout his Texas stay.

He and Margaret leased the 400-acre Van Zandt farm on the outskirts of Fort Worth. It proved an ideal place for entertaining and playing cowboy. Paul soon purchased a golden palomino and a large pony for riding about the wheatfields. His new friends and neighbors began to give him pearl-handled .45s, silver belt buckles, prize livestock, and fine horses. And the special awards and citations grew to fill an entire room at the country house.

After being elected a Texas Ranger, Paul was sworn in as mayor of Fort Worth for an hour—an unprecedented gesture. Surrounded by reporters and municipal officials, he announced that as acting mayor, he decreed that each city department should have a good orchestra and that policemen should walk their beats with songs in their hearts. He heard cheers when he proclaimed summer dress for all city employees: short sleeves for men and shorts for ladies. Questioned about taxes, he replied, "Out at Casa Mañana we got a song for that—The Eyes of Taxes Are Upon You."

That fall a statewide Paul Whiteman Week culminated in a concert at the University of Texas in Austin with Paul and the boys on the bandstand. On the morning of the program Paul addressed a joint session of the Texas state legislature which, at Paul's suggestion, passed a resolution to supply schoolchildren with music textbooks. Later Governor Allred, in recognition of the part Paul had played in calling Texas to the attention of the nation, appointed him a lieutenant colonel on his official staff. Paul responded by saying, "If I had my way, I would buy a big ranch, quit fiddlin', and ride Texas horses."

Not to be left out, the Fort Worth Chamber of Commerce gave him a pair of spurs in solid silver inlaid with gold; they were inscribed, "With the hope that he may spur himself into the affections of the World as he has into the affections of our folks."

On that occasion Paul gave a brief but heartfelt talk. It sounded as if he were facing a midlife, midcareer crisis.

> I am a Texan because you made me one of you . . . I came down here a man sorely in need of spiritual uplift. In Texas I have found it. Even success and fame that I have worked so hard to obtain had begun to lose their glamour. But the remarkable friendliness which met me on all sides brought me a new outlook on life. I am bound to Texas by irrevocable ties, and so deeply do I feel the Texas spirit that I do hereby appoint myself your musical ambassador.

Paul was not the only one for whom the summer offered a chance at new ties and affection. Dr. William Crawford was a frequent visitor to the Whiteman household, taking care of Paul and his family. The kindly doctor soon fell in love with Margaret's sister, Ivy, who had been handling public relations and secretarial chores for Paul and had lived and traveled with the Whitemans for several years. Ivy and Bill were constantly seen dining and dancing at the Casa Mañana, and they attended many parties together. Before the end of the year they were married at the city hall in St. Louis, where Crawford had attended medical school.

Other romances blossomed on and about the bandstand at the Casa Mañana. Roy Bargy planned to marry Virginia MacLean, one of the Dixie Debs, a vocal trio Paul had hired for his Sunday programs. Durelle Alexander fell in love with Edmund Van Zandt, the son of Paul's landlord. The young man followed her to New York, and after a long engagement they were married in Texas in 1939. Whiteman's staff arranger, Ken Hopkins, journeyed from New York to Texas on several occasions that summer. He would turn out two or three arrangememts a week for the band, particularly for Ramona. "Latin from Manhattan" was among the most popular.

On the comeback trail Paul and his 1931 orchestra prepare to entertain at the Edgewater Beach Hotel, Chicago. Female vocalists include Mildred Bailey and Miss Muriel LaFrance. *(Courtesy of Glenn Osser)*

Jane Froman at the NBC Chicago microphone in 1931, tries conducting with one of Paul's batons. *(Elmer Ellis Library, University of Missouri at Columbia)*

Paul and Margaret Whiteman strike a pose shortly after their marriage in August 1931. *(Courtesy of Margaret L. Whiteman)*

Margaret expresses pleasure at a slim husband, following a concert in the early 1930s. *(Courtesy of Margaret L. Whiteman)*

Walking Horse Farm in Hunterdon County, N. J.: White-man's large country "ranch" from 1938 to 1958. *(Courtesy of Margaret L. Whiteman)*

Whiteman works with director Busby Berkeley and with Mickey Rooney in MGM's *Strike Up the Band*. The movie signaled Paul's retirement in 1940. *(Courtesy of Howard Hays)*

Out of retirement by late 1940, Paul rehearses his new band for an opening in Miami. Mike (left) and bass player Artie Shapiro are the only holdovers from the past. Musicians include Artie Friedman on sax and George Wettling on drums. *(Courtesy of Margaret L. Whiteman)*

Whiteman alumnus Jack Fulton visits Pops during engagement at Chicago's Chez Paree. *(Courtesy of Jack Fulton)*

When Adolph Deutsch left Paul for greener fields in Hollywood, Ken took his place. He and the recently divorced Ramona were married later in 1936.

As the weeks sped by, the band played for all kinds of special occasions. There were salutes to such Texas towns as Denton, Dumas, and Galveston, tributes to Will Rogers and to community service clubs, talent contests for Texas young people, and presentation balls for Fort Worth debutantes. As a final gesture Paul conducted his orchestra and the Fort Worth Symphony on November 3 in a typical Whiteman program of Gershwin, Grofé, and Still.

Just before Whiteman boarded the train for New York by way of Springfield, Missouri, he learned that nearly a million and a half people had visited the centennial celebration. Many seasoned fairgoers were calling it the best exposition of its type in the nation's history. There was talk of repeating the fair the following summer. Billy Rose had plans for an aquacade in Cleveland in 1937; this lavish production led to his participation in the 1939 World's Fair in New York.

Before and after the stay in Texas business was not entirely as usual for Paul and the band. The month he started his Woodbury radio show a sizable and important chunk of music was pulled from the air. Warner Brothers' music publishing unit decided to withdraw from ASCAP. The producer believed that since its subsidiaries—Harm's, Witmark, and Remick—accounted for nearly a quarter of ASCAP's business, it should get a heftier slice of licensing fees. Warner's decided to handle its own negotiations with broadcasters, and in the meantime it withheld its music from radio. Every musician and performer lost the use of the works of such popular composers as Jerome Kern, Rodgers and Hart, Sigmund Romberg, and the Gershwins.

Paul, like everyone else, had to look to other publishers for material and this included a substitute for his theme, *Rhapsody in Blue*. At first Warner Brothers permitted Paul to continue using the identifying tune, since it was consiered a "musical work" rather than a pop number. NBC, however, fearing legal repercussions, refused to agree.

Whiteman scouted around for a new signature tune. Adolph Deutsch wrote a new tune, which Paul immediately decided to name "Margo"—for the newest member of the Whiteman family—as a sign of how much he liked it. After four years of marriage Paul and

Maggie had adopted a three-year-old child. The new daughter, Margo, would grow up in the limelight often thrust on the children of celebrities and would herself pursue a career as a Whiteman "discovery."

But the listening public did not have a chance to miss its favorite music for long. Warner Brothers settled the dispute with ASCAP within six months and returned to the fold by midsummer. Paul lost no time in brushing up on the *Rhapsody*.

Whiteman's records continued to sell well in 1935 and into 1936. The gang cut a dozen sides, including "Awake in a Dream," "Wah-Hoo," "Gloomy Sunday," and "There's a Small Hotel."

Paul and a number of other musicians were increasingly annoyed at the use of their recordings by radio stations day after day without authorization or payments to the performers while royalties went to composers and publishers. Although most labels carried the warning, "Not licensed for radio broadcast," stations ignored the restriction and blatantly spun any and all records. A number of major radio performers curtailed their recording activities. Among them was Fred Waring, who also made up his mind to sue for performance payments for each Waring record played on the air. Fred first took action against WDAS, a Philadelphia station, and won an injunction. As president of the National Association of Performing Artists, Waring encouraged other leading recording artists to go to court and back legislation to protect against unauthorized use of recorded material.

Whiteman, Walter O'Keefe, Don Voorhees, Frank Crumit, and Lawrence Tibbett filed suits against commercial firms which, they alleged, used their records on radio programs. Paul acted against the WBO Broadcasting Company, owner of WNEW in New York, home base for such fast-rising disc-jockey shows as Martin Block's *Make Believe Ballroom*. Don Voorhees sued Audio Scriptions, Inc., for pirating his performances directly from the air, another practice Whiteman and others sought to stamp out. These bootleg recordings were often modified and altered to attract sponsors who thus had the use of the artist's talents without having to pay them.

A spokesman for WNEW replied to the Whiteman suit. "We just go ahead and play any record we feel like using, as we have done for years. We will utilize records constantly as a source of program material, and most artists are glad to have us do so. We have no arrangement with Whiteman or any other artist for the use of their recordings. Many stations of the country use records as we use them.''

For nearly five years court proceedings granted limited and regional relief for Whiteman and Waring. Only Voorhees's case and similar actions against radio bootleggers and pirates were totally sucessful. Ultimately, in December 1940, the United States Supreme Court declined to review the decision against Whiteman handed down by the Circuit Court of Appeals. Judge Learned Hand wrote, ''Copyright in any form, whether statutory or in common law, is a monopoly. It consists only of the power to prevent others from reproducing the copyright work. WBO Broadcasting Company has never invaded any such right.'' Thus, Paul and his coplaintiff, RCA Victor, lost their suit to control their recordings and restrict them, if so desired, to noncommercial use in private homes.

Paul's involvement with the control and production of music also took him in another direction in 1936. Together with Fred Waring, Guy Lombardo, Abe Lyman, and Jack Denny, he formed a music publishing company, Words & Music, Inc. They began by purchasing an inventory of songs from the firm of Davis, Coots, and Engle. The most productive tune in its catalog, ''Dream a Little Dream of Me,'' paid the rent, but little else. The Dana Suesse–Billy Rose hit, ''The Night Is Young and You're So Beautiful'' from the Case Mañana Revue later added handsomely to the business. Overall, the firm generated few moneymakers. Paul soon quit as a partner, and Waring eventually became sole owner.

By the mid-1930s Paul's office in New York was overflowing with orchestrations and scores, press books and phonograph records. The collection represented a valuable and unique record of over fifteen years of the Whiteman organization. Storage had become an increasingly costly problem, as Paul complained to his lawyer and financial adviser, David Pollack. Pollack mulled over the disposition of the important memorabilia during a summertime motor trip through New England. As he drove his car into the Berkshire Mountains of northwestern Massachusetts, he came to small, picturesque Williamstown and Williams College. He learned that the college, founded in 1793, had a student body of some 850 men.

The following day Pollack explored the bucolic grounds of the college on his own and came away feeling that he had spent his time well. He would urge Paul to turn over his collection of arrangements, scripts, records, and instruments to Williams College; the donation could make it a center for the study of American music.

David Pollack approached Paul by giving two reasons for his suggestion. Paul would become a leading benefactor of a small and grateful institution, which—Pollack quickly added—had done little academically in the field of music but had great potential in that area. Moreover, the gift would provide a sizable and continuing tax benefit for the Whiteman family.

After visiting the campus, Paul agreed to the proposal and asked Pollack to sound out the college. Paul's press aide, Estella Karn, had worked for Williams's president, the historian Tyler Dennett. This personal element was a help in persuading the school to accept memorabilia of such a popular and contemporary nature.

In late October 1935, after long and careful discussion by the trustees, Dr. Dennett announced the gift, adding that the college intended expanding its music department and making the collection accessible to scholars of popular American music. At roughly the same time Paul asked permission for a concert to raise funds for a wing to house his collection of several thousand scores and hundreds of records and books. "I realize you are a little crowded for space, but I think we could raise a goodly sum," he wrote.

While Paul had no family ties to Williams College, several sons of prominent Denver families were enrolled there. Senator Lawrence C. Phipps sent two sons, Allan and Gerald, to Williams in the early 1930s. Wilberforce knew of the senator's high regard for the school and was aware that Denver students regularly studied there.

Early in 1933 Professor Whiteman had written to Paul about a possible concert for the Williams students. Allan R. Phipps, the senator's older son, had asked Wilberforce's help in persuading Paul to perform a Concert of Modern Music for Williams. "They have had the Cleveland and Detroit symphonies," Wilberforce wrote, "and Paderewski whom they paid $3,100. They would not want you to play dance music but give a program like the one you gave in Carnegie Hall. He thinks your orchestra and the kind of concert you give would attract one hundred percent of the student body. That is his wish."

The 1933 concert never took place, and Whiteman had undoubtedly forgotten the proposal by the time David Pollack finished negotiating with Williams. At the formal announcement Paul gave the credit for his gift, not to his attorney, but to David Diamond. The recent Whiteman scholarship winner had complained to Paul that he could not find a school where he could study semiclassical music. Paul delightedly told him that Williams would be filling this void. He added that his gift would include the original manuscript of *Rhapsody in Blue*.

To build an endowment fund for the collection, the Whiteman band traveled to Williamstown in May 1936 for a benefit concert in Chapin Hall. Paul arrived in an enormous white Packard roadster, which had difficulty maneuvering the narrow campus roads. The luxurious automobile caused a sensation among the students, as did the appearances of sultry Ramona in a glittering, tight-fitting gown. Paul attracted a full house and raised $1,250. After the concert the band went on vacation, while Paul remained on the campus for several days.

Buoyed by the enthusiastic response of the Berkshire audience, Paul suggested a similar benefit program in New York later that year to underwrite the costs of the wing to house his collection. Williams readily agreed to the plan and began organizing a major event. Paul decided to conduct his own players along with the Philadelphia Orchestra, which would share the proceeds with Williams. He scouted for new compositions and decided to premiere the program in Philadelphia with the Philadelphia Orchestra at two subscription concerts on November 27 and 28.

When Paul returned to his Essex House apartment from Texas in early November, Williams and its prominent New York alumni had molded the concert into an elegant winter gala. Various regional and junior committees formed, held teas and luncheons, courted society publicists and columnists, and gave lavish dinner parties for well-known figures about town. Extensive and costly promotion and advertising helped to sell every seat in the house, bringing in $35,000 at the box office.

Paul gathered the two orchestras, the Williams College Glee Club, a baritone, a harpist, four kilted bagpipers, and Deems Taylor to act as program commentator. The mammoth proceedings on December 1, 1936, delighted the formally dressed spectators. A show worthy of the Whiteman name, it turned classics into popular tunes and blues into highbrow themes.

The harp presentation by Casper Reardon showed the evolution of swing music by employing his own treatment of the "St. Louis

Blues." Adolph Deutsch's "Essay on Waltzes" covered favorite melodies by Strauss, Gounod, Chopin, Beethoven, and Tchaikovsky. And Van Phillips contributed a lively composition, "Thank You, Mr. Bach."

The most talked-about entries in the latest Whiteman modernistic sweepstakes came from three important composer-arrangers, two of whom had regularly contributed to the organization. Deutsch's *Scottish Suite* utilized five folk melodies. The final section brought forward a quartet of bagpipes in full regalia to add an authentic climax. William Grant Still once again contributed a well-crafted piece titled *Ebon Chronicle*. Of the three new numbers, *All Points West*, a symphonic narrative by Rodgers and Hart, gained the most attention. Performed by the orchestra and baritone Ray Middleton, it depicted through monologue and recitative the frustrations of a Grand Central Station train announcer who never goes anywhere and then meets a violent, melodramatic end when he gets caught in gunfire between a prisoner and the police. Paul's association with Rodgers and Hart on *Jumbo* had led them to try their hand at one of Pops's concerts.

Though it was somewhat sentimental and melodramatic, the piece allowed the writers to expand their score. "We wanted to escape the conventions that hedge in the musical comedy song," Richard Rodgers explained. "Also we got pretty tired of writing about nothing but love."

Paul pleased his standing-room-only audience, but both he and the Williams trustees were incensed when they learned that expenses ran to astronomical levels. The benefit program netted only $6,000 to be shared equally by Williams and the Philadelphia Orchestra's pension fund. With so little left to pay for housing the Whiteman Collection, Paul wrote out a personal check for $4,750 and sent it to Williams.

Very little was added to the collection until after the Second World War. In 1946 Professor Roy Lamson, who had joined the Williams English department in 1938 and, as a Harvard undergraduate, had played clarinet in the Gold Coast Band with John Green, became the first curator. He persuaded Whiteman to have his staff resume work on the project in New York.

In 1947, while he was preparing materials to send to Williamstown, Paul discovered that Ferde Grofé's original score for *Rhapsody in Blue* had disappeared. A photostat of poor quality had been substituted. Paul investigated that matter and learned that Grofé had donated the valuable score to the Library of Congress without any consultation with Whiteman. Paul was furious, vowing once more never to speak to Grofé again. He directed his lawyers to sue his associate and the Library of Congress. But his counselors pointed out that Williams College would have to become a party to the suit, in view of the gift made in 1935. The trustees declined to become involved, fearing that such action might harm the important relationship between the college and the Library of Congress. Still outraged, Paul had no choice but to let the matter drop.

Nevertheless, Paul shipped six tons of memorabilia to the Whiteman archives in 1948. Boxed in forty-one packing cases, the material was stored in the basement of several campus buildings as the task of cataloging began.

Paul had other things on his mind back in 1936. The once promising Woodbury radio series lost favor about midway into its second twenty-six weeks and never regained a solid audience. Paul quickly recruited a hillbilly act from the *Ziegfeld Follies* of 1936 to stimulate interest and continuity. Judy Canova, her sister Annie, and her brother Zeke offered comic relief with a touch of homespun harmony. The popular tenor Frank Parker also made frequent appearances, even traveling to Fort Worth for several shows. But on Sunday evenings listeners were entertained by Jack Benny, Eddie Cantor, and Phil Baker, followed by classical and semiclassical programs including the *Ford Sunday Evening Hour, General Motors Concert,* and *American Album of Familiar Music.* By the time Whiteman came on at ten o'clock, the audience was tired of radio. Although he followed Walter Winchell on the same network, Paul's rating was less than half of his *Kraft Music Hall* ratings a year earlier. Just weeks after the Williams–Philadelphia Orchestra benefit the Woodbury contract ran out and was not renewed. With the major source of regular income gone, Paul had to face immediate personnel changes. His chief recourse took the form of "farming out" his soloists to other bands and shows and collecting talent or manager's fees.

Many of Paul's star performers resented being treated as commodities. This feeling quickly led to the departure of some Whiteman bandstand regulars. Ramona was the first to leave. She had sued to break her $125-a-week contract, accusing Paul of exploiting her "as if I were a slave or some inanimate chattel subject to all his whims, desires, and wishes." Paul's Artists Management Bureau, the singer-pianist complained, got $300 to $500 a week for services she performed elsewhere, while she had to be content with a mere $25 or $50. The courts ruled against Ramona and held her 1934 agreement valid. Paul, however, willingly released his popular soloist that winter. With the help of her husband, Ken Hopkins, she formed her own band and picked up a WOR radio series. Hopkins believed that she had made a mistake in leaving Whiteman. His feeling was confirmed when Ramona quickly slipped from national prominence.

Approaching eighteen, Durelle Alexander wanted to cast off the little-girl image and perform as an adult band vocalist, with a salary to match. Paul agreed to tear up her $75-a-week contract; the action would help to cut his payroll. Durelle quickly joined Al Donohue's band at the Rainbow Room. By 1939 she was singing with Eddy Duchin and his popular orchestra.

Veteran sax player Charlie Strickfaden requested a leave of absence early in 1937 to settle some family matters in California. He never rejoined Pops but remained in Los Angeles, where he both managed real estate holdings and worked as a film studio musician.

Though Goldie also left to form his own band, he returned to Paul later that year with his trumpet.

The King's Men slipped out of the stable as well. Ken Darby complained of the paltry compensation paid his group and especially himself as arranger, accompanist, and coach. Moreover, Paul held the reins as a manager, pocketing 10 percent of all outside earnings.

"It's not fair to be so exploited," Darby grumbled.

"Read your contract," Paul pointed out.

The King's Men owed much of their success to Whiteman, but they had little to show for it. As the year unfolded and no financial gains were forthcoming, Ken and the others decided to revoke their contract, even though it meant that they could not sing elsewhere. They headed for their native California in mid-1937 to wait it out. Months passed before a letter arrived from Paul.

"This is to advise that we cannot recognize nor accede to such cancellation," it stated. "If you persist in this wrongful attitude in refusing to recognize the existing contract, we will take action." But the King's Men would not give in. Finally Paul made it known that he would not stand in their way. Margaret wrote to Ken.

Delighted to hear of the birth of your son. Paul and I send heartiest congratulations. Sorry we did not see you while on the Coast. We tried to get you several times without success.

We wanted to tell you that if you and the boys settle your
personal loans outstanding, you will remember, and if you forward checks, we will cancel your contracts. Of course, we
have a perfectly good case against you, and we would win.

Ken, Jon, Bud, and Rad each sent a check for $170.45, thus end-
ing their association with Whiteman. The quartet soon joined the
weekly radio show of Fibber McGee and Molly; they stayed with
the popular comedy team for over fifteen years and acted as a summer replacement one year. From time to time they also worked at
film studios and in concerts. Ken's many talents led to posts as
musical associate at Disney and Fox, where he won Oscars for his
contribution to the motion pictures *The King and I, Porgy and Bess,*
and *Camelot.*

By the spring of 1937 most of Paul's vocalists had left or were
headed toward the exit. Whiteman had cut back to a sixteen-piece
dance band with Bob Lawrence as chief vocalist. Without radio
ties, Paul took to the road. First stop: Chicago, and a long engagement in the Gold Coast Room at the Drake Hotel.

Paul's arrival in the Windy City was acknowledged with a welcoming reception and parade. Pops's alumni and friends and a unit
of the 122nd Field Artillery Lancers gathered at LaSalle Street Station to meet the Whiteman train. Among the welcomers were Henry
Busse, Jack Fulton, Charles Gaylord, and Chicago's Charter Jubilee
Queen, Lorraine Ingalls. Scores of greeters accompanied the band
as it drove to the Drake, where Paul was proclaimed King of Music
by the city.

Paul acknowledged the honors with a loud "Whew!" Once more
Chicago would soothe his wounds and restore his confidence. In
November he returned for another booking at the Drake, this time
with a coast-to-coast late-night Mutual radio pickup and two new
singers, Marion Manners and Jimmy Brierly.

The absence of a major prime-time radio series hurt the band.
Since 1932 it had been on the air at least once a week for a national
sponsor, bringing in over $300,000 a year. Rumors abounded; Paul
claimed that he turned down five major offers. In 1937 he wrote to
a potential backer.

I have felt for a long time that to continue on the air with
mixed programs is musical suicide, especially as I stand more
or less as the sponsor for our type of music. The advertising

agencies and sponsors have arrrived at the conclusion that just musical programs do not rate with a high percentage. You and I know that this is a lot of bosh, as music still is a pretty swell institution, and most of the programs in vogue today had their origin with the musical show. We know that Major Bowes just revamped my old Pontiac program with the amateurs, and pretty near all the stars popped out of musical shows to take shows of their own. However, we agree that there isn't any straight musical program that rates very high at the present time, although straight symphonic programs can rate about twelfth.

Paul proposed a radio deal that would emphasize his outfit as the all-American versatile Whiteman Wonder Band. Not a symphony, not a brass band, and not a swing band, it would play at three—symphonic music, marches, and swing tunes.

I have lots of program ideas, which will always be tied up with publicity as it will always be news to know how the old masters will be played for the first time in new groupings of instruments. I originated the "hit of the week" on the Kraft program. After playing hit tunes each week for eleven weeks on the program, the continuity man for Kraft thought the idea had no merit. However, this was good enough for Lucky Strike, and for the Lucky Strike Hit Parade ever since.

Brimful of program suggestions and ideas for special features, including a segment on the new sounds of the electrical guitar, organ, cello, and other instruments, Paul hoped to snare a big nationally known backer, such as his former sponsor, General Motors.

If you can find anybody who has vision and guts enough to match mine, although the guts department is not as big as usual, I will fly, drive, walk, or crawl to talk to him.

While seeking a gutsy partner, Paul continued to play one-night stands so as not to have to "dip into the family exchequer."

He jumped at the chance to return to Fort Worth and a second summer of the Frontier Fiesta. Amon Carter had wanted Whiteman back with Billy Rose's new revue at Casa Mañana. Paul was worried over the bite in his fees taken by the renting of a hotel suite or a house. Carter offered to turn over his country place to the Whitemans for the run of the show. They took up residence, rent free, in the handsomely furnished farmhouse surrounded by large oaks and thousands of acres of land. Carter staffed his Shady Oaks Farm with a cook, maid, gardener, and handyman. Margaret brought along five-year-old Margo and a nanny.

Paul loved the Texas outdoors and the Texan's belief in doing everything in a big way. He helped his ranch neighbors to round up calves, hung around saddle shops in town, ate barbecued sides of beef and black-eyed peas at prairie cookouts, and rode the range under the Western moon. "They didn't treat me like a bandman," he told his city friends. "They treated me like a cowman—not so good at riding and roping as they were, maybe, but a cowman."

Before summer ended Carter gave his tenant some land on a nearby lake. The Fort Worth publisher urged Paul to build a ranch house on the property. A guy living on the south side of Central Park with four or five horses clustered in city stables needed a country place to get away from the bustle of Broadway. Not a bad way to spend the rest of your life, if it came to that.

Paul thought it would be like going home.

The summer in Texas again brought honors to Paul and the band. They traveled to the area's colorful rodeos, played at charity dances, and greeted a continual stream of celebrated visitors. The Casa Mañana show itself—a musical dramatization of best-selling books—proved less successful. Dancer Harriet Hoctor replaced Ann Pennington. Everett Marshall was the only star performer to return with Paul.

Some 1,500 miles west of Fort Worth, George Gershwin was in Hollywood working on nine songs for a new picture to be called *The Goldwyn Follies*. It featured singers Kenny Baker and Helen Jepson, dancer Vera Zorina, and comedians Edgar Bergen (with Charlie McCarthy) and the Ritz Brothers. In late June, Gershwin collapsed at the studio and was taken to the hospital for observation but released. X-rays, following a second attack, revealed the presence of a virulently spreading brain tumor. In spite of immediate surgery, thirty-eight-year-old George Gershwin died on Sunday, July 11, 1937. Ira and Leonore Gershwin were at his bedside.

News of George's death went out on the radio by Sunday noon. When Paul heard the announcement at the Carter farm, his initial shock turned into disbelief, then anger. He needed to be alone. He saddled one of his horses and rode out into the open wilderness of the Texas plain. His thoughts turned to his young friend and collaborator. Both had worked to discover new paths for their music and to raise it to higher levels. Paul wondered how different his life would have been without the *Rhapsody*. After that wintery afternoon at Aeolian Hall thirteen years earlier, Gershwin and Whiteman had been a unique team, and their partnership had given a tremendous boost to both careers. Now George was gone. There would be no more gala concerts with Gershwin at the piano, no more intricate and sparkling melodies and themes with the Gershwin touch.

Paul reined his horse to a halt and gazed across the countryside. Tears filled his eyes. Slowly he turned the animal in the direction of the farmhouse, and sadly he rode back to the stable.

18

Swing Wing

Gershwin's music of the Jazz Age endured very nicely into the next decade. Paul played it with unfailing regularity; George's works never disappeared from his repertoire. But by the middle of the 1930s a new sound captured the listeners and diminished Paul's popularity. Swing—dance music laced with jazz—shook the Whiteman throne. Long identified with early jazz and big-band syncopation, Paul discovered that, in the words of the Duke Ellington song, "It Don't Mean a Thing If It Ain't Got That Swing."

The swing era was born in the late summer of 1935 in the city where the jazz era had begun for Paul. At the Palomar Ballroom in Los Angeles, Benny Goodman was nearing at the end of an unsuccessful cross-country tour. The engagements generated little enthusiasm for Benny's fourteen-piece band, which had been formed a year earlier in New York for supper-club bookings and a radio series. If the band was going to fold, Benny felt, it might as well end by playing what Goodman and his musicians wanted to play. They put aside the sweet waltzes and subdued foxtrots and pulled out their snappy arrangements by Fletcher Henderson and other jazz-bent musicians. "King Porter Stomp," "Sometimes I'm Happy," "Blue Skies," and "Sugar Foot Stomp" exploded from the bandstand. The audience gave a shout, became truly alive, and surged around the band. The dancers roared with approval. The swing era had begun, with Benny as its king.

In the sixth year of the country's economic depression and the third of Washington's New Deal young people were ready to pick

221

up a new sound and make it their very own. Swing struck a responsive chord. Potential swing fans had been conditioned by performances of little-known studio and staff musicians who played popular tunes with a jazz twist during the late 1920s and early 1930s. Glenn Miller, Tommy and Jimmy Dorsey, Red Norvo, Artie Shaw, and others had served apprenticeships as anonymous sidemen. Led into the kingdom by Benny Goodman, these players joined him in the celebration of swing.

Many of the swing leaders had worked in the Whiteman band and had gained experience in ensemble playing. Most had left to freelance when radio grew in popularity. Paul had no doubts that Tommy Dorsey, his former trombonist, would one day lead a band of major importance; but he and many others would not have believed that Goodman, a scholarly-looking clarinetist, had the makings of the phenomenal King of Swing. Goodman, in fact, was one of the few top-ranking players in New York who had never been on Paul's payroll.

Swing had been heard for some time, particularly in the large bands of Jimmie Lunceford, Don Redman, Duke Ellington, and Jean Goldkette. Glen Gray's orchestra at the Casa Loma came closest perhaps to extracting a commercial Goodman swing sound. The orchestra, twice the size of the early jazz bands, performed with specific written arrangements. Paul rightly stated that long before Benny's reign, he shouted to his band, "Swing it, boys, swing it!" whenever he wanted action. It was a catchy phrase that linked up with a whole new era.

Paul pointed out that swing was an "intensification of the jazz motif," and in order to "swing it," a band emphasized the offbeat. Swing music, he found, aside from certain minor improvements, is "not so very far removed from the tunes strummd out by the Original Dixieland Jazz Band, the California Ramblers, or Louis Armstrong, which marked other eras of the jazz age."

In 1935 Whiteman's outfit certainly did not qualify as a swing band. Nor was it a sweet-music unit along the lines of Wayne King, Guy Lombardo, and Jan Garber. And it tried to avoid appearing as a novelty band, gladly surrendering that designation to Horace Heidt.

Inevitably Paul gave in to the day's demands by forming a swing unit within the band. In May 1936 this band-within-a-band participated in one of the earliest swing concerts, a benefit for the Musicians' Emergency Relief Fund. Paul directed his own unit featuring Jack and Charlie Teagarden and Frankie Trumbauer. They shared the stage with swing groups from Glen Gray, Fred Waring, Bob Crosby, and Adrian Rollini, as well as those formed by five Pops alumni—Tommy Dorsey, Red Nichols, Red Norvo, Bunny Berigan, and Joe Venuti. A week later Paul sent his "swing wing" to a Sunday-evening swing session at the Imperial Theatre. Again many of the same musicians played, staying close to the traditional Dixieland or New Orleans jazz. Every inch of the theater was occupied for what was billed as New York's first swing concert. The surprise hits of the evening were Red Norvo and his Swingtette— with Mildred Bailey, who was still married to Norvo, as vocalist— and Artie Shaw and his String Swing Ensemble. Shaw garnered the only encore of the concert with his own composition, "Interlude in B Flat." Stopping the show, he joined the ranks of big-band leaders almost overnight.

The hot-music crowd, especially on college campuses, was dropping Paul. The swing-conscious set looked to the Dorseys, Goodman, Cab Calloway, and Jimmie Lunceford. Students from UCLA to Harvard rated these bands tops. They were buying out supplies of swing records, frequenting clubs where swing was played, and driving miles to hear and dance to swing bands. College proms and dorm dances signed up the Pied Pipers of hot music. If college students were to be believed in 1936 and 1937, Paul might as well have abdicated as King of Jazz.

Alfred Butterfield, writing in the *Harvard Crimson,* noted that such names as Waring, Whiteman, Bernie, and Rudy Vallee have "a familiar ring to Harvard ears. They would draw here," he wrote, "and Waring much the best of the lot. They are a little outside our orbit, though. . . . Rudy puts on one of the best air shows, as he did last year at the freshman smoker, but the Connecticut Yankees once got a barrage of grapefruit from Harvard students. He wouldn't get it now for two reasons. Those that went to hear him would go for his show, and they wouldn't be disappointed; those that want good music would stay home."

Frequenters of the popular clubs along Manhattan's Fifty-Second Street sought the latest in swing—and got it from a string of highly capable musicians including Red McKenzie, Dave Tough, Wingy Manone, John Kirby, Count Basie, and Eddie Condon.

Swing was sweeping the country, from remote roadhouses to

midtown hotels. Paul could no longer ignore its all-encompassing presence. After a year filled with many one-nighters but virtually without radio work, he sought full membership in the ascendant swing club.

In December 1937 the Whiteman band played an engagement at the Coconut Grove in Los Angeles. On New Year's Eve it inaugurated a new radio series with an emphasis on big-band swing. Sponsored by Chesterfield cigarettes, the show made a play for a young audience—current and potential smokers. By then Camel cigarettes was sponsoring Benny Goodman every Tuesday at ten, while Raleigh's presented Tommy Dorsey each Friday. Liggett & Myers, makers of Chesterfields, had just ended a radio season with Hal Kemp. Whiteman now offered an opportunity to bring along many of his older fans, with the additional promise of capturing the country's youth.

Originating on the West Coast, the new CBS series—*Chesterfield Presents*—fell into the trap of parading Hollywood personalities before a microphone and having them do things the public never knew they did. Connie Boswell played the saxophone; Burgess Meredith sang a self-written song; Francis Lederer performed on the harmonica; Sylvia Sidney did a parody of her film *Dead End*. Comedian Oliver Wakefield shared the duties of master of ceremonies with Paul. The maestro got some unusual reactions on his role after the opening show. Crosby wired, "Hi, Pops. You sound just like me on the air. Who taught who in this business?"

The music, especially the swing selections, was lost under the novelty acts. After four or five programs the sponsor's agency knew that it had problems. The show was moved to New York and acquired a new producer. CBS agreed to assign the man behind its innovative *Saturday Night Swing Club* to Whiteman's show. Phil Cohan, formerly head of the music department of Paramount Pictures at its Astoria studios and a capable saxophone player in his college days, returned the proceedings to their original concept. Swing from a big band with much emphasis on vocal arrangements succeeded in achieving good ratings; the standings, in fact, were equal to Benny Goodman.

One of the first joint decisions of the cigarette sponsors and the pipe-smoking Cohan was to move the show around the country and broadcast it from wherever the band had bookings for personal appearances at dances and other special events. The second was to open it up to an audience in the CBS Playhouse on those occasions when the band performed in New York.

Cohan also lined up Paul Douglas, a CBS staff member and swing enthusiast, to serve as the regular announcer. The vocals gained from the hiring of Joan Edwards and the Modernaires. A real New Yorker, Joan was born in Manhattan and majored in music at the city's Hunter College. As the niece of showman Gus Edwards, she fell into singing pop tunes at parties and on radio. Rudy Vallee invited her to do guest appearances on his show several times, and nightclub work in Florida followed. Then, when she was nineteen, Joan auditioned for Whiteman and won the coveted slot of featured vocalist with the band, and, in turn, at least two songs a week on *Chesterfield Presents.* Among the dozen or more female vocalists Whiteman used with the band, only Mildred Bailey outshone Joan as a versatile artist and magnetic personality. From Pops's bandstand Joan moved on to Broadway, then to her best-remembered association, costarring with Frank Sinatra on the radio *Your Hit Parade* of the early 1940s.

The Modernaires, a close-harmony quartet with a flair for swing numbers, was another wise choice. Consisting of Chuck Goldstein, Bill Conway, Hal Dickinson, and Ralph Brewster, the group stepped into the saddle shoes of the departed King's Men. They proved that Pops could pick talented combos as well as individuals.

Whiteman and Phil Cohan quickly built the orchestra into a highly respected "swinging" outfit. Some of the foremost practitioners of the big-band sounds of the swing era came on the bandstand. There were George Wettling on drums, Al Gallodoro on saxophone, Artie Shapiro on string bass, Buddy Morrow and Miff Mole on trombone, Bob Cusamano on trumpet. Frankie Trumbauer, however, had left a year earlier to organize a band with trumpeter Mannie Klein. At the start of the Second World War, Trum abandoned music for a job as a test pilot and administrator with the Federal Aviation Authority, having first taken up flying as a teenager in St. Louis.

Cohan asked violinist Al Duffy to do a jazz spot on "Limehouse Blues." When everyone liked the number, Duffy received an offer to become a fulltime player; Pops remarked, "Why can't we get to do something like this ourselves?" As a member of the band, Duffy was one of the four violinists in the swing wing's Swingin' Strings, which also included two violas, a bass, a guitar, and a celeste. Another member, violinist and concertmaster Julius Schachter, met Joan Edwards during the run of the Chesterfield show; they were married in 1942.

Kurt Dieterle came back to the Whiteman fold to work in the Swingin' Strings after a three-year break. He remained for the run of the radio series.

Pops soon added other swing units within the orchestra. The Bouncing Brass and the Saxophone Socktette satisfied still more members of the swing set. He picked a handful of arrangers to provide musical variation, paying more than $1,000 a week for special material. Contributors included newcomers Fred Van Eps and Morton Gould and veterans Bill Challis and Roy Bargy. Paul still delivered a musical melange that tried to satisfy all tastes, from the swing addicts to those who liked the concert touch.

A carefully planned and well-written program, *Chesterfield Presents* required eight hours of actual rehearsal for a thirty-minute broadcast. Guest artists—performers who were making waves in the sea of swing—were selected with care. Artie Shaw, Bobby Hackett, Walter Gross, Raymond Scott and his Quintet, the Andrews Sisters, and Joe Venuti took to the mike. Paul remembered an earlier success by guest Stuff Smith, when he introduced "I'se a Muggin' " on the air during the Woodbury show in 1936. The black fiddler won raves from listeners and convinced Paul that a "hot" specialty act could serve several purposes. On the Chesterfield show he expanded this guest segment into a major feature.

In January 1939 Joan Edwards gained a singing partner. Tenor Clark Dennis had worked on bandstands with Orville Knapp and Raymond Paige on the West Coast and on radio with the *Breakfast Club* and *Fibber McGee and Molly* from Chicago. An avid golfer, he spent many hours a week on the links. One afternoon, on a course near Chicago, he met his golfing partner's sister, Jane Vance, who had recently left Whiteman's troupe. They started to date. Clark made a special recording of "Begin the Beguine" with Roy Shields's orchestra; when Jane heard it, she sent it to Paul in New York.

Pops liked the tenor voice on the record and offered Jane's friend a contract at $500 a week if he was willing to move to New York. Jane wired Clark's acceptance of the extraordinarily large salary and added that she would be coming along. Clark and Jane planned to be married.

Clark Dennis always had at least one featured solo on the Chesterfield show, and usually a duet with Joan Edwards on such songs as "This Can't Be Love," "Let the Punishment Fit the Crime," and "Say It Isn't So."

As planned, the radio program did travel. Broadcasts from Tampa, New Orleans, Baltimore, Chicago, and numerous other locations were frequent. The program often tied in with tobacco-festival dances in North Carolina, junior proms in New England, and Mardi Gras carnivals in the Gulf states. Leslie Lieber, a CBS publicist, ended up working both behind the scenes and on the bandstand. Les had long played the penny whistle as a hobby. One summer day he mentioned his skill to Phil Cohan, who gave him an audition as they sat on the CBS fire escape to catch a cool breeze. Les and his two-and-a-half-octave penny whistle became a special feature of the show.

In May 1938 Pops asked Les to play a special new arrangement of "The Parade of the Wooden Soldiers," for orchestra and penny whistle. The arranger, Irving Szathmary, lived in Brooklyn; Les set a time to rehearse with him at his apartment in Brooklyn. On the way to Szathmary's place, he ended up lost in a labyrinth of Brooklyn streets. After two hours he finally telephoned Szathmary from a cigar store, explaining that he was lost and could not see him that night.

"What key is your penny whistle in?" Szathmary asked just before he hung up.

Les played at bit over the phone to give him an idea. He continued to play major segments of the familiar piece while Szathmary listened and ran back and forth to work key measures out on his piano.

A cluster of people soon gathered near the phone, wondering what in the world was going on. The performance over the telephone inspired Szathmary; he quickly completed a fine arrangement for Pops and Les and his penny whistle.

Midway through 1938 Paul and the orchestra took time out from broadcasting and traveling to play a special concert. On July 11— the first anniversary of George Gershwin's death—Paul and his men gathered at Lewisohn Stadium for a memorial concert. A record 19,000 people jammed the amphitheater to hear Whiteman and the New York Philharmonic pay tribute to the late composer.

The selections offered a balanced and comprehensive retrospective of Gershwin's productive career. They included his show tunes and his film contributions, his concert works and specialty numbers. The orchestra played *An American in Paris, Three Preludes for Piano, Rhapsody in Blue,* and *Rhapsody No. 2,* a none-too-successful revival of the 1931 successor of the original work. Roy Bargy was the soloist. The Modernaires and the Lyn Murray chorus handled the lyrics on "Sascha, Jascha, Mischa, Toscha" and "That Certain Feeling." Maxine Sullivan recalled *Porgy and Bess* with a vocal interpretation of "Summertime," and Gershwin's Hollywood period with "Nice Work If You Can Get It."

Highlight of the evening, for the audience and the critics, was one of Whiteman's earlier discoveries, Jane Froman. Her deep rich voice charmed the gathering as she sang "The Man I Love" and "It Ain't Necessarily So." Paul's radio vocalist from Chicago had taken his advice and traveled East to Broadway, where audiences could see one of the most attractive young singers in the business.

Much of the stadium program had been broadcast the previous afternoon by Paul's orchestra and soloists and Howard Barlow and the CBS Symphony. There were a number of musical tributes to Gershwin that day. NBC's *American Album of Familiar Music* presented an all-Gershwin memorial broadcast, with Frank Munn singing the composer's last hit, "Love Walked In," Elizabeth Lennox rendering "Who Cares?" and Munn and Jean Dickenson harmonizing on "Maybe."

After Gershwin's death in 1937 there had been two memorial concerts. The one at Lewisohn Stadium, conducted by Ferde Grofé and Alexander Smallens, featured Todd Duncan and Anne Brown from the cast of *Porgy and Bess* and Ethel Merman, star of *Girl Crazy.* The Hollywood Bowl concert had seven conductors, including Victor Young, Nathaniel Shilkret, and Jose Iturbi, and Fred Astaire, Al Jolson, Lily Pons, and Gladys Swarthout as soloists. But on the first anniversary of Gershwin's tragic death, many of his comtemporaries wanted to honor his memory with special programs, again, setting a precedent whereby all-Gershwin concerts would be regular events both on radio and in concert. Because of his close association with George and his music, Whiteman was often asked to conduct and plan the programs.

During 1938 Whiteman's popularity increased his tendency to self-indulgence. Flush with renewed success on radio and in personal appearances, he eagerly joined the heavier drinkers in his band. He often grabbed Jack Teagarden as a companion in a marathon round of elbow bending. In fact, Paul so often sought his presence that Jack protested.

"It doesn't look good. The boys will think you're playing favorites."

"I'm paying you, ain't I?" Whiteman snapped. "Ain't I paying you?"

Teagarden admitted he was.

"Then come along and don't give me any backtalk."

At other times Paul drank alone. Just before a Chesterfield broadcast from Detroit he slipped into his hotel bathroom, presumably to wash up. He discovered a telephone next to the tub and ordered liquor, instructing room service to deliver the bottle to the back entrance of the suite to bypass his worried producer, who had already found several empty bottles in Paul's quarters.

When he was eventually brought out of the bathroom, Paul asserted over and over, "Don't worry, old boy, I won't let you down." In spite of all he had to drink, he did manage to get through the program.

The orchestra always protected Paul and always seemed to forgive him. The musicians acted as a benevolent Gestapo, keeping tabs on him and alerting Margaret when he disappeared for an unusually long time between meetings or rehearsals.

Margaret had talked with medical experts about Paul's periodic bouts with the bottle; his system seemed to demand liquor from time to time. He would begin to get restless and agitated. If he was at home, Margaret had a method of dealing with him. She would stock the bedroom with a dozen bottles of liquor and mixes and tell him to go ahead and drink all he wanted. Then she would lock him in the room, making sure that any objects or gadgets that could possibly do him any harm had been removed. In three or four days Paul would "get it out of his system" and emerge from the bedroom happy and relaxed.

When he was away from home, things were not that well controlled. During an engagement—and spree—in Detroit, Paul emerged from a limousine and fell against the side of the car. He started to turn, then grabbed for the back fender, again losing his balance. Clutching the car, he rolled completely around the rear of it onto the opposite side, where an open door brought him back into the limo. No slapstick comic could have done it better.

After his three-day benders Pops would suffer pangs of remorse.

"Why do I do these things? Why do I let my friends down?" he would plead. Totally contrite, he would swear that this had been his last bout. Then, in the next breath, he would wonder if science could one day replace his body's malfunctioning "plumbing" with new "parts." "When they do," he mused, "I'll probably go out and ruin it all over again."

When he was drunk an occasional mean streak surfaced. While riding with a publicity aide in a taxi in a midwestern city, he spotted a hunched-over old man in the distance. As the vehicle approached the poor fellow walking on the side of the road, Paul rolled down the window and, without rhyme or reason, shouted, "Get out of the way, you old son of a bitch."

Paul's companion tried to forget the incident, but it stuck in his mind as an ugly, irrational act. Margaret learned to live with his transgressions and phobias. Often they were amusing to others, but not to her. "Everyone gets a kick out of Pops. Everyone's always covering for him," she observed again and again with perfect accuracy.

Paul's publicists were unable to make the country perceive Paul as a swing leader, but they were successful in tagging him the Dean of Modern American Music. With that broad designation, he could expostulate on any kind of music. Using the assistance of "ghosts," he began writing articles for a variety of publications, ranging from *Down Beat* and *Etude* to *American Cavalcade* and *Rotarian*.

When the popular weekly magazine *Collier's* invited him to select an "All-American Swing Band," he relished the task. Realizing that he was going out on a limb because every musician and swing fan had definite ideas on the subject, Paul admitted that his preferences were no more valid than anyone else's—"but I'll fight for my selections." About one-third of his choices fell on members of his own band and former members. They were Jack and Charlie Teagarden, Al Duffy, Jimmy and Tommy Dorsey, Frankie Trumbauer, Joe Venuti, and Matty Malneck. "There is a technique connected with swing music just as there is with any kind of music. Every man I'm picking on my All-American team, except one, is a fine reader of music, a man who has mastered the fundamentals of music and who had gone beyond that technique to add something of his own."

In addition to his band alumni and three current members, Paul's swing group included Benny Carter (alto sax), Louis Armstrong,

Mannie Klein, and Roy Eldridge (trumpet), Carl Kress (guitar), Bobby Haggart (bass violin), Chu Berry and Ed Miller (tenor sax), Jack Jenney (trombone), Benny Goodman and Artie Shaw (clarinet), Gene Krupa and Ray Bauduc (drums), Eddie South (violin), Adrian Rollini (vibraharp), and Tito (accordion). For keyboard he picked Bob Zurke and Art Tatum (the blind pianist who, as Paul noted, could not, therefore, read music). All in all, Paul knew which musicians were swinging in 1938.

Whiteman's knowledge and perception made little impression on old Wilberforce. The octogenarian came to New York on a visit and remained unconvinced that jazz or swing had anything to offer. "I hate jazz and swing music and I despise crooning—there is no art in any of them," he remarked. "I wouldn't go out of my way to hear Paul play swing. But if I *must* hear it, I would rather hear it the way Paul does it. All the same, I like Paul's manner of playing new things. He is modern, and I am not. Deems Taylor . . . once told me that my son knew more about a modern orchestra than any other man living today. Everything in the world today is chaotic, even music, and Paul's great idea is that out of the modern music things will arise which ought to be preserved."

Wilberforce came to New York several times that year. After Elfrida's death the ranch was sold and he moved back to Denver. Wilberforce opened a voice studio, planned student recitals, and helped to arrange auditions in Manhattan for a number of his young students.

Paul had a new recording contract to show his father. Since its founding in 1934, Decca had wanted Whiteman as an artist. The firm signed Bing Crosby, Guy Lombardo, and the Dorsey Brothers at the beginning, but the recording company had to wait four years until Paul's agreement with Victor expired. The arrangement with Decca included Paul's swing aggregation and featured Joan Edwards, Clark Dennis, Jack Teagarden, and the Modernaires as soloists. After a gap of eighteen months new Whiteman recordings appeared with "My Reverie," "While a Cigarette Was Burning," "All Ashore," and "Heart and Soul." Decca also recorded many Gershwin concert numbers, including *An American in Paris, Rhapsody in Blue* (with Bargy), and the *Concerto in F.*

Paul was riding high. He felt that the time was right for another inquiry from the podium, "Is there such a thing as American music?" On Christmas night a large segment of the jazz world gathered in Carnegie Hall for Whiteman's Eighth Experiment in Modern American Music. The concert came on the heels of an instructive examination by Benny Goodman into the rise of jazz and swing in New York,

John Erskine, a musicologist and author, joined with Benny and his orchestra at Town Hall to trace modern dance music from early ragtime to the jazz period and into the era of syncopated jazz. The latter period, Erskine explained, gave rise to Paul Whiteman "with his carefully syncopated jazz, grounded in musical intelligence." The evening really took off when Goodman moved "into the groove" with his quartet, and brought down the house with "Lady Be Good," "I Know That You Know," and "One O'Clock Jump."

At Carnegie Hall on December 25 Whiteman stayed clear of swing except for two interludes with two of its leading practitioners— Artie Shaw and Louis Armstrong. Shaw played his own composition, "The Blues." Trite, but brilliantly executed, reported *The New York Times*. Armstrong performed with the Lyn Murray Singers on "All Over God's Heaven" and "Shadrack," but he was virtually ignored by the critics.

A half-dozen new, somewhat overdressed, works failed to create any surge of excitement in the sold-out house. For example, Paul's idea of presenting a series of short orchestral pieces on the subject of bells, soliciting individual contributions from Duke Ellington, Fred Van Epps, Bert Shefter, Walter Gross, Roy Bargy, and Morton Gound, resulted in a commonplace potpourri. Richard Rodgers's new *Nursery Ballet* was dull; Grofé's *Trylon and Perisphere*—a tribute to the approaching New York World's Fair—lacked direction; Raymond Scott's *Three Ideas for Quintette and Orchestra* only briefly amused; Nathan Van Cleave's *Opus I, Number 1* was overwritten.

Unwisely perhaps, Paul offered Gershwin's unfinished "Cuban Overture" with Rosa Linda at the piano. On surer turf, he closed the concert with *Rhapsody in Blue*.

Of the bulk of the program the *Times* could only write, "This stuff has all been heard before under other titles. It is music that once was jazz, trying to be something better than its own swell self. It is music that has scorned its musical heritage, cut its social roots, and fallen for the empty glamour of vaudeville virtuosity. It has clothed innocent tunes in pretentious tonal raiment, and awaited the coming of the second 'Rhapsody in Blue.' "

The performance was the last of Whiteman's experiments in the concert hall. Eight times in nearly fifteen years he had gambled for high stakes. He had won big and gloriously the first time out, but he had never again equaled the impact he made in 1924. Paul never lacked for a capacity audience and critical appreciation for his experimental endeavors; but he did fail to match his polished virtuosity with solid creativity.

Four days after the concert Whiteman opened at Loew's State Theater on Broadway in a revue called *The Rhythm Rodeo*. He topped the bill with old favorites, modulated swing music, and a jitterbug dance contest. During one matinee performance Jack Teagarden kept glancing at his watch. A single tune remained to be played. When the band finished the number, Big T carefully cleaned his horn and placed it in the case. His brother Charlie watched in bewilderment. "Where are you going?" he asked.

"Home," Jack happily replied. "My five-year contract ran out a couple of minutes ago. Now I'm gonna start my own swing band."

"We've got another show tonight," Charlie reminded him.

"Miff Mole can handle both parts." With this, Teagarden walked toward the door, where Paul was standing. "So long, Pops. I know you had plans for me. And thanks."

An astonished Paul was, for once, at a loss for words—not to mention at a loss for a fine horn.

The upturn in Whiteman's finances renewed his hopes of owning a working ranch or farm. His two summers in Texas had made him realize how much he missed living in the country, surrounded by land and cattle and horses. Amon Carter's gift of a homesite near Fort Worth seemed to have given him an ideal place to build, but Paul was sensible enough to realize that his work necessitated a home near New York.

In the spring of 1938 he and Margaret seriously looked for a farm. They found a 147-acre rural retreat in Hunterdon County, New Jersey. Situated seventy miles from the city and near the town of Rosemont, the property consisted of two old stone houses and several dilapidated barns and outhouses. The view from the main building took the Whitemans' breath away. To the west there was a panorama of the stately Delaware River and the heavily wooded Pennsylvania hills. The farm also provided an immediate place for Paul to keep his horses, long confined in city stables. Paul envisioned a re-creation of his father's Colorado ranch, complete with cows, pigs, and chickens. Paul, Jr., would have his own room, and Margo would really blossom.

Paul, Jr., had spent occasional school vacations with Pops after the divorce from Vanda. The boy's happiest times, however, were spent at his grandparents' place in Colorado. But trips West, away from schools and city apartments, ended when Wilberforce moved back to Denver.

From the time Paul, Jr., was very young, Vanda insisted that the boy be sent to boarding school. At first, he was enrolled at the prestigious Black Foxe Military Institute in Los Angeles, where his classmates included the sons of Charlie Chaplin, Buster Keaton, and Jack Robbins. Paul, Jr., resented being sent so far away from both his mother's and his father's homes. Paul seemed unaware of his former wife's maneuverings; he saw only an apparently healthy boy, who seemed eager to carry on the family's musical tradition. During the summer of 1934 Pops added Paul, Jr., to his organization as a summer attraction at Manhattan Beach. The ten-year-old boy in short pants led a group of youngsters scouted by Pops and rehearsed by Roy Bargy. They played for several weeks at the New York resort. As the drummer, Junior held the spotlight. However, he avoided practice at the least excuse, believing that as Paul Whiteman, Jr., he did not have to work very hard. "When they put that spotlight on me, I'll show 'em," he would say.

It was not easy having the same name as America's biggest showman. Tremendous pressure was placed on the boy to emerge as a musical personality. Junior basically lacked the talent, drive, and judgment necessary to compete among natural and better-trained musicians, especially those who had passed the rigors of a Whiteman audition. Junior was a placid boy with a faraway gaze. Paul felt that a summer at the new farm would really straighten the boy out—make a man of him.

As Margaret and Paul took title to their farm, they dreamed of filling the homestead with children. Margo was not enough for all their love. Within a month or two they heard of a baby available for adoption. They filled out the necessary papers and journeyed to Massachusetts to bring the child back to New York. An aide at the medical center accompanied them to the nursery, where they saw the baby for the first time. The boy was pitifully tiny and unusually scrawny. The nurse explained that the infant would require a great deal of medical attention and supervision; a burden for any mother, he would probably never be able to lead a full and normal life. Paul was hesitant about taking the baby, but Margaret picked him up, eager to give him whatever help he needed, regardless of the burden and ultimate outcome. Paul agreed that the infant required a good home, and, in typical Whitemanese, he said, "Okay, wrap it up."

A nursery was soon added to the Essex House duplex for little Richard Whiteman, called Dickie.

The New York apartment was enlarged, renovated, and remodeled nearly every year. It had started out as four rooms, and doubled in size during the 1930s. Margaret designed the decor to resemble a summer garden with the suggestion of a cool and peaceful wisteria arbor in the entrance. She added white wrought-iron arches, purple walls, and grayish purple rugs. White brackets held pots of ivy against the walls. Most of the furniture was Victorian, with the frames painted white and the upholstery in cream, yellow, or blue silk. The dining room continued the garden motif, with a broad wallpaper border of green ivy running around the room and two pedestals flanking a white console marbleized in green and white, each bearing a vase full of deep-green huckleberry leaves. All but Paul's western-style room carried out the impression of fresh, open, green country. In less than a year the Whitemans would have the real thing; work on the farmhouse was progressing according to schedule as 1938 drew to a close.

Proceeds from a heavy schedule of one-nighters, strenuous weekly broadcasts (with late-night repeats for the West Coast), out-of-town theater engagements, periodic recording sessions, and convention bookings filled Whiteman's pockets with the necessary cash to pay for the continual influx of bills to revamp the farm and maintain his city apartment.

Of all his engagements in 1939, Paul's appearance at the Southwestern Exposition and Stock Show in Fort Worth pleased him most. It was old home week as the band played twice daily at the show and nightly at a café on the grounds. Paul even brought two of his horses to Texas to enter in competition.

In October 1939 ASCAP celebrated its twenty-fifth anniversary with a Swing Night at Carnegie Hall. The association's president, Gene Buck, asked Paul to open the concert. The audience, who had come for swing, merely tolerated Whiteman's musical display. They were eager and anxious for the real thing. Benny Goodman

took charge and filled that need, earning an overwhelming response
from the crowded hall. Fred Waring and a large chorus followed.
He conducted novelty numbers from a marvelous collection of
voices. But the jitterbugs were none too happy; they wanted action.
Along came Glenn Miller, whose band, rumor had it, was now the
most popular in the land. When Miller began to play his trombone
and pointed its bell directly at the audience, the gesture acted as
an invitation for them to scramble into the aisles for dancing. He
gave them "Little Brown Jug" and several other pop tunes. "What
has this guy got that Benny didn't have?" someone asked a jitterbug. "Nothing, really," she replied, "except that this guy has a
lot more brass."

With Glenn and Benny getting the lion's share of accolades from
jitterbugs, Paul and the gang hoped for a warmer reception at the
Corn Palace Festival in Mitchell, South Dakota. The annual celebration—which paid tribute to a good harvest of corn, wheat, rye,
and other grains—took place in a large auditorium suitably decorated inside and out with corn and grain mosaics.

Paul owed the booking to Roy Bargy's wife, Virginia MacLean.
Her father, Wallace MacLean, managed the Corn Palace show and
asked Whiteman to play during the festival. Virginia's father and
Paul hit it off too well when they met at dinner at the MacLean
home. Before, during, and after the meal, MacLean and Paul
downed round after round of drinks. Paul continued on into the
next day and through the week. Bargy ended up doing all the conducting until the last night.

That evening Pops felt duty bound to appear and mustered up
enough energy to climb onto the bandstand. He acknowledged the
applause and cheers of the crowd on the dance floor. As the music
filled the large hall, Paul's eye caught the unique decorations. Bun-
dles of corn stalks and mounds of pumpkins stood in every section
of free space. Without thinking, Paul picked up a good-sized pumpkin and tossed it on the dance floor. Its seed-laden insides splattered
in every direction. Hearty laughs followed. Pleased at the reaction,
he grabbed a small squash and heaved it into the audience. Next
he grabbed a pumpkin and a squash—using both hands—and threw
them at the feet of the dancers. By the end of the evening the floor
was a gooey mess and Pops wasn't much better. By now the local
townsfolk were outraged at his behavior and refused to pay his full
fee for the engagement.

Margaret, summoned from New York, arranged to have Paul meet her in Chicago. To her amazement, chagrin, and annoyance, Paul had shaved off his famous pencil-thin moustache. Her first task consisted of painting on a moustache, using a mascara brush. Paul had a date to play, and no one would acknowledge his presence without this vital identification.

When Liggett & Myers heard of the pumpkin-throwing episode at the Corn Festival, they called a meeting with the agency in New York, wondering whether the time had come to terminate Paul's services when his contract ran out.

Once under Margaret's steely eye, Paul pulled himself together in time for an opening at the Hotel New Yorker in November. As he was rehearsing for the engagement—which included radio pickups—he received word that his father was seriously ill with pneumonia. He rushed across the country to Wilberforce's bedside. When Wilberforce rallied slightly, Paul returned East. Soon after he opened at the New Yorker, Phil Cohan told him that the Chesterfield series would end on December 20, 1939. The cigarette people had decided to sign up Glenn Miller and his orchestra, for a fee that came to over $100 per minute of air time. The sponsor also wanted Paul's Modernaires, and before long the popular quartet joined Miller's aggregation.

As the holidays approached, Paul was again summoned to Denver and his father's bedside. He flew out and spent five hours at the hospital before returning East.

On Sunday morning, December 17, Ferne telephoned her brother to discuss their father's condition. Wilberforce was unconscious and in serious condition. Paul had been in an alcoholic haze for days, expecting the worst and fortifying himself for another plane journey to Denver. He immediately reserved a seat on a westbound flight leaving shortly after noon. During the stopover in Chicago he left the plane for a drink or two, and the aircraft departed without him. An hour later Paul was in a private plane he had chartered to fly him directly to Denver. While he was in the air, his father breathed his last. Five years earlier, Paul had rushed West to his mother's hospital bed, had also stopped briefly in Chicago, and had also lost the battle against time.

Family history records some words Wilberforce is claimed to have spoken to his son. The Professor, suffering from pneumonia, had been in an intermittent coma, only occasionally recognizing his family and physician. When Paul arrived at his father's bedside, the old man's eyes opened and stared in Paul's direction. He faintly mumbled, "Now what have you done?"

As the decade of the 1930s was entering its final days, Paul's disillusionment with the big band scene and swing was acute. He felt that his orchestra had a limited future in the swing era. He had tried to capture the attention of the country's youth. But the young people realized that he was not one of them; he looked as if he belonged to another age, when the Model T and Prohibition were new. When he came to the bandstand dressed in the colorful garb of contemporary swingsters and mugging like a teenager, his older fans were alienated. Most of the young jitterbugs considered him an aging relic.

Now, fifty years old, he also felt unable to endure the pace and discomforts of the road and weeks of one-nighters. With Margaret's encouragement, he made up his mind to give up the band.

Margaret had traveled less and less with Paul once it became clear that young Dickie could not leave home. She hovered over him constantly. Though he grew weaker and demanded more of her time, she seldom complained. Convinced that the boy would benefit from the country air and surroundings, she insisted on moving to the farm and she lived there permanently as soon as the house was habitable.

Paul looked forward to semiretirement. He had earned his rest. Over the past twenty years he had earned more money than any other conductor anywhere, at any time. In the Depression year of 1938 alone his organization had grossed more than $600,000. Many one-nighters paid $4,000 or $5,000, setting box-office records for the band business.

Whiteman decided to set out in early 1940 on one final five-month tour of theaters in twenty-seven cities in the East and Midwest. Thereafter he would stick to guest appearances and special engagements, keeping a nucleus of musicians on call.

The ultimate decision to break up his established organization hurled the already exhausted Pops into a state of depression. A few days after the new year began, he disappeared from the bandstand and New York. On January 9, 1940, he was discovered, under the name James Black, as a patient in a Long Island hospital. Authorities at Nassau Hospital refused to describe his illness except to state that it was not serious. Paul alone knew the real cause and the possible cure.

19

Travelin' Light

Paul left the hospital at the end of a week. The diagnosis was exhaustion, compounded by several months of excessive drinking. In mid-January 1940, Paul was back with the band for a tour of theaters in twenty-seven cities. This final road trip would nearly last five months. On April 2, shortly after his arrival in Cortland, New York, Paul was too weak to go on stage. Roy Bargy took over the conducting chores; Goldie served as master of ceremonies. Paul quickly returnd to New York, where he entered a hospital. Again the diagnosis was exhaustion. After a week of confinement he was released to rejoin the band. The tour ended in New York on May 30, and the band officially broke up.

With the pressures of leading a band full time lifted from his shoulders, he took an increasingly active part in the remodeling and modernization of his New Jersey "ranch." He retained its former owner as overseer and set him up in one of the houses on the property. The main house, a stone dwelling, had been built in 1787 by Joseph Reading, son of Governor John Reading of New Jersey. Whiteman named his place Walking Horse Farm in honor of his favorite horse, Walkalong. Before long he planned to expand the tract by buying an adjacent farm. When that deal went through, his property embraced over 600 acres of tillable land and forest. He soon referred to the real estate and the incessant talk about its running expenses as Agony Acres on Swinging Jaw Bend.

Within a year or two the farm became a thriving operation. Paul and his tenant farmer added a herd of Aberdeen Angus cattle, nearly

400 hogs, and several riding horses. Corn and barley covered much of the acreage as well. With the assistance of agricultural experts at Rutgers University, Paul also began a soil-conservation program. It entailed crop rotation, along with the construction of an enormous drainage ditch and contoured sloping at a cost of nearly $5,000.

Paul devoted much of his time and energy, as well as money, to Walking Horse Farm. He made frequent trips from New York, often stopping on the way at Colligan's Inn in nearby Stockton to drink and chat with its proprietors and customers. His commuting to the farm was interrupted by a commitment on the West Coast. Before the band officially broke up, Paul had agreed to appear in a film musical slated for production in 1940. With this in mind, he had kept four key men on standby—Al Galladoro, Harry Goldfield, Charles Teagarden, and of course, Mike Pingitore. The rest of the film orchestra would be recruited in Hollywood.

On June 7 Paul, accompanied by Margaret's sister, Ivy, and her husband, Dr. Bill Crawford, faced a musical welcome at Los Angeles airport. The head of the local musicians union led a small band as the visitors walked toward the terminal.

"How did they know about your arrival?" asked Crawford.

"It's been in all the papers," Paul replied. "And besides, the leader of the group, Spike Wallace, used to work for me."

Meeting Paul were representatives from MGM, the studio that had hired him for a role in the musical *Strike Up the Band*. The agreement called for five days' work at a fee of $30,000, plus expenses for Paul and the Crawfords during their stay at the Hollywood Roosevelt Hotel. It was a fair amount, as Paul admitted; but it was peanuts compared to Hollywood fees ten years earlier, when everything, even the lampposts, were made of solid gold.

During the years Whiteman was away, movie musicals had briefly fallen out of favor. Then, with Warner's *42nd Street*, they entered on a popularity that gave no sign of diminishing. However, the all-star revues of the early talkie days were outmoded. Audiences demanded solid plots performed by established actors and musicians in carefully crafted productions. A growing number of these films were being shot in Technicolor as the process continued to improve.

Every major studio released an average of one feature a week. And the productions under way in 1940 reflected the industry's commitment to quality, diversity, and innovation. Alfred Hitchcock was shooting *Rebecca*, which would win the year's Oscar for best picture. Orson Welles had begun production on *Citizen Kane* at RKO. *Our Town, Abe Lincoln in Illinois, The Great Dictator,* and *The Philadelphia Story* were among that year's crop.

Bing Crosby had become a big box-office draw as a singer and was winning laughs as a comic sidekick to Bob Hope in the first of the Road pictures. At Universal, where Paul luxuriated as the King of Jazz, W. C. Fields, his old costar from the *Scandals,* was king of the lot. Walt Disney toiled over *Fantasia,* a cartoon feature introducing Fantasound, a method of putting three sound tracks on the film. Paul was intrigued with Disney's achievement of giving recorded music a sense of depth. "Music as we know it," Paul said, "has a sense of width and height."

At MGM two dozen films were in production. Among them were *Northwest Passage,* with Spencer Tracy and Robert Young; *Pride and Prejudice,* featuring Laurence Olivier and Greer Garson; *Waterloo Bridge,* starring Vivien Leigh and Robert Taylor; and *Boom Town,* with Clark Gable and Claudette Colbert. A handful of Andy Hardy, Dr. Kildare, and Maisie pictures also utilized the Culver City sound stages. MGM's high-grossing musical operations were preparing a half-dozen entries with such draws as Fred Astaire and Eleanor Powell (*Broadway Melody of 1940*), Jeanette MacDonald and Nelson Eddy (*New Moon*), and Lana Turner and George Murphy (*Two Girls on Broadway*). Paul soon joined Mickey Rooney and Judy Garland on the set of *Strike Up the Band,* a follow-up to the successful *Babes in Arms.*

Directed by Busby Berkeley, the movie bore no resemblance to the Broadway show of the 1920s on which it was supposedly based. Aside from its title song by the Gershwins, the musical numbers came chiefly from the team of Roger Edens and George Stoll. Producer Arthur Freed and Edens contributed the best tune, "Our Love Affair," which was nominated for an Academy Award but lost. Douglas Shearer, the sound engineer, did, however, win an Oscar for the picture's track.

The energetic Mickey Rooney was at the top of his form playing the leader of a high-school band competing in a talent show. The contest idea stemmed from the popular radio amateur hours. Naturally Whiteman played the host of a nationwide radio talent search. Playing himself with and without his orchestra, Paul frequently required retakes as he flubbed the few lines the script assigned to him.

"The only thing that bothers me," he remarked to Dr. Crawford, "is these speeches I'm supposed to say. I can remember music all right. But when I get before that camera, I simply can't remember the words."

In a scene with Judy and Mickey, Paul muffed his lines a dozen times. On the thirteenth try, sweating and with all the people on the set holding their breath, he got the words out correctly. Mopping his brow, he hightailed it to his dressing room, where Crawford joined him. Paul was delighted to see his brother-in-law. "Whew! I'm glad I brought you along, Bill. If they're behind schedule on this picture, they might say I'm not physically fit and hold up production. But I've got you to say I'm fit as a fiddle."

The day after Paul finished his part in *Strike Up the Band* Crawford met him at breakfast. The doctor did a double take as he stood looking at Paul. Whiteman had shaved off his moustache.

"Why did you do that?" Crawford asked.

"The studio thinks they're going to get some publicity pictures of me on the set tomorrow. I'm not about to do it. This way they can't make me work and we can have some fun before we head back East."

Paul joined the rest of his family at the farm. He drove regularly to his New York office, where Jack Lavin still managed his affairs and those of the artists who remained under contract. As the summer droned on, Paul became restless and edgy. Something had gone out of his life that he missed fiercely. The conferences, the auditions, the telephone calls, the jokes, the gossip—he wanted to be a part of those activities. The pace and excitement, the fanfare and acclaim—they had shaped his existence for too long.

One day, after baling hay, he came into the farmhouse and said to Margaret, "I'm gonna get another band together and have Jack line up some bookings." In the fall of 1940 Whiteman and a new band resurfaced from one of the shortest retirements in show-business history.

Mike Pingitore got the word at his home at Grantwood, New Jersey. Drummer George Wettling and string bass player Artie Shapiro also returned to the Whiteman fold. Within a month Paul and Jack had gathered the nucleus of a new band and had begun rehearsing. Toots Camaratta supplied arrangements and helped form the outfit. The group brought together in late 1940 included Danny D'Andrea on saxophone and Murray McEachern on trombone; both had played with the Casa Loma orchestra. Murray doubled on a half-dozen instruments, including alto sax and violin, and filled the shoes of assistant conductor.

Paul needed still more key men to front a balanced, cohesive unit worthy of his name. He sought a replacement for Roy Bargy, who had joined the Lanny Ross radio program as conductor. Paul and his scouts spotted pianist Buddy Weed in Teddy Powell's band. Actually, the occasion was a rediscovery. A year earlier, Buddy had appeared in a swing contest on Tommy Dorsey's Kool cigarettes radio program; Chuck Goldstein of the Modernaires had taken the audition record of Buddy's impressive talent to Pops. But when Weed took Pops up on an invitation to sit in with the band at the New Yorker, Paul had fallen off the wagon in preparation for a flight to his sick father's bedside; Buddy never got a chance to play.

Now Paul imagined pianist-arranger Buddy Weed as his new Roy Bargy, perhaps a "coming Gershwin" he could mold. Buddy certainly knew the Gershwin repertoire, and it was not long before he became a leading and worthy interpreter of *Rhapsody in Blue*.

Lavin had booked the band for its debut in January 1941 at Ben Marden's new Colonial Inn in Hallandale, Florida. Paul rushed to put the finishing touches on the group. One of the last musicians hired was a young alto sax player from Brooklyn. He had solid professional experience playing with Hank Sears's band at Child's Restaurant in the basement of the Paramount Theater and with Zinn Arthur's orchestra at Roseland.

Paul first heard Alvy West over his car radio. Whiteman was impressed with Alvy's sax solo improvising on "The Woodpecker Song" broadcast during a remote of Arthur's group from the St. George Hotel. He called George Simon, editor of *Metronome* magazine, to have him track down the sax player for an audition.

Alvy lived with his parents in Brooklyn and regularly practiced in the living room. He did not like to be disturbed and never answered the phone. He would say, "Even if it's Paul Whiteman, tell him I'm not interested and hang up."

One day Whiteman's office did, indeed, call; Pops wanted to see the man who'd done the solo on that woodpecker number. Alvy went to the office, full of doubts about whether he would fit in and overly humble. Paul asked him how he would do on the clarinet cadenza of *Rhapsody in Blue*.

"Mr. Whiteman, I'd practice awfully hard. I'd study it and study it."

It was not the answer Paul was waiting to hear. "Well, son, some other time then."

A crestfallen Alvy left the office and headed back to Brooklyn. He wondered how he could explain the loss of such a fabulous opportunity to his parents. Disabled at birth with a crippled right arm, he worried about competing with other sax players who did not need specially adapted instruments.

Two weeks later a friend told him that he had landed a choice job—solo sax player with Paul Whiteman. That really hurt. But he had added, "Since I'm leaving Richard Himber's band, there'a spot open. I've set up an audition for you. Alvy."

Alvy appeared at the rehearsal hall only to discover a mass audition. Every sax player in the city had come. He refused to be a part of it. He was finally persuaded to go inside and get it over with. Alvy walked in, and to his surprise discovered Whiteman in the room.

Alvy went straight to his chair, took out his horn, and opened the music of "To a Wild Rose." He and the band began playing. During the piece Himber moved from the back of the room to join Whiteman. They put their heads together, and snatches of words reached Alvy's ears. "I want him."

"No, you already have one of the best."

"I need him badly."

At the end of the audition Whiteman spoke. "Meet me in my office after rehearsal."

When Alvy again faced Paul, he said, "I want you. Himber's taking back my new sax player. What's your price, son?"

"It would be presumptuous to name an amount. I'll leave that to you."

"I'll take care of you, son. We're married for life."

West joined Whiteman with a mere handshake, not a written contract. For the remainder of Paul's career he brought in Alvy whenever possible. "He treated me like a son for the rest of his life. When I got serious with a girl in California, he asked to meet and talk with her. After we were married, he kept up with our family. We never lost touch."

Yet at Alvy's first rehearsal with the band he was not so sure he wanted to travel with Pops. Alvy arrived early and ran into Mike sitting alone on the side of the room. "The old man is drunk," Mike growled. "And when he's drunk he's mean."

In his naivete Alvy went to Jack Lavin. "I'm not going with the band to Florida."

"Why?"

"Because Mr. Whiteman drinks."

"Don't worry, Alvy, I'll make sure Mr. Whiteman doesn't drink again."

Unbeknownst to Alvy, Paul's doctors had given him an ultimatum that week: if he did not stop drinking, he would not live very long. Paul sobered up remarkably fast that winter, and he worked hard.

The band that emerged turned out to have the best dancing beat of any Paul had led in years, and he was back in the big leagues. Paul opened at the Colonial Inn with a revue starring Sophie Tucker, Harry Richman, and Joe E. Lewis. In spite of his usual first-night jitters, he appeared in control and relaxed as he backed the veteran headliners. There were three floor shows nightly, in addition to his own dance sessions. As part of dance sets Whiteman experimented, none too successfully, with dubbing in the voices of Bing Crosby, Connee Boswell, Mildred Bailey, and Morton Downey, all former proteges. He inserted their records into the Whiteman arrangements, explaining that, though they could not be there in person, they had "sent their voices down."

In *Variety's* Band Reviews, Abel Green called the new Whiteman aggregation as modern as 1941.

New blood, fresh arrangements, peppery rhythm and thoroughly solid in every respect. Proving that neither time nor tide can dim the King of Jazz. Excepting for Mike Pingitore who, Whiteman states, will always have a job with him, it's all fresh Local 802 fodder. It's a zingy setup of four violins, four reeds, four brass, five rhythm including a crack Cuban drummer [Willie Rodriguez] when the band converts into an equally fancy smaller unit for the congarhumba tempos. The four strings become seven through doubling by the reed section. There's also a relief pianist to round out the eighteen personnel in addition to Ann Sutherland who chants a nice vocal.

The country had a chance to see and hear a "new" Paul Whiteman that winter and spring. The band played engagements in Miami,
Fort Meyers, and Orlando, before heading to other cities in the
South and East. In March Paul returned to New York to make a
few changes before opening at Chicago's Chez Paree in May. He
had added Frank Howard, a former singer with Charlie Spivak, to
the group, and now he sought a new female vocalist. He auditioned
a slew of them and settled on Dolly Mitchell. He also reorganized
the band as George Wettling and reedman George Poliakin left.

The month Paul opened in Florida the industrywide broadcast
licenses with ASCAP expired. The group looked for a sizable boost
in fees. Radio stations and networks reacted by forming their own
performance-rights society, Broadcast Music, Inc. (BMI). Broadcasters prepared for ASCAP's blackout of its huge inventory of
popular songs by trying to find other sources of music so as to
make radio independent of ASCAP's copyright pool. Since Paul
was not on the radio except for an occasional remote pickup, the
blackout had little immediate effect on his repertoire. However, he
looked for a substitute for the *Rhapsody* to use as a theme. "Margo"
no longer suited the times. He chose a thoroughly contemporary
tune by composer-arranger Larry Wagner. Called "Whistler's
Mother-in-Law," it had been brought to Paul's attention by Murray
McEachern. Paul remembered Wagner as the freelance arranger
used for most of Durelle Alexander's light ballads and novelty tunes
during the Woodbury series. The band used the new signature melody before ASCAP settled with the country's broadcasters in mid-
1941, but the substitute theme never became identified with Pops.

Whiteman opened in Chicago on May 16, 1941, for a long engagement. Twenty-five-year-old Murray McEachern gained tremendous attention by playing in succession alto sax, trombone,
violin, clarinet, and trumpet. His rendition of "Only Forever" on
alto sax gained him a huge following, and Paul predicted that one
of these days the Canadian-born McEachern would give dance-band
leaders a run for their money.

Near the end of the Chez Paree booking Paul received an urgent
call from Margaret. Little Dickie had suffered a serious relapse in
his battle against nephrosis, for which there was no cure. Off and
on for more than a year his body had swelled up with water as his
kidneys failed. The three-year-old child required nursing day and

night. Margaret devoted all her time to him, giving up virtually everything to comfort the youngster through the ordeal.

When Margaret's call came in early July, Paul immediately flew home. Paul passed the seemingly endless hours of the journey by staring out the window watching cloud formations. They seemed pink as a baby's skin and reminded Paul of poor Dickie, who called him "Papa moon." In midair he had a premonition that he was too late. In fact, his young son died before Paul's plane landed.

Paul could not linger long in New Jersey. The band had to rehearse for a tour from Pennsylvania to California. Many of the dates brought in less than top dollar, but overall because of close bookings the outfit was making some money. Paul hoped to record again; it had been eighteen months since he had last cut any sides. His contract with Decca had run out not long after he recorded a half-dozen numbers based on a New York theme, "Manhattan Serenade," "Metropolitan Nocturne," and "Side Street in Gotham" among them.

The prospect of a radio connection appeared more promising. In late August Paul's office worked out details; beginning on October 7 Whiteman would costar with George Burns and Gracie Allen on their Tuesday night NBC program from Hollywood. Lever Brothers was planning to introduce Swan Soap—"the new white floating soap eight ways better than old-style floating soap . . . it lasts and lasts." Lever had allocated a large budget for the comedy show. Paul and the band were elated to land the coveted job with the popular comedians, who were starting their tenth year on the air. Although the job required that they settle on the West Coast for a while, the men were eager for the extra money and the exposure. Paul made plans to bring Margaret and Margo and the Whiteman household staff to California.

By the first week in September the band was in the Far West, booked into Elko, Nevada, during the state's livestock show and fair. From there it headed north to Seattle for a twelve-day engagement before opening at the prestigious Rose Room in San Francisco's Palace Hotel.

Paul quickly set an attendance record in the city where he had first ventured into popular music. The crowds poured into the Rose Room for dancing, and the interest in Pops's new band led the hotel to schedule a Saturday afternoon Tea Dance. As a gesture of welcome, the mayor of San Francisco, Angelo J. Rossi, presented Paul with yet another key to the city.

The men were earning bigger checks. Every Monday night after the last set at the Palace, they boarded a special double-decker sleeper bus for Los Angeles to do the Tuesday radio shows with Burns and Allen. A relic from earlier days of bus travel, the vehicle provided bunks, so that the troupe could sleep en route. Because Paul hated to fly and the train timetable did not mesh with late-night travel, the bus offered the only means to get to Hollywood in time for a late-morning rehearsal.

The pace was grueling—most of all for Paul, who played a part in the weekly script and had to review his lines as well as rehearse the opening theme, the transitional music, the scene ending "tags," the closing piece, a featured band number, and a solo by tenor Jimmy Cash. Even after the Rose Room engagement ended, commuting from the San Francisco area continued when Paul accepted a brief engagement at Sweet's Ballroom in Oakland. Alvy West remembered that booking; it ended on a low note for him.

In the early hours of the morning, as the sleeper bus unloaded at the NBC studios at Hollywood and Vine, Alvy discovered that his horns were missing. The baggage handler swore that they had never been loaded onto the bus in Oakland. Alvy was beside himself—the instruments had been stolen. He went immediately to Whiteman and explained what happened.

"I don't care," Paul snapped. "Go across the street to Lockie's music store and when it opens, get a new horn."

Alvy fretted about the loss of his specially designed alto sax. Now he had to adjust to a normal instrument. He preferred not to play at all, but Paul insisted, counseling that it was not the end of the world. Meanwhile he spread the word about the theft of the custom-made horns. Herb Caen wrote the loss up in a San Francisco newspaper, pointing out that no one would dare to fence these specially made instruments. Return them to the ballroom; no questions would be asked, the newspapers urged.

Exactly two weeks later Alvy received a call from Sweet's. The horns had been dropped in the ballroom; the manager was bringing them to Los Angeles for delivery to an overjoyed Alvy West.

Whiteman augmented his radio work with one-nighters as distant as Phoenix. Then he settled into the Florentine Gardens on Hollywood Boulevard. Reunited with producer N. T. Granlund, Paul and the band backed an exotic floor show of sensational-looking chorus girls. All the boys remembered one scantily clad chorine in particular . The sultry Yvonne De Carlo stood out in the entrancing line of beauties.

More arrangers were needed to deal with the large volume of song material. Two musicians within the band, sax player Dan D'Andrea and trumpeter Monty Kelly, regularly worked out arrangements. But they were soon joined by two Hollywood musicians engaged for the radio shows—Felix Mills and Joe Glover. Fashion-conscious Joe came on the scene dressed in a Norfolk jacket and an Alpine-style felt hat with a beaver tail set in its ribbon. His jaunty appearance was augmented by a distinctive moustache and Vandyke beard. Paul took one look at him and quipped, "Whaddaya know—Christ in *Esquire*."

Paul still needed a chief arranger for the band and sent for Jimmy Mundy in New York, one of the few black musicians to be a regular member of an all-white outfit. He had joined Benny Goodman in 1935, writing "Sing, Sing, Sing" for the King of Swing two years later. A tenor-sax player with Earl Hines in the 1920s and early 1930s, and later the leader of his own band, Mundy contributed two other big hits to the swing era, "Jumpin' at the Woodside" and "Air Mail Special." Mundy spent a year with Whiteman in Hollywood; when he joined his organization, Paul refused bookings that necessitated different accommodations for him.

When the band began to work at the Florentine Gardens, Sunday-morning script rehearsals for Burns and Allen were started. Since Paul had a speaking part in the show as a humorous, or "jive-talking," musician, he participated in these reading sessions with the costars, announcer Bill Goodwin, vocalist Jimmy Cash, and cast members Dick Ryan, Edith Evanson, and Irving Lee. Paul received his share of laughs, often from ad libs. One critic called him the "most sensational newcomer" to the program. "His music is superb but his unique brand of 'jive talk' is more spectacular." Paul had finally overcome his fear of talking at a microphone; he even enjoyed his part in the dialogue on each broadcast.

On the first Sunday in December, Paul arrived at NBC Studio B to join the cast, scriptwriters, and producer. He apologized for being several minutes late and holding up the rehearsal. Then he announced, "While we were driving over here, we had the car radio on and heard that the Japanese bombarded Pearl Harbor out in Hawaii. It looks like we're in the war."

The stunned group was not prepared. The war in Europe had seemed very far way to most of them, and certainly self-contained. America blessedly was not involved. All that was changed now as they considered the possibility of an attack on California. Their minds raced from the words on the script to the calamity and devastation awaiting the West Coast from a possible sneak air attack or sabotage. They worried about their families and became suddenly aware of the fact that they had sons of draft age.

The Federal Communications Commission decreed that all Los Angeles radio stations must shut down and go off the air. This blackout would prevent approaching enemies from pinpointing objectives by radio and help local monitoring outposts to locate the enemy. "When the air is clear," FCC inspector Frank Burris explained, "our own 'listening in' is simplified." After nineteen hours of silence the ban was lifted.

The producer, Glenhall Taylor, quickly called for a rehearsal for the Burns and Allen broadcast on Tuesday, December 9. The words of Eleanor Roosevelt in the morning newspaper stuck in his mind. She advised America to pull down the blackout shades, turn on the radio, sit back, and enjoy some laughs. At the final run-through, Taylor made many last-minute rewrites and changes. At one point George Burns said, "We'll probably have to ad lib the whole show."

"We can write the dialogue on a slate," remarked costar Gracie Allen.

"Nope," added Paul. "We'll put the gags on plate glass, so the audience can see through them."

In the following months NBC and Lever Brothers took the popular program and its thirty minutes of laughs and music out of the studio. Broadcasts were picked up from army bases, naval stations, and other military installations throughout California.

The record business, aware there would be shortages of materials very soon, rushed to cut as many records as possible. Whiteman joined the singers and musicians crowding into studios on both coasts.

No longer tied to Decca, Paul agreed to Victor's suggestion that he record a couple of sides with the company studio orchestra. On February 7 he brought in a Jimmy Munday tune called "Well Digger's Breakdown" and a vocal duet by Dolly Mitchell and Wingy Manone titled "A Zoot Suit." Victor also reestablished Whiteman in the catalog that year by issuing a souvenir album of eight sides made in 1927.

In the early months of 1942 two old Whiteman pals took the daring step of forming a record company in Hollywood. Johnny Mercer and Buddy DeSylva, together with an executive in the electrical industry, Glenn Wallichs, organized a firm that would draw upon the musicians and singers based in and near Los Angeles. Wallichs, who had started as a radio and camera repairman in Hollywood, managed the new company, which bore the name Capitol Records.

Mercer urged Wallichs to sign up Whiteman at a substantial guarantee. The prestige of his name, even after twenty years, would add luster to the new company. Capitol's three principal owners decided to use Paul on the first releases. Augmented by Billy Butterfield on trumpet, the band recorded four current tunes—"I've Got a Gal in Kalamazoo," "I've Found a New Baby," "The General Jumped at Dawn," and "Serenade in Blue." Two months later, in June, the band returned to make discs with three noteworthy vocalists. Johnny Mercer and Jack Teagarden sang "The Old Music Master," and Billie Holiday (using her nickname, Lady Day) vocalized on "Travelin' Light." It was originally an instrumental piece by trombonist Trummy Young, who wrote it with Jimmy Munday— both had been with Earl Hines in the 1930s. Mercer had added lyrics after he heard Paul rehearse the number. When he had studied the song, Pops asked that Billie record the tune. It was tailored into a slow ballad to capture her sultry quality. Trombonist Skip Layton gained label billing for the opening and closing stretches. On the flip side Whiteman added a run-of-the-mill arrangement of the Mercer–Kern song "You Were Never Lovelier," with a refrain by Paul's trumpeter Larry Neill.

Paul's line-up of musicians in the Capitol studios that June 12, 1942, comprised the last of his own bands. In addition to violinists Dave Newman, Harry Azinsky, and Saul Blumenthal, who were not used that day, the players were:

TRUMPET; Monty Kelly, Larry Neill, Don Waddilove.
TROMBONE: Murray McEachern, Skip Layton.
SAXOPHONE: Alvy West, Dan D'Andrea, Lenny Hartman.
BANJO: Mike Pingitore.

PIANO: Buddy Weed.
DRUMS: Willie Rodriguez.
BASS: Artie Shapiro.

Whiteman's Capitol releases made little impression on buyers. They barely broke even; only Billie Holiday's disc generated interest and eventually became a collector's item. Capitol's biggest hit in the early months of the war turned out to be a boogie-woogie number by pianist Freddie Slack and his orchestra. "Cow Cow Boogie," with a vocal by Ella Mae Morse, launched one of the catchiest tunes of the year.

That summer the president of the American Federation of Musicians, James C. Petrillo, served notice on recording companies; no more phonograph records could be cut with his union members after July 31 unless the manufacturers guaranteed that their discs would not be played in jukeboxes and on radio. In essence, Petrillo was urging musicians to discontinue all recordings; they were making the live musician seem obsolete. Only vocal records without instrumental accompaniment or solos could be produced. To all intents and purposes the ruling ended the long and productive recording career of many orchestras, including Whiteman's. By the time the strike was settled in late 1944 Paul had moved on into other areas of the entertainment field.

His association with Capitol could easily have turned out differently. When the company was getting off the ground, Johnny Mercer urged Paul to invest in the business; he only wanted a few thousand dollars. Paul, however, could not visualize a serious competitor to Victor, Decca, and Columbia. He believed that Capitol would go the way of so many record companies he knew of: Majestic, Pathe, Cameo, Gennett, and Perfect had had only fleeting successes. Mercer's company, he thought, had hardly any chance of staying in the moneymaking groove. As it turned out, the early investors made millions when the company was sold to EMI in 1956.

Paul was surprised and delighted that his buddy Mercer made the Capitol label tops among record makers. In the 1940s it signed up a blockbusting array of stars including Nat King Cole, Peggy Lee, Andy Russell, Stan Kenton, Margaret Whiting, Betty Hutton, Jo Stafford, Mel Torme, and the Pied Pipers. Paul came back to the fold in a modest way. Dave Dexter, a company executive, asked him to participate in Capitol's *History of Jazz* project, encompassing forty sides featuring many noted musicians. Paul rounded up a sizable number of his earliest players—including Mueller, Gott, Grofé, and Pingitore—and recorded "Wang Wang Blues" note for note as they had played it some twenty-five years earlier. Paul conducted a second group of oldtimers, including Matty Malneck, Perry Botkin, and Elmer Smithers, on his 1927 hit, "San." Still later, with the arrival of the long-playing disc, Capitol brought together Paul and pianist Leonard Pennario for a recording of *Rhapsody in Blue*. Roy Bargy came in to do the ground work on what turned out to be a highly creditable and popular rendition of the Gershwin classic.

Gershwin's music struck a patriotic chord during the early war years. He had captured the sounds, tempo, and nuances of Broadway, the concert stage, and Tin Pan Alley, as well as such geographical and ethnic areas as Harlem, the South, and Cuba. With the fifth anniversary of Gershwin's death approaching, the Los Angeles Philharmonic asked Whiteman to conduct an all-Gershwin benefit concert. Paul drilled the orchestra for days, until the results satisfied him. Using his own men as a small nucleus, he rehearsed the compositions as if they had just been written and were entirely new to everyone. As he surveyed the large aggregation from the podium, some classic Whiteman wisecracks emerged. "If you guys approached Beethoven the way you approach Gershwin, Beethoven would stink, too." To achieve a certain effect he said, "Now, this is very soft, fellows. It's in the lullaby department. So make with the 'Hansel and Gretel.' " When that failed to make a deep enough impression, he added. "If you guys don't quit trying to make like Jericho with the studio walls, I'm gonna stuff grapefruit in those lousy horns!"

The concert had been organized to shore up the Philharmonic's dwindling reserves. Bing Crosby, Harry James, Dinah Shore, and the King's Men had been signed up; Oscar Levant was asked to play *Concerto in F* and *Rhapsody in Blue,* but his sarcastic response to the fact that he was always being asked to play the two old Gershwin standards and nothing else made Paul give the assignment to Buddy Weed. The program opened with a eulogy read by the movie actor, Edward Arnold. It closed with selections from *Porgy and Bess* sung by Crosby and Shore. In between, Whiteman and his guest artists performed an array of the best known of Gershwin music.

The concert proved a financial and critical success. San Francisco's Symphony Orchestra went into action to bring the program to its Civic Auditorium. On February 20, 1943, Paul conducted a repeat for the benefit of the symphony. Another sell-out, it brought in $40,000—a record for a one-night program, surpassing the previous high of $27,000 for soprano Mary Garden. The program had changed very little from the earlier line-up. Bing and Dinah were back on stage with the King's Men. This time Edward G. Robinson read the eloquent tribute to Gershwin, and Jesus Maria Sanroma played the piano solos (in the interval, Buddy Weed had joined the army).

Paul joined other bandleaders and musicians aiding the war effort by selling bonds, visiting military hospitals, and helping GI recruitment drives. He was also asked to serve as an advisor to the War Department's Special Services Division. By the late summer of 1942 Paul had lost several more musicians to Uncle Sam. Once again he was ready to toss aside his baton. As the second season on Burns and Allen approached, he disbanded the orchestra; his men were headed elsewhere. Jack Lavin also left, to join the Disney studios as a casting director.

Burns and Allen switched to the CBS network, which agreed to hire studio musicians to work with Paul. He had, however, retained Mike and Alvy to keep some continuity and familiarity in the Whiteman sound. As the war entered its second year, Paul was occupied with the weekly broadcast and with plans for special concert appearances. One of the more unusual and certainly most talked about undertakings came about in Carnegie Hall just a month after the Gershwin program in San Francisco.

George Burns and his writers had concocted a running gag in which Gracie would begin taking piano lessons with the whimsical notion of one day playing in a concert hall with an orchestra. Gracie's efforts at the keyboard were woven into every program. Ultimately the plot had Gracie planning for her big debut.

The original episodes were aired during regular broadcasts from the CBS Hollywood studios. But then it was decided that an actual concert would be held in New York and would also serve as a wartime fund raiser. For the event, which included works by Gershwin and Cole Porter, Paul brought Bargy and other key players. Felix Mills came up with an arrangement for the occasion; he developed an orchestral pattern built on Gracie's attempts to play the scale. Dubbed by the orchestra the Concerto for Scale and Clinker, it opened with an octave, the last note a wrong one. Gracie pantomimed the keyboard motions on a miniature piano, her hands not visible to the audience. Whenever she hit the clinker on the scale, the orchestra picked up the note and repeated it over and over, as a device to move into the familiar strains of "Night and Day" and the Anvil Chorus from *Trovatore*. After a half-dozen pages of this, Gracie at last conquered the scale. All eight piano notes were played perfectly and without accompaniment. The performance netted a sizable sum for the American Red Cross.

Back in California, Paul conducted the Gracie Allen *Piano Concerto for Index Finger*, as it was now known, at the Los Angeles Philharmonic Auditorium on April 1 and 2. Other concerts—featuring Gershwin scores—took him to Pasadena and San Diego in early spring. Then, to open the Hollywood Bowl summer season on July 4, 1943, Paul presented an all-American program of composers and performers. He shared the podium with Captain Meredith Willson and Ferde Grofé, both of whom conducted compositions of their own. Soloists included pianists Ray Turner and Louis Alter, vocalist Ginny Simms, and "keyboard artist" Gracie Allen. Works by Sousa, Herbert, Gershwin, W. C. Handy, Charles Wakefield Cadman, and Rodgers and Hart delighted the large audience. The evening ended with Paul's leading a medley of service songs sung by a group called the Bombardiers.

Whiteman had managed without his orchestra to establish himself as a leader of concert orchestras—a guest conductor who could bring together in one program something to please everyone. And music lovers old and young flocked to hear him present familiar semiclassics, "hot" specialties, waltzes, and pop tunes.

The continuing popularity of Gershwin's music had led movie moguls to think about filming his life story. Back in 1938 Warner Brothers had already announced that the studio's latest discovery, John Garfield, would play George in a movie authorized by the Gershwin family. Warner's hired Clifford Odets to prepare a script; Ira attended the first story conference and made so many notes after hearing only the first page or so that he decided he could only turn his back and let the scriptwriters do what they wanted. The project stalled for several years. Then, in 1941, Ira again tried to help by giving a series of interviews to the latest set of writers assigned to the story. Eventually very little of his first-hand information was used.

Producer Jesse L. Lasky indicated that there could be no Gershwin biography without *Rhapsody* and that there could be no *Rhapsody* without Whiteman. Lasky had a verbal agreement with Paul concerning his part in the film.

Casting and production began in late 1942. More than eighty sound-stage settings and 3,000 extras were ultimately used. The studio cast the twenty-eight-year-old Robert Alda as Gershwin, with Joan Leslie and Alexis Smith depicting two of the many women in his life. The movie *Rhapsody in Blue*, which ran for almost two and a half hours, ended up as a pedestrian and inaccurate account of the composer's life and times. The redeeming elements of the film were the glorious Gershwin melodies, the superb photography, and the marvelous array of real-life supporting players.

Oscar Levant, George White, Al Jolson, Hazel Scott, Anne Brown, and Pops all played themselves to good advantage. Jolson, in particular, brightened up the screen by performing "Swanee," Gershwin's first big hit. (Al's appearance resulted in the filming of his own biography, *The Jolson Story*, and one of the greatest comebacks in the history of show business.)

Rhapsody in Blue, which occupied Paul for several months, reunited a handful of the Whiteman players of the 1920s—Charles Strickfaden, Mike Pingitore, Harold McDonald, Mischa Russell, Henry Busse, and Ray Turner. They peformed with about fifty other studio musicians in the highlight of the film, the complete performance of *Rhapsody in Blue*. Oscar Levant played the title work as well as *Concerto in F*, while all other piano selections were dubbed by Ray Turner for Robert Alda.

Paul as himself injected authenticity into the biography. He was seen at Carnegie Hall conducting *135th Street*, at Aeolian Hall with *Rhapsody*, at Lewisohn Stadium with an all-Gershwin concert, and in various backstage scenes. The film, a commercial success, served its purpose as a wartime patriotic salute to an American musician.

Rhapsody in Blue was released in June 1945 after six months of previews for the Armed Forces. Long before it opened, Paul romped through a minor musical at Republic Pictures. The studio cast its biggest vocal star, Constance Moore, in a nostalgic cream puff called *Atlantic City*. To give the picture authenticity it signed old timers Joe Frisco, Belle Baker, Buck and Bubbles, Al Shean, and Gus Van. Paul, none too eager to make this movie, asked for a high fee, hoping the producers would refuse. To his surprise, the small studio agreed to his request of $50,000. The quickly made film was shot in the spring of 1944 and released in August. Paul enjoyed working with such supporting players and specialty acts as Louis Armstrong, Jerry Colonna, and Dorothy Dandridge.

The Burns and Allen broadcast went off the air in May 1943 for the customary summer break. As the studio door at CBS closed, another opened down the street at NBC. On June 6 Chase and Sanborn Coffee sponsored *Paul Whiteman Presents*, a thirteen-week summer replacement for Bergen and McCarthy. The show starred Pops and newcomer Dinah Shore and featured announcer Bill Goodwin.

By 1942 Dinah had become the outstanding female blues singer in the country. Her regular appearances on the Eddie Cantor radio show and many Bluebird recordings had made her a star on the rise. As she handled the chores of program hostess with charm and assurance, she provided the perfect balance to the weight and longevity of Paul's credentials and career. She actually had filled in as Pops's band vocalist for several nights at the New Yorker Hotel in late 1939.

It is easy now to see why *Paul Whiteman Presents* has been called a landmark in variety shows. Nearly every program of the series welcomed an alumnus of Pops's organization. Beginning with Henry Busse and his trumpet solo on "When Day Is Done," the broadcasts brought back Matty Malneck, Johnny Mercer, Jack Teagarden, the Modernaires, Roy Bargy, Jimmy Dorsey, and Mike Pingitore. Such comic headliners as Eddie Cantor, Olsen and Johnson, Ed Gardner, Jimmy Durante, Bert Lahr, William Gaxton and Victor Moore, Red Skelton, Lou Holtz, and Burns and Allen became Sunday evening guests.

Paul's most remarkable coup was to persuade Bing Crosby to join the reunion of the Rhythm Boys on the Fourth of July broadcast. Bing agreed as a favor to Pops; afterward he remarked, "Now we're even." Apparently it took a lot of nerve for him to face Al Rinker and Harry Barris again, let alone sing with them. Both were bitter at having been ignored by their former partner. Al had not seen Bing since the trio broke up in the early 1930s; Barris had seen him only once, some eleven years earlier. Nevertheless, the trio performed effortlessly and with little rehearsal on the hit they had created back in 1927, "Mississippi Mud." The broadcast also offered a satirical sketch on their first audition with Paul. Dinah played Paul's secretary in the skit, which tossed in some current jokes about Bing's race horses. Thirteen years later, when Paul commemorated his fiftieth year in show business, the segments were reproduced in a multidisc anniversary record album—the only part of the all-star LP that could not be newly recorded, chiefly because Bing was no longer interested.

The Rhythm Boys never sang together again. Briefly it had seemed like old times to Pops, but as Harry Barris would always say when urged to get in touch with Bing, "I wouldn't waste a dime calling him."

At the end of the Chase and Sanborn series on August 29, Paul had a commitment in New York. Margaret and Margo had been hastily packing and closing up the rented house in Beverly Hills; they were both anxious to return home to the farm.

Paul's two-year stint in California had kept him busy with successful radio contracts, a major motion picture role, a dozen Gershwin concerts, a handful of new recordings, and many weeks of hotel and nightclub bookings. In the midst of his activity, he broke up the band, keeping two or three old players on standby. Even without the band, Paul's momentum hardly slowed. He was about to enter a new and challenging phase of his career—one that seemed a natural step for this man whom everyone in and outside the business recognized as the dean of American music and the monarch of mass entertainment.

20

Blue Notes

During Whiteman's visit to New York to do the Gracie Allen Carnegie Hall concert, he worked out the details of a project that would bring him back East to a new job. He met with the officers of a radio network which was emerging as an independent chain. The Blue Network had its roots in the earliest transmitters in the country and had grown into a chain of over 160 station affiliates. The outfit now sought an executive who would bring leadership and prestige to the musical aspect of the revamped broadcasting system. It was mandatory for the chain to assert its programming individuality and financial viability.

For some fifteen years the Blue Network had operated in the shadow of its sister company, the Red Network. Both had come into being in 1926, when the National Broadcasting Company first went on the air and divided affiliates and wholly owned stations into two distinct chains. NBC linked New York station WEAF to the heavily sponsored Red Network and made the nearby Westinghouse outlet WJZ the flagship station of the less commercial Blue.

In the 1920s WJZ gave many established artists and aspiring performers their first opportunities to perform. Opera star Anna Case was a featured soloist on special pickups. Broadway comedians George Jessel and Ed Wynn paused briefly at its mike. The harmonizing Happiness Boys and sportscaster Ted Husing discovered the new medium and stayed. In the years WJZ broadcast from studios in Aeolian Hall from 1923 to 1927, the station lured a young singer named Milton Cross to an announcer's job. Remote pickups of Paul Whiteman and other dance bands also sporadically filled hours of broadcast time.

NBC's coast-to-coast Blue Network became known for programs that emphasized fine music (Chicago Civic Opera, Boston Symphony), public service (*National Vespers, America's Town Meeting of the Air*), and education (*National Farm and Home Hour, Music Appreciation Hour*). Lacking the Red chain's star-studded comedy and variety shows, it had to fill out the broadcast day with low-keyed community-oriented features that built a loyal though smaller following.

Behind the revamping of the Blue Network into a dynamic and enterprising broadcasting company was a man who had made a fortune from the Life Saver candy business. In the early 1940s Edward J. Noble turned from mint manufacturing to other areas to invest his millions. Radio attracted his interest, and he became the first individual to own a national radio network.

This purchase was made possible when RCA began to look for a buyer for its NBC Blue chain in 1941, after the FCC ruled out the ownership of more than one station in a market or operation of more than one network by the same interests. The following year Noble bought the Blue for $8 million. To satisfy government regulations, he agreed to sell New York station WMCA, which he had bought in 1940 from Donald Flamm. Noble's decision to acquire the Blue operation was well-timed. Paper shortages and wartime limits on magazine and newspaper size brought in new advertisers and boosted radio profits.

By 1943 a growing array of major sponsors had linked up with Blue Network shows—Coca Cola and *Spotlight Bands;* Jergens and *Walter Winchell's Journal;* Kellogg and *Breakfast at Sardi's;* Bristol Myers and *Duffy's Tavern;* Miles Laboratories and *The Quiz Kids;* Sloan's Liniment and *Gangbusters;* Hallmark and *Meet Your Navy.* Sustaining, or unsponsored, programs featured Ella Fitzgerald, Wilbur Evans, and the Ink Spots. In addition, the network broadcast many programs connected with the war effort: *Wake Up America, John Freedom, This Is War, Chaplain Jim of the U.S.A.,* and *Weekly War Journal.* The network's weakest area was evident to Noble, president Mark Woods, and program vice president Phillips Carlin; the chain needed variety and popular-music shows. Blue executives and department heads met to determine how to fill the gap. They agreed to hire someone who would take charge of all musical programs presented by the network and act to produce new shows.

With nearly twenty-five years' experience as a conductor and impresario and a dozen seasons on various network shows, Paul Whiteman won everyone's approval. "We thought he was the best man for the job for our new network," Mark Woods recalled. "I had watched his career. He was one of America's best-known and best-loved musicians. People had confidence in him, and after he took the post of Director of Music of the Blue, he did things rapidly, thoroughly and with a certain flair. We became personal friends, and I was very fond of him." On hearing of Pops's move into the job, Ken Darby of the King's Men voiced the sentiments of most Whiteman alumni. "I never wondered about Paul being able to stay in the business, because he *was* the business."

On March 17, 1943, Paul accepted the position. He would be in complete charge of all sustaining musical programs, and acting in a supervisory capacity, he would plan new programs of music and cooperate in the production of musical programs with sponsorship possibilities. His annual salary would be $50,000 with additional fees for conducting network shows.

In September, after he had completed his Hollywood obligations, Paul, Margaret, and Margo drove across the country to the farm. Paul immediately assumed his duties at the Blue Network. Pops presided over a group of more than sixty-five staff musicians, including Vladimir Brenner, Alex Drasein, Rosa Rio, Harry Edison, Al Gallodoro, Arthur Rollini, and Nat Levine. The network conductors were Paul Lavalle, Joseph Rines, and Josef Stopak. Frank Vagnoni handled the chores of assigning people to various programs. Among the commercial musical shows in the fall line-up were *The Chamber Music Society of Lower Basin Street, The Metropolitan Opera Audition of the Air*, the Guy Lombardo Orchestra, the Metropolitan Opera Broadcasts, and *The Morton Downey Program*. There was clearly much room for expansion.

Within the Whiteman household, Paul, Jr., was facing the military draft. Nearing his twentieth birthday, he had completed his education with some difficulty. He had been a mediocre student who evidenced no interest in college. Music and show business continued to fascinate him, even as he put aside his drummer's sticks to join the army.

When Paul, Jr., entered the Air Corps, Pops hoped that basic training and military discipline would toughen him and give him direction. In the meantime he could only wait and wonder. Pops's young brother-in-law, Ivy's husband, also joined the service. Bill Crawford left Texas to serve as a medical officer in the Navy. Paul and Maggie saw much of Ivy during the war as she spent long periods at the farm until Bill was discharged, in 1946.

Paul himself was happily at work on the farm as well, raising vegetables, grain, and cattle for the war effort. His duties as Blue's music director were given high priority as the communications industry and the government recognized the morale value of escapist entertainment.

Paul's work at his Radio City offices for the Blue demanded long hours. Not infrequently the day was made even longer by his aversion to crowded spaces. Time after time he refused to enter an elevator occupied by more than three or four passengers. On other occasions he would not ride above the eleventh or twelfth floor. The phobia complicated meetings and schedules within the high-rise RCA Building; luckily most of his work confined him to the first eight floors.

In December 1943 Paul went on the air with a new show called *Philco Radio Hall of Fame,* where he conducted a network staff orchestra using several of his alumni and arrangements tailored to fit his style. Each week the Blue chain's first major variety program since it had broken away from NBC featured a half-dozen guest stars from the stage, screen, and radio. The Sunday series included salutes to performers who qualified for the *Radio Hall of Fame.* Abel Green, editor of *Variety,* selected the artists who would appear in what was the equivalent of a weekly Academy Awards. The opening broadcast, with announcer Glenn Riggs and commentator Deems Taylor, starred comedians Red Skelton and Frank Fay, vocalists Harriet Hilliard and Ginny Simms, and the all-black cast of the new Broadway musical, *Carmen Jones.* Journalist Quentin Reynolds appeared to announce the Philco Corporation's gift of $25,000 to the Army Relief Fund.

One of network radio's earliest advertisers, Philco had aired such pioneering programs as *The Philco Hour of Theater Memories,* with Jessica Dragonette, and the Philadelphia Orchestra concerts conducted by Leopold Stokowski. After a lapse of several years the company decided to sponsor a coast-to-coast series as part of its campaign to keep the name before the public. Philco was looking ahead to the postwar period, when the company would be manufacturing home appliances, including television sets.

Paul was given carte blanche to hire practically any entertainer he wished. During the first three months Whiteman showcased some of the biggest and brightest names ever heard on the air, from Fred Allen, Lauritz Melchior, Fannie Brice, Helen Hayes, Kate Smith, and Martha Raye to Garry Moore, Joan Fontaine, Hildegarde, George Jessel, Tallulah Bankhead, and Groucho Marx. Such stars as Frederic March, Elizabeth Bergner, and Jennifer Jones appeared in scenes from current plays and films. Originating from the network-owned Ritz Theatre in New York, the broadcasts attracted hundreds of ticket seekers, especially GIs passing through town. At least once a year Paul and the show settled in Hollywood for a period to bring on such movie stars as Jeanette MacDonald, Frank Morgan, Ronald Colman, Bob Hope, Judy Garland, Jack Haley, Dale Evans, George Murphy, and Betty Hutton.

An audience-building feature became part of the full-hour broadcasts in 1944. During his early years, Paul had introduced and popularized so many hit songs that it was decided to inaugurate a "Now and Then" segment. A small combo from the orchestra played the original arrangement of such tunes as "Avalon," "Sweet Sue," and "Whispering," complete with Mike on the banjo. The same selection was played by the full aggregation in an embellished contemporary scoring. Eddie Condon, the jazz guitarist, was in the audience to hear the intricate current rendition of "Sweet Sue." He nudged his companion to complain. "They're always asking me: 'Where's the melody?' Now, I'm asking, 'Where the hell's the melody up there with those guys?'"

The "Now and Then" segment proved to be good listening. Audiences looked forward to it as to a "Lucky Strike extra" on the *Hit Parade*. Nearly all of Whiteman's popular repertoire of the 1920s was used except, for obvious reasons, "Japanese Sandman"; this was no time to remind the audience of the enemy. Occasionally the actual Whiteman recordings had to be studied and copied to recreate the original sound of the band.

One day Richard Osk, a publicist for the network, came up with the idea of pretending that Paul did not own some of the original records. Listeners were asked to write in if their collections included a particular recording. First one to send the serial number would receive a war bond. "Of course, Whiteman or the network actually had the record," Osk revealed. "But it was another way to promote war bonds." Everyone connected with the show was amazed at the response. People had really bought those records, and now they were tuning in the show in great numbers.

In June, as a thirteen-week summer break for the *Hall of Fame,* Paul signed such promising new performers as soprano Eileen Farrell, the vocal rhythmic group of Hi, Lo, Jack, and the Dame, and singer Bob Johnstone. For contrast he brought in old-time accordionist Charles Magnante and the Memphis Five jazz combo. To keep listeners up on the invasion of Europe, announcer Kelvin Keech injected the latest dispatches from the front.

Paul still had his eye on new talent for his Philco broadcasts. A tall, blonde singer from Virginia who specialized in such "unsophisticated" songs as "Let Him Go, Let Him Tarry," "The Lass with the Delicate Air," "Dance with the Dolly," and "Grandfather's Clock" caught his attention. Evelyn Knight's soft and haunting style was ideal for the small, chic Blue Angel nightclub, where she had made her first New York appearance. Deems Taylor introduced her on the *Radio Hall of Fame* with the words, "She's the Cinderella of the nightclubs whose unsophisticated songs and refreshing personality stopped New York's smart set in its tracks." Evelyn skyrocketed on radio as costar of the Lanny Ross show and in jukeboxes as an artist for Decca Records.

During a 1944 war-bond tour, Paul discovered a classically trained pianist with a knowledge of jazz and pop tunes. Private Stan Freeman was part of a GI orchestra that featured guest artist Oscar Levant and filled in whenever Levant, the perpetual hypochondriac, was unable to perform. Whiteman invited Freeman onto a Philco program; for his radio debut Freeman would play *Rhapsody in Blue.* Freeman's performance brought him acclaim and led, after his military service, to a debut at Carnegie Hall and guest appearances with symphony orchestras in Washington, Cincinnati, and New York.

A young, untrained choir singer in an Armenian church in Chicago took her first step toward nationwide popularity and work with Whiteman in April 1943. Kay Armen had been augmenting her wages as a ticket seller at a movie house by singing with a band at a Chicago ballroom. With perfect pitch and a steel-trap memory for words and music, she began to pick up radio assignments. A

scout for station WSM in Nashville invited her to join the staff at
$35 a week.

At WSM the dark-haired, heavy-set singer, who replaced Kitty
Kallen, sang for hours every day. Pop tunes, traditional numbers,
folk songs, hymns—she did them all, from Monday morning to Saturday night. While singing with Beasley Smith's orchestra at the
station, she attracted the interest of the network. On January 1,
1944, Kay arrived at the Blue in Radio City and immediately headed
for a microphone and a half-dozen assignments. Three weeks later,
when Georgia Gibbs dropped out of a *Philco Hall of Fame* show,
Whiteman turned to Kay. She bowed with Pops on January 23. It
was not long before she served many radio sponsors on programs
broadcast from ABC and other networks. In 1947 Kay became part
of the musical team that propelled the quiz show *Stop the Music*
into the top ten radio shows and gave ABC its biggest postwar
show.

Whiteman used Kay regularly. She required no coaching and little
rehearsing; Paul liked such quick studies. Kay's excursions with
Pops on the road for all-Gershwin programs, however, proved to
be ordeals. An engagement to conduct the Detroit Symphony, with
Kay and Earl Wild as soloists, brought out the worst in Paul. On
yet another drinking spree, he turned boisterous and crude. Somehow he led the orchestra through the program, but his behavior
took its toll on everyone, incuding Kay, who could never again
respect the maestro.

Another Gershwin concert—this time in Patterson, New Jersey—
turned sour for Kay and baritone Bob Johnstone. Whiteman's
booking office had set up the engagement for them. Kay agreed to
sing for $350. The box office cashier, however, ran off with the
proceeds, and she ended up with ony $50 for her work. Paul, she
believed, could have made up the difference. But he didn't, and
another similar episode left her disenchanted with Whiteman's
ventures.

Not all of Paul's discoveries cut the mustard. He engaged one
pop singer on the basis of his audition record. On the day of the
show Paul conducted the orchestra and cued the young baritone
on his part. Through numerous rehearsals the singer continued to
hit wrong notes.

With the broadcast only a couple of hours away, Paul had to
show off the previously announced guest to best advantage. (Shows

were live in those days.) Later he remarked with obvious embarrassment to his producer and engineers, "His record sounded good. Gee, how did I know he was so lousy?"

In September 1944 ABC and Philco increased the number of stations carrying the program from 165 to 194. In addition twenty-two Canadian outlets picked up the show, making it the top commercial line-up in radio, according to *Variety*. That fall Paul brought in Abe Osser as an assistant. A graduate of the University of Michigan, Abe had studied piano and violin. After he came to New York in 1936, he arranged for Charlie Barnet, Bob Crosby, and Bunny Berigan. As a teenager he had tuned in the broadcasts of Whiteman, little thinking that one day he would be Paul's right-hand man.

Osser regularly rehearsed and conducted Paul's men, and as a network staff musician, he contributed arrangements. For over twenty years he was a fixture at the station and Paul's closest associate. Pops hated the sound of Osser's name and played crude word games with it. Finally he said to Abe, "Let's do something about it. There's room for improvement, especially if it's spoken quickly."

Paul borrowed the first name of announcer Glenn Riggs and came up with the professional name Glenn Osser. Abe liked it. The transition from one name to another was carried out smoothly until the time Paul strained his arm and could not conduct the orchestra. Osser was assigned the task. Just before air time Paul, his arm in a sling, stepped on stage to introduce his assistant to the studio audience. After explaining his inability to lead the band, Paul announced, "And now I'd like to introduce a new and very capable individual—my assistant conductor, Ab . . . er, Glenn Osser."

The two first names became intermingled in his mind. Momentarily confused, Paul gestured toward the wings where Osser was standing and ordered, "Come out here, Abe!" Later Paul remarked to Osser, "Maybe I should just call you Glabe."

The Blue Network studio musicians included Bobby Hackett and Billy Butterfield on trumpet, George Wettling on drums, and Felix Giobbe on bass. Paul regularly gave them solo spots to display their talents. At one particular rehearsal, when Pops had a problem capturing the right sound balance from the rhythm section, Giobbe truly suffered for his art. The band went over the piece again and again to make it as perfect as possible for the live broadcast. Giobbe never seemed to get his fast, jazzy bit quite right. After six run-throughs everyone was thoroughly irritated with Paul's attempts to surmount the technical difficulties. On the seventh try Giobbe, instead of playing the correct notes on the string bass, thumped out the unmistakable theme of Chopin's "Funeral March." On hearing the deep *dum-dum* notes from his bassist, a red-faced Whiteman blew up with uncharacteristic anger. "You're wasting time, goddamn it!"

Paul's time was indeed at a premium during 1944. Along with the weekly Philco broadcast, he was developing new network programs, making guest appearances on radio shows and at war relief events, and shooting *Atlantic City*.

At the end of the year Paul, Maggie, and Margo arrived in Hollywood for six weeks of Philco broadcasts from the West Coast. The half-dozen shows from California came to be considered among the very best of the series. On December 17, 1944, Philco presented *"Life Magazine's* cover girl of the week" and star of the new musical *Meet Me in St. Louis,* Judy Garland, who shared the microphone with Lum and Abner, Les Paul, Jerry Colonna, and announcer Jimmy Wallington. A high point of the show was an original poem by program writer Mort Lewis. Judy read his sentiments, and everyone's dream of a peaceful Christmas. While Paul conducted Irving Berlin's "White Christmas," Judy spoke, "I'm dreaming of a peaceful Christmas, and so are you . . . and there are times when it may seem far off . . . But it will come. It *will* come!" As she recited the last lines, she burst into tears, moving many in the audience to do the same.

On December 24, Paul gathered Orson Welles, Bing Crosby, and the King's Men for a Christmas Eve show. On New Year's Eve the *Radio Hall of Fame* gave listeners a special treat: an adaptation by Mort Lewis of the Jerome Kern–Oscar Hammerstein–Edna Ferber classic, *Showboat.* Kathryn Grayson and Allan Jones starred, and Helen Forrest and Charles Winninger played supporting roles. The hour-long production was the first radio interpretation of the musical in more than four years; *Lux Radio Theatre* had offered a version in 1940 with Irene Dunne, Jones, and Winninger.

Mort Lewis was quite proud of his adaptation and managed to get hold of Kern's telephone number. "Mr. Kern, I've written a new adaptation of *Showboat*, and it's going to be on the air tomorrow. I would like your opinion of it."

Kern promised to listen. The show went off well, and Lewis called the composer as soon as he got home. "Whiteman really loused up my music with those arrangements of his!" Kern stormed. He had not paid the slightest attention to Mort Lewis's script.

Shortly after *Showboat,* Paul became involved with yet another unusual radio undertaking. "I've got some musical ideas I'm crazy about trying out," he announced. "Radio is a brand-new medium for music. There's been music written for ballet, opera, movies, and various other familiar mediums, but there's never been any important music written for radio. In radio, a composition must say a whole lot in seven or eight minutes. You can't give many two-hour concerts. I'd like to get a group of about fifteen serious composers who would concentrate on writing radio music. It won't be easy—but believe me, if it doesn't work at first, we'll keep on trying."

Paul visualized a dozen or so short pieces, five or six minutes long each, miniature *Rhapsodies.* Once again he was searching for a new Gershwin—a popular composer who, if properly encouraged, could provide music in concert forms.

In 1944 Whiteman persuaded the Blue Network to establish a Creative Music Fund to commission gifted young composers to write in capsule form something between a song and a symphony. The fund provided an advance sum to musicians toward radio presentation of new pieces in a new series, *Music Out of the Blue.* The network retained first broadcast rights and, for a period of one year, performance rights. Composers who accepted the commission assigned all royalty rights to the Blue Network until the initial advance had been recouped.

Paul chose the composers on a noncompetitive basis. Those who accepted were Roy Harris, Leonard Bernstein, Aaron Copland, Igor Stravinsky, Paul Creston, Morton Gould, David Rose, Richard Rodgers, Ferde Grofé, Peter De Rose, Duke Ellington, Eric Korngold, and Victor Young.

"If we get four really good things out of the thirteen compositions, we shall be doing well, and if we get six, we shall be doing awfully well," Paul explained. "They will be run at twelve o'clock at night, so if they are too bad few people will know it. If the public responds favorably, these symphonettes may get further hearing in concert halls—and the fund may be set up permanently for subsidizing still more."

During the fall of 1944 most of the commissioned composers contributed works to the broadcasts, which featured a number of other artists eager to give their latest compositions a hearing. Roy Harris conducted his *Piano Concerto* and *Free Fantasie on Rock of Ages.* Copland's *Letter from Home,* Korngold's *A Merry Overture,* and Creston's *Dawn Mood* were aired in September and October. Theodore Weingand presented *Variations on a Hot Lick,* Paul Lavalle contributed *Manhattan Rhapsody,* and Leroy Anderson came out with *Jazz Pizzicato.*

Morton Gould's composition, *Pops' Serenade,* was dedicated to Paul; Richard Rodgers worked on a concert waltz, *Tales of Central Park;* David Rose created a Latin American piece called *Dance of the Spanish Onion,* Victor Young introduced *Stella by Starlight,* and Alex Templeton contributed *Insect Suite.*

Of the original thirteen composers, Stravinsky provided Whiteman with one of the more ambitious and imaginative pieces, a Russian-flavored folk scherzo. His work, begun in 1943, was originally a wordless choral duet called *The Second Trio.* Rewritten and orchestrated for Whiteman's band, it emerged for its radio bow as the *Scherzo a la Russe.* Nearly twenty years earlier Whiteman had offered a commission to Stravinsky, at the time of the Russian composer's first visit to the United States. He had considered it seriously, but his commitments as guest conductor of the New York Philharmonic ruled out an excursion into the Whiteman organization of 1925.

Paul recalled the visit of French composer Maurice Ravel to a Whiteman rehearsal in 1928. Ravel had been so impressed with the sound of the orchestra on records that he had insisted on meeting and hearing Paul during his trip to America. Paul believed that if Ravel—who had died in 1937, after a long, debilitating illness—had been active in the 1940s, he, too, would have contributed to *Music Out of the Blue.*

Whiteman's Music Fund rekindled the hopes of those who wished for more originality in the music heard over radio. The brief series provided opportunities that rarely came to composers. Only the Columbia network's earlier efforts, in 1937, to bring works especially created for the air by such composers as Walter Piston, Aaron Copland, Louis Gruenberg, Howard Hanson, and Roy Harris showed that the medium had some interest in truly contemporary serious music.

By the 1945 *Music Out of the Blue* faded along with the network's

old name. Edward Noble and Mark Woods changed the Blue network into the American Broadcasting Company. Still facing sluggish
billings and generally limited station coverage, ABC added more
stations in major markets and began to develop its own new programs, a function the other major networks had long since abandoned to advertising agencies. Woods hoped that by originating
shows, ABC could prevent advertisers from moving them to NBC
and CBS as soon as the programs gained real popularity. The network's biggest break came when it picked up Bing Crosby and his
coast-to-coast broadcasts.

Tired of keeping regular radio engagements, Bing wanted to
prerecord his shows. By cutting three or four shows a week, he
would free up time for his race horses and his ranch in Nevada.
Kraft, his sponsor since 1936, refused to take such a risk. Moreover,
both NBC and CBS maintained a strict ban against "canned" shows
and refused to transcribe Crosby. ABC, without a rigid stance that
prohibited recorded programs, grabbed Bing for its network. In this
effort the network had help from Paul. Whiteman had already utilized electrical transcriptions on the *Philco Radio Hall of Fame* to
permit more convenient scheduling of guest artists and to correct
any "fluffs," or mistakes.

ABC and Paul sold Philco Corporation a Wednesday night spot
for Bing's new series, *Philco Radio Time,* which was taken from
sixteen-inch discs, recorded at roughly half the revolutions per
minute of standard 78-rpm recordings. Neither the sound quality
of the broadcasts nor the weekly ratings suffered from this major
departure from live airing.

In a sense Paul turned his weekly variety show over to Bing. In
return he received a vice presidential post within Philco. As an
officer of the company, with a salary of approximately $25,000 a
year, and as an executive of ABC, he was, in a manner of speaking,
once again Bing's boss. Since most of Bing's shows were recorded
on the West Coast, Paul and his former crooner crossed paths infrequently. And that was the way Bing probably wanted it.

Paul's Philco programs lost much of their initial appeal during
the final season. The Hall of Fame concept was modified to embrace
a new theme. The show focused on rising talent, people who were
climbing a *Stairway to the Stars*. With that new title the series featured vocalist Martha Tilton, backed by Paul's band. A native of

Corpus Christi, Texas, Martha had won initial acclaim as a singer with Benny Goodman; she stayed with the King of Swing for three years. Following an appearance at the New York Paramount and a stint for the USO to the South Pacific, she decided to go on as a single act. For Whiteman she shared the microphone with new-comers George Shearing, Mindy Carson, Vic Damone, Norman Paris, and Jack Paar. No one was more grateful for the chance to work on radio than Paar. At the end of his spot, he broke down in tears at the thought that Whiteman had given him a chance to be heard by millions of listeners.

Paul devoted most of his time to radio, refusing all theatrical engagements except his annual appearance at the Capitol Theatre in New York and a recording session for Capitol Records of *Rhapsody in Blue* with Earl Wild, then an ABC staff pianist. In late 1945 ABC put on a special anniversary show, *The First Twenty-Five,* built around Paul's music since he had broken into the big time in 1920. As the network's director of music, he could point to a number of ABC musical programs that had stemmed in part from his efforts. These commercial ventures included *Sunday Night Serenade, Johnny Thompson Show, Sammy Kaye Serenade, Club Time,* and the Detroit Symphony Orchestra broadcasts.

The war was over. Paul, Jr., was safe, and so was Ivy's Bill. Paul thanked God and, along with millions of other Americans, felt that his country had played its most important role.

When his Philco affiliation ended in the late spring of 1946, Paul was eager for a short concert tour. He wanted to get back on the road and meet his public again. Using a few key men from his radio orchestra and augmenting them with local musicians, he scheduled a handful of all-Gershwin concerts. He added two of his radio discoveries, Mindy Carson and Bob Johnstone, and Earl Wild to serve as soloists.

Mindy, a nineteen-year-old singer from the East Bronx, had auditioned for music publisher Eddie Joy and made a demo recording of the tune "Rumors Are Flying." Harry Cool, about to bring his orchestra to the Glen Island Casino in Westchester, New York, heard the record and hired her sight unseen, to fill the job as female vocalist. Mindy, who bore a striking resemblance to actress Ingrid Bergman, had a way with a song. Johnny Messner engaged her for his orchestra at the McAlpin Hotel Grill. Then Joy decided that the time had come for her to audition for Whiteman. Paul signed her for an ABC appearance. After a few broadcasts he made her a permanent addition to *Stairway to the Stars*.

Bob Johnstone sang on local stations in Nashville before journeying to New York in 1944. Pops heard him and signed the twenty-seven-year-old vocalist to a contract with the *Philco Hall of Fame*. After seventeen weeks with Whiteman, Bob was drafted. He rejoined Paul when the war was over.

Earl Wild came on the tour with Pops as soloist on the Gershwin piano selections. He had achieved national fame in October 1942, when Toscanini had picked him to perform *Rhapsody in Blue* with the NBC Symphony (Benny Goodman played the clarinet cadenza). This was Toscanini's first significant venture into popular music and his first program of all-American music. American-born and wearing the uniform of the United States Navy, Earl added the ideal patriotic touch. As a teenager with the gift of absolute pitch, he had played celeste and glockenspiel in the Pittsburgh Symphony. An energetic child prodigy, he was able to read anything at sight. He came to New York to study with Egon Petri, and in 1937 he became a staff pianist and arranger at NBC. On radio he played under Walter Damrosch, with Mischa Elman, and alongside other great figures. He regarded his five years at NBC as among the most important of his early years.

In late 1942 Earl entered the Navy as a musician first class. He gave numerous special performances, including a solo recital for President Roosevelt at the White House. He played nineteen different concertos with the Navy Symphony Orchestra and was honored by being chosen to play in the Western premiere of Dimitri Shostakovitch's *Piano Trio in E Minor,* which was heard over the ABC network. After his discharge Wild appeared as soloist on a number of major radio programs, including a dozen performances with Whiteman at ABC. He disliked outside concert appearances with Whiteman, but as an employee of ABC he could not refuse to play these additional dates with the network's musical director. Earl remained at ABC for nearly twenty-five years while simultaneously pursuing a successful career on the concert stage.

Paul, Earl, and the rest of the small troupe traveled from New York westward, giving Gershwin concerts in a dozen cities. On July 13, 1946, they appeared at the Hollywood Bowl. On the West Coast, Paul initiated a sustaining ABC program called *Forever Tops*.

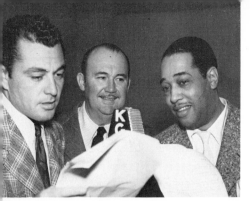

Back in Los Angeles in 1941, Paul concentrates on radio work, here with Tony Martin and Duke Ellington. *(Courtesy of Margaret L. Whiteman)*

A sell-out audience in San Francisco's Civic Auditorium listens to the 1943 all-Gershwin program led by Whiteman. *(Courtesy of Margaret L. Whiteman)*

Paul lends a hand to Leonore Gershwin as she christens the Second World War ship *George Gershwin* at San Pedro, California. Participating in the launching are film producer Jesse L. Lasky (center) and playwright Marc Connelly (with cigarette). *(Courtesy of Leonore and Ira Gershwin)*

At Coda Cottage in 1966 Paul and Margaret hold walking sticks for a midday stroll. *(Courtesy of Margaret L. Whiteman)*

The final stop for the King of Jazz—the Whiteman mausoleum, Ewing Church Cemetery near Trenton, N. J. *(Courtesy of Paul Hutcoe)*

The New Paul Whiteman Orchestra plays vintage Pops arrangements in London, October 1974. T small group in front consists of (left to right) Harry Gold, Paul Nossiter, Dick Sudhalter, and Ke Nichols. *(Courtesy of Dick Sudhalter)*

It highlighted favorite songs that had stood the test of time. For vocalists he chose Johnny Thompson, a baritone, and Eugenie Baird, a recent singing partner of Bing Crosby on the *Kraft Music Hall.* A product of the big-band era, she had sung with Tony Pastor, Jan Savitt, and Glen Gray in the early 1940s and recorded for Decca and Bluebird. In the fall Paul brought her back to New York, where his new series continued for the remainder of 1946. For the next two or three years Eugenie was on call as Pops's chief band and concert singer.

Paul started off 1947 with a two-week tour that opened in Syracuse, New York, in mid-January. His nucleus of musicians and soloists included Eugenie, Earl, Johnny, Mike, Al, and a recent addition, trumpeter Phil Schapiro (who a dozen years later would hire Pops). Dates in Michigan, Indiana, Ohio, Maryland, and Virginia, as well as Toronto, brought Paul to cities he had not visited since the 1930s. At the first concerts, Paul would stand in the lobby before his performance, greeting and chatting with people. But after the first few, the tour lost its luster. Pops became bored and tired; his back hurt from traveling and conducting day after day. As a result, he increased the tempo of virtually every number on the program to bring the concert to a close and end his misery.

"I was singing the torch song, 'The Man I Love,' almost in march time," Eugenie remembered. "Paul, who I always called Pappy, wanted to get each show over with. I pleaded with him: 'Couldn't we slow it down a little bit, Pappy?' It didn't do much good. Finally, during a performance of *Rhapsody in Blue,* Earl Wild looked up from the keyboard and yelled, 'Too fast! Too fast!' "

Eugenie actually wanted to quit the tour before it reached Washington, D.C. Besides contending with accelerated tempos, she was becoming a nurse to Paul. In Detroit, while preparing for a special engagement in nearby Grosse Point, Paul ran into a convention of mailmen at his hotel. They invited him to their hospitality suite for a drink—and Paul was not seen again. With the concert fast approaching, Eugenie tracked him down and broke up the party. Then she had to call the hotel bellboys to get Pops back to his own quarters and see to it that he washed, shaved, and dressed. Paul appeared on the podium that night, but all he wanted to conduct was *Rhapsody in Blue* over and over and over. Luckily clearer heads prevailed.

Audiences were never bored by Earl's performance of the

Gershwin composition. It "blazed with keyboard color" as he brought out "every phrase and tone quality of the work," according to the music critic of the *Detroit Free Press*.

By 1947 Paul had advanced to a vice presidency at the American Broadcasting Company. His performing chores on radio that spring included a series, without a fee, for the National Guard, to promote enlistments. He also continued the weekly *Paul Whiteman Show*. On the managerial level he judged a composers' competition, "Concerto for Doubles," for entries written for orchestra and two or more solo instruments played by one person. Thomas J. Filas of Chicago won Whiteman's $1,000 prize; Paul performed the winning piece with Al Gallodoro on sax and clarinet on April 3, 1947.

Whatever else he did, Paul never stopped trying to improve the sound quality of orchestral broadcasts. He experimented with placing mikes in various locations, segregating the violin section to bring out special effects, and adding echo chambers to compensate for dead spots.

Also in 1947, a whole new form of expression opened for Paul. That at the age of fifty-seven Whiteman should cap his long career seated at a microphone and surrounded by stacks of ten-inch records struck many as a comedown as sad as Babe Ruth's playing out his string with the Akron Dodgers. Disc jockeys had been spinning platters and chatting at microphones since the earliest days of radio, and at many small stations they became personalities. For years they had lived on the fringes of the industry, staying up all night routinely playing records for petty cash and less prestige. Then, in 1935, a year after Martin Block joined New York's station WNEW, he filled in between on-the-spot reports from the Lindbergh kidnap trial with recorded music. Instead of coming forth with a random selection, Block broke his airtime into segments of ten or fifteen minutes each and programmed his records in the same way the networks played their live music. He gave listeners three or four numbers by Red Nichols or Ben Pollack before moving on to Benny Goodman or Glen Gray. Audiences found his organized approach and knowledgeable delivery to their liking. Sponsors discovered his growing popularity and turned to him to sell their products. As Block prospered with what he soon called *The Make-Believe Ballroom*, others turned to his trade. Al Jarvis on KFWB in Hollywood and Arthur Godfrey at Washington's WTOP had already made local reputations with similar formats.

During the Second World War, the GI disc jockey reigned at

makeshift radio outposts in far-flung locales, even aboard ships on the high seas. The entertainment thus provided was accessible and instantaneous. All it took was a stack of popular records, a turntable, and a record spinner with a congenial manner of speaking. Back from the war, ex-servicemen kept up the habit of tuning in to disc jockeys who played the latest pop releases. Yet only the small, unaffiliated stations seemed to offer what these listeners were seeking in the way of current music. Broadcasters began to realize that there was room for many more Martin Blocks on the dial—even on the flagship stations.

In 1946 and 1947 some of the biggest names in radio entered the disc jockey sweepstakes: Tommy Dorsey, Duke Ellington, Ted Husing, Kate Smith, Rudy Vallee, Bea Wain, and Andre Baruch. And the potential for big money from an array of sponsors enticed major performers and programmers. In his dual capacity as both radio executive and broadcaster, Whiteman joined the growing herd.

The actual logistics of how Paul became dean of American disc jockeys is another story. Early in 1947 Charles "Bud" Barry, ABC program director, was looking for a Saturday-morning program for WJZ in New York. He came up with a test record featuring popular vocalist Mary Small and songwriter Vic Mizzy as disc jockeys, but then decided to expand coverage to the network's six key cities outside New York—Chicago, Philadelphia, Detroit, Washington, San Francisco, and Los Angeles. To hit all six, he needed a major personality.

At the same time Campbell Soup had asked ABC for a daytime radio format, and the sponsor liked Barry's suggestion. Barry had unsuccessfully approached a number of music, stage, and film personalities when into his office walked Whiteman. Recognizing a bonanza when he saw one, Barry asked, "Whiteman, how would you like to be a disc jockey?"

"Don't be crazy," Pops said.

Barry persisted. Paul agreed to think it over. He came back the next day. "Would I have to read the commercials? I've never done that in my life."

"Yup," said Barry. He took Paul into a studio to make a test record. ABC's musical director was unaware the mike was open from the start, so that preliminary remarks, wisecracks, and stories were also recorded.

"I want to capture the real Paul Whiteman," Barry explained.

"The one everyone in the music business knows, with his humor and informality and colorful gab. No one's done it yet."

When he heard the playback of that first record, Paul capitulated. Barry built a show around Paul especially for Campbell, but in the end the sponsor dropped the option. With the potentially hottest disc show burning a hole in his hands, Barry was eager to sell it fast. He and ABC's sales manager invaded the offices of scores of clients and agencies in a dozen major cities in six weeks. Their hour-long presentation often had five showings a day. In the spring of 1947 the Borden Company sponsored *Borden's Musical Revue,* with Paul functioning as disc jockey. This was a trial run, but by mid-May the hour was sponsored in four fifteen-minute periods.

Paul quickly grew enthusiastic about the project and became convinced that disc-jockey shows had come to stay. The very existence of such a form of entertainment, it seemed to him, revealed the great interest people had in music and their eagerness to turn to it as a respite from other forms of radio fare. Maybe the secret of the disc jockey's popularity lay merely in the suspense of waiting for the next tune. Then again, this interest might demonstrate the vitality of all music, whether live or canned. Perhaps it presented an immediate, vicarious means of escape from the regular routine. The contact with a familiar and friendly voice might carry the listener along through the day or night. No doubt all these elements, Paul thought, contributed significantly to the disc jockey's rapid rise.

Whiteman decided to make his usual full-blown entrance. He took to the air on June 30, 1947, as host of *The Paul Whiteman Club* and the first coast-to-coast disc jockey with an hour-long program every weekday afternoon. Broadcast over an expanded chain of 228 stations from three-thirty to four-thirty, the show brought the biggest time sale in the history of radio. Replacing Borden as sponsor, four companies paid nearly $6 million to have Paul hawk their wares for one year.

ABC brought into the fold Camel Cigarettes, Premium Crackers, Wesson Salad Oil, and Nescafé Instant Coffee. Each carried a fifteen-minute segment of the show. Paul agreed to handle the commercials, as did every other disc jockey. Indeed, the sponsors were heavily sold on the basis of Whiteman's folksy manner when he pitched his sales talks. At the start Paul's commercials were rather casual and unrehearsed. Soon after the series bowed, for example, Pops delivered a discourse on Nescafé.

My wife, Maggie, makes a wonderful cup of coffee with Nescafé Instant Coffee, and you, too, can make a wonderful cup. You know what you do? You just take a little ol' tea-spoonful of that Nescafé, put it in a cup, pour hot water into it. Stir it for a couple of seconds, and you know what ya got? The greatest little ol' cup of hot water you ever tasted!

Prerecorded commercials read from a prepared script by Paul and staff announcers gradually replaced Paul and his ad libs and his inclination for putting his large foot in his mouth.

The format of *The Paul Whiteman Club* ideally suited the master music maker. Pop tunes dominated the hour, with old favorites, collector's items, and very light operatic and classical numbers worked in for variety. Of course Paul's own records were inserted from time to time. Whiteman had firsthand knowledge of much of this music, together with a long and close association with many of the country's leading singers and instrumentalists. Playing re-cordings of songs he had helped to popularize led naturally to back-stage anecdotes and to stories about the selections and the artists known only to an insider. And these in turn brought in the per-formers themselves as guests, usually in prerecorded interviews. Ethel Merman, Guy Lombardo, Mel Tormé, Tommy Dorsey, Jane Froman, Dinah Shore, Eddy Duchin, and countless other celebrities were more than willing to talk on the show.

In its review of the first broadcast, *Variety* noted that the program "put disc jockeyism into long pants." As such shows went, the journal added, "the verdict is in Pops' favor . . . In terms of after-noon programming to counter the NBC-CBS soap opera technique, its entertainment value can't be minimized—and that goes for Whiteman as a saleman." *Variety* pointed out that it represented a wide jump for a maestro rooted so deeply in show busienss, "but he makes the hurdle into out-and-out commercialism with a finesse and inoffensiveness that must certainly back up ABC's conviction that integration of disc jockeyism and personality can add up en-tertainment and box office at the corner store."

What may have sounded easy and casual actually represented many hours of preparation by a large staff. Paul's entourage for the daily stint included producer Bud Barry, director George Wiest, writer Bernard Dougall, announcer Doug Browning, commercial rewrite man Edward Ehrich, contact man Lester Lewis, publicity aide Richard Osk, three engineers, and four secretaries. *The Paul*

Whiteman Club carried multimillion-dollar billings. Thoroughness and professionalism were the keynotes.

Also behind the scenes was a twenty-two-year-old record librarian who, with Paul's help, turned a hobby into a full-scale job. A few years earlier, during the run of the *Philco Hall of Fame,* Paul was searcing for one of his early discs for the weekly musical feature "Now and Then." Hundreds of people wrote in to offer their records of the long-lost "Do You Ever Think of Me." One letter from a young soldier at Camp Hood, Texas, added that he had every record Whiteman ever made. The teenage GI was Joe Franklin.

After the war Joe looked Paul up, hoping for a job as an assistant. Until that day he helped to select records for Martin Block and Andre Baruch, and of course he loaned them discs from his own extensive collection. Paul brought Franklin into ABC as staff librarian and gave him the nickname Little Joe. It would be Joe's special task to search out one or two examples of unusual performances and songs for each show. Joe wasted no time in bringing Pops a prize specimen for the opening broadcast. The future television talk-show host and nostalgia buff carried into the studio a 1917 pressing of Eddie Cantor's "That's the Kind of Baby for Me." Cantor remained Little Joe's all-time favorite performer.

Paul also tagged Joe the Young Wreck with the Old Records. He gave him the chance to pick records for entire shows, which had an audience of nearly nine million people from California to Maine. Pops was proudest of his discoveries, his proteges. He remained loyal to his old musicians, too. When bandleader Art Mooney came on the program as a guest and asked about using a banjoist for an upcoming MGM record date, Pops didn't hesitate a second in recommending his old pal, Mike Pingitore. The Mooney disc turned out to be one of the year's biggest sellers—"I'm Looking Over a Four Leaf Clover," with "Baby Face" on the flip side.

Franklin's counterpart in the publicity department was Richard Osk, who generated major press coverage for Paul's latest venture. Many feature stories in national magazines appeared during the early months of the show; most critics agreed that *The Paul Whiteman Club* brought distinction to one of the most discussed professions in radio. A week or so before Paul began his program, Edward Barrett, the editor of *Newsweek,* asked his young radio reporter what was new in the field. "Nothing really," was the reply. "Just another disc jockey show in the works, with Paul Whiteman as the DJ. But that's about all.''

It happened that Paul Whiteman was one of Barrett's idols. "That's great," he exclaimed. "We'll make it a cover story.''

On July 14, 1947, the magazine ran a full-color cover photo of Paul ("Jazz King to Disc Jockey"). A nattily dressed, happily beaming Paul was holding up a shiny disc as he sat before a cluster of recordings, a turntable, and a large ABC table mike. The three-page story in the "Radio" section described the emergence of the disc jockey from "the cocoon of the local station to become the rich butterfly of the networks" and retold Pops's unparalleled show-business career. ABC, in third place among the four networks and outpacing only the Mutual Broadcasting System, luxuriated in the national limelight. The coverage led to other big features in such widely circulated magazines as *Redbook* and *Parade*.

Paul's latest success led to a ghost-written book on the record business and record collecting. The project began as a promotional effort by a record company, which planned to include guidelines on starting a library of popular and classical discs. Someone came upon the idea of tying the book to Whiteman and his long association with the record industry and his current acclaim as the world's first network disc jockey. Called *Records for the Millions,* the book reflected Paul's musical development and ideas, and, of course, it gave a plug to *The Paul Whiteman Club*. It was an excellent reference for anyone who wished to start a basic and well-rounded record collection.

During his stint as a coast-to-coast platter spinner, Paul failed in one respect—he could not persuade Bing Crosby to appear as a guest on the show. Virtually every other big-name singer and musician sat at Paul's mike. But Bing had little use for disc jockeys anywhere and took particular offense at small-time disc jockeys who would spin his records and pretend, or half pretend, that he was in the studio by launching a line of patter. "Hey, look who just walked in, none other than Bing Crosby. Got a song for us, Bing? Gee, that's swell. Folks, he's gonna give us 'Pennies from Heaven.' " Having sold his public personality on his various national shows, Bing resented the scores of radio nonentities who pretended to their audiences that he was making personal appearances on their programs when he was actually a thousand miles away.

Soon after Paul started his series, Bing came to New York to do several shows at ABC. "It would give our show a great beginning," Paul told his staff. When it was suggested that Bing might not want to do it, he brushed the thought aside.

"One thing about Bing," he said, "his head's never gotten bigger, only his heart."

After Bing's arrival at Radio City, Paul walked into the studio where Bing was recording. He had already suggested that Bing do a guest spot. "Hi, Paul," Bing said coolly, never taking his eyes from the music. Paul took the hint. He decided to discuss the matter with Bing's brother Everett and settle it one way or another. But Everett could do nothing. Paul made another attempt to line up Bing; again he was turned down. Because Paul had been so set on Bing's appearance, Osk asked Paul to try once more to persuade Crosby to give five minutes of air time to his old boss.

"I've tried enough." Paul was bitter. "And I'm never going into his studio and get treated like that again."

As far as Paul was concerned, Bing's head had now grown considerably bigger than his heart.

Throughout this time Paul's income had grown. His share of the six-million-dollar show came to $4,000 a week, or $800 a broadcast. In early 1948 he received the highest salary save one at ABC; only Don McNeill of *The Breakfast Club* surpassed him, at a salary of $180,000. If *The Paul Whiteman Club* had continued into a second year, Paul's network compensation would have exceeded a quarter of a million dollars and placed him third (behind Arthur Godfrey and Lowell Thomas) in salaries paid by any radio or television network. Roy Bargy once remarked, "Paul Whiteman needs money like the rest of us need oxygen. God just supplies it."

Once the novelty wore off, Paul's show faced criticism from a large segment of his daytime audience—housewives. They considered his accent phony and his choice of words unduly condescending. He talked down to his female listeners, calling them "honey chile" and "baby." Some women thought his sloppy grammar distracting and undignified. His delivery of commercials didn't sound sincere. "Just putting it on thick for the radio audience," remarked a listener. "No man of his caliber could really believe what he was saying about Nescafé," wrote another. Others did not find Paul very interesting. He seemed to ramble on, mentioning names and places that meant nothing to most homemakers.

In 1948 the show was tightened up and revised to allow the regular program announcer to handle most of the commercials. The choice of songs and artists, too, was revamped to bring them more into the mainstream of what listeners expected from popular music.

The results proved disappointing. To make matters worse, a dispute between recording companies and the American Federation of Musicians, which climaxed in a recording ban effective January 1, 1948, cut off the supply of new discs for many months.

Even at $800 an hour, Paul tired of the daily preparation and prerecording, especially the continual revisions and changes for each of the four sponsors. On top of that, several advertisers were looking into television, now that ABC was planning to start TV broadcasting. *The Paul Whiteman Club* was displaced after a full year and a run of more than 250 hours on the air.

As the program neared its end, Paul invited Osk to lunch at the English Grill at Rockefeller Center as a gesture of appreciation for all of the fine press coverage the show had garnered. During the meal, talk turned to politics in that year of approaching presidential elections.

"Paul knew music, but politics was not his forte," Osk remembered. "His views were rather shallow and to the right. But after a few drinks, he thought he could size up the political-economic scene pretty well."

Their discussion continued as the two walked into the RCA Building. Paul stood with his back to the escalator in the first-floor lobby. "Everybody wants to make fifty bucks a week nowadays," he complained. As he raved on, a uniform guide led a group of tourists down the escalator behind Paul.

The guide was saying proudly, "As we go through Rockefeller Center, we may from time to time see certain celebrities—and there's one right now! Paul Whiteman!" Like a musical counterpoint, Pops rumbled, "What the hell are we arguing about, Dick? Why stew about politics? Really there's only two things a guy wants. He wants to get drunk and he wants to get fucked."

The last word had reached the ears of the tour group as Paul turned toward the cluster of visitors. Red-faced and suddenly more sober, he smiled sheepishly and quickly walked away, happy, for once, to go into the protective confines of an elevator.

21

Calling All Kids

The front gate of Walking Horse Farm was a welcome sight each Friday evening as Paul drove up Rosemont Road. He looked forward to his weekends away from stacks of records and pages of scripts. The challenges, problems, and chores of farm life were a respite from Radio City. In winter, there were high snowdrifts to be plowed through; in summer, fields of lush alfalfa to be cut down. Paul called the main dwelling his farmhouse. Actually it was a gentleman farmer's well-appointed lodge. By the late 1940s the Whitemans had added to and expanded the original stone house into a very large and custom-designed home. It was decorated as a diverse blend of a Park Avenue penthouse, a Western ranch, a New Orleans mansion, and an early Colonial dwelling. A porcelain chandelier from Austria shed light on saddlelike chairs from Texas. Yet all the elements seemed to complement each other.

The courtyard became a spacious forty-foot living room with high windows framed in white wrought iron. They opened out on a terrace with a wall of native stone and rock. To one side was a sundial with the inscription "I count none but the sunny hours." Just beyond this was a sixty-foot swimming pool. Tons of dirt were bulldozed around the sides of the pool to form slopes to its edges. Planted with grass, it appeared set in the natural terrain.

Along the winding path leading to the front door Paul had installed a row of old-fashioned street lights. On each side of the entrance he placed a brightly painted carousel horse. The gabled marquee at the gateway to the property was a real source of pride. A square cupola with louvered sides rested atop the shingled roof of the structure—a surprise Christmas gift from the members of his orchestra at ABC.

Although the farm never made any money for the Whitemans and rarely broke even, Paul and Margaret were proud to point out that there was no mortgage, and that everything on the land was paid for.

Paul's love of pitching hay, hammering loose boards, sawing wood, hoeing cornfields, and driving his tractor made him a down-to-earth neighbor and a readily accepted resident. The community proudly called attention to his farm as a fine example of what a newcomer to the area could do. Paul, in turn, contributed his talent and time to community projects. Not long after he joined the ranks of disc jockeys he had occasion to participate in one of the area's most successful and widely heralded recreational undertakings—a project Pops spearheaded with such dedication that it opened up another new phase of his career.

Juvenile delinquency, both actual and potential, captured the attention of much of the country in the immediate postwar years. When the guns cooled off, Americans had jobs and money. Over fifty-three million people were working and unemployment stood at less than 2 percent. After a decade of the Depression and the Second World War, the children could once again be indulged. Material wants were answered; disciplinary restraints and social curbs were understandably lifted. The results proved unfortunate in many communities. Street fights, automobile accidents, drinking episodes, shoplifting incidents—most town and villages faced them week after week. But few localities did anything about changing the conditions that led young people into trouble and into what was broadly called juvenile delinquency.

There wasn't much for boys and girls to do on a Saturday night in New Jersey's Hunterdon County. Parents frequently handed their kids a few dollars, saying, "Go have yourselves a good time." The good time often consisted of drag racing on highways and illegal drinking in back alley roadhouses, and more than a few car smash-ups resulting in injured, maimed, and even dead teenagers.

With a fifteen-year-old daughter who was becoming part of that scene, Paul decided to do something about it. "I'm sick of hearing so much talk about juvenile delinquency and nobody doing anything about it," he exclaimed. "The kids aren't having any fun on Saturday night. Maybe they go to the movies and straggle home about half-past nine. But some don't go right home—and end up in places not so good.''

In the fall of 1947 Paul joined a group from nearby Lambertville who felt that the village needed more recreation for the kids. They formed a committee to look into activities that would keep their young people busy and off the streets. As a musician Paul associated Saturday night with a dance. He urged the community to hold such a weekly dance as a proper outlet for the local boys and girls. The group agreed to begin raising funds to build an outdoor dance pavilion the following spring; but Paul and William Losch, a Lambertville businessman, wanted faster action. They arranged to borrow the recreation hall at St. John's Catholic Church for a Saturday night record hop. Word of the event spread among teenagers, and several hundred appeared at the neighborhood get-together on Halloween weekend. Young people from twelve to nineteen filled the hall as Paul stepped up to a microphone and announced, "Okay kids, let's dance.'' Then he signaled the record spinner to go to work. He also put the bite on his radio sponsors. National Biscuit Company supplied crackers, Nescafé provided instant coffee, and Philco contributed the phonograph and amplification equipment. Since the dance pleased both the youngsters and their parents, the gatherings continued every Saturday night through the winter. By early summer money had been raised with the help of the Rotary Club to expand the outdoor recreation park.

The success of the Lambertville parties started Paul thinking about expanding on the idea. He believed that it could work in countless communities across the country. "I look at it this way," he explained in an interview for the New York *Herald-Tribune*. "Every town's got a town hall; there are school bands if no other music is available . . . So if the dads and mothers really stir themselves they ought to be able to get the local theater and nightclub people . . . to let talent drop by for a few numbers. Good clean fun for kids just doesn't happen; it has to be organized —by older people—and everybody's got to plug it.''

During his network broadcasts, Paul talked of his hopes that the teen dances would spread from coast to coast. In 1948 at least fifteen communities across the United States picked up Pops's idea and started providing Saturday night recreation as a means of combating juvenile delinquency. And every Saturday Paul came to St. John's

Hall to preside as master of ceremonies. Often he brought such well-known performers as Patti Page, Carmen Cavallaro, and Mindy Carson. In turn, he plugged their records that week on his coast-to-coast disc jockey show.

Margo was at her father's side every Saturday night. Vivacious and attractive, she handled the selection of records for dancing. She relished the job, and all week long she looked forward to sharing the limelight with Pops. One Saturday in midwinter Paul fell ill with a cold and had to stay home. Margo, who had watched her father's style as master of ceremonies and all-round greeter, took over his post. Completely at ease and poised, she slipped into the role of a glib and amusing disc jockey like a needle falls into a record groove. By all reports she was the hit of the evening, and Paul began to look at her with different eyes.

The rather comely, somewhat precocious, and very indulged Margo had spent her formative years in Hollywood and in New York. In the mid-1940s, when she was twelve, she was enrolled in Marymount School in Manhattan, a prestigious Catholic girls' academy. "I'm trying very hard to grow up," she wrote her parents during her second term, "but it doesn't look like I'm making it." She daydreamed of the farm and her own horse. Soon she had a mount called Beauty, but she pleaded for a palomino. "If I got Beauty in good shape and made a good horse out of her, would you sometime get me a horse something like Roy Rogers's Trigger?" She promised to turn a new leaf, to do well at school, and to be a good Sugar Plum—Paul's pet name for her. The Shirley Temple of Walking Horse Farm, Margo lived like a princess; but now she was about to take the first step toward leaving the Good Ship Lolli-Pops.

Discovering a promising young performer at his very hearth, Paul decided to bring Margo to Radio City for a broadcast celebrating his fifty-eighth birthday on March 28, 1948. Charles Barry liked what he heard from Margo as she sat before the microphone and helped Pops spin records. Impressed by her spontaneous and cheery responses to Paul's introductions of records and his lead-ins to commercials, Barry easily convinced Pops that, given her pleasant personality and fine speaking voice, she had the makings of a radio performer. Less than two months after the birthday broadcast Margo signed a contract with ABC, making her mistress of ceremonies for a sustaining series called *Tomorrow's Tops*. The agreement provided Margo with a weekly stipend of $200. Produced and written by Madge Tucker, the program showcased teenage professional talent each Monday evening at nine. It replaced Pops's new series, a talent quest called *On Stage, America,* which moved to Wednesdays.

Margo was helped considerably by Glenn Osser and his orchestra and by announcer Jimmy Blaine, who provided the ebullience and upbeat demeanor necessary for a variety show. Of the half-dozen youngsters on the first broadcast, little Robert White, a potential full-voiced Irish tenor, lived up to expectations. His dad, Joseph White, the Silver Masked Tenor of early radio, had coached him well.

That summer Margo emerged as an actress as well. She played a minor role in a summer-stock production, *The Gilded Cage,* at the Bucks County Playhouse in New Hope, Pennsylvania, across the Delaware River from the farm. The venerable actor Sidney Blackmer starred in the comedy which gained considerable publicity by Margo's presence.

At nearby movie theaters Paul's latest (and last) feature film drew music fans. *The Fabulous Dorseys*—the life story of Jimmy and Tommy Dorsey— again reunited on screen Paul, Mike, Henry Busse, and the Dorsey brothers. Otis L. Guernsey, Jr., film critic of the New York *Herald-Tribune,* wrote that the playing of the music in the United Artists release "has been staged with variety and visual interest . . . but the story is just a bare outline of the Dorseys' rise to fame."

With Margo, Paul was certain he had a rising star in the family. Looking back at his clan's track record, he should have been a bit dubious of real stardust. There had been many false hopes before. Margaret's niece, Ivy's attractive daughter by her first marriage, might have made it. Known as Dorothy Atkins, she sang over New York's WMCA, accompanied the Whiteman band as a soloist on a southern trip, and then made her Broadway debut in the musical comedy *Roberta*. But at the age of nineteen, in 1935, she threw it all aside by eloping with a doctor. Then, there was Emerson Frome, one of Margaret's many cousins, who was coached and preened to enter the family "business"—motion pictures. Margaret secured small parts for the boy in a few early talkies. Emerson decided to become a dancer when movie musicals took over many sound stages. After Paul became a member of the family, he worked periodically with the band. A few more doors opened, but no breaks came Frome's way. When Whiteman joined the Casa Mañana production in Texas, he found a spot for Emerson in the chorus. During rehearsals Frome took it upon himself to attempt to unionize the dancers. His action brought down the wrath of Billy Rose. Paul, too, was hard pressed to explain what had come over Margaret's young cousin. The episode was the beginning of the end of a career that never really was.

Paul Whiteman, Jr., grew up surrounded by virtually every musical instrument conceived, from accordion to zither and ranging from king-size to lilliputian. He reached for a violin while still in short pants, only to discover that it was beyond his artistic grasp. He tried and discarded various brass and reed instruments. Then he took up the drums; percussion appeared to be his forte. After he entered the military in 1943, the Air Force assigned Paul, Jr., to an entertainment unit, undoubtedly capitalizing on his name. With extra money coming regularly from home, he indulged in liquor and then drugs. Almost an addict, he seemed to recover just before his discharge from the service in March 1946. Soon he began appearing at Paul's rehearsals. From time to time he would sit in on the drums. That fall Pops agreed to let him work with the orchestra on stage at the Capitol Theatre.

Interviewed backstage, the twenty-two-year-old appeared ill at ease and shy. He stared at the floor and seemed anxious to get away. His father did most of the talking. "Junior asked me if he could play this engagement with me when he got out of the Air Force last spring. I told him he could if he worked on my farm this summer. And, boy, you should have seen him work. He's a better farmer than I am. He's a good musician. I'm kind of proud of him."

Finally Paul, Jr., looked up and politely suggested that his dad had better wait a while before boasting about his talents. "After all, I haven't done anything so great. Lots of people play the drums." He explained that he needed experience but was hopeful that one day he would have his own band.

That one day came up fast. Two months later, in December 1946, Paul Whiteman, Jr., and his orchestra opened at the Iceland Restaurant in Manhattan. In the audience were Paul, Glenn Osser, and members of his ABC band. Not only was Margaret there, but so was Vanda, who had remarried. She joined the Whiteman table. Junior's combo—consisting of two reeds, a trumpet, bass, Hammond organ, and drums—played a smooth society beat. The Iceland ballyhooed the Whiteman name and insisted that Paul, Jr., use *Rhapsody* as a theme. Paul, Jr., was a bit bewildered by the whole experience. He was waking to the reality that it took more than shaking a stick to lead a band. *Variety* noted that the group's danceable styling should bring a booking in a classier spot without much trouble. But that eventuality did not materialize, and Junior fell by the wayside when the music world realized he could not live up to his famous name. It was cruelly observed that he did not even seem good enough for the old man to keep him on *his* bandstand.

Dorothy, Emerson, and now Junior. They all slipped out the stage door without leaving much of a trace. But Margo—Margo would be different, Paul told himself.

The instant success of the Lambertville record dances gave rise to a Paul Whiteman teen club chapter in nearby Flemington, New Jersey. The club met in a high-school auditorium, where Paul and Margo stopped every Saturday night as the second stop on their disc jockeying itinerary. Another chapter soon emerged in Sloatsburg, New York, and from time to time father and daughter journeyed north to its parties. Paul now conceived the idea of a nationwide dance session to be broadcast each Saturday night playing uninterrupted band music from nine to midnight. He envisioned teenagers gathering in big cities and small villages to tune in to his smoothly moving dance programs—at no cost.

Whiteman failed to sell ABC on such a weekly show. But one of the network affiliates did lend a sympathetic ear. Pops was familiar with a children's program at WFIL in Philadelphia called *Magic Lady Supper Club*. Produced by the station's educational director, Edmund "Skipper" Dawes, the show contained the nucleus of a teen-club format not unlike the record hops Paul had helped to organize. Dawes's major discovery, a young singer named Eddie Fisher, appeared regularly.

The WFIL management believed that Pops's idea had merit. During the discussion stage, however, ABC coincidentally entered network television broadcasting, using WFIL as its Philadelphia outlet. Quickly the emphasis switched to video programming.

Paul, who had made his first TV appearance in 1947 with Dave Garroway, had surveyed his prospects in the new medium many years earlier. Television in a rudimentary form had been around before he went to Hollywood for *The King of Jazz*. During the 1930s Paul thought of television as a hit-and-miss affair—a potpourri of sights with sounds not unlike the very early experiments in talking motion pictures. At the end of the decade NBC began commercial telecasts with the opening of the 1939 New York World's Fair. The four or five hours of television broadcasting each day persuaded few people to buy receivers and even fewer to buy air time.

The end of the war, however, completely changed the outlook. NBC, CBS, and Dumont quickly inaugurated regularly scheduled commercial programs from major cities. Nevertheless, in 1946 less than thirty TV stations were on the air in the entire country. Two years later, in 1948, ABC had added TV operations. As a network vice president, Paul had participated in the opening-night telecast from the Palace Theatre on Broadway, an appropriate setting for the video vaudeville that was to follow in the postwar years.

Paul had inaugurated ABC telecasting by conducting *Rhapsody in Blue*. New to the medium, the network geared up for its debut amid last-minute confusion, frayed nerves, and false cues. For his part, Paul was instructed to turn to the viewing audience and deliver some words of welcome after leading a few bars of the Gershwin score. Just minutes before air time Paul stood on stage looking for a microphone. He called over the young stage manager.

"There's no mike on stage for me," Paul pointed out.

"Don't get temperamental with me, Whiteman," the nervous manager replied.

"Son, have you ever conducted *Rhapsody in Blue?*"

"No."

"Well, you're about to, because I ain't."

Paul handed him the baton and walked off stage. A microphone quickly appeared at the side of the podium—in time for the TV opener.

Sizing up future broadcast prospects along with Philadelphia's television capabilities, Paul joined with Skipper Dawes to expand the projected radio teen show into a full-fledged TV event. After more than a year of Saturday-night dances for New Jersey bobby-soxers and their dates, he easily carried off the role before video cameras. Margo followed at his side.

Paul Whiteman's TV Teen Club first appeared in program listings in March 1949. Beamed from a National Guard Armory in Phila-delphia, it attracted a massive turnout of young people, who jammed bleachers set up in the arena. Several thousand kids descended on the telecast every Saturday evening. After each actual telecast, which lasted from eight to nine, they danced to the music of a big band for two or more hours. The televised portion featured eight or nine teenage acts—singers, instrumentalists, and dancers—introduced by Paul and Margo.

It was apparent that Paul had lost neither his keen interest in discovering new talent nor his unusual enthusiasm for young people. Now, with television, Pops paraded before a nationwide audience hundreds of talented teenagers who wanted a crack at show business. And music teachers, dramatic coaches, and dancing instructors noticed a change in their students' attitude. Previously some had had a lukewarm interest in performing. Now, with the *TV Teen Club* on their television sets, many were thrilled at the idea of appearing on the screen and hurried to board a trolley to the armory to try out for the show. Pops was giving the lie to the old saw that Philadelphia closed for the weekend.

That city had already built a parochial tradition as a talent booster. At one of the early radio stations, WCAU, Stan and Esther Broza produced the *Children's Hour*, sponsored by Horn and Hardart Restaurants. It was a launching pad for hundreds of young performers, including Eddie Fisher, Ezra Stone, and Elliot Lawrence. The long-running series lasted into the early TV period. By then Whiteman's show had picked up the mantle. Later, in the mid-1950s, Dick Clark, who had appeared with Pops, carried on as the Pied Piper of teenage dancers. His *American Bandstand* brought rock to millions of late-afternoon boppers, fruggers, and strollers as guest performers would lip sync along with the recorded music. Chubby Checker, Frankie Avalon, Bill Haley, Fabian, and Freddie Cannon were lifted to stardom by coming on Dick Clark's TV show over ABC.

Paul brought in many large groups of performers for his teen club. The armory was the scene of a demonstration by a marching band of seventy high-school musicians, a choir of fifty, a dozen square dancers, a high-stepping chorus line, and a hundred young singers—adolescent mayhem, but Paul loved it. A teenage jury helped to judge the weekly winners. The grand prize for any young performer who won first place for five consecutive weeks was a Nash Rambler automobile. Many applicants were selected outside Philadelphia through auditions held by department stores, civic and social organizations, and ABC affiliates carrying the show.

Nino Pantano entered a competition at the Abraham & Strauss Department store in Brooklyn in July 1949. A voice teacher urged the thirteen-year-old tenor to enter Paul's competition. Nino sang Figaro's aria from *The Barber of Seville,* tied for first place with two accordion-playing brothers, and was invited to Philadelphia for a TV appearance. Introduced as a "boy Caruso," Nino won the first week and returned for two more shows to sing popular tunes. He was offered a weekly job on the teen club, but Nino's teacher felt that work as a pop singer would ruin his voice for a career in opera. He studied the classical repertoire for a spell, but soon gave up his music studies to become a public-school teacher.

Others lasted longer in the limelight. Young Junie Keegan turned up as a contestant during the early days of the program, sang one song to overwhelming acclaim, and almost caused a stampede in the armory. She came back to win week after week, until Pops persuaded her mother to let Junie sign a $200-a-week contract to sing on the teen club and other Whiteman shows.

Carol Ellis, a high-school cheerleader from Detroit, flew to Philadelphia after being chosen locally to compete as an announcer on the Whiteman talent show. She emerged a winner on the program, and during the post-telecast dance she won a jitterbug contest. "How strange the accents of the Philadelphia station staff sounded," Carol recalled, "and I probably sounded as odd to them."

As a result of her success with Pops, she decided on a career in television and majored in broadcasting at the University of Michigan. After two years as a weather girl, announcer, and continuity writer at WAVY-TV in Virginia, she had her own show over New York's WNBC and appeared on the Merv Griffin Show, many TV specials, and commercials.

Some of Carol Ellis's contemporaries who also progressed from Pops's show to real stardom included Peter Nero, Leslie Uggams, Diahann Carroll, Bobby Rydell, Pat Boone, and Wayne Newton.

Three teenage singing brothers bearing the name Crosby, however, never made the auditions. Pops heard Lindsay, Philip, and Dennis Crosby at a small club near New Hope one summer. After they performed, the trio came to his table to discuss the act's potential. Though Paul was not impressed by their work, he politely offered suggestions to improve their routine. When it came time to pick up the check, one of the Crosby lads reached for it, saying, "It's about time a Crosby paid for a drink. You picked up enough bills for my old man."

Paul grabbed the check from his hand. "Let me tell you something, kid. If you weren't Bing Crosby's son, you couldn't sweep the floors in this place."

With that, Pops got up and walked out.

Meanwhile the success of the various Delaware Valley teen clubs aroused the interest of Justin Herman, a documentary film producer and writer. The Philadelphia native had recently returned from various projects on the West Coast and now decided to work on short subjects in the picturesque and unusually neighborly region north of his historic city. *The Lambertville Story,* shot on location using actual residents and kids, brought to audiences throughout the United States the saga of one community's solution to its juvenile problems. Paul and Margo "starred" in the eleven-minute short, which Paramount released. On screen father and daughter appear on horseback at the farm and at an outdoor teen dance. Paul narrated the story of how he spearheaded the drive for a recreational outlet for youth. He turned over his $500 compensation to the Lambertville Recreation Center.

By 1949 Paul had gained a fair degree of exposure in short films. He appeared in two March of Time editions—*Upbeat in Music* (1943) and *It's in the Groove* (1948). *Rural Rhapsody,* a general-interest featurette, included Paul as owner-manager of his large New Jersey farm, and *Musical Miracle* presented him in an eleven-minute short with singer Patti Clayton. All these films helped to build up his confidence for the demanding and fast-paced television work about to come his way.

Margo, however, did not make that major move into the television studios of New York. Busy with singing, dancing, and piano lessons, the energetic co-emcee had also discovered boys. One of her steady beaus, a student at the University of Pennsylvania, was also a part-time assistant director of her show. Thomas C. Haas and Margo became inseparable during the first year of the TV teen club. At Thanksgiving they announced their engagement, and they were married on February 3, 1950, in a simple ceremony in the rectory of St. John's Church. Only nine persons, all family members, attended. Foregoing a reception, Margo and Tom sped off to a brief honeymoon in Atlantic City.

Now a married teenager—Margo was a bride at seventeen—she could not, of course, continue to hold her assignment as cohost of the TV teen show. Besides, approaching motherhood ruled out television appearances. Later that year Pops became a Grandpops when Margo gave birth to a son, Thomas, Jr. Two daughters, Cindy and Nancy, followed in the 1950s.

Nancy Lewis, a seventeen-year-old singer, succeeded Margo on the Saturday night telecasts. Paul's heart was broken. The career of his Sugar Plum had lasted less than two years; she was the last of the Whiteman–Livingston clan to attempt to carve a niche in show business. It is worth speculating on how young Margo would have fared if marriage had taken a back seat. *Paul Whiteman's TV Teen Club* enjoyed a solid five-year run, leaving the air in March 1954. Margo would have been only twenty-one.

Some two years before Paul first faced a TV camera he wrote to the radio editor of *The New York Times* predicting that television would lend a great impetus to the enjoyment of music in America if producers used taste in projecting their ideas. "Chances are that our first year of music by television will be quite a conglomeration of experiments, ranging from artistic attempts to interpret music visually to a few outlandish exhibitions of bad taste; and the audience will, as usual, vote for the winning techniques by means of that well-known secret ballot called the dial."

Paul raised questions about the ways TV could be adapted to best project music. Few broadcasters were giving the subject much thought in early 1947.

Should cameramen be permitted to crouch behind every flute player? Or should the audience in the home be satisfied to have a peanut heaven view of the orchestra, with a front row microphone pickup?

Will the Disney Fantasia technique be used, so that you, in the dining room, will hear Beethoven's Fifth accompanied visually by an echelon of llamas doing the breast stroke across a bowl of borscht?

Paul considered TV another form of showmanship. It would make new demands on performers, as had been the case in the early days of motion pictures and radio. "As sound and color affected the motion picture field, so will television bring about a vast change in radio. It will be a new test, and with a more discriminating public than ever before, performers literally will have to be 'on their toes.' "

After six months with the TV teen club Paul was ready to launch his own variety show at ABC-TV. The network needed the likes of Pops to compete with the popular and top-rated Milton Berle's *Texaco Star Theater* on NBC and Ed Sullivan's *Toast of the Town* on CBS. The smaller Dumont chain beamed Jack Carter and *Cavalcade of Stars*. ABC's chief draws in 1949 were *Stop the Music*— a radio quiz show converted to TV—and the Roller Derby.

American Broadcasting now had the space, if not the means, to enter television in a bigger way. Its operations moved from the RCA Building uptown to a cluster of old, nondescript buildings between Broadway and Central Park West. Performers and employees jokingly called the location the Levittown of radio, after the housing development in the potato fields of Long Island. To many performers the facilities carried a quaint aroma. After making some inquiries about the neighborhood, they discovered that the new ABC television center on West Sixty-Sixth Street had formerly housed a stable. It was one of the few spots in mid-Manhattan with enough ceiling height and floor space to give the electricians and cameramen adequate elbow room.

In this onetime riding arena, roughly the size of a football field, Whiteman inaugurated the first television musical show to approach the staged musical numbers turned out so effortlessly in the movies. *Paul Whiteman's Goodyear Revue* utilized this, the biggest TV studio in the world, to produce an extravaganza. Sets, costumes, choreography, camera work, and the overall entertainment impact rivaled almost anything turned out by the major Hollywood film studios.

Paul wanted a Ziegfeld approach to his variety show—large scale, bigger than life, no holds barred. He got it, along with the job of host and on-camera orchestra conductor. The split-second visual cues were so demanding that Paul gladly turned over the extensive conducting chores to Glenn Osser. The musicians were seated on platforms at several levels arranged in the shape of a V. Osser actually did most of the baton waving out of camera range, hidden behind a large section of Paul's high podium.

The weekly show was built around vocalists Earl Wrightson and Maureen Cannon, a singing chorus, dancers coached and led by Valerie Bettis, and one or two guest stars. But it was the execution and staging that set the offering apart. Much of the credit was due to the efforts of producer Ward Byron. He had written a dozen or so radio shows for Whiteman in the mid-1940s while producing the popular *Fitch Bandwagon* and traveling the country to bring the biggest name bands to radio audiences. Just before joining ABC-TV, Ward was in charge of the *Chesterfield Supper Club* with Perry Como at NBC. Because he was an occasional writer for Whiteman shows, Pops considered him a "ghost" writer and called him Spook.

Paul's new show, Byron's first assignment at ABC, became an unforgettable experience in his long career, which had begun in the NBC music department in the late 1920s. "An important element in the productions were the sets," he explained to this author. "Created by a young architect, James McNaughton, they outdistanced virtually every other television studio set of the period. McNaughton thought out his designs in pure television terms. This meant extending the perspective out onto the floor of the stage itself. The result was added dimension for the viewer at home and infinitely greater comfort for the viewer's eyes."

Each set was built in three days at a modest cost of about $2,500. Usually the set included scenes painted on a fifty-foot-wide canvas cyclorama and on thirty-foot columns of cloth suspended from the ceiling gridiron. McNaughton's tricks resulted in the illusion of three-dimensionality for production numbers set against an underwater grotto, a full-rigged pirate ship, an Oriental harem, and a western ranch.

An unconfirmed story concerns a visit to the set by Pat Weaver, an early NBC-TV executive and the creator of the *Today* show. He viewed a rehearsal for a Christmas show that created a Dickensian village along the walls of nearly the entire studio. The cameras were placed in the center so as to pan the set in a full circle. Weaver walked through and looked on in amazement, repeating, "This is spectacular . . . spectacular . . . spectacular." About six months later NBC produced its first big musical variety show; the network called it a spectacular.

The lavish sets for the comparatively tiny video screen also caught the attention of editors at *Life* magazine. For the June 12, 1950, issue, they photographed the building and assembling of scenery for a Roman Forum sequence; fun-loving Paul was snapped wearing a toga as Nero with his fiddle.

The demands of live television left only seconds for costume changes and camera positioning. Paul was faced with switches from a tuxedo to a pirate costume or from Tudor king back to the tux during any one half-hour telecast. Bill Brown, the director, set up a small dressing room just off stage for Pops. During one show he had to strip right down to his shorts and get dressed in another costume. He had barely taken off his jacket when Brown called, "Pops, where are you? Aren't you through?"

"No," came Paul's voice through the dressing area partition.

"Hell, I allowed forty-five seconds."

"My God, Bill, I'm an old man. I can't even get my fly open in forty-five seconds."

The *Goodyear Revue* dictated split-second timing, particularly for the dance numbers. Choreography was an integral part of nearly every segment. In fact, Paul's show is recognized as the first TV series to fully exploit dancing. When Valerie Bettis worked out her routines, she made the camera a key component. Until that time dancing had come to the TV screen much as it was presented in the theater—straight on—interrupted only by occasional downstage closeups. Trained as a modern dancer, Bettis had worked with Hanya Holm, the Ballet Russe, and her own Dancers Studio. On Broadway she scored a triumph when she appeared as Tiger Lily in the 1948 revue *Inside U.S.A.* At ABC, in association with Jim McNaughton, she staged her routines in terms of depth, surmounting many of the physical limitations on dance in television. Her deftness overcame the usual sensation that the dancers were being crammed into the screen. "She also has capitalized to an astonishing degree on the merit of simplicity in the dance," observed *New York Times* television critic Jack Gould, "without any severe sacrifice in artistic ingenuity. Here by all odds is a superior job." Valerie Bettis's success with Pops led her to choreograph many specials on TV. But few of her later routines surpassed such specially choreographed video segments as the full fifteen-minute rendition of *Rhapsody in Blue* and her interpretation of Ravel's *Bolero*.

Paul was content to let his show speak for itself; he kept his introductions appropriately brief, in contrast to most variety-show hosts. He gave his guest artists—Connee Boswell, Victor Borge, Margaret Whiting, Peggy Lee, Mel Torme, Mimi Benzell, Rosemary

Clooney, Connie Russell, Jessica Tandy, Lina Romay, and others—those extra minutes that many hosts used for their own introductory chatter.

Moreover, Whiteman eliminated the studio audience. With a stage cluttered with cameras and cables and technicians, spectators would have had a difficult time seeing anything anyway. Besides, an audience and its response would have taken up essential space and a valuable chunk of the thirty minutes of air time. In a musical show such as this, an audience could only break the mood and lightning speed of Paul's finely honed production numbers.

No matter how well prepared they were, the cast and crew of the *Goodyear Revue* faced all the pitfalls and foibles of live telecasting. Paul always used cue cards for his opening and closing remarks; every word was written out and printed on large poster boards. At the sign-off of one show, the boy working the cards held them off camera as usual, for Pops to read.

"Don't forget, folks, to look in next week," Paul said, peering at the bottom words on a card. The young man flipped it over for Paul, who continued, "There will be swimming at Palisades Amusement Park." The stagehand had held up the wrong cue card. The show went off the air while audiences wondered what Pops was planning for his next show. A special remote from a swimming pool?

At the usual post-show conference on one particular Monday the sponsor's representative had a bone to pick. The broadcast had featured a New Orleans French Quarter scene, with a sexy female leaning against a lamppost. The man from Goodyear complained that, because of the performer's dress and actions, the show had seemed to be catering to whores.

"So what?" was Paul's instant response. "Whores buy tires."

Critics, columnists, the sponsor, and show-business leaders loved the program. Even the tire commercials won praise. But in general, audiences were lukewarm. Home viewers were geared to watching Berle, Sid Caesar, Ed Sullivan, Red Skelton, and Ken Murray in vaudeville settings. "The program was too artistic," Glenn Osser observed. "It was way ahead of its time. If color TV had been available and if fewer competing variety shows had existed in the early 1950s, it probably would have achieved high ratings and lasted years beyond the 1951–1952 season."

Another factor in the show's demise stemmed from radio, still a healthy and mature member of most households. Opposite Paul on Sunday evenings, Jack Benny overpowered the *Goodyear Revue*. It would be a year or two before live network radio folded; meanwhile, Benny, Crosby, Hope, and Fibber McGee and Molly kept it going.

After the Goodyear show expired, Paul's TV activities chiefly centered on his teen club, until March 1954. At that time, he was poised to begin a new ABC series, another talent-hunt called *On the Boardwalk,* broadcast on Sunday nights. Amateur contestants of all ages were welcomed on the hour-long program. Pops aired the show from his old foxtrot turf, Atlantic City.

Early in 1954 he chanced to meet a New Jersey politician who told him that the resort city was interested in becoming a focal point for major network-television broadcasts. The boardwalk attracted many performers of varied talents and degrees, along with thousands of vacationers each week. With the city fathers of Atlantic City Paul worked out an arrangement whereby the city contributed about $5,000 per week to the telecast from the Steel Pier. Cables linked it to the nearest ABC terminal, Philadelphia. However, neither Atlantic City nor Philadelphia rose to compete with the primary TV centers, New York and Los Angeles.

Paul's weekly trips to the seaside resort during the summer of 1954 stirred up ideas for new TV shows. He suggested that ABC televise the Miss America Contest from Atlantic City. His old sponsor, Philco, agreed to pick up the tab. Pops came into the proceedings as a judge, and along with him were Osser as conductor and ABC-TV personality Bert Parks as host.

On the Boardwalk was dropped after three months—no significant loss to the entertainment world. Pops soon triggered interest at CBS-TV in his genial presence as a summer replacement for the highly popular Jackie Gleason. Titled *America's Greatest Bands*, the show featured four different famous dance orchestras each Saturday night. Pops played emcee to such diverse aggregations as Rudy Vallee and Count Basie, Xavier Cugat and Art Mooney. Apparently the idea came from Gleason, a self-styled musician and would-be conductor of pop tunes. Noting that people at the movies were happy to watch bands for an hour or more, he believed that TV audiences would be no different.

The Gleason–Whiteman venture was an ideal insert for the summer months. Viewers did watch the big bands; some even danced to the music, just as they had in the days of early radio. Paul cut a new record album, *Fred Astaire's Cavalcade of Dance*, full of vintage favorites for turkey trotting or bunny hugging in the living room. Coral Records released the long-playing record.

Paul and Gleason soon produced a pilot for a projected full-season series. During the taping, Paul was on the podium, though pint-sized conductor Ray Bloch was actually kneeling in front of him, out of camera range. Paul, who always wore a large gold ring with an egg-sized stone, gave a downbeat—and hit Block on the head, knocking him out cold. The proceedings came to a halt while he was revived. Block got off the ground, but the proposed show never did.

Plans were announced for yet another Paul Whiteman show, but at the last moment NBC canceled them. ABC, too, had intended to present Pops in a new series; it was also dropped as the TV industry cast about for quiz shows and Westerns to fill prime time.

In the shuffle Paul had already bowed out at ABC in May 1955. His departure came when he agreed to do *America's Greatest Bands* for the rival CBS network. ABC released him from a long-term pact. His close ties with Jackie Gleason Enterprises raised questions at his home base. With his plans for a variety-musical show, Paul felt that his executive position at ABC was not justified. But after 1955 his TV exposure narrowed to a handful of guest appearances on NBC's *Talent Scouts,* Ed Sullivan's *Toast of the Town,* and the *Bell Telephone Hour.* Concert bookings kept Paul busy and in public view. Thus, actual retirement was still a long way off. The years ahead brought new opportunities and endeavors, some in the concert hall and recording studio, others at the race track and on the skeet field.

22

Roadrunner, Sharpshooter

Gershwin concerts, anniversary recordings, and auto accidents kept Whiteman in the news even after his television and recording activities ended. Margaret, whose career had finished twenty-five years earlier, seemed happier now that Pops's involvement in show business had lessened. The family and the farm were her first priorities. It had to be a very important occasion before she would travel with Pops. One of the reasons for this reluctance lay in one journey that ended in near-disaster.

In midwinter of 1949 Margaret and Paul had boarded the Orange Blossom Special to return north from a radio-industry meeting in Florida. They had had two relaxing days of train travel and were on the last leg of the trip, passing through Virginia, when they were suddenly thrown to the floor of their compartment. At sixty miles an hour, the speeding train had jumped the rails near Fredericksburg. Ten coaches of the seventeen in the all-Pullman flier were derailed. Several toppled to the side of the roadbed. Paul escaped injury, but Margaret suffered bruises and cuts on her arm and shoulder. She was carried to a local hospital, where stitches were taken. Margaret left the emergency room later that day, and the Whitemans rented a car to continue their journey home—to an empty home, as far as Margaret was concerned.

In her mid-fifties, Margaret still wanted a family. With Margo's sudden departure, as a bride, the nest was completely empty. Paul, Jr., nearing thirty, showed no signs of settling down to a steady job. Most of his occasional visits to the farm spelled trouble or disharmony. During one such stay he accidentally shot himself in the chest with a .38 caliber revolver while "cleaning" it. He was taken to a Trenton hospital, and the wound was found to be superficial. Junior recovered.

"Mag's wearing her Mother Hubbard again," Paul joked to friends when he told them of her plans to adopt more children. In 1951 she and Pops started proceedings to fill the nest. Early the following year two daughters joined the household—ten-year-old Jan and five-year-old Julie. Although Paul kidded his wife about being a mother at her grandmotherly age, he seemed to enjoy haivng a young family again. Following a visit by Margaret and the girls to his office, he remarked to Glenn Osser, "The best luck a man can have is to have a nice family."

Margaret's desire to raise another set of youngsters was fulfilled. As she had since their marriage, she advised Paul on his professional commitments and kept a tight rein on family finances. He admired her talents as both a homemaker and a bookkeeper. But those roles all too often demanded her presence away from his side, and he missed her wifely companionship and attentiveness.

Not long after the adoption of Jan and Julie, one of Paul's musical family members took gravely ill. Mike Pingitore, who had retired to California just before the *Goodyear Revue* started, had cancer. Paul telephoned him every other day until his death in North Hollywood in October 1952, at the age of sixty-four.

Then, fourteen months later, on Christmas Eve 1953, Paul's sister, Ferne, suffered a fatal heart attack at the age of sixty-seven. She and her husband, Paul Smith, had moved from St. Louis to Fort Worth, where they were neighbors of Ivy and Bill Crawford. Paul Smith had died a year or two earlier and Ferne increasingly became part of the Crawfords' lives. Dr. Bill served as both her doctor and the executor of her estate. Childless, she left her entire fortune of about $50,000 to her brother.

A saddened Paul was now into his fourth decade as a headliner. Conducting before thousands of spectators, he showed no signs of slipping in popularity; the public remained interested in him and his music. In June 1953 he opened in a show at the Hotel Last Frontier in Las Vegas. He performed nightly for three hours, assisted by Roy Bargy and his TV teen talents: singer Nancy Lewis, drummer Bobby Gregg, and comic Dave Barry. In July the show moved to Reno's Mapes Hotel.

In 1954 he accepted an invitation to be a guest conductor at a reception given by Dag Hammarskjold, the Secretary of the United Nations, for diplomats at the UN headquarters. Nearly 4,000 people, representing sixty nations, attended. Other entertainers who took part included Helen Hayes, Victor Borge, Edgar Bergen, and Douglas Fairbanks, Jr.

Gershwin concerts with Pops continued their momentum into the 1950s. Whiteman again conducted in the Hollywood Bowl in July 1954 at a tribute to George and Ira. He set an attendance record for the three-concert series; a total of 57,000 people bought tickets. Roy Bargy appeared as piano soloist, and a new Pops discovery, Shirley Harmer, sang. A twenty-one-year-old mezzo-soprano from Toronto, she had concentrated on radio and TV work in Canada. Paul had brought her to the United States for performances on his and Dave Garroway's shows. With the voice of a Dinah Shore and the looks of a Grace Kelly, Shirley seemed to be headed for a big career. Paul did his best to groom her for stardom, but she never reached the top. Meanwhile she and Paul returned to the Hollywood Bowl for another Gershwin night in 1956. André Previn handled the piano parts.

Paul's concertizing—for a minimum fee of $2,000 a performance—took him to Denver in 1954. It was his first visit to his native city since the death of his father fifteen years earlier. Paul and Margaret arrived at Union Station from Los Angeles, to be greeted by Saul Caston, the conductor of the Denver Symphony, who had invited Whiteman to lead the orchestra at the annual Red Rocks Music Festival. In his usual gregarious manner Pops looked over the city and pronounced it "still the same old place." A few thought they detected a touch of bitterness. Paul, it seemed, had felt that his home town should have done something over the years to honor him and his band as had Chicago, Detroit, Philadelphia, San Francisco, and other cities. In Denver he felt overlooked and unappreciated. In any event, Paul drew the largest crowd at the music festival, packing the theater on July 30. He felt a thrill at conducting in the place where he used to hunt rattlesnakes and go picnicking.

In 1955 he conducted a Gershwin concert at Carnegie Hall. It was sponsored by the George Gershwin Memorial Foundation of B'nai B'rith Victory Lodge to commemorate the thirty-first anniversary of the premiere of *Rhapsody in Blue*. Paul led the ABC

Symphony Orchestra, while Shirley Harmer and pianists Buddy Weed and Bruce Steeg appeared as soloists. The program was repeated a year later in the same hall for the same sponsor. For the 1956 benefit Harmer and Weed were joined by soprano Vivian Della Chiesa and baritone Jack Russell in selections from *Porgy and Bess*.

Whiteman's concerts and other appearances were now arranged and managed by Peter Dean, a New York agent who also handled Buddy Weed and Shirley Harmer. Paul had first met Peter when he was a high-school student in New York. Dean had auditioned as a singer at a youth talent search in the early 1930s. Intoxicated with jazz and the big-band sounds, Dean spent many hours as a kid at the Savoy Ballroom and Apollo Theatre in Harlem, where he got to know Chick Webb, Duke Ellington, Teddy Hill, and other regulars. As an adult, he turned to managing the performers he admired so much.

One day in 1953 Dean's doorbell rang. When his mother answered it, she saw a large hulk of a man. She immediately recognized the visitor, and the visitor struck her speechless. "Peter . . . ," was all she could get out. At that moment a hat sailed across the living room. Peter looked up to see Pops in the entrance way.

"Mrs. Dean," Whiteman said, "I've been watching your son work for a couple of years. Do you mind if I hang my hat here for the rest of my days?"

From that day on, Peter Dean functioned as Paul's manager. He admits to learning more from Pops than from any other person he ever worked for or with, before or since. It was also a job, he soon learned, that demanded his attention or presence anywhere, any time.

Late in August 1955 Peter received a call while visiting in Stamford, Connecticut. Summoned from the tennis court, he heard Buddy Weed's voice on the other end. "You better get up here to Fairfield. The old man's rolling."

Several days earlier Paul had driven from the farm to southern Connecticut for rehearsals and preconcert promotion for an all-Gershwin summer pops concert on the athletic field of Fairfield University. He had arrived on Wednesday to join a parade of celebrities to the nearby Bridgeport City Hall, where Mayor Jasper McLevy presented him with a gold-plated key to the city. On Thursday he made radio appearances to spur ticket sales. The event on Friday night would benefit the victims of the recent Connecticut floods, which had devastated much of the state the previous two weeks.

During the course of these activities many old friends were at hand, eager to buy Pops a drink. Later, alone at his motel, he stocked up on liquor and continued to imbibe. By the time of the rehearsal late on Friday, it was all he could do to keep falling off the conductor's stool.

At the sight of Peter Dean, Paul snapped in a loud voice, "What the hell are you doing here?" Paul knew that his manager would do anything to stop him from drinking; he had faced the consequences many times. Dean had realized that as Pops had grown older, his drinking led more and more to abusive behavior, even fights with Margaret.

Dean spotted the local chief of police and his contingent, who were assigned regular duty at the concert field every week. He suggested that they guide Pops to the backseat of a patrol car. The police dutifully transported Whiteman to his motel room and to bed. Meanwhile Peter Dean discovered several bottles of whisky stashed under the hood of Paul's red sports car. Dean carried the liquor into the bathroom, where he proceeded to empty the contents into the sink. Paul heard the gurgling sound, jumped from his bed, and darted into the bathroom. He seized Peter's arm in an angry torrent of profanity. Peter yelled to the cops, who rushed in and saved him from imminent injury.

Elizabeth Lennox Hughes, the program chairman and a former singer, expected a record-breaking crowd of 10,000, the largest in the eight-year history of the summer concerts. Her committee considered Paul's appearance crucial. He had to be revived. The police suggested plenty of fresh air. They guided him out of the motel, propped him up in the back seat of a patrol car, opened the windows, and drove him all over the town. He seemed to get hold of himself as the hour approached for the performance, which was delayed by a monumental traffic jam on all roads leading to the university.

Whiteman opened the concert with Gershwin's "Cuban Overture," then conducted Shirley Harmer in selections from Gershwin's work in Hollywood. Throughout the number, he clutched his side and back. Suddenly he wheeled dizzily on the podium and started to fall. Stagehands and police rushed to the podium and caught him just before he hit the floor of the outdoor band shell. They helped him to the wings.

Buddy Weed came out to finish the selection. Then, against the advice of several physicians in the audience who had scurried backstage to treat him, Paul returned to complete the first half of the program.

The intermission served to introduce a dozen figures from motion pictures, radio, stage, and television who had been instrumental in promoting the benefit. Backstage, Elizabeth Hughes conferred with Peter Dean, who suggested that Paul's collapse might have stemmed from more than drinking—perhaps he was seriously ill. Gus Haenschen, a well-known radio conductor, was summoned from the audience and asked to extend the intermission by leading the orchestra and Hildegarde in selections the two had performed just a week earlier at a Fairfield pops concert. Haenschen agreed to salvage most of the regular program while Pops remained stretched on a cot in his dressing room, guarded by four or five cops.

For the final number Gus took up the baton for *Rhapsody in Blue,* with Weed at the piano. They were halfway through the work when Paul, hearing the strains of his theme, groggily came to, pulled himself from the cot, and stumbled toward the cops. He mumbled that he had to go to the men's room. A friend volunteered to guide him. He helped Paul unzip his fly and then held his penis while he urinated. Rezipped, Paul pushed everyone aside and rushed on stage just as Haenschen was leading the musicians through the final section of the *Rhapsody.* Paul bumped Gus off the podium with a brusque shove of his shoulder. The startled Haenschen nearly fell to the floor and stumbled off to the wings.

Like a big bird Paul raised his arms and led Buddy and the players into the final part of the familiar Gershwin work. The audience went absolutely wild. At the conclusion it jumped to its feet, cheering, yelling, applauding. The King of Jazz had recovered. He could not deny his subjects the thrill of watching him bring to a climax one of the greatest of popular American works, the opus he had helped to inspire and create. Pops was the hero of the night, the talk of the town.

The concert had been broadcast by two local radio stations. These airings, which picked up the change of conductors, helped to spread reports that Paul Whiteman had dropped dead. The backstage telephones rang without letup as reporters from New York inquired whether or not Pops had played his last concert. When Paul heard about it, he jabbered, "The story got around I had dropped dead. Now wouldn't that be wonderful if I died before this wonderful audience? But just put the soil over me lightly."

In the interim Peter Dean had called Margaret. "Meet me in New York at the Gotham Hotel," was all she could say.

The ovation still ringing in his ears, Paul took off in his car for Manhattan. An hour later he returned to the motel. "I don't know where I'm going," he explained to Peter. "Please come with me. I know you won't drive my little car, but you can hold on to the wheel, and if I start to cross the white lines, you get us back in the lane."

Peter reluctantly agreed. "Okay Pops. But only if you keep to thirty-five miles an hour all the way to New York."

In the lobby of the Gotham Hotel, Paul spotted Margaret and bolted out a side door. "Get out of my way," he barked. Prepared for another bad scene, she had alerted their doctor to track him down in the one or two all-night bars in the area. The physician located Paul in a saloon on Fifty-Fourth Street. He managed, after a few drinks with him, to bring Whiteman back to the hotel, sedate him, and get him into bed—where he slept for three full days.

Peter Dean believed that Paul's drinking became more problematic as he got older. "About every three months something would set him off and he'd drink nonstop for days. In between, he could go for long stretches without touching a drop."

Whiteman made headlines periodically when he mixed drinking with driving. Sober, he was a fast, reckless driver, especially when he was speeding along the New Jersey roads in a high-powered car. Intoxicated, he was a menace; he was hospitalized with minor cuts and bruises following several car crashes. Once, when in his words, "something went wrong with the steering wheel," he hit a telephone pole. Another time his car collided head on with another vehicle in Philadelphia. Another episode ended in a jail cell in Reading, Pennsylvania, when, on a charge of intoxication and profanity, Paul had pulled into an American Legion post for drinks, became unruly, and took a swing at a policeman.

His bookings suffered. He failed to appear at an event at New York's Waldorf-Astoria Hotel when he stumbled upon a group of convivial bankers from Denver. Engaged by the Chrysler Corporation to perform in Detroit, he arrived absolutely drunk, then proceeded to throw up on his hostess, and ended the evening rolling down a flight of steps. People persisted in joking about his very severe problems; one observer quipped that Pops was certainly keeping up with the times as a rock and roller.

In truth he had taken notice of the latest style and beat in music in 1956. Of rock and roll he said, "It's all right. Some of that rock stuff is pretty good—especially when the guys grab some good chords on their guitars. Of course it's nothing new to us; it's strictly Chicago two-beat, with church shouting, only they've changed 'Jesus' to 'love.' "

When Elvis Presley burst onto the pop scene, Paul took a close look, sized him up correctly, and didn't write him off. "That guy is a symbol to a lot of kids with troubles . . . I think Presley's got the inner talent if it's handled well, but he'll have to develop his style in order to stay on top, like Crosby and Sinatra have."

Pops also predicted some basic changes in the orchestration of rock and roll. "They'll get tired of that one-or-two-guitar sound, and eventually they'll add fiddles and saxes and brass, like we did when we started the big-band business."

Paul even accepted an invitation to act as emcee for a concert by Bill Haley and the Comets in Jersey City. But the mayor and two city commissioners refused to permit the controversial music in their local stadium because of possible riots. Rock-and-roll stars, Paul firmly believed, were as deserving of their acclaim as the idols of earlier years had been. Although Whiteman was asked to emcee rock concerts during the 1950s, he himself made no plans to perform the sounds of Elvis, Jerry Lee Lewis, and Bo Didley.

Coral Records, a firm founded in the postwar years, expressed an interest in capturing the Whiteman sound using the newer recording techniques of the LP era. In 1954 the company signed Paul—who in turn brought in Buddy Weed and Earl Wild—to record twenty-five oldies to be issued on three separate microgroove discs. In 1956 Paul's old friend Enoch Light invited him to record for his new company, Grand Award Record Corporation. Light, a sweet-style hotel bandleader and violinist in the 1930s, met with Pops to discuss a repertoire. Ever mindful of anniversaries and milestones, Paul said, "Ya know, I think it's time to make a fiftieth-anniversary album."

Pops and Enoch decided to record a lot of the old tunes that were identified with or were arranged especially for Whiteman's musicans. Mike, Bix, and Busse were gone, but there were plenty of alumni around. Although most of them were under contract with other companies, Light made the necessary arrangements, given the assurance that all of them would be happy to see the project realized and perhaps take part.

In September 1956 a group of Pops's former stars gathered in New York for several days of recording some of the tunes they had helped their old boss to popularize. In the studio were Johnny Mercer, Jack Teagarden, Jimmy and Tommy Dorsey, Joe Venuti, Charlie Margulis, Al Gallodoro, and Buddy Weed. Working for the minimum union fee, they happily cut special tracks for the two-volume set. Unable to fly East, Hoagy Carmichael, backed by Van Alexander's orchestra in a Hollywood studio, contributed his "Washboard Blues." Flat broke, Teagarden needed money to travel from California; Paul sent him $750. When Bing Crosby, the most successful and affluent Whiteman alumnus, refused to participate, Paul scouted around for unissued material of his old Rhythm Boys. He came up with a transcription of the radio broadcast reunion of July 4, 1943, from *Paul Whiteman Presents*. Bing, Rinker, and Barris agreed to let Paul use "Mississippi Mud."

The high-fidelity recording captured all the soloists at the top of their form, especially Teagarden on "Basin Street Blues," "Lover," and "Jeepers Creepers" (with Mercer) and Venuti on "How High the Moon" and "Autumn Leaves." Weed played the *Rhapsody* in such a way that Paul was convinced that the original spirit and feeling of the work—or as he put it, "the nervous energy and movement"—were recaptured.

The four twelve-inch LPs were supplemented with fifteen pages of program notes by George Simon. The album sold well, and in a short time it became a collector's item—helped in part by the sudden and tragic death of Tommy Dorsey the week the set was released, followed by Jimmy's death six months later in June 1957. Tommy's trombone solos on "My Romance" and "The Night Is Young" and Jimmy's saxophone on "It's the Dreamer in Me" were the last selections recorded by the Dorseys.

The carefully chosen repertoire and skillful hi-fi techniques of the anniversary album encouraged Grand Award to issue further Whiteman recordings. Paul and Joe Venuti cut a collaborative effort called *Fiddle on Fire*. A record of ten Hawaiian melodies followed, then two LPs of standards titled *The Night I Played 666 Fifth Ave-*

nue and *Cavalcade of Music,* respectively. They signaled the end of Whiteman's prolific output on discs for nearly every major label in the record business.

In 1956, Paul's fiftieth year in show business, Denver, where he had felt slighted over the years, honored, not the celebrated native son, but his distinguished father. The Denver Board of Education chose to name a new four-million-dollar elementary school for Wilberforce Whiteman. Because of the Professor's devotion to music among young people, the city's public schools had made a permanent place for music education in the curriculum. Thousands of youngsters had studied and learned through his efforts. Those who remembered his work recalled his frequent comment to his pupils, "Maybe you can't learn to make good music, but you can learn to listen to it and be happy listening."

On May 1, 1956, the city and its board of education dedicated the 600-student building on East Fourth Avenue. Paul was asked to represent the Whiteman family. The event coincided with Denver Music Week, which paid tribute to both father and son. Paul and Margaret came to Denver for several days of special activities. Paul conducted a citywide sixth-grade chorus of 4,500 voices—a choral group founded in the early 1900s by Wilberforce for a benefit concert to buy shoes for the needy. Paul also led an elementary-school string orchestra, a high-school symphony, and a citywide high-school band, as well as other vocal and instrumental aggregations.

Paul won some share of acclaim. The Denver Music Educators Club held a dinner in his honor at the Denver University Student Union. The Denver Musicians Association presented a plaque of appreciation. And the West Denver Historical Society made Pops an honorary member. After years of international recognition and honors, his hometown was finally beginning to acknowledge his contributions to music. The celebration soothed his bruised feelings and erased to some extent what he felt as slights in the past. In 1976 in Denver the National Music Council, Colorado Federation of Music Clubs, and EXXON unveiled a Bicentennial plaque commemorating Whiteman's inauguration of "a new era of concert music known as 'symphonic jazz.' " Colorado Day at the Kennedy Center for the Performing Arts in Washington was dedicated to Paul that year.

After the opening of the Wilberforce J. Whiteman School, Paul's thoughts were filled with memories of his parents. He began composing a song for "the finest mother any boy ever had." He called the waltz that evolved "Mother Dear" and added words to the melody. "She left me a legacy of love and faith and wit," he remarked when the tune was published in time for Mother's Day in 1957. "She encouraged me in my career and was vastly pleased when at sixteen I became principal viola of the Denver Symphony."

Paul recorded the song with vocalist Bob Eberly, formerly with Jimmy Dorsey. Pops had written to Bing urging him to record "Mother Dear." Without commenting on the merits of the decidedly sentimental number, he dismissed the request in his typically aloof and cool manner, claiming that his recording days were just about over. In fact, he recorded dozens of albums during the next twenty years, virtually until his sudden death from a heart attack in 1977.

"I think I'm over the hill now," Bing wrote. "The pipes aren't the same, and singing has become a chore rather than a pleasure and a joy. I think you'd be much better off, and so would the people who are promoting the program (for Mother's Day), to get a younger singer, one with a little more popular appeal—someone like Pat Boone, maybe."

Paul made one last effort to change Bing's mind. "I'll admit it was a little commercial on my part to want you to do it. However, I didn't feel the sentiment of the song was too sloppy, and they wanted to run your picture in the American Weekly, and are boosting up the printing that week to 11 million . . . So I thought singing another mother's song might have been a nice thing."

Paul added a few comments on Bing's singing. "I can't agree too much about your singing, or being over the hill, because I think the one you did with (Grace) Kelly was pretty great. Although you might not win a high note contest with Lanza, you're still my boy. I think I told you the story once, that when Johnny Johnston told me he had heard some of your records and you were sounding pretty old (that was 20 years ago), I said I didn't know about how old you were getting, but I did know that when you rolled over just before you died, you would, if you know what I mean, [do] a song better than he was singing them now."

During 1956 and 1957 Paul's half-century on the podium attracted the attention of disc jockeys and newspaper columnists from coast to coast. He went far and wide for interviews that focused on his past successes as well as on the anniversary LP record.

His travels to radio and TV stations often fit in with his newest pastime—sports-car racing. Automobiles had intrigued him as a boy. He once rode with Barney Oldfield in his two-cylinder Winton racing auto. He admired Eddie Rickenbacker and Ralph De Palma and journeyed to the annual Indianapolis Memorial Day championship whenever possible. In later years, after driving large cars, ranging from a Stutz Bearcat to a Duesenberg, he switched to small sports cars, usually a Jaguar or a Porsche. With a greater amount of leisure time in the late 1950s, he traveled south to attend the Daytona races.

At the Florida beach resort he met Tom McCahill and Bill France, stock-car promoters, who were anxious to gain attention for the beach-road track. They invited Paul to join the board of the Daytona International Speedway, with the official title of director of sports-car competition. He headed south two or three times a year. On occasion he drove alone in his Corvette to Daytona by way of Fort Worth. At the Big D track he participated in Sports Car Club of America races and for the annual Speed Week, donating the Whiteman Trophy for sports-car racing. In 1957 Paul helped with the Florida races at New Smyrna Beach, where 100-mile events were held on a 2.4-mile blacktop course. Paul himself got the feel of the track by racing around its curves in a Mercedes at a 100 or more miles per hour.

To have a convenient and mobile base while attending these racing events, Paul purchased a caravan trailer. The Hillman wagon allowed him to park next to the track and set up his living quarters within the sound of whining, snarling engines. The caravan's sides and cab doors advertised the track and Paul with the words "Daytona International Speedway" and "Pops' Pub" and the well-recognized Whiteman caricature. Paul's vehicle headed south nearly every winter well into the 1960s.

Whiteman's interest in and enthusiasm for sporting guns brought him nearly as much fun—and almost as much press coverage—as sports-car racing. In the 1930s he had flirted with deep-sea fishing and golf. He had organized Paul Whiteman's Marlin and Tuna Club for early morning rod-and-reeling off the Jersey coast. Its members included Red Norvo, vocalist Ed Smalle, bandleader Jolly Coburn, and Red Nichols. Next Paul tried golf in a big way, joining four or five courses and buying five sets of matched clubs. "I went at it real hard," he observed. "Of course, during the time I was involved, I kept trading off the different sets of clubs, or buying new ones. But no matter how hard I looked, I was never able to find a set of self-playing golf clubs. I always ended up by not being too good.''

Then Paul took up trapshooting. He bought a fine, expensive gun at Abercrombie & Fitch, and in typical Whiteman fashion, he went at it hammer and tongs. He started a club and as many as forty sportsmen joined. Paul became one of the best overall shots in the group. He built a small but professional trap and skeet range of his own and rigged about 15,000 watts of lights so that he and his friends could shoot at night. When the president of Philco, Jimmy Carmine, heard about the shooting activities on the farm, he gave Paul an air-conditioned clubhouse for the range. In 1955 Paul won the first Duck Shooting Championship of America at the Amwell Shooting Preserve in Ringoes, New Jersey. Flushed with success and pride, he donated an annual Paul Whiteman Trophy.

By the time he withdrew from shooting, he had amassed a collection of a half-dozen quality-built Purdey, Browning, Woodward, and Beretta guns. In 1964 he sold his prized collection on consignment at Abercrombie & Fitch; but he never lost his interest. When Eugenie Baird visited the Whitemans during Paul's last years, he took advantage of Margaret's momentary absence to whisper, ''I got 300 dollars that Maggie doesn't know about, and I'm gonna get another gun. I've got the money hidden in a box.''

Approaching seventy (and still driving sports cars at over eighty miles per hour), Paul continued to look for work on stage, accepting engagements and bookings from one corner of the country to the other. During 1958 he played to tens of thousands of concertgoers and nightclub patrons. In February of that year he conducted the Utah Symphony in an all-Gershwin program. In April over 900 standees heard his concert in Tucson, Arizona, and a capacity crowd turned out in Chicago's Orchestra Hall. ''I can still conduct as many symphonies as I want,'' he remarked to a Chicago reporter. ''I've been pretty lucky. I never was a romantic figure. I didn't sing. But my type of guy doesn't get washed up so easy.'' He still had the old touch. ''It was a good show, deserving of the kind of response it received,'' said Robert C. Marsh of the *Chicago Sun Times*.

Pops returned to Chicago in August as guest of honor at the annual Chicagoland Music Festival. Seated in an open car, he made his entrance into Soldiers' Field, where he conducted the *Rhapsody*.

At the close of the evening his portrait was pictured in fireworks. The same week he pulled out his scores of Gershwin favorites for Minneapolis's Music under the Stars festival.

Sandwiched between these concerts, a musical occupied Paul in Las Vegas and Los Angeles. When he accepted the engagement, Paul had assumed that the show would consist simply of another band fronted by him plus a handful of specialty acts. He soon learned that he was to appear in a nostalgic revue called *Newcomers of 1928*. A trite plot—a rocket ship journeyed backward in time to land on earth in the year 1928—was saved by swiftly moving, opulently mounted scenes with Paul and a quartet of old "names": Harry Richman, Rudy Vallee, Buster Keaton, and Fifi D'Orsay. A cast of thirty-five singers, dancers, and showgirls explored the Roaring Twenties to the delight of Desert Inn patrons. Paul and the *Rhapsody* were a musical highlight that evoked deafening applause night after night during a six-week run. Producer Jackie Barnett took the show to Hollywood, to Miami, and back to Las Vegas at Christmas 1958.

Shortly after the Whiteman family returned to the farm in early 1959, Paul received word that the White House requested his presence as guest and master of ceremonies for a special music program. He would introduce music by Gershwin and songs by Victor Herbert, to be played and sung by Buddy Weed, Earl Wrightson, and Eleanor Steber, a leading soprano of the Met. The gala reception given by President Dwight Eisenhower for President José María Lemus of El Salvador on March 10 featured vocal selections from *The Red Mill, Eileen, Sweethearts,* and *Naughty Marietta.* Harold Eugene "Buddy" Weed —as he was listed in the program—played a magnificent *Rhapsody in Blue* and accompanied Steber and Wrightson. After the final vocal number Vice President Nixon came over to Buddy at the piano, shook his hand, and remarked, "You're a hell of a pianist, but I can see your forte is accompanying singers." Buddy walked away wondering why anyone would want to give such a verbal slap to an artist.

That night at the White House capped Whiteman's varied undertakings in the decade of the 1950s, and it may be seen as a fitting end to a long career that, for all intents and purposes, was drawing to a close. Paul now turned to putting his house in order in several ways, and this meant giving up the comfortable old farm.

23

Coda Cottage

"**E**very blade of grass looks up at me and says 'Goodbye,' " said Paul after he decided to give up Walking Horse Farm in 1958. After twenty years in the Hunterdon Hills he found the large operation increasingly expensive to run and farm help more and more difficult to find. He had hoped that Paul, Jr., and Margo and Tom might build houses of their own on the property. When he realized that they were not interested, he felt that the place had outgrown its owner. "If some nice fellow comes along and wants to buy it, I'll be willing and happy," he often said. "Far better than subdividing the land into smaller farms. But I know I'm going to miss the place."

Margo's marriage showed signs of breaking up in the late 1950s. With three young children to tend to, she gradually became disenchanted with homemaking and looked around for an opportunity to revive her career in some form. Margaret took over the care and education of the Haas youngsters while Margo tried to "get her act together."

One day she received an offer from television station WNHC in New Haven, Connecticut; the program director wanted her as a weather girl for the two evening news shows. Attractive and personable, Margo Whiteman left Pennsylvania to start her comeback. After the first few days of her nightly broadcasts, she would disappear from the studio to arrive back just minutes before airtime. Frequently someone from the studio who went to look for her found her in a nearby bar. Many of her breaks between broadcasts were spent drinking heavily. The program director and the station manager did what they could to cover for Margo, but it was inevitable that the station would discover it had a problem on its hands. Finally Paul was summoned to retrieve his daughter. When Margo spotted Pops at the studio, she flew into a rage, realizing that he would be taking her home and thus ending her hopes for a return to show business. Adrift in a deepening maelstrom of alcohol, Margo received the best possible therapy and care. Paul tried everything, but nothing helped. He wrote her off and literally closed the door, perhaps too soon. By the 1980s, Margo had remarried and became a New Jersey State Certified Health Aide. Her work centered on health care for the elderly living in the Princeton area.

Paul, Jr., stumbled along as a part-time musician, then struggled as a freelance painter. Drug addiction plagued his existence. Committed to institutions, he drew pictures of himself under a big thumb or incarcerated in a cell provided with an enormous lock and key. Undoubtedly these sketches reflected his feelings toward his father. Neither Junior nor Margo, it seemed, could be counted upon to stand on their own two feet.

Then, in 1958, Margaret's mother died in her eighty-second year. Full of energy and wit until nearly the end, Eda had run the farmhouse during the frequent travels of her daughter and Paul. Her absence, more than anything else, brought it home to Paul that it was time to move. When Lloyd Westcott, a dairy farmer, lost his own property to a state reservoir and heard that Paul's farm was going on the market, he took a close look at the property. Westcott met Paul's price of roughly $400,000 for the large compound. The deal allowed the Whitemans to live on the property for about six months. That period of final good-byes to his land was heartwrenching for Pops. "The good old farm," he said time after time. "Boy, I'm gonna miss it."

Shortly before he moved, Paul signed a contract with Simon and Schuster for his life story. The publishers brought in a well-known author, Stephen Longstreet, to write the book, based chiefly on Pops's taped reminiscences. Longstreet also spent a week or two with Margaret and Paul, who picked him up in New York after he flew east from his home in Los Angeles. Paul seemed bored, according to Longstreet, and welcomed an opportunity to chat at length and, with a guest in the house, to drink a bit more than usual. Pops's biographer worked on the manuscript for months. Then Margaret sat down to read what had been written by her husband and the author of *Real Jazz, The Devil Is a Lady,* and the book of the musical *High Button Shoes.*

When Margaret had finished, she went to Paul. "You're not going to have this published! There's too much on your wild escapades, your mini-marriages, and your crazy drinking! And all that stuff about Chicago, drugs, and gangsters! I won't have it in print." But her suggested cuts robbed the story of its impact.

Since Longstreet, Margaret, and Paul were unable to agree, the project was dropped and Paul returned his advance to Simon and Schuster. During the 1960s other biographers approached the Whitemans with ideas for books and films. But each time Margaret demanded editorial control and final approval. In Margaret's view, Paul had to be portrayed without any significant blemishes or tarnish. Every would-be chronicler of the King of Jazz faced an unsurmountable roadblock.

The autobiography pushed aside, Paul packed away cartons of career memorabilia. Most of the Walking Horse Farm furnishings were temporarily put in storage as Paul and his family headed West to Los Angeles for the winter of 1959–1960. Upon their return they rented a neighboring farmhouse for the time it took to virtually rebuild a house across the Delaware River in New Hope, Pennsylvania. Situated on a hill in a grove of dogwood trees, the two-story custom-built dwelling offered ample room for Paul and Margaret and four youngsters ranging in ages from six to nineteen. Margaret had not lost any of her interest in looking after the next generation. She continued to bring in foster children and to find permanent homes for them among her friends. Close to twenty such youngsters passed through the Whiteman household.

Paul, now nearly seventy years old, insisted on his own quarters, away from the noise and the comings and goings of the rest of his family. He found them in what he whimsically called the root cellar—the entire downstairs area, cut into the back slope of the hill. Here he enjoyed the serenity and quiet he had longed for. The area provided him with a recreation den along with a bedroom and bath. Sliding glass doors separated the rooms from the grounds, with their flowerbeds and an outdoor barbecue.

Upstairs, after ringing the doorbell that chimed the first four notes of the slow theme from the *Rhapsody,* a visitor passed through a spacious entrance hall into a comfortable informal living room with a fireplace whose mantel was adorned with large hurricane lamps.

Between these lights was an Impressionistic painting by Covar-rubias illustrating the *Rhapsody in Blue*.

The New Hope house bore the picturesque address of 6 Great Oaks on the Windy Bush. Paul immediately tagged the new house Coda Cottage, certain that it would be the place where the "closing chords" of his life would be played. Most often Paul could be found in the recreation room listening to recordings of the classics he loved so well and had played in his youth. He would relax with a pack of Luckies or light up one of the pipes in his large collection. Happy at Coda Cottage, nevertheless he missed his horses, his cat-tle, and the sounds and smells of the farm. Occasional professional bookings still got him out of New Hope and kept him in public view.

At the nearby Music Circus, run by St. John Terrell in Lam-bertville, he conducted ten performances of *A Night of George Gershwin*. (The producer wired Ira Gershwin to ask if he would come East from California as an added attraction. Ira telegraphed back, "I'm afraid I would be not an added attraction, but an addled attraction.") Paul also opened the 1960 Illinois State Fair in Spring-field with a similar program. On Pops's seventieth birthday in 1960, Revlon sponsored a television tribute to which Jack Teagarden, Peggy Lee, and Bing Crosby contributed a song or two. Buster Keaton performed a pantomime act with the honored guest. Harry Reser stirred some memories with his banjo. Peter Nero was the piano soloist on the *Rhapsody,* once again the highlight of the show. "But Pops Whiteman seventy years old?" questioned veteran radio-television reporter Ben Gross. "The calendar has played a dirty trick. We who danced and sang to his tune in that long ago simply refuse to believe it."

In October Paul returned to Denver to conduct a concert at a convention of the Retail Druggists' Association. The following year he appeared at several industrial shows and concerts, as well as on the *DuPont Show of the Week,* where he narrated a salute to music of the 1930s. Phil Schapiro, his former trumpet player and now a producer, brought him to Stony Brook, Long Island, to con-duct a special Gershwin anniversary program at the community's Dogwood Hollow Amphitheatre. In 1962 he was named Man of the Year by the Press Club of Atlantic City; the New Jersey Senate, citing him as "one of the outstanding men of America, presented him with a license plate bearing the designation POP-1. He taped a discussion on jazz with Dave Brubeck at WLOF-TV in Orlando, Florida. And during a visit to Fort Worth he participated in an entire day's tribute to his career over radio station KJIM.

Occasionally on these travels–and, earlier, during tours and one-nighters—a maitre d' in a hotel dining room or eating establishment would call his suite or arrive in person to invite Paul and his party to dinner. The maitre d' would seat Paul and his group near the entrance in the most visible area to gain the greatest possible publicity value. Paul assumed that he was the manager's guest and that the meal was on the house. All too often, however, Paul was presented with a sizable tab. On one occasion when a restaurant wooed him and then stuck him with a bill, its manager asked Paul as he left, "How old are you now, Pops?" He snapped back loudly, "I'm not half as old as that god-damned steak you served me!"

By the 1960s not many of the younger people recognized Whiteman. The famous moustached visage, the large impressive bearing, and the snappy, colorful wardrobe hardly registered with the under-thirty set. It often bothered Paul that he was no longer known by every waitress and sales clerk in the country. Fast-fading fame and publicity drove Pops into periods of depression, marked by heavy drinking. His brother-in-law believed that he missed the excitement, the camaraderie, and the trappings of show business. Paul once remarked to him, "The biggest mistake I made, Bill, was giving up the band when Maggie said I should."

In 1962 Paul suffered breathing and respiratory problems. After weeks of putting off going to a hospital, he finally agreed to take tests. His illness was diagnosed as virus pneumonia. "It's one of those things which either kills you in two or three days," he said, "or worries you to death for weeks." The following March he again contracted pneumonia while he was attending sports-car races in Florida. He spent seventeen days in a Miami hospital, where he celebrated his seventy-third birthday with a bevy of nurses at his bedside. Just before he fell ill, he had agreed to conduct a pops concert of the University of Miami Symphony Orchestra that June. He later canceled his appearance because of illness and a nagging fear that he would forget a cue while on the podium.

Back on his feet in late April, Paul decided to remain in the warm, Florida climate. Margaret, herself ailing from the flu, had already returned to Pennsylvania to recuperate. Paul drove to St. Petersburg to visit with his old pal, Guy Lombardo. Lombardo's orchestra and its "sweetest music this side of heaven" was the drawing card at Port-O-Call, a popular dining and dancing spot. Paul discussed a possible partnership with Guy and the organizing of his own band as an alternate attraction at the restaurant, but nothing came of the idea. Paul may have been concerned over the diminished popularity of big dance bands and of dancing itself. "People got so wound up with singers," he told a Pennsylvania reporter that year, "they went to a place just to listen. They started to stand around listening, and they quit dancing. We killed ourselves. We were out of business, when they could go someplace and sit down and listen."

With another winter approaching, Margaret suggested that the family settle in Palm Springs, California. They drove to the desert resort and their newly purchased home adjacent to the Canyon Country Club. Julie, as well as Margo's daughters Nancy and Cindy, were enrolled in school there for the next three semesters. Their brother, Tom Haas, Jr., spent most of his boyhood with his father's family. Twenty-year-old Jan Whiteman had married Daniel D. Martino in September 1961 in Trenton. Margaret urged Paul to consider selling Coda Cottage. But he soon found that Palm Springs was not interesting if you were not a golfer. Paul's professional acquaintances were few and far between, and those he knew best only visited on weekends. He could not get involved with the local lifestyle, and soon he began driving the two or more hours to Hollywood, where he would meet such old cronies and friends as Phil Cohan, actor Bill Frawley, and restauranteur Bob Cobb. They asked him why he disliked Palm Springs so much. "Because there ain't no Toots Shor's there," he replied bitterly.

After a year of idleness and introspection Paul fell into a state of acute depression. Dr. Crawford was summoned. Realizing that Paul needed immediate care, he took him to Fort Worth for hospitalization. The family joined him there at the end of the school term in May 1965. They understood that his illness required prolonged treatment and a long recuperation under the watchful eyes of Dr. Bill and Ivy, as well as Margaret. She leased a furnished apartment in Fort Worth, where they remained until the following June. The year spent in Texas was looked upon by Paul's family as the most depressing period of his entire life. Surely Paul felt that way, too.

Although not a religious man, Paul began raising questions about the "unknown." Margaret and several Texas friends suggested that he seek the spiritual through the study of Christian Science. He visited a practitioner in Fort Worth, read the prescribed texts, and from time to time called for guidance. The practitioner found him a humble person, sincere and untiring in his quest for faith.

While Paul worked his way out of the depression, his former wife, Vanda Hoff Unger, now divorced, was the target of a poisoning plot in San Francisco. For a year or more her nephew, William Cootes, Jr., had secretly administered carbon tetrachloride to her food during his almost daily visits to the apartment where she lived alone. Vanda began to suffer from a liver ailment and entered a convalescent hospital. One day, in August 1964, a nurse saw Cootes pouring a substance into his aunt's coffee. The nurse alerted a doctor, who ordered a laboratory analysis.

Authorities learned that Cootes was a conservator of Vanda's estate. Nearly $30,000 in cash and five expensive pieces of jewelry from her safe-deposit box had vanished—along with the nephew. A nationwide police search discovered the rings and brooches in several cities. That same week Cootes, a child psychologist, was found dead in a San Francisco hotel room. A suicide, he died of an overdose of pills. In the meantime Vanda recovered from her ordeal and moved back to an apartment in her native city. From time to time Paul sent money to Vanda, whose resources had been exhausted by chronic illness, excessive drinking, and her nephew's thievery. Margaret continued sending occasional checks until Vanda's death in the late 1970s.

By January 1966 Paul, too, had sufficiently recovered to make a public appearance at the opening of the William Edrington Scott Theatre in Fort Worth, along with Zsa Zsa Gabor, Gordon MacRae, Gian-Carlo Menotti, and other celebrities. The applause for the grand old man of jazz was the loudest of all. But he was more than a celebrity; he was already a legend. That month, as a cold January wind blew across a graveled parking lot near the site of the old Casa Mañana, Paul gazed at what remained of the Texas Centennial. He joined a group of local officials to break ground for an addition to a new, aluminum-domed Casa Mañana. Standing only fifty or so feet from where he had conducted for Billy Rose in 1936 and 1937, Paul remained silent for a moment or two, then suddenly laughed. "We had a forty-five-minute wait each night between the first and second shows. Every night I would have a washtub full of chicken salad brought in from a restaurant. And rolls. And a case of beer. The showgirls, and all the cast, gathered around. They ate and they drank. They called it the Whiteman Club.''

In June 1966 Paul returned to New Hope in the company of Dr. Crawford. His Bucks County neighbors welcomed Paul after nearly two years away in California and Texas. He was a guest of honor at the annual party opening the Lambertville Music Circus and at the midsummer Governor's Night there. About selling his Pennsylvania home he said, ''I don't know why I ever thought of such a thing. That's my home.'' Coda Cottage was taken off the market, and the For Sale sign went up in Palm Springs. He would remain a Bucks County baron.

After his return to Pennsylvania, Pops's associates wanted to honor him at a dinner in New York. Ward Byron spearheaded the event, but he decided to check out Paul's health first. Ward saw Whiteman and Margaret at Peter Dean's office one morning. He seemed in good shape to Ward, but he had expected more spark from his old boss. Near the end of the meeting Paul asked Dean to call the St. Regis and make luncheon reservations.

''Could you make reservations at one o'clock for Mr. and Mrs. Paul Whiteman?'' Dean dutifully spoke into the telephone. After a pause, he said, ''No, Mr. and Mrs. . . . no, not Whitman. Paul Whiteman.'' Again Dean spoke. ''Whiteman. W-H-I-T-E-M-A-N. Paul Whiteman and his wife for . . . Yes, that's right.''

Paul heard Dean's efforts across the room and shouted, ''Tell that rock-and-roll son of a bitch to drop dead!''

Ward immediately thought to himself, Pops is his old self; he'll be okay.

Later that week Ward telephoned Margaret at New Hope to set a date for the surprise tribute and to discuss the details of getting Paul there. A day or two later Paul came into New York and ran into Ward.

''Spook, I thought we were good enough and close enough friends so you wouldn't go behind by back. If you wanted me to do something, you could have come to me directly. You don't have to go through Maggie on a thing like this. I resent it.''

It seems that during Ward's call to New Hope Paul had picked up an extension phone and overheard the conversation.

''All I was doing was checking out how well you were doing, Pops,'' Ward explained. ''And I'd rather ask Maggie to be the judge of that.''

Paul misunderstood the nature of the special dinner; he believed that the broadcasters wanted him to conduct an orchestra at the tribute. He became embarrassed as he learned the true nature of the program, but by then he would not admit his confusion. "Always come to me on these things," he blustered and then refused to attend the dinner, which was quickly called off.

One celebration that did come off was a salute by the New Hope Historical Society to its resident "king." On his seventy-seventh birthday nearly 300 people honored Paul at a dinner dance in the Playhouse Inn. While a small combo played the songs that had made him famous, Paul reminisced about Gershwin, Crosby, the Dorseys, and many alumni of his band. "If I started life again, I'd probably let my hair grow long and form a rock group. Rock-and-roll is improving a lot. It's slowing down; it isn't as noisy as it was. The bands are beginning to play better chords. And the Beatles: they've done some lovely things."

The Whitemans brought one special guest to the formal bash—May Singhi Breen, the widow of songwriter Peter De Rose. Paul called De Rose, who had composed "Deep Purple" for him, "the greatest friend I ever had." After being introduced by former band member Jimmy Carmichael, Paul said, "At seventy-seven, there is so much to be grateful for. I am humble tonight—I've never been humble before."

A month before the birthday gala Paul's and Margaret's youngest daughter, Julie, married David Kelley, a Navy veteran with the Princeton Aviation Corporation. At the reception in the River's Edge restaurant on the banks of the Delaware, Paul listened to the accordionist and violinist he had hired to play background music. When they played "Wonderful One," he suddenly borrowed the violin and teamed up with the accordion player. "He likes to hear it and play it when he's having a good time," Margaret remarked to a guest. It was the last time he would hold a violin to his chin.

At seventy-seven he also made made known the fact that he would no longer conduct. "All I do is creak," he said. "And without my hat, these days I look like an old turtle that ought to pull its head back in its shell. I don't like these 'wattles' either," he added, pointing to his jowls. The physical assaults of age annoyed him, but he still got a kick out of being gruff about them.

Youth and the new generation were foremost in his mind that year of Vietnam fighting and draft-card burning. "There's nothing wrong with today's kids except bad examples we have set. Kids have some nice inside sentiments. They are too smart for the mess they're inheriting. Most of them are pushing for something better."

Paul maintained that he did not particularly care for reminiscing. But he talked to any reporter and interviewer who expressed an interest in his career. And when he started to talk, he became a great monologist. The arrival of a reporter was a welcomed event; it gave shape to the day that often lacked direction or a schedule. The absence of daily routine frequently bothered Paul. "I would be better if I did have one. Then I'd know what I was gonna do."

Inactivity stimulated an increase in his drinking as the 1967 Christmas holidays approached. He missed the big Yuletide parties he had given for his men in the band and later for the staff musicians at ABC. The old gang was scattered all over the country. The arrival of Christmas cards from many of them pleased him, then depressed him. To ward off a crying jag, Paul would get into his car and drive across the river or go into town for a round of drinks. He seemed headed for another of his monunmental benders as Christmas Day came and a week of year-end parties filled the last days of 1967.

Then, in the predawn hours of December 29, Margaret awoke from a deep sleep to the sound of the buzz of the intercom telephone. She groped for the receiver at her bedside. The voice on the other end was Paul's, and he was in trouble.

"Mag," he groaned. "I've got terrible chest pains. I need help. I think this is it."

Margaret immediately called the family doctor who, in turn, summoned a rescue squad. She hurried downstairs to Paul's bedroom and helped him to get into some clothes. He was already wearing his favorite knitted slippers, shaped and decorated to resemble riding boots. By the time Paul and she were dressed, the paramedics had arrived with a stretcher and resuscitation equipment.

Glancing at the stretcher, Paul asked, "Do I have to lie in that thing? Can't I walk?"

The squad assured him that it was best not to walk. Alert and calm, Paul followed their instructions. Before leaving, he turned to his granddaughter Cindy and said, "Take care of your grandmother. She needs your help." The ambulance sped toward the Doylestown Hospital, and Paul joked a bit with the men about their racing skills. They brought him in by the emergency entrance at

4:30 A.M. Twenty minutes later, with Margaret and his doctor at his side, Paul's heart stopped.

Among the first telephone calls Margaret made that morning was one to Ivy and Bill. She would make no arrangements until they could join her in New Hope. With New Year's Eve falling on the approaching weekend, Margaret and Bill Crawford planned services following the holiday. News of Whiteman's death appeared in the afternoon edition of the Doylestown *Daily Intelligencer*. By the following day obituaries and photographs of Pops appeared on the first page of newspapers from New York to San Francisco. *Variety's* Abel Green wrote a full-page account of Paul's career for the January 10 edition. In virtually every headline he was tagged the Jazz King, who had reigned supreme as a hero of the Jazz Age.

On New Year's Day more than 100 people gathered at a funeral home in Doylestown to pay their respects to their friend and neighbor. The service itself was held the following afternoon at Frank Campbell's in New York. Over 250 mourners attended, including bandleaders Guy Lombardo, George Olsen, and Xavier Cugat, and composers Abe Olman, Johnny Marks, Noble Sissle, Rudolf Friml, Eubie Blake, and Lou Alter, and such Whiteman associates as Joan Edwards, Ward Byron, and Peter Dean. Many messages poured in from Hollywood. Among the tributes was one from Bing. "He was my benefactor. He was a giant in the music industry and advanced the quality of American music in the early days when jazz was just catching on."

During the service, concert pianist Leonid Hambro softly played the slow theme of the *Rhapsody in Blue*. Six former Whiteman string players from the ABC orchestra rendered Paul's favorite song, the poignant and moving "When Day Is Done." Along with the music, two eulogies of Pops, the musician and the man, touched the mourners. Herman Kenin, president of the American Federation of Musicians, and Stanley Adams, president of ASCAP, spoke. "Paul," noted Adams, "raised popular music from the basement to the penthouse. To some he is a legend; to others an ideal. To all a man worthy of respect and abiding affection."

Not present was Ivy, who was not well enough to leave Texas. More noticeably absent was Paul, Jr. When he was asked if he wished to attend, he sent word from the psychiatric institution where he was confined. "Why should I? What did he do for me?" Nine years later, he died in a rehabilitation institution at the age of fifty-two. He had been married only briefly and had no children. There appeared to be no one to mourn his passing.

On Wednesday, January 3, as a layer of snow covered the ground, Paul was brought to the Ewing Church Cemetery near Trenton, New Jersey. At the end of a path, covered by a ribbon of carpet for the occasion, stood a granite-and-fieldstone mausoleum resembling a small chalet. Commissioned by Margaret when little Dickie had died twenty-six years earlier, the structure already held her mother, and Ferne and Paul Smith by now.

Through the bleakness of the winter morning Dr. Crawford, Margaret, her daughters and grandchildren, and a cluster of friends walked behind the pallbearers to the portal of the Whiteman mausoleum. Inside, the names on the four crypts recalled memories of Denver, the Essex House, Hollywood, Walking Horse Farm, Fort Worth, and a dozen other places. Now the bright and colorful spirit that had traversed them had ended his earthly tour. Pops—the big man with the big band—was home from the road.

24

The Quintessential Pied Piper

By the 1960s *Rhapsody in Blue* had a long association with Paul Whiteman. It was his artistic signature, played by his orchestra thousands of times over a span of forty years. Whiteman and others had performed it as a choral piece, as a jazz trio, as a military march, as a Grecian ballet, as a harmonica solo—virtually every instrument or combination of instruments had rendered it. Whiteman and Gershwin had shared this well-loved composition in all its variations and modifications. But with Paul's death, the Whiteman-commissioned *Rhapsody* was, in a sense, "reclaimed" by its late composer. Less and less would Whiteman and the 1924 Aeolian Hall masterpiece be linked. Composer George Gershwin lived on through his *Rhapsody* and other works; conductor Paul Whiteman barely survived the collective memory of his audience.

During 1968, however, in the immediate retrospective of Paul's career, a number of musical organizations paid tribute to Whiteman. The Washington National Symphony and its conductor Howard Mitchell dedicated a program of symphonic jazz by Carpenter, Milhaud, and Gershwin to Paul, noting "his vision in sponsoring the most influential piece of music yet written in the United States, the *Rhapsody in Blue*." The concert was repeated at Lincoln Center in New York, where Mitchell told the audience that jazz and dance music would not have reached the concert stage so soon, had it not been for Whiteman. "None of the music on today's program would have been written if there had not been Paul Whiteman."

The Stony Brook Music Festival recreated the outdoor concert conducted there by Paul in 1963. Producer Phil Schapiro brought together Glenn Osser and Buddy Weed for this all-Gershwin program. Margaret, her daughters, and her granddaughters were in the audience that evening and shared in the posthumous acclaim. They would not be present at future recreations in the 1970s.

Richard Sudhalter, a musician, musical historian, and author, conceived the idea of putting together a band that approximated the original Whiteman aggregation of 1928. Using orchestral scores borrowed from Williams College and gathering some thirty musicians, he gave performances in 1974 in England of the vintage arrangements of Challis, Malneck, Satterfield, Hayton, and Grofé. The group—called the New Paul Whiteman Orchestra—appeared on radio and television, and were recorded. The British remained enthralled with early jazz, which Americans had introduced and made preeminent.

For a presentation in New York on October 29, 1976, Emery Davis bankrolled Paul Whiteman Rediscovered and conducted a twenty-five-piece orchestra. Featured soloists included Raymond Jackson, Dick Hyman, Al Gallodoro, Jim Maxwell, Johnny Mince, and Sudhalter (on a Bix-like cornet), as well as six vocalists led by Larry Carr (on Bing's songs).

The program was a success in New York, where it drew many musicians and fans. But it failed to create much excitement in Philadelphia, and plans for additional engagements were dropped.

It was readily apparent that the original sounds of such leaders as Glenn Miller, Tommy Dorsey, and Benny Goodman—with their singular identities—outlasted the big-band era. But Paul, in his great diversity, failed to develop a distinctive "swing." Certain bands live on through their phonograph records, but Paul's did not wear well. A prolific output on wax and vinyl hardly ensured long-playing immortality.

Margaret felt that she and her advisers were the only ones who could adequately and properly perpetuate the Whiteman legacy. They visualized a tremendous interest in Pops—a surge of activity that would bring fees and royalties directly into their hands. When that enthusiasm failed to materialize, especially after the Sudhalter endeavors in 1974 and 1976, Margaret lost interest in working with promoters.

Fortunately she had no financial worries. Her control of the bank books during her thirty-six-year marriage had saved Paul from a big financial comedown. She had invested in annuities which ensured a comfortable retirement for both of them. Paul's will, executed seven weeks before his death, also guaranteed her well-being. He simply left everything to her outright. There were no bequests to individuals or charities, with the singular exception of the Whiteman Collection, which gained the remaining musical scores, arrangements, and records in his possession.

Margaret and her granddaughters Cindy and Nancy Haas continued to live in Coda Cottage at New Hope. In the early 1970s Margaret never let up on her personal crusade to ensure Paul's place in the annals of popular music. She wanted posterity to remember him as the monarch of music, not as the court jester, the stag-room story teller, and the backstairs inebriate.

She grew increasingly senile, requiring constant attention. When it became apparent that there was no hope for recovery, the house at Great Oaks on the Windy Bush was sold. Margaret entered a nursing home, where she received close and solicitous care for the remaining years of her life. Marriage to the big and boisterous ringmaster of a musical circus had perhaps taken its toll.

From the earliest days of Paul's career people tried to explain what made him a show-business giant, a national celebrity, and a world figure.

Born on the eve of America's ragtime era, Whiteman developed into an astute musician and an inspirational conductor. Then he adapted syncopated jazz to a large scale and presented it to a growing public. The idea was not only new but also revolutionary. The country was eager to receive it. Mass entertainment developed to spread it. "Lacking any one of these factors," wrote musicologist Doron K. Antrim in the 1930s, "Paul might still be driving a taxi in Denver or playing viola in the San Francisco Symphony Orchestra. When Paul signed the Victor contract, he signed the credentials that made him the world's ambassador of jazz."

Whiteman gave the world a new sound—fast, modern, strident, and all-American. "Paul," recalled Charlie Strickfaden in his last years, "imparted to audiences a series of aural sensations, rhythmic extremes, melodic poise, cultural shock through unheard-of harmonies, and fresh humor in instrumentation."

"I never believed that jazz was as bad as the symphonists thought it was," Whiteman once remarked, "nor that symphony was as bad as the jazz lovers thought it was. There ought to be a common ground, and I helped find it." He was a master of lending the classical atmosphere to popular music. He showed that a dance band could play with the precision, delicacy, and technical brilliance of a symphony. As such, he became the most important single force in American music in the 1920s and 1930s.

Fred Waring summed up Pops's legacy at the time of his death. "He printed special arrangements of jazz-like music, played them in concert halls, and made them acceptable to listen to. He put together a new idea of instrumentation and made it into dance music. I think everybody in the popular music business should say a prayer of thanks for Paul Whiteman every night."

Visually, Whiteman added class and dignity to the podium. Impeccably dressed and tall, he stood out. Yet beneath the veneer he was more showman than disciplined musician. He was fascinating to watch, and that was part of his aura. From tea dances to swing sessions, from arias to blues, from nocturnes to riffs, Whiteman delighted audiences of all ages and tastes for longer than most other purveyors of melody.

More significantly, as the Pied Piper of Jazz Age youth and its offspring, Paul had a keen ability to tune in on new, emerging talent. He discovered more major musicians and singers, as well as orchestrators and arrangers, than any other impresario of his time. A catalytic force, he attracted, encouraged, and developed these artists to an extraordinary degree. Dozens went on to lead their own bands. More than 300 musicians played from his bandstand. And he made them first-class citizens; no longer would they be treated like low-paid gypsies and servants.

Whiteman introduced scores of singers, including the biggest names in the business. His arrangers created some of the best scores of the period; he made their role increasingly important—one of his most vital contributions to popular music. Composers, too, who passed through his organization produced ground-breaking and distinctive works.

Paul Whiteman was the most influential person in the careers of many musicians and associates. He approached people with a friendly, outthrust hand and life itself with a jovial, upbeat outlook. Furthermore, he had an innate gift of charming everyone, from shoeshine boys to heads of state. Like the words on the sundial at his Walking Horse Farm, Pops tried to count "none but the sunny hours."

Selected Bibliography

Anderson, John Murray. *Out Without My Rubbers*. New York: Library Publishers, 1954.

Anger, Kenneth. *Hollywood Babylon*. New York: Dell, 1975.

Antrim, Doron K., ed. *Secrets of Dance Band Success*. New York: Famous Stars Publishing Co., 1936.

Baral, Robert. *Revue: The Great Broadway Period*. New York: Fleet Press Corp., 1962.

Basten, Fred E. *Glorious Technicolor: The Movies' Magic Rainbow*. Cranbury, N.J.: Barnes, 1980.

Bernays, Edward L. *Biography of an Idea: Memories of Public Relations Counsel*. New York: Simon & Schuster, 1965.

Berton, Ralph. *Remembering Bix: A Memoir of the Jazz Age*. New York: Harper & Row, 1974.

Carroll, Carroll. *None of Your Business, or My Life with J. Walter Thompson*. New York: Cowles, 1970.

Crosby, Bing. *Call Me Lucky*. New York: Simon & Schuster, 1953.

DeLong, Thomas A. *The Mighty Music Box: The Golden Age of Musical Radio*. New York: Hastings House, 1980.

Dexter, Dave, Jr. *Playback*. New York: Billboard Publications, 1976.

Dorsett, Lyle W. *The Queen City: A History of Denver*. Boulder, Colorado: Pruett Publishing Co., 1977.

Durante, Jimmy, and Jack Kofoed. *Night Clubs*. New York: Alfred A. Knopf, 1931.

Eberly, Philip K. *Music in the Air*. New York: Hastings House, 1982.

Edward, H. R. H., Duke of Windsor. *A King's Story*. New York: Putnam's Sons, 1947.

Ewen, David. *George Gershwin: His Journey to Greatness*. Englewood Cliffs, N.J.: Prentice-Hall, 1970.

Flemmons, Jerry. *Amon: The Life of Amon Carter, Sr. of Texas*. Austin: Jenkins Publishing Co., 1978.

Fowler, Gene. *A Solo in Tom Toms*. New York: Viking, 1946.

Fuld, James J. *Book of World Famous Music*. New York: Crown, 1946.

Gross, Ben. *I Looked and I Listened*. New York: Random House, 1954.

Jablonski, Edward, and Lawrence D. Stewart. *The Gershwin Years*. Garden City, N.Y.: Doubleday, 1958.

———. *The Encyclopedia of American Music*. Garden City, N.Y.: Doubleday, 1981.

Johnson, Carl. *Paul Whiteman: A Chronology (1890–1967)*. Williamstown, Mass.: Whiteman Collection, Williams College, 1977.

Kinkle, Roger D. *The Complete Encyclopedia of Popular Music and Jazz 1900–1950*, Volumes 1–4. New Rochelle, N.Y.: Arlington House, 1974.

Kreuger, Miles, ed. *The Movie Musical: From Vitaphone to "42nd Street."* New York: Dover, 1975.

Lewine, Harris. *Goodbye to All That*. New York: McGraw-Hill, 1970.

Lombardo, Guy, with Jack Altshul. *Auld Acquaintance*. Garden City, N.Y.: Doubleday, 1975.

Lopez, Vincent. *Lopez Speaking*. New York: Citadel Press, 1960.

Osgood, Henry O. *So This Is Jazz*. Boston: Little, Brown, 1926.

Phillips, Cabell. *From The Crash to The Blitz, 1929–1939*. New York: Macmillan, 1969.

Ramsey, Frederic, Jr., and Charles E. Smith, eds. *Jazzmen*. New York: Harcourt, Brace, 1939.

Randall, Monica. *The Mansions of Long Island's Gold Coast*. New York: Hastings House, 1979.

Raymond, Jack. *Show Music on Record from the 1890s to the 1980s*. New York: Frederick Ungar, 1982.

Rust, Brian. *The American Dance Band Discography 1917–1942*. Volumes 1 and 2. New Rochelle, N.Y.: Arlington House, 1975.

———. *The Dance Bands*. London: Ian Allan, 1972.

Sanford, Herb. *Tommy and Jimmy: The Dorsey Years*. New Rochelle, N.Y.: Arlington House, 1972.

Schuller, Gunther. *Early Jazz: Its Roots and Musical Development*. New York: Oxford University Press, 1968.

Schwartz, Charles. *Gershwin: His Life and Music*. Indianapolis: Bobbs Merrill, 1973.

Shapiro, Nat, and Nat Hentoff, eds. *Hear Me Talkin to Ya*. New York: Rineholt & Co., 1955.

Shepherd, Donald, and Robert F. Slatzer. *Bing Crosby: The Hollow Man*. New York: St. Martin's, 1981.

Simon, George T. *The Big Bands*. New York: Macmillan, 1967.

———. *Simon Says: The Sights and Sounds of the Swing Era*. New Rochelle, N.Y.: Arlington House, 1971.

Smith, Jay D., and Len Guttridge. *Jack Teagarden: The Story of a Jazz Maverick*. New York: Da Capo Press, 1976.

Stearns, Marshall. *The Story of Jazz*. New York: Oxford University Press, 1956.

Sudhalter, Richard, and Philip Evans, with William Dean-Myatt. *Bix: Man and Legend*. New York: Schirmer Books, 1975.

Taylor, Glenhall. *Before Television: The Radio Years*. Cranbury, N.Y.: Barnes & Co., 1979.

Waring, Charles H., and George Garlick. *Bugles for Beiderbecke*. London: Sidgwick & Jackson, 1958.

Wheeler, Keith. *The Townsmen* in The Old West series. New York: Time-Life Books, 1975.

Whiteman, Margaret Livingston, and Isabel Leighton. *Whiteman's Burden*. New York: Viking, 1933.

Whiteman, Paul, and Leslie Lieber. *How to Be a Bandleader*. New York: McBride & Co., 1941.

———. and Mary Margaret McBride. *Jazz*. New York: J. H. Sears & Co., 1926.

———. *Records for the Millions*. New York: Hermitage Press, 1948.

General Index

Songs and Compositions

Places

Chronology

1890—Born in Denver, Colorado on March 28.
1896—Margaret (Marguerite) Livingston, fourth and last wife of Paul
    Whiteman, born November 26 in Salt Lake City, Utah to John
    and Eda Frome Livingston.
1907—Hired by the Denver Symphony Orchestra as a violist.
1908—Elopes with chorus girl, Nellie Stack. Marriage annulled in 1910.
1914—Leaves home for San Francisco, where he finds a job with the
    Panama-Pacific Exposition orchestra.
1915—Secures a chair as violist with the San Francisco Symphony.
1917—Becomes intrigued with ragtime music and adds to his income
    by playing in Barbary Coast cafes.
1918—Quits the Symphony to "study" jazz. By spring he is accepted
    for duty in the U.S. Navy as a bandmaster at Mare Island, near
    San Francisco.
1919—Forms a dance orchestra for Fairmont Hotel's Rainbow Lane
    room in San Francisco.
    Organizes his "original" band at the Alexandria Hotel in Los
    Angeles.
1920—Opens at the new Ambassador Hotel in Atlantic City.
    Records for the first time when Victor signs him to a contract in
    August.
    "Whispering" is released, quickly selling over a million
    pressings.
    Opens at New York's fashionable Palais Royal in September.
1921—Plays a long run at the Palace Theatre, the leading U.S.
    vaudeville house.
    Marries and divorces Alfrica "Jimmie" Smith.
1922—Makes debut in a Broadway show, George White's *Scandals of
    1922,* with music by George Gershwin.
    Weds dancer Vanda Hoff at New York's City Hall on
    November 4.
1923—Appears in London musical revue and nightclub during five-
    month stay in England.

1924—Organizes "An Experiment in Modern Music" on February 12
at Aeolian Hall for which he commissions Gershwin's *Rhapsody
in Blue*.
Begins the first of many extensive tours throughout the U.S.
Paul, Jr., born on May 30.
1925—Conducts Gershwin's jazz opera *135th Street* and Ferde Grofé's
Mississippi Suite at Second Experiment in Modern American
Music on December 29 at Carnegie Hall.
1926—Writes the book, *Jazz*, with Mary Margaret McBride.
Embarks on March 31 on a European tour throughout Great
Britain and the Continent.
Hires Bing Crosby and Al Rinker, the nucleus of the band's
Rhythm Boys.
1927—Opens the Club Whiteman on Broadway.
Adds former Jean Goldkette band musicians: Bix Beiderbecke,
Frank Trumbauer, Bill Rank, Steve Brown, Jimmy and Tommy
Dorsey, and Bill Challis.
1928—Signs a recording contract with Columbia.
Conducts Third Experiment in Modern American Music on Octo-
ber 7 at Carnegie Hall, which features Gershwin's *Concerto in F*.
1929—Begins weekly radio series, *Old Gold–Paul Whiteman Hour*, on
February 5.
Travels with 33-piece band on the Old Gold Special train to
Hollywood.
Signs Mildred Bailey, the first female vocalist with a big band.
Starts work in *The King of Jazz* at Universal Studios.
1930—Appears as an on-stage attraction with George Gershwin at the
Roxy Theatre premiere of *The King of Jazz*.
Cuts ten musicians and arrangers from organization as bookings
drop and U.S. depression worsens.
1931—Opens at Chicago's Edgewater Beach Hotel.
Marries fourth wife, film actress Margaret Livingston, in
Colorado on August 18.
Returns to RCA Victor with new recording contract.
Introduces Ferde Grofé's *Grand Canyon Suite* at Chicago's
Studebaker Theatre.
1932—Begins long engagement at New York's Biltmore Hotel.
Conducts Fourth Experiment in Modern American Music at
Carnegie Hall, with composer-pianist Dana Suesse.

1933—Returns to Carnegie Hall for Fifth Experiment on January 25, featuring John Green's *Night Club*.

Launches NBC radio series, *Kraft Music Hall,* with Al Jolson.

Presents Sixth Experiment, with works of William Grant Still and Dana Suesse.

1934—Establishes Elfrida Whiteman Scholarship in memory of his mother. Prize won by David Diamond for *Sinfonietta*.

1935—Conducts Seventh Experiment at Robin Hood Dell, Philadelphia.

Returns to Broadway in Billy Rose's *Jumbo* at the Hippodrome.

Donates scores and career materials to Williams College to form the Whiteman Collection.

1936—Plays at the Casa Mañana during Fort Worth Frontier Centennial in Texas.

1937—Re-engaged for the Fort Worth celebration where on July 11 learns of the death of George Gershwin.

Inaugurates new radio series, *Chesterfield Presents,* with emphasis on swing performed by Trumbauer, Jack and Charlie Teagarden, Al Gallodoro, Miff Mole and The Modernaires.

1938—Signs recording contract with Decca.

Conducts Eighth (and last) Experiment at Carnegie Hall, on December 25.

Purchases Walking Horse Farm near Rosemont, New Jersey.

1940—Breaks up band for semi-retirement on New Jersey farm.

1941—Organizes new band, which bows in Florida in January.

Three-year-old adopted son, Dickie, dies.

Joins radio program of Burns & Allen in Hollywood.

1943—Signs contract to appear in *Rhapsody in Blue,* film biography of Gershwin.

Becomes musical director for the Blue Network, later known as ABC.

Originates the *Philco Radio Hall of Fame.*

1947—Broadcasts *The Paul Whiteman Club,* the first coast-to-coast network disc jockey show.

Initiates Saturday night teenage record hops for New Jersey neighbors.

1949—Enters television with *TV Teen Club,* co-hosted by daughter Margo.

Inaugurates TV musical series called *Paul Whiteman's Goodyear Revue* at ABC.

1954—Conducts Gershwin concert at Hollywood Bowl, setting attendance record of 57,000 for three-concert series.

1955—Hosts a summer TV series, *America's Greatest Bands.*

1956—Celebrates 50th year as professional musician with release of Grand Award anniversary album.

1958—Appears in revue, *Newcomers of 1928,* at Las Vegas.
Sells New Jersey farm and prepares to move to newly-built Coda Cottage in New Hope, Pennsylvania.

1959—Serves as emcee at White House musicale at request of President Eisenhower.

1962—Spends the first of several winters in southern California.

1967—Honored on 77th birthday with a dinner-dance by New Hope Historical Society.
Dies at Doylestown Hospital on December 29, and interred in Whiteman mausoleum in Trenton on January 3, 1968.